S0-DUG-013

THE CULTURE OF STRANGERS

---

*Globalization, Localization and
The Phenomenon of Exchange*

G. Eric Hansen

*Bill
with regards
Eric
5/15/02*

University Press of America,® Inc.
Lanham · New York · Oxford

Copyright © 2002 by
University Press of America,® Inc.
4720 Boston Way
Lanham, Maryland 20706
UPA Acquisitions Department (301) 459-3366

12 Hid's Copse Rd.
Cumnor Hill, Oxford OX2 9JJ

All rights reserved
Printed in the United States of America
British Library Cataloging in Publication Information Available

Library of Congress Cataloging-in-Publication Data

Hansen, G. Eric.
The culture of strangers : globalization, localization,
and the phenomenon of exchange / G. Eric Hansen.
p.   cm
Includes bibliographical references and index.
1. Culture. 2. Social evolution. 3. Social systems. 4. Exchange.
5. Globalization. I. Title.

HM621 .H36 2002
306—dc21   2002018729 CIP

ISBN 0-7618-2205-4 (pbk. : alk. paper)

♾™ The paper used in this publication meets the minimum
requirements of American National Standard for Information
Sciences—Permanence of Paper for Printed Library Materials,
ANSI Z39.48—1984

In Loving Gratitude for My Mother
Kathleen Hearty Hansen
and
In Memory of My Father
Andrew Eric Hansen

*The world about us would be desolate
except for the world within us.*

— Wallace Stevens

CONTENTS

ACKNOWLEDGMENTS

A work with the scope of this book owes a debt to many individuals, who as friends, mentors, colleagues and students inspired it.

As an undergraduate at Lawrence College I was first exposed to the history of ideas and the importance of a historical imagination by William A. Chaney. The world of philosophy was opened to me by Herbert Spiegelberg, who played an important role in introducing phenomenology to Americans during the 1940's and 1950's. William H. Riker was my teacher in government, and an important guide in understanding positive and normative statements in the social sciences. Mojimir Povolny was both realist and idealist, critic and activist in the field of international affairs, and director of my senior thesis, which focused on globalization before the term itself was coined. Lawrence Steifel introduced me and a whole generation of students to the values of art history and criticism as a vehicle for understanding the various worlds of humanity. Douglas M. Knight, an inspiring polymath, provided a model of learned culture.

As a student of Allan B. Cole at the Fletcher School at Tufts University I came to share his love of things Asian, especially China and Japan. Leo Gross was a challenging mentor in the fields of international law and organization, and a seminal influence in my understanding of globalization.

My encounters with Hannah Arendt when I was on the faculty of Wellesley College, and she a visiting professor there, are among the most vivid of my memories of intellectual discovery. Her work and ideas always lurk in the shadows behind my own, and form a subtext for this book.

The years I spent at the Massachusetts Institute of Technology were lived in the tension between realism and idealism at a time when these were both most in conflict and most in accord in university life. Ithiel de Sola Pool, with whom I disagreed about almost everything in foreign policy, was nevertheless a courageous and indefatigable advocate for his positions, and notable for his unending willingness to interact with students and faculty during the trying debates surrounding the Vietnam War. I recall him as a model of the civility which this work commends.

Without the invaluable assistance of Susan Peabody this book, which she patiently formatted, would not have gone to press. UPA associate editor Diana Lavery was always available and very helpful from the beginning of the editorial process. Very special thanks go to Michael Schement and Daniel Smith for their computer expertise, especially with graphics. The Faculty Development Fund and the School of Economics and Business Administration at Saint Mary's College of California were generous in their financial support. Colleagues and students at Saint Mary's read, approved and disputed this manuscript at various stages, and made writing it an intellectual adventure. Its shortcomings, alas, are mine alone.

My European mother and my Middle Western father met and married in New York City in the 1930's. Their life together and my own with them is a beloved memory of global horizons, by sea and air. This book is dedicated to my parents because the journey it charts began with them in every way.

GEH
San Francisco
June 2001

PERMISSIONS

(pp. 35-36) Quotation from James Balwin, *Go Tell It on the Mountain* (Dial Press 1953) courtesy Bantam Dell Publishing Group and Doubleday.

(p. 43) "The Kula Ring (map)," from *Argonauts of the Western Pacific* by Bronislaw Malinowski, copyright 1922 by Bronislaw Malinowski, (c) 1961 by E.P. Dutton. Used by permission of Dutton, a division of Penguin Putnam, Inc.

(p. 72) Graphic plan of Beijing and (p. 174) drawing of Culemborg from *Design of Cities,* by Edmund Bacon, copyright (c) 1967, 1974 by Edmund N. Bacon, used by permission of Penguin, a division of Penguin Putnam Inc.

(p. 87) Graphic of Chinese market structure from G. W. Skinner, "Marketing and Social Structure in Rural China," *Journal of Asian Studies* (November 1964), reprinted with permission of the Association for Asian Studies, Inc.

(p. 89) Floor plan of Chinese house from Lucian W. Pye, *China: An Introduction,* 4th ed. Copyright (c) 1991 by Lucian W. Pye. Reprinted by permission of Pearson Education, Inc.

(p. 108) Graphic "Optical Correction in Greek Architecture," from Banister Fletcher, *History of Architecture,* 17th ed. courtesy of Butterworth-Heinemann.

(p. 109) Site plan of the Athenian acropolis reprinted from Constantinos A. Doxiadis, *Architectural Space in Ancient Greece* (1972) courtesy of MIT Press.

(p. 109) Drawing of the Athenian acropolis from Kent C. Bloomer and Charles W. Moore, *Body, Memory and Architecture*, p. 110 (1977) reprinted by permission of Yale University Press. Copyright (c) Yale University Press, 1977.

(p. 117) Floor plan of 5th century Athenian house reprinted from Rodney Young, "An Industrial District in Ancient Athens," *Hesperia* XX (1951), figure 34, courtesy of American School of Classical Studies at Athens.

INTRODUCTION

> The objectivity of the world — its object- or thing-character — and the human condition supplement each other; because human existence is conditioned existence, it would be impossible without things, and things would be a heap of unrelated articles, a non-world, if they were not conditioners of human existence.
>
> — Hannah Arendt

Globalization in all of its dimensions has provoked much discussion over the last decade. "The forces of global integration are a great tide," proclaimed President Clinton, "inexorably wearing away the established order of things." The fall of communism in Europe and the crisis of capitalism in Asia are evidence of global trends challenging "the established order." Simultaneously, the usually less noticed forces of localization are transforming other social landscapes. The rise of regionalism in Europe and elsewhere is evidence of this trend. While many commentators have noted the dynamics of international relations, economic factors and/or failed policies as explanations for these historical events, few have looked at the role of culture. As a teacher of international management I had recognized the importance of culture in the development of business values and in understanding global trends, and the need to expose students to cultural analysis in an organized way. The very amorphousness of ideas about culture made it difficult to present, in a relatively short time, a systematic approach to them. If the ideas were presented at a level of abstraction necessary to convey their conceptual importance, they had little relevance to students. If they were more concrete they became impressionistic and lacked intellectual rigor. In preparing this study I have tried to establish the right tension between a systematized approach and one that will provoke thinking about the practical implications of cultural values.

Recently Samuel P. Huntington has helped to stimulate substantial discussion with his thesis that modernization and Westernization are not the same thing, and that there is no reason to assume that "societies with modern cultures should be any more similar than are societies with traditional cultures."[1] In making a distinction between what is modern and what is Western Huntington marks an important analytical divide, first identified by Greek thought, which distinguished between what is inherent (*phusis*) and what exists as a matter of convention (*nomos*). Encapsulated within the concept of "the West" is the presumption of a unique historical process, which accounts for the fact that a relatively few societies bordering the North Atlantic dominate much of the world's commerce in goods, ideas and values. Simultaneously, the concept of "the modern" suggests a much more abstract, pervasive, but no less powerful set of influences which are transforming life on the planet. By distinguishing between the Western and the modern we are separating the contingent from the transformational, what is accidental in history, from that which is universally operative beneath these contingencies. In attempting to understand historical development we attempt to cut through the accidental and contingent in search of some unifying phenomena. If history is to be more than one wag's postmodern definition of it ("Just one damn thing after another") we need analytical tools which will separate the unique Western development from the basic forces which more broadly shape collective human experience.

Modernization is one such analytical tool, and many theories of modernization locate themselves within cultural interpretation. Sociologist Daniel Lerner in his important work, *The Passing of Traditional Society*, argues that modernization can be a "unifying principle" of analysis. Modernization is indeed different from Westernization at certain levels, but since Westernization is itself a variation on a fundamental process called "modernization," any modernization of society will inevitably bring about more than superficial Westernization as well. He asserts: "This observational standpoint implies no ethnocentrism. As we shall show, the Western model of modernization exhibits certain components and sequences whose relevance is global."[2] Looking toward the ultimate unity of human experience, we must develop models which sufficiently generalize that experience so that meaningful comparisons can be proposed.

The fashion for "deconstruction" and relativism in contemporary intellect — one consequence, I believe, of the broadly deligitimizing social disorders of a generation ago — is being challenged by the older, and in my view more substantive, vision of unitary knowledge. Socio-biologist Edward O. Wilson has revived the early nineteenth century term "consilience" in rejecting the idea of an inherent division of knowledge or borderline between the natural sciences on the one hand and the social sciences and the humanities on the other. He asserts that this division issues from unfounded assertions of an "epistemological discontinuity" between ways of knowing, which makes these fields artificially autonomous. Instead, he proposes,

> At the heart of this borderline is the shifting concept of culture and its hitherto puzzling relation to human nature — and then to the general inherited properties of individual behavior. In the spirit of the natural sciences, the matter can be expressed, I believe, as a problem to be solved. It is as follows: Compelling evidence shows that all culture is learned. But its invention and transmission are biased by innate properties of the sensory system and the brain. These developmental biases, which we collectively call human nature, are themselves prescribed by genes that evolved or were sustained over hundreds of thousands of years in primarily cultural settings. Hence, genes and culture have coevolved; they are linked.[3]

To generalize effectively in matters of human values and culture is ultimately to take a stance in consilience, the alignment of all knowledge in common patterns of understanding. The nexus of consilience in understanding human evolution seems to me to lie in the unique capacity of humanity for abstraction. It is this biologically based capacity of brain and mind ("hardware" and "software," so to speak) which accounts for how a creature so unspecialized in other physiological ways — even to the point of lacking a skin which adequately protects it from the elements — has mastered its environment so profoundly. The ability to function symbolically gave man the ability to manipulate the material environment in ways utterly unique to himself, and it provided the basis for reflection, the ability to think about thinking, which allowed abstraction itself to be carried to yet undiscovered limits.

The confluence of genetic evolution in the brain with cultural evolution in the mind has produced what we describe at any place and point in time as "human nature," intrinsically oriented toward comprehending the world, including the self. Cosmologist Carl Sagan wrote, "Natural selection has served as a kind of intellectual sieve, producing brains and intelligences increasingly competent to deal with the laws of nature. This resonance, extracted by natural selection, between our brains and the universe may help explain a quandary set by Einstein: The most incomprehensible property of the universe, he said, is that it is so comprehensible."[4] In co-evolving with the universe, a natural sympathy — almost musical in its character — between human imagination and the material environment developed as well. Humanity's engagement of the world in abstract thought is the result of this natural evolutionary sympathy expressed in what the great Jesuit paleontologist Pierre Teilhard de Chardin called "the noosphere."[5]

In adopting these perspectives in the study that follows I also acknowledge my debt to existential psychology, described a generation ago by one of its leading practitioners, Abraham H. Maslow as, "new ways of perceiving and thinking, new images of man and society, new conceptions of ethics and of values, new directions in which to move."[6] My method shares with the psychological and philosophical existentialists the belief that humanity experiences life as a question, or as an enterprise which requires dialectical engagement with it. In this view, the ground of being from which humanity begins and sustains this life project is biologically based and the same in all humans. It is in fact the substance of our humanity. It is this shared nature, not genetic differences or cultural differences, which ultimately defines us individually and collectively as human beings, and which makes it possible for us to communicate with one another beyond time and cultural circumstance. Adapting a concept from the linguistics of Noam Chomsky, I am suggesting that all human beings possess a fundamental and universal grammar of existential engagement.

In Chomsky's very influential formulation, our capacity for language is inborn and governed by biologically based linguistic structures.[7] This universal grammatical structure is identical in all human beings regardless of cultural differences in the rules of formal language. This universal grammar also links the capacity for symbolization to one of man's most potent bio-cultural capabilities, speech. The human cultural tool kit, based in the capacity for symbolic abstraction, especially the capacity for language, issues from and shapes the human engagement of the experienced environment. While all humans share what Chomsky called "syntactic structures," these biologically based structures reveal themselves in actual languages which are cultural artifacts. The linguist Benjamin L. Whorf asserted about humankind: "His thinking itself is in a language — in English, in Sanskrit, in Chinese. And every language is a vast pattern system, different from others, in which are culturally ordained the forms and categories by which the personality not only communicates, but also analyzes nature, notices or neglects types of relationship and phenomena, channels his reasoning, and builds the house of his consciousness."[8] Whorf's assertion encapsulates a theme of this work — that human culture embodies two sometimes contrary elements: human singularity and human plurality. Underlying formal language are global structures which characterize much of humanity's life as a species; also located within language are those variations which reflect the diversity of human experience. Human existential engagement is mediated in and through language in both global and local forms. This existential engagement is experienced on two phenomenological levels, the personal and the social.

On the personal level, again citing Maslow, human beings all seek, as a condition of their humanity, ultimate "self-actualization." The impulse is toward "full-humanness, the development of the biologically based nature of man, and therefore is (empirically) normative for the whole species rather than for particular times and places, i.e. it is less culturally relative."[9] Maslow thus proposes that, "We have, each of us, an essentially biologically based inner nature, which is to some degree 'natural,' intrinsic, given, and in a certain limited sense, unchangeable, or at least unchanging."[10] In Maslow's developmental model, based on a "hierarchy of needs," human personality develops in a systematic way, dialectically engaging both the limits and the possibilities of the environment, to realize certain inherent needs: for life, for safety and security, for belongingness and affection, for respect and self-respect, and for self-actualization. This series is not random. Each serial need rises from, and in organic relation to, other needs — and always within an actual, total social context. This formulation proposes that, as each of these needs is more fully engaged and satisfied, higher needs unfold in a process of self-discovery. Every need is consequently viewed as a universal paradigm of human life seen at one level of experience. This development, while in no sense inevitable, is systematic, one need and the values associated with it providing the basis for organic growth into higher need fulfillment. Each need is fulfilled individually but also socially, and thus culturally, as the formal environment creates the possibility for each need in the hierarchy to be more fully experienced, identified and sustained. This is also a process of ever more complex, mediated abstraction; each human need is satisfied at higher levels of mental functioning, which in turn require more complex symbolic systems rooted in an evolving culture.

While there is no inevitability to this process, there is much to propel it. In fact, the inability of individuals and of societies to evolve into higher states of being and cultural fulfillment can be regarded as the basis for a sort of on-going individual and social crisis. Existential psychology tends to view such lack of growth as the source of both psychopathology and sociopathology. Maslow asserts:

> Certainly it seems more and more clear that what we call 'normal' in psychology is really the psychopathology of the average, so undramatic and widely spread that we don't even notice it ordinarily. The existentialist's study of the authentic person and authentic living helps to throw this general phoniness, this living by illusions and by fear into a harsh, clear light which reveals it clearly as sickness, even tho [sic] widely shared.[11]

Society, like individuals, can endure long periods of near-malignant dormancy — a stasis within which cultural effeteness casts a pallor over all movement toward spontaneity and innovation, a paralysis in which form invariably eclipses substance. Humanity's capacity for symbolization can be the path into deep individual and social illusion if existential engagement of the environment is not vigorous and continuous. Dynastic Egypt and China, and more recently the Soviet Union, often had these static characteristics, a paralyzing localism which made responses to the momentous changes taking place in the global environment very difficult.

Human beings at the social level develop within systematic paradigms which frame relatively coherent cultural value systems. As the word "paradigm" suggests, I am persuaded by the arguments of sociologists like Talcott Parsons and Robert N. Bellah that thought seeks integration around fundamental normative structures which create a morphology of ideas and values as nearly systemic as that found in individual organisms. In the Parsonian model these elements interact at a number of levels which he calls "action systems." A social system interpenetrates with other action systems: "Because of such interpenetration, each of the other action systems (Culture, Personality, Behavioral Organism) constitutes a part of the environment — or, we may say an environment — of a social system. Beyond these systems are the environments of action itself, standing above and below the general hierarchy of facts that control action in the world of life."[12] While each action system can be analytically distinguished, it must always be viewed in organic relation to those other action systems with which it functions. Consequently, just as human beings do not have wings, and could not have wings, given the structure and interdependent shape of our biology, structures of social thought viewed holistically and systematically tend to include, and to exclude, certain ideas and values as they seek integrated organization. After the Newtonian revolution in physics, for example, Aristotle's ideas became difficult to sustain because their universal ontological context had been irrevocably altered. In Thomas Kuhn's famous formulation, there had been a "paradigm shift." Newton's mechanics were, in turn, fundamentally challenged by the revolutions in quantum mechanics and relativity theory. As a result, the use of Aristotle's "natural law" arguments or Newton's mechanics can be persuasively coherent only when apprehended in isolation. What is lacking in these formulations is their systematic and necessary relation to those dominant paradigms in science and philosophy which have shaped human life since the seventeenth century.

People tend to think paradigmatically as a consequence of thinking abstractly. Every abstraction is itself an effort toward an ordered system of understanding. Thus, contemporary human beings who confirm in their everyday lives the reality of powerful technologies made possible by the new paradigms are unlikely to long reject their inclusion in most aspects of their lives. This is only relative, of course. There is a phenomenon called "cognitive dissonance," and it is not invariably resolved by individuals changing their conceptual frameworks when faced with phenomena which contradict them. There are human beings who, for example, live obviously modern lives in many ways while simultaneously affirming such beliefs as Biblical inerrancy or astrological prediction. But such people also tend to make themselves peripheral to the dominant culture and its paradigms by inhabiting highly localized subcultures which reinforce values distinguishing them from a larger, unbelieving world.[13]

I propose a model of cultural development which, paralleling Wilson, Maslow, and Parsons, assumes that human beings live in cultural worlds or paradigms which are systematically directed toward inner coherence as they deal with fundamental categories such as matter, individuation, action, space, time, and motion, which together shape the phenomenon of exchange. In this formulation, human societies shift paradigmatically as environmental and internal dynamics of change in combination impel them toward fundamental reinterpretations and rearrangements of these basic, normative categories. The model also asserts a systematically impelled movement from more basic and primal cultural states to more advanced and complex ones as the lower-order needs common to all animals, such as safety and physical sustenance, are eclipsed by the more distinctly human higher needs of sociality where individuals are affirmed in more complex roles and hierarchies based on esteem, and ultimately self-esteem and self-actualization. This also reflects the passage from what psychologist Rollo May called conditions of "mere life" to "higher life."[14] The individual and the social interact as the bio-cultural impulses which animate the former are shaped by the forces issuing from the latter. In short, we are always both dynamically individual and social in intertwined combination.

Human beings, I suggest, create meaning as the necessary consequence of experiencing their environments. Man is a meaning-making animal. Our environments would be, as Hannah Arendt has asserted, only "a heap of unrelated articles — a non-world" if humanity did not extract meanings, systems of normative order, from it.[15] The creation of meaning constitutes the heart of the phenomenon of exchange, the existential process through which human objectivity and subjectivity define one another in expressing values. These meanings become the agents through which environments are transformed into worlds, places where objects and events are ontologically connected, and condition the experience of the human beings who inhabit them. *Homo sapiens* creates and recreates his worlds, as his worlds create and recreate him. As anthropologist Clifford Geertz suggested, human symbolic worlds are both "models of" and "models for" reality, giving "objective conceptual form to social and psychological reality both by shaping themselves to it and by shaping it to themselves."[16] I have identified those created and creating realities in four interpenetrating worlds of experience which shape human beings, and which are shaped in turn by human encounter. In each of these paradigmatic realms the phenomenon of exchange is expressed differently. The mercantile exchange in goods, which is central to a business society, emerges fully in one of these realms, which I define as "the civil world."

This formulation, like all such schemes, should be understood for what it is: an attempt to model reality in order to further intellectual dialog. I understand the dangers of intellectual dogmatism which sometimes arises from such modeling, certainly those connected in the past with the works of Marx and Freud. What I offer I offer in the spirit of Bellah, a social theorist of both imagination and modesty, whose thoughts on one of his own attempts at paradigm-building I echo: "Construction of a wide-ranging evolutionary scheme like the one presented in this paper is an extremely risky enterprise. Nevertheless such efforts are justifiable if, by throwing light on perplexing developmental problems, they contribute to modern man's efforts at self interpretation."[17] The four worlds of human cultural experience which I identify are the primal, the traditional, the civil and the individual. Each world rises from and is conditioned by the reality of its predecessor. There is nothing inevitable about this passage. Primal societies may exist relatively unchanged for millennia if their environments remain unchanged. The artifacts left by the very isolated Aleut aborigines 10,000 years ago are indistinguishable from those made in the last century. The essential contours of traditional China, its canons of custom, art and belief, were in place two thousand years ago and may not have significantly changed at all except for unavoidable contact with the outside world, especially the West. At the same time, I am proposing that each state in development requires the preceding one to give it coherence. Consequently, there could be no traditional society without the primal society which precedes it (and which it incorporates), or a civil society without the traditional society from which it issued. The world of the individual is, to me, not fully comprehensible outside the context of civil society.

This developmental model may be characterized as a pyramid, rising from a primal base within which society meets its most basic survival needs to its apex in high culture, paralleled by an individual needs hierarchy based in the primal requirements for life and security, rising to an apex in self-actualization. Psychologist Erich Fromm has distinguished between lower order "scarcity-pleasure" and higher order "abundance-pleasure."[18] The lower order pleasures associated with the satiation of physical needs and appetites are distinguished in his theory from the penultimately human pleasures of creation and insight. This model also assumes that the individual and his society are synergistic. "His culture provides the raw material of which the individual makes his life," said anthropologist Ruth Benedict. "No individual can arrive even at the threshold of his potentialities without a culture in which he participates. Conversely, no civilization has in it any element which in the last analysis is not the contribution of an individual."[19]

The pyramid aptly models these parallel hierarchies for another reason. A phenomenon of increasing density is at work in its structural dynamics. As one moves from its base to its apex a principle of compression supplements a principle of more mediated abstraction. As we shall see, the growing density of human populations (and thus the complexity of their interactions) plays a critical role in the transition from one world to another. Each demographically promoted transition up the hierarchy is enabled culturally by an increased ability of human beings to understand and to shape their worlds in more intellectually mediated and abstract terms. This reflects an evolving process by which human beings, individually and collectively, more actively adapt their environments to themselves by embedding their wills and purposes within them, rather than more passively adapting themselves to their environments, which are experienced as givens. I am thus describing evolution from a life centered in habit and reaction, to a life centered in purpose and action. I am also describing human lives initiated in highly local circumstances evolving into global perspectives.

THE WORLDS OF CULTURAL EXPERIENCE

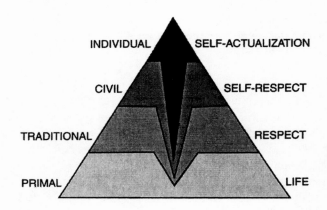

INDIVIDUAL   SELF-ACTUALIZATION

CIVIL   SELF-RESPECT

TRADITIONAL   RESPECT

PRIMAL   LIFE

Figure Intro 1: The worlds of cultural experience can be characterized as an evolving pyramid within which four paradigmatic realms interpenetrate. At its base is the primal world within which the most basic of human needs for life and safety are engaged and reflected in cultural interpretation. Above this is the traditional world, characterized by roles and rules within value hierarchies. The respect of one's superiors, inferiors and peers is the dominant human motive which characterizes traditional culture. The civil world which supersedes traditional society is characterized by ties resting in the consent of autonomous persons. It is a world of reason, negotiation and contracts, which together promote the need of human beings for self-respect, esteem in their own eyes. At the summit of the cultural pyramid is the world of the individual. It is here that the penultimate human existential need, for self-actualization, is satisfied in creation and insight. In each of these worlds the phenomenon of exchange, including the exchange of goods, is understood and expressed culturally in different ways. None of these cultural worlds exists independently of the others. Individual human beings and social systems inhabit these worlds simultaneously. Their interpenetration accounts for some of the dynamics of psychological and social life.

In the course of human evolution nature selected for those capacities, such as speech, which promote complex sociality. Nature also selected for those brain characteristics which promote ever-greater capacities for symbolic abstraction. In the process of doing this, nature evolved the biological basis for the individual, himself an ultimate abstraction as well as the summit of a process of demographic compression. The individual and his world are the final extrusions of social density.

While each of these four worlds of human experience has its own paradigmatic integrity, a vital center which shapes the contours and textures of its culture, none of these worlds exists independently of the others. Individuals, and social systems, inhabit each of these worlds simultaneously. It is their interpenetration which accounts for some of the dynamics of both psychological and social life. The civil world, for example, contains many elements which are animated by the primal and the traditional. What makes the civil world uniquely itself are the dominant civil norms and modes which characterize it. This is an important point to stress at both the individual and social levels. We do not as individuals entirely surrender the primal need for physical safety and sustenance because we advance to psychological modes centered in the need for peer esteem or self esteem.

At the social level every society has distinctive elements drawn from each world, but derives its character from dominant norms issuing from one of them. Some observers of contemporary Japan have called it a modern civil society because its political, social and economic institutions — constitution, elections, political parties, press, courts, bureaucracy, business groups, banks, corporations, etc. — seem so similar to those of civil societies in the West. I shall argue that Japan is fundamentally animated by values characterizing the traditional world. Its imported civil characteristics function, in my formulation, peripherally to the dominant traditional mode. Thus, my cultural model will suggest that Japan is neither fundamentally Western nor fundamentally modern.

In writing this study I have been self-consciously catholic in my approach. When one addresses a subject as complex and elusive as culture one has to be specific in the focus of one's analysis, and at the same time must inevitably outline many important themes using literary, linguistic and artistic images, the insights of anthropology and sociology, and a fundamentally historical frame of reference as one seeks uniformities in duration. My approach suggests that in cultural analysis one has often to seek a whole greater than the parts. Geertz's work in cultural interpretation introduced the concept of "thick description," and distinguished it from "thin description."[20] "Thin description" minimally, cautiously, and "objectively" describes human activity, while "thick description" places any human activity within an interpretive whole of cultural intentions and meanings. This study is a thick description of the phenomenon of exchange, an understanding of economic relations framed within other human meanings.

My model is often focused on the elements which characterize the transitions from one dominant cultural world to another. My thesis is that each of these worlds has a powerful integrity, and that their individual gravities do not permit easy movement into other modal orbits without a very compelling interaction of external and internal forces. Societies and human beings individually are complex exchanges of the forces of stasis and change, of growth and decay. Because stasis and entropy tend to be the dominant forces, change is not entirely seamless nor is it consistently graduated. Borrowing a term from the evolutionary biology of Stephen Jay Gould, change is more characterized by long periods of relative stasis interrupted by periods of rapid reconfiguration in a process of "punctuated equilibrium." The historical passage from one world to another — for example, from primitive, pre-dynastic Egypt to the traditional society of the Old Kingdom, and from traditional archaic Greece to the civil world of the classical era — occurred relatively rapidly. Social morphologies seem to follow some of the same rules as biological ones: the requirements of internal organization and coherence motivate rapid systemic change into new states of equilibrium.

Existential psychologists sometimes use the terms "growth" and "defense" to distinguish these simultaneous and often contending processes in individual psychology. The organism seeks growth to accommodate changes in the experienced world, while at the same time defending achieved structures of normative integration. J.W. Burton asserts, applying general systems theory:

> System change and adaptation are well understood in biology; survival of species depends upon adjustment to environmental alterations. The possibilities are elimination, or survival in an altered form. The two processes, maintenance and adjustment, interact, and the outcome depends upon the level of adjustment required by environmental change, and the system's ability to alter.[21]

A system's boundaries describe the outer limits of a system's functioning in terms of the other systems with which it interacts. The phenomenon of exchange is experienced at these boundaries where systems interact with one another.

Systems attempt to maintain their individual integrities through a complex process of maintenance and adjustment, simultaneously moving out to control the environment from which forces of change come (i.e., other experienced systems), and adapting internal subsystems to maintain systems coherence as external forces are accommodated. "It is the boundaries of systems that respond to the environment," says Burton, "and it is out of this response that change occurs."[22] Individual psychological systems, and social systems, seem to experience crisis when unable to manage this complex exchange process of maintenance and adjustment, defense and growth. How systems understand where and how boundaries are most appropriately drawn, and how exchange is consequently to be managed, is one measure of a successful strategy of survival and growth. The tension between the impulses toward globalization and contending impulses toward localization is often a reflection of this underlying dynamic.

One of the social roles of intellectuals, in particular, has been to function at the boundaries of various systems — social, scientific, esthetic, religious — managing change by proposing (and opposing) alternative patterns of normative integration. Sociologist Edward Shils described the inherent ambivalence of intellectual life, a complex dialectic of creativity and conformity, and its contribution to social change:

> The process of elaborating and developing further the potentialities inherent in a 'system' of cultural values, entails also the possibility of 'rejection' of the inherited set of values in varying degrees of comprehensiveness. In all societies, even those in which the intellectuals are notable for their conservatism, the diverse paths of creativity, as well as the inevitable tendency toward negativism, impel a partial rejection of the prevailing system of cultural values.[23]

The element of contingency in cultural change, always a counterpoint to systematic evolution, was expressed by Max Weber in his theory of the charismatic. The charismatic intellectual — from Socrates to St. Paul, from Luther to Lenin — often provides the catalyst for change, when systemic boundary conditions make societies ripe for it, by providing the locus of adhesion for individuals and groups seeking alternative orientations in cultural matters. It is at the boundaries of systems that individuals and societies feel the powerful pull of the differing and contending worlds of human experience — one set of forces directed toward the familiar past, and another directed toward possible futures. There is also a metabolic element in exchange — the transactions in which substance and process transform one another — which gives human culture its unique dynamism. The twin forces of globalization and localization are only dimensions of this deeper capacity for exchange at various levels of human experience. The four worlds which I describe are treated in equilibrium with an eye toward those powerful exchange dynamics operating at the systems boundaries that govern transitions, and mark this metabolic movement from one world to another.

This study takes as its central concern the relations between culture and commerce. Transactions in goods are presented as extensions of the dominant exchange norms in each of the four paradigmatic worlds which I discuss. Economic exchange evolves from primal and local conditions, in which markets play little or no part, to civil and global conditions where markets dominate other social relations. This scheme implicitly, at the very least, puts me into an adversarial stance to those who posit that commerce, at all times and in all places, is governed by the same economic laws. I do not deny the usefulness of various economic models in understanding goods transactions, but I see commercial relations as essentially a dependent variable, shaped by the dominant exchange values which govern differing cultural systems. Adam Smith brilliantly described, in systematic ways, the organization and function-ing of economic relations within the civil culture of his time. Much of what he had to say still illuminates economic relations in contemporary civil cultures like our own. The application of classical liberal economic models like Smith's to primitive cultures such as those of the Amazon basin is, on the other hand, a very different matter.

The debate between formalist and substantivist conceptions of economics is an old one. This work is substantivist. Like anthropologist Marshall Sahlins, it views economy as "a category of culture rather than behavior, in a class with politics or religion rather than rationality or prudence: not the need-serving activities of individuals, but the material life process of society."[24] The rational, self-interested man basis of classical economics is being challenged by those who believe that larger social and cultural forces play a critical role in the way individuals and groups make economic choices. "An important shifting of the ground in theoretical economics is taking place," asserts economist H. Peyton Young of the Brookings Institution. "There's a greater willingness to consider social forces and interactions as essential for understanding how goods are distributed, but this work still lies outside the mainstream."[25]

The word "globalization" is a term that refers to those expansive forces, principally economic and technological in origin, which have challenged national borders, institutions and cultures.[26] Globalization is usually associated with the activities of transnational corporations, but the phenomenon is a pervasive subtext to all human exchange in the contemporary era, as in pre-vious eras. The forces of globalization were inherent within the first man-ifestations of private enterprise in ancient societies. Business activity by its very nature transacts and transgresses boundaries, including those of kinship, of government and of geography. No sooner had the world's first merchant been recorded in third millennium BC Sumeria than he appeared with his goods in the Indus valley a thousand miles away.

Included within globalization are two other associated impulses: those of "localization" and of "delocalization."[27] Localization describes the processes through which the forces of globalization are accommodated, resisted and absorbed, and given expression in any particular context. As Saskia Sassen expresses it, "Globalization can be deconstructed in terms of the strategic sites where global processes materialize and the linkages that bind them."[28] The Worldwide Web is a good example of a globalizing force which has been almost universally localized in every region and continent. Delocalization describes the more negative processes through which localized elements — economic, social, cultural — in any of their expressions are more deformed than transformed by globalizing trends which extract them from their particular contexts. The loss of sectors within individual economies, without a parallel upgrading of workforce skills and the provision of new jobs for displaced workers, is an example of delocalizing consequences attending globalization. Ideally, the forces of localization and of delocalization would be symmetrical within globalization. Every delocalizing tendency would be accompanied by a localizing element which maintains a dynamic equilibrium as social and economic systems transform themselves by adapting to the globalizing forces crossing their boundaries. This ideal is seldom achieved. Consequently, some social systems, especially in their nation-state expressions, find themselves experiencing a persistent net delocalization. The erosion of integrity and autonomy — economic, political, social and cultural — which accompanies persistent delocalization underlies the protests against globalization, of which those that ritually accompany the meetings of the World Trade Organization, and the International Monetary Fund/World Bank, are only the most dramatic and most noticed.

All societies experience these asymmetrical forces of localization and delocalization as the phenomenon of globalization continues to transform the world into what Paul Dicken calls a "global space-economy."[29] The 1970's were a particularly difficult time for the United States as well-paying industrial jobs were lost, and as inflation and declining productivity eroded an economy and the lives of those who had experienced a post-World War II prosperity unparalleled in history. As the nation adapted to these trends, and as the extraordinary economic expansion of the 1990's counteracted many of them, it was also clear that the asymmetry between localizing and delocalizing forces was persisting. The delocalization of well-paying industrial and white-collar jobs was not always paralleled by the provision of alternative, comparable employment, and many Americans enjoy a lower standard of living, what Thomas I. Palley ironically termed "plenty of nothing," now than a generation ago as a consequence.[30]

But it is elsewhere, particularly in the less developed world, that these delocalizing forces attending globalization have had their most negative effects. In places like Mexico the agricultural sector, which had provided a livelihood to a large portion of the population, was undermined by the globalization of commodity markets. The result has been a net decline in real commodity prices over the last quarter of a century, causing the collapse of many small farms. Commodity production, especially agriculture, had been delocalized with no symmetrical localization of those globalizing trends which maintain and improve living conditions. In only a limited number of sectors in Mexico, particularly petroleum and electronics manufacturing, has economic localization occurred. The massive emigration from the countryside to the cities, and to the centers of global localization in Europe and North America, accounts for much of the instability about which we are reminded daily in the media. In places like sub-Saharan Africa this delocalization has eventuated in social chaos and the destruction of human substance on an immense scale. A continent almost entirely dependent economically on commodities, especially agriculture, has been delocalized to the point where food must now be imported.

Some social and political systems attempt to thwart the effects of delocalization, while simultaneously entering the globalized economic system. Japan is a good example of a society which, at least in the short run, has managed to reap the advantages of participation in the global economy, while isolating itself from many of the delocalizing elements which have created unemployment and widely disparate income levels in other societies. The role that culture plays in enabling this response to globalization is a central focus of this study. Whether this social strategy is a tenable long-term solution to the problem of globalization is another. Other societies, such as our own in America, are not as culturally homogeneous as Japan. A number of differing cultural modes co-exist, often uneasily, within the social matrix. Each of these cultural modes is adapted, or maladapted, in differing measures for dealing with the impact of globalization. Those who most fully participate in America's dominant civil culture have most successfully adapted to globalization, with its twin localizing and delocalizing impulses. Others, like America's black underclass, have found their cultural modes woefully inadequate to confront the delocalizing trends which began to impact the American economy in the postwar period. Still other groups, like the first generations of middle-class Southerners, and of immigrant Catholics and Jews, find themselves increasingly inhabiting a cultural "no man's land" as their traditional social values are delocalized by these culturally transforming trends inherent in globalization. The domestic American "culture war," which I explore in detail, is consequently, in part, a localized reflection of the global "clash of cultures," asserted by Huntington

At the center of human life abides the phenomenon of exchange. The human capacity for exchange is an extension of the existential impulses toward development in all of its dimensions. Within the exchange relations of language human beings express the character of their connections with their surrounding world. Through the exchange of sentiments and values humanity forms dynamic bonds with that world. The creeds and institutions human beings create are manifestations of their understandings of these bonds. The exchange of goods in social relations represents a variant of this fundamental human capacity for growth and self-realization in exchange.

Human culture is the expression of the complex matrix of exchange relations among people at any time and place. Commercial relations, as only one expression of this larger phenomenon of exchange, consequently have a fundamentally embedded cultural character.[31] Human culture may be understood as the sum of the values and means by which people, in their myriad exchange relations, attempt to interpret and to realize themselves. The economic expression of any culture will thus reveal certain common elements intrinsic to the exchange of material goods, as well as other characteristics representing the total constellation of values which typify any culture in its particular expressions. Economic relations ultimately cannot be understood in isolation, the expression of laws which are self-contained, universal and constant. Culture and commerce always exist in dynamic and evolving relation.

Individual persons invest in their environments in various ways as a means of defining themselves and of realizing their values. Those investments — spiritual, intellectual, emotional, social, political and economic — express themselves in exchange relations informed by the total array of values which they seek to actualize. Any individual act of economic exchange is thus always an investment of the self as well as a transaction in goods.

Human beings interactively create the worlds in which they seek to actualize their values. These worlds to various degrees accord and conflict with the worlds other human beings have created. Humanity becomes estranged from itself as a whole phenomenon as various human worlds and their attendant values evolve along differing paths. Human exchange is thus characterized by both cooperation and contention as these estranged worlds encounter one another. Human culture is the evolving means by which groups of human beings seek the sustained common ground which promotes an existence which is inherently social as well as individual; which ultimately accommodates both those perceived as fellows and those perceived as strangers. Economic values, as an extension of these common cultural understandings, express in unique ways the human capacity for both conflict and concord as human worlds enter into conversation. Exchange always occurs in environments which express the resistance and the accommodation which are central to human lives lived both individually and socially. Civility, the culture of those who understand the significance of living among strangers, in both its localized and globalized expressions, embodies and institutionalizes, always imperfectly, this tension among alternative human values arising from multiple worlds.

Contemporary commercial relations, in their globalized expression, reflect the great power of integrative technology and the human values which both created it and are shaped by it. These values originated within the exchange relations which evolved in the Western world over centuries of development. They reflect the attempt of individuals and groups which interacted within Western civilizations over many centuries of evolution to define and realize their values. Economic and social development at the global level should be understood as an extension of this continuing quest for the realization of a body of cultural values. Some cultural value systems will be more congruent than others as this process of global integration proceeds. Rather than "celebrating cultural diversity" planetary humanity needs to reflect on the consequences of the basic incompatibility of some value systems with others as their exchange relations become more frequent and more substantial. The human capacity for both cooperation and contention forms a pervasive subtext of the phenomenon of globalization.

With the exception of Japan (a significant, but only partial, exception) no non-Western culture has evolved a mature business society — one in which the great masses of the population actively participate. As the new millennium begins the same Western societies which have dominated the commerce in goods, ideas and values during the last few centuries continue to play this role. In the face of assertions about the challenging rise of new economic regions, such as those of East Asia, and of non-Western values, such as those associated with Islam, there is still no substantial evidence that those societies or their indigenous values have made any significant impact on the basic forces which continue to shape the future of the planet. These transforming forces, especially those associated with science, technology and commercial culture, continue to originate in the West. Other societies, such as Japan, to the extent that they participate at all in this ongoing global transformation do so by adopting (or adapting) Western cultural values. Effective participation in the globalized economy and its associated social and institutional structures takes place to the extent that these values become modal in any society. Those societies which have least successfully adopted (or adapted) these values, such as those of sub-Saharan Africa, participate least in the world economy and those trends which continue to transform it — with disastrous consequences for millions of people.

No culture is monolithic. Individual cultures have located within them numbers of elements which cohere with various degrees of success. Some national cultures, *viz.* Japan, have achieved a very high degree of cultural coherence: the basic values of the socio-economic elites are widely shared throughout Japanese society. Other societies, such as our own in America, are characterized by widely differing degrees of participation in the values of the dominant civil elites who shape the allocation of resources, and their associated institutional and communication structures. Among other things, this means that the Japanese people have broadly shared in the benefits of participation in the global economy, while Americans have benefited with wider variation, depending in part on the complex of cultural values with which they are most closely associated. Conversely, it also means that Americans have had to evolve and to defend a culture of strangers, of civility, which permits the coexistence of these contending social strains, while Japan has little such experience. This implies that Americans may have greater success *in the long run* in accommodating global pluralism..

These premises have determined the structure of this study. This *Introduction* presents a basic model for cultural interpretation. It presents what I term "worlds of human experience" in an evolutionary scheme. Each of these defining cultural worlds or paradigms is subsequently treated separately in parts *I* through *IV*. This model suggests that each paradigmatic world is governed by defining clusters of cultural values, including those associated with transactions in goods. It further suggests that mature business societies are associated with a constellation of cultural values which are associated with one of these worlds, which I call "the civil world," the culture of strangers. In addition, this analysis suggests that individuals within particular societies participate to various degrees in each of these worlds, and that their successful participation in business activity is conditioned by the nature of this experience. In particular, some Americans participate with a high degree of success in our dominant business culture and its globalized expressions because of their complex associations with civil society and its values. Other Americans participate far less so, with resulting hardships, because of their association with values deriving from the primal or traditional worlds. This issue is treated at length in

Part VI as a contribution to the important public debate over the decline in "civility," and over issues of social equity, especially those related to poverty, employment and "multiculturalism." Japan is also examined in some depth, in *Part V*, to assess the degree to which this global economic power has been "modernized," "Westernized," or even authentically "globalized."

This approach to understanding cultural values and their development places them within what phenomenologist Martin Heidegger called a "referential totality." It suggests that culture can best be understood using the insights of a number of disciplines: history, anthropology, economics and psychology, certainly; but also linguistics, literature and the arts. Within this approach the phenomenon of exchange becomes a master metaphor for understanding the complexity of the ways human beings invest themselves and create value, that is, create "culture." Johan Huizinga used play as such a master metaphor to understand human culture a generation ago. Exchange and play are related phenomena. The word "play" derives from the Germanic *pflegen*, "to take care of" in the basic sense of "to bestir oneself, to be busy." The business at the core of commercial culture is the playful element within it. "The spirit of playful competition is, as a social impulse, older than culture itself and pervades all life like a veritable ferment,"[32] wrote Huizinga in *Homo Ludens*.

This study attempts to map the developmental process of competitive exchange to its full fruition in a globalized civil society and a commercial culture within which individuals realize their values.

NOTES TO INTRODUCTION

1. Samuel P. Huntington, "The West: Unique, Not Universal," FOREIGN AFFAIRS (Nov./Dec.1996) p. 29; his full study was published as THE CLASH OF CIVILIZATIONS AND THE MAKING OF WORLD ORDER (New York: Simon & Schuster, 1996); see also his edited collection (with Lawrence E. Harrison) CULTURE MATTERS: HOW VALUES SHAPE HUMAN PROGRESS (New York: Basic Books, 2000); these issues are treated from an economic perspective in David S. Landes, THE WEALTH AND POVERTY OF NATIONS (New York: W.W. Norton & Co., 1998)

2. Daniel Lerner, THE PASSING OF TRADITIONAL SOCIETY, (New York: The Free Press, 1964), p. 46

3. Edward O. Wilson, "Is Everything Relative?," *The Wilson Quarterly* (Winter 1998) pp. 17-18; anthropologist Clifford Geertz had made the same point in his essay, "The Growth of Culture and the Evolution of Mind," published a quarter century before in THE INTERPRETATION OF CULTURES (New York: Basic Books, 1973); Wilson's full exploration of these issues is to be

found in his CONSILEINCE: THE UNITY OF KNOWLEDGE (New York: Alfred A. Knopf, 1998)

4. Carl Sagan, THE DRAGONS OF EDEN (New York: Ballantine Books, 1977) p. 243

5. Pierre Teilhard de Chardin, THE PHENOMENON OF MAN, Bernard Wall, trans. (New York: Harper Brothers, Publishers 1959): Teilhard posited that evolution occurs simultaneously on three interdependent levels: geological (the "geosphere"); the biological (the "biosphere") and the mental (the"noosphere"). Stanford University cosmologist Andrei Linde also has speculated that "consciousness, the very hallmark of humanity, could be an intrinsic part of the universe - as fundamental to the warp and whoof of creation as space and time." George Johnson, "Science and Religion: Bridging the Great Divide," THE NEW YORK TIMES (June 30, 1998), p. C4

6. Abraham H. Maslow, TOWARD A PSYCHOLOGY OF BEING, 2nd ed. (New York: Van Norstrand, 1966), p. iii

7. Noam Chomsky, SYNTACTIC STRUCTURES (The Hague: Mouton & Co., 1957); Stanislas Dehaene, a French psychologist, has recently made a parallel claim for an inherent human "number sense," encoded by evolution in genes. HOW THE MIND CREATES MATHEMATICS (Oxford: Oxford University Press, 1997).

8. Benjamin L. Whorf, "Language, Mind and Reality," in John B. Carroll, ed. LANGUAGE, THOUGHT AND REALITY (Cambridge, MA: The MIT Press, 1956), p. 252; see also, Steven Pinker, HOW THE MIND WORKS (New York: WW Norton, 1997)

9. Maslow, *op.cit.,* p. vi.

10. *Ibid.,* p. 3

11. *Ibid.,* p. 16

12. Talcott Parsons, SOCIETIES: EVOLUTIONARY AND COMPARATIVE PERSPECTIVES (Englewood Cliffs, NJ: Prentice-Hall, Inc., 1966), p. 8

13. Leon Festinger and his colleagues' work, WHEN PROPHECY FAILS (Minneapolis, MI: University of Minnesota Press, 1956), documents the activities of a millennial cult which, having predicted the date and time of the world's end, only became more internally cohesive and evangelistic when the appointed time for "The End" failed to produce the predicted result. Because the *need* to believe generates the belief, the failure of the belief only generates a *greater* need to believe. Many fundamentalist religions isolate their members from the surrounding society so that belief is not compromised by experienced reality.

14. Rollo May, THE DISCOVERY OF BEING (New York: WW Norton & Co., 1983), p. 10

15. Hannah Arendt, THE HUMAN CONDITION (New York: Doubleday Anchor Books, 1959), p. 11

16. Clifford Geertz, "Religion as a Cultural System," in THE INTERPRETA-TION OF CULTURES, *op.cit.,* p. 93

17. Robert N. Bellah, "Religious Evolution," AMERICAN SOCIOLOGICAL REVIEW (June 1964), p. 374

18. Erich Fromm, MAN FOR HIMSELF (New York: Holt, Rinehart & Winston, 1947), Chap. 6

19. Ruth Benedict, PATTERNS OF CULTURE (Boston: Houghton Mifflin Company, 1934), pp. 252 - 253; This synergy is not without its tensions, as Freud suggested: "A good part of the struggles of mankind center around the single task of finding an expedient accommodation - one, that is, that will bring happiness - between this claim of the individual and the cultural claims of the group." CIVILIZATION AND ITS DISCONTENTS , James Strachey, trans. (New York: WW Norton & Company, Inc. 1961), p. 50

20. Clifford Geertz, "Thick Description: Toward an Interpretive Theory of Culture," in THE INTERPRETATION OF CULTURES, *op.cit.* Literary critic Stephen Greenblatt suggests that "Thickness is not in the object; it is in the narrative surroundings, the add-ons, the nested frames." "The Touch of the Real," in Sherry B. Ortner, ed.,THE FATE OF 'CULTURE,' (Berkeley: University of California Press, 1999), p. 17

21. J.W. Burton, SYSTEMS, STATES, DIPLOMACY AND RULES (Cambridge: The University Press, 1968), pp. 16 - 17

22. *Ibid.,* p. 17

23. Edward Shils, "The Intellectual and the Powers," in Philip Rieff, ed., ON INTELLECTUALS (New York: Anchor Books, 1970), p. 32

24. Marshall Sahlins, STONE AGE ECONOMICS (New York: Aldine De Gruyter, 1972), p. xii

25. Bruce Bower, "Yours, Mine and Ours," SCIENCE NEWS, March 28, 1998, p. 205; Young, together with Samuel Bowles, Herbert Gintis and Robert Boyd, participates in an interdisciplinary group of social scientists interested in the role of values in the formation of economic preferences. Under the auspices of the MacArthur Foundation they are commissioning "ultimatum games," conducted with groups around the world. Ultimatum games are experiments designed to test the critical role that concepts of *fairness* play in bargaining decisions.

26. There is a large and growing literature on the phenomenon of globalization. A provocative account of this process is Richard J. Barnet and John Cavanagh, GLOBAL DREAMS: IMPERIAL CORPORATIONS AND THE NEW WORLD ORDER (New York: Simon & Schuster, 1994)

27. These twin forces, under different terms (e.g. *dispersal* and *concentration*) have only in the past decade received the attention they deserve. See, for example, Paul L. Knox and Peter J. Taylor, eds., WORLD CITIES IN A WORLD SYSTEM (Cambridge: Cambridge University Press, 1995)

28. Saskia Sassen, "The Impact of the New Technologies and Globalization on Cities," Lo, Fu-chen & Yeung, Yue-man, eds. GLOBALIZATION AND THE WORLD OF LARGE CITIES (Tokyo: United Nations University Press, 1998), p. 392; "Localization," as a phenomenon, and as a noun, should be distinguished from "localized," an adjective which describes things or events in their isolated social or geographical contexts.

29. Paul Dicken, "Global-Local Tensions: Firms and States in the Global Space-Economy," ECONOMIC GEOGRAPHY (No. 70, 1994)

30. Thomas I. Palley, PLENTY OF NOTHING (Princeton: Princeton University Press, 1998)

31. It was the work of Karl Polyani which brilliantly introduced, in 1944, the phrase "socially embedded market," which I have adapted here. Cf. THE GREAT TRANSFORMATION (Boston: Beacon Press, 1980)

32. Johan Huizinga, HOMO LUDENS (Boston: Beacon Press, 1950), p. 173

PART I

THE PRIMAL WORLD

The moment we clearly realize this essentially compulsory movement of property — compulsory because it is set in a dynamic framework and is the mechanism by which certain fixed relationships between individuals are visualized and authenticated — then a number of traits of the economic life of primitive people, which has always sorely troubled investigators, become clear.

— *Paul Radin*

CHAPTER ONE

PRIMAL IMMEDIACY

The duality of subject and object in human perception is almost entirely absent in the primal world. The primal imagination does not easily distinguish between an objective reality and a subjective self. The boundaries between self and world are too fluid and ill-defined to sustain this perceptual stance. The primal world is natural in the sense that the self and nature are almost co-extensive. The self is as much an object of nature as nature is an object of self. Primal humanity consequently lacks subjectivity to the extent that it does not habitually contemplate an interior and autonomous world of the self with its own ground of truth.

The primal world is the realm of intimacy, of unmediated exchange. The relations which characterize parents and their children, lovers with each other, or humans with their companion animals or deeply familiar places, are essentially primal. There are few boundaries within these intimate relations, and relations deepen as boundaries dissolve within them. Modern languages tend to embed, as a condition of their modernity, the subject-object duality, and as a consequence often fail as vehicles to convey the essence of primal relations.[1] This is certainly true of English in which the intimate second-person singular "thee" (equivalent to the French "tu" or German "du") dropped from the language in the seventeenth century as Britain emerged as the premier global economic power. Thus, attempting to describe primal relations often requires its own vocabulary and grammar. Philosopher Martin Buber attempted to formulate such a vocabulary and grammar to describe primal relations, and was inevitably led to an almost poetic mode of expression to overcome the subject-object duality of contemporary expression, and to convey the immediacy of primal exchange. For him a "primary word" is artfully composed of word combinations from modern language to expose the essence of subject-object relations in their unmediated state. Buber's formulation of primal relations in his classic and influential work, *I and Thou*, suggests the primal by using an essentially poetical language:

> Primary words do not signify things, but they intimate relations.
> Primary words do not describe something that might exist independ-
>   ently of them, but being spoken they bring about existence.
> Primary words are spoken from the being.

Buber uses the word combination "I-Thou" to refer to an unmediated state of identity between subject and object. He uses the combination "I-It" to refer to that first state of separation between subjectivity and objectivity, where each of these begins to rest on its own existential ground. Thus "I," and being itself, is always relational.

> The existence of I and the speaking of I are one and the same thing.
> When a primary word is spoken the speaker enters the word and takes
>   his stand in it.[2]

The primary word *I-It* is spoken from a consciousness which posits the otherness, the *not-me* of the object of exchange, as when I *talk about* my beloved. The primary word *I-Thou* is spoken from a consciousness which posits identity between myself and another which obviates otherness, as when I *speak to* my beloved.

The underdevelopment of the subject-object duality inclines primitive peoples, that is those peoples whose cultures are most centered in primal modes, to address nature as simultaneously an extension of self, and the self as an extension of nature. These are of one spirit; they share the same essence. The playful fluidity of this relation between nature and self permits manifestations of nature to be viewed as personalities in the same way that the self is viewed as natural. Primal people make differing distinctions than modern people between human and animal, for example. For these peoples, animals are assumed to share the same essential spirit as do humans. Animals are therefore addressed as one person to another, account being taken of different forms and habits, rather as adults deal with children as fellow humans with different forms and habits. Among the Ojibwa Indians, before an animal could be hunted and killed, "permission had first to be asked of the animal, and apologies made to it afterwards."[3] This same etiquette is observed among the Bushmen of the Kalahari in Africa. Aesop's ancient animal fables treat animals as if they are essentially the same as humans, with the same merits and foibles. Other natural phenomena (trees, rivers, mountains) are likewise personified in the primal realm.

Among primal humanity a common spirit world penetrates and unites the known cosmos. People are connected to people, and people to the natural world by a common inhabitation of spirits, which flow ceaselessly in and out, around and among, all of perceived reality. This means that a rock or a tree is a spiritual entity as much as any human. These are often apprehended as *Thou,* where modern humans apprehend an *It*. Indeed, in the primal world the same spirit which inhabits an animal can take up residence in a human, or a spirit once resident in a human can find abode in a tree. The subject-object duality in which spiritual reality is confined to self and other humans, while nature is viewed as inert unless moved by objective laws, is a modern view of the world completely at odds with the experience of primal humanity. Anthropologist Henri Frankfort, echoing Buber, asserted:

> The world appears to primitive man neither inanimate nor empty but redundant with life; and life has individuality, in man and beast and plant, and in every phenomenon which confronts man — the thunderclap, the sudden shadow, the errie and unknown clearing in the wood, the stone which suddenly hurts him when he stumbles while on a hunting trip. Any phenomenon may at any time face him, not as "It," but as "Thou." In this confrontation, "Thou" is not contemplated with intellectual detachment; it is experienced as life confronting life, involving every faculty of man in reciprocal relationship. Thoughts, no less than acts and feelings, are subordinated to this experience.[4]

In the Shinto religious system of Japan, the world is perceived to be infused with *kami*, which are the subject-object of spiritual exchange. The primal origins of Shinto are nowhere better illustrated than by the difficulties which philologists have in defining *kami*. D.C. Holtom adumbrates the reality of *kami* as follows: "...it may be said that kami is essentially an expression used by the early Japanese people to classify experiences that evoked sentiments of caution and mystery in the presence of the manifestations of the strange and the marvelous. [...] In this sense it has an undifferentiated background of everything that is strange, fearful, mysterious, marvelous, uncontrolled, full of power, or beyond human comprehension."[5]

In the primal world, abstract thought takes mythopoetic form. Mythmaking is the means by which the enormous richness and importance of humanity's exchange encounters with its own spirit(s), the spirits of others and the material world can be narrated, that is given coherent form in a story. Because this world is apprehended so complexly at so many undifferentiated levels, the logic of modern science and its narrations is not understood. This is so precisely because in contemporary scientific thinking one truth may exclude others; substantive and analytical boundaries are usually clearly drawn. Myth-making is, in the words of theologian Mercea Eliade, "multivalent."[6] Seemingly inconsistent and contradictory elements are often combined in the same myth. Egyptologist John Wilson used the term "consubstantiality" to describe a myth-world in which there are, for example, at least two distinct and differing Egyptian creation stories.[7] The sky is understood as both the overarching body of a goddess, Nut, and also the manifestation of the god Horus (and of his consort, Hat-hor). Reality is consequently more contextually imagined than in modern societies.[8] The impulse toward a universalized, integrated and systematic scheme of thought, where truth is less contextualized, is highly muted.

The powerful immediacy of primal exchanges with the surrounding world requires a story — less an explanation than a retelling of encounters with nature in a poetic narrative, which gives them reality. Capturing the fullness of the encounter requires non-rational, or at least pre-rational, means of apprehension and narration. A Dakota Indian shaman explained his conception of God in these words:

> Everything as it moves, now and then, here and there, makes stops. The bird as it flies stops in one place to make its nest, and in another to rest in its flight. A man when he goes forth stops when he wills. So the god has stopped. The sun, which is so bright and beautiful, is one place where he has stopped. The moon, the stars, the winds, he has been with. The trees, the animals, are all where he has stopped, and the Indian thinks of these places and sends his prayers there to the place where the god has stopped and wins help and a blessing.[9]

The primal religious sensibility is monistic, and thus not other-worldly. Robert N. Bellah, an influential theorist of religious development, says that, "Primitive religions are on the whole oriented to a single cosmos — they know nothing of a wholly different world relative to which the actual world is utterly devoid of value."[10]

Mythopoetic thinking is not scientific in the modern conception, but it functions in the primal world in much the same way. Primitive humanity, the generic form of being for the great majority of millennia during which *homo sapiens* has existed, is fully human: as intelligent and imaginative as any contemporary human being. The primal imagination structures the relations between man and nature, man and man, man and society, including economics, using the structures of thought accessible to it given very limited but nonetheless very complex experience. French anthropologist Claude Levi-Strauss argued that totemism plays this sort of role in many primitive societies. He asserted that

> ideas and beliefs of the 'totemic' type particularly merit attention because, of the societies which have constructed or adopted them, they constitute codes making it possible to ensure, in the form of conceptual systems, the convertibility of messages appertaining to each level, even of those which are so remote from each other that they apparently relate solely to culture or solely to society, that is, to men's relations with each other, on the one hand, or, on the other, to phenomena of a technical or economic order which might rather seem to concern man's relations with nature.[11]

In conceptualization, and in narrative, the primal imagination orders in complex ways the world of nature, its plants and animals, its mountains, and streams, and this ordering parallels and is often consubstantial with very complex kinship typologies which relate humans to one another. These relationships are acted out in story, chant and dance, the playful ceremony capturing a universe of values and meanings.

Primal experiences and the mythopoetic modes which often accompany them are not, to repeat, restricted to humans most of whose lives are lived in a primal world. Contemporary people in modern societies continue to use poetry to express complex, multivalent truths not as easily conveyed by other forms of expression. Walt Whitman, America's first great poet, spoke in what is essentially a primal voice. He opens his *Leaves of Grass* (1855):

> I celebrate myself,
> And what I assume you shall assume
> For every atom belonging to me as good belongs to you.
> [...]
> Mine is no callous shell,
> I have instant conductors all over me whether I
>   pass or stop,
> They seize every object and lead it harmlessly
>   through me.[12]

At the same time, Whitman was very much a modern man, his sense of freedom and optimism giving full evidence of it. The mythopoetic disposition among primitive people shapes the important concepts of will and fate differently. Primal humanity is fatalistic in the sense that the world is seen as so full of wills, of causality which is so complex, that it cannot be even fully perceived, let alone controlled. Primal humanity can easily believe that circumstance is largely controlled by unknown wills. The result is a life centered in habit and reaction, rather than action. Purpose, as it is understood by contemporary people, is very underdeveloped. Rather, in a fateful world a primal life is what anthropologist W.E.H. Stanner called, "a one possibility thing."[13] From birth to death events in primal life unfold with a kind of inevitability which makes individual purpose and will existentially meaningless. Modern people, like Whitman, are willful in the sense that they tend to believe that since only they have will, the rest of nature can be understood, controlled and directed through human purpose. Modern humanity consequently is not inclined really to believe in fate. Mortimer Adler deleted fate from his list of the most persuasive and enduring Western ideas on the grounds that in the modern world the idea is no longer as vital and persuasive as it was, for example, to the Greeks.

The pervasiveness of the spirit world, which unites primal humanity to its natural environment, shapes its view of utility. Objects of nature are not really "objects" at all, but rather fellow subject-objects. The particular spiritual quality of the object determines how it is to be understood, approached, and used. Among the primal people of Polynesia each natural entity has a *ta pu* (taboo) which determines its relations to people: when it may be used; how it may be used; and who may use it. Certain feathers of certain birds may only be worn by members of the chiefly class. The *ta pu* of the feather and the *ta pu* of the chief are uniquely compatible. It is forbidden to others. The Omaha Indians distinguish between themselves and white people in that, "Indians never pick flowers." That is to say, Indians never pick flowers for pleasure. For plants "have sacred uses known (only) to secret owners."[14] Each plant has a particular spiritual character which engages itself to particular people with whom it has a sort of kinship. Only they may use this plant. Plant and animal classifications of primitive people, often tied to totemism, are extraordinarily elaborate and detailed. Plants, for example, are divided into hundreds of species and sub-species not only on the basis of a system of morphology, but also on their perceived relations with either of the sexes or with particular individuals who may be related to them or named for them.

In the primal world, thought, action and words are united by the spirits which animate them. There is no thought or spirit which does not manifest itself in the world. Among the Hopi Indians thought is believed to traffic with the material world, and *thought intensity* or concentration responsible for the degree of effect in material outcomes. In the extreme case, among aborigines of Australia the world of dreams, "The Dreaming," is thought to be the *real world*, and the waking state only an extension of this world of dreams. Other primitive people also see dreams as essential conveyers of reality. Which is to say that these people make no distinction between the interior reality of consciousness and the exterior reality of the world, or at least, psychoanalysis notwithstanding, a distinction very different from our own.

Words, too, are indistinguishable from the reality they describe. To say the thing is to invoke its essential spirit. Name-giving is an act of spiritual exchange dynamically joining speech with the encountered world as a form of possession. In the Biblical creation story the first man participates in creation and is given dominion over it: "and whatsoever Adam called every living creature, that was the name thereof." [Genesis 2:19] To name something is to transact its form and reality. In one telling, the Egyptian primordial god Ra created himself by naming the parts of his body. *In the beginning was the word.* Even mentioning the name of a dead person is forbidden in some societies for fear of the deceased's spirit taking up residence in the speaker. Other cultures fear mirrors or photography because these capture the spirit as well as the image of the person. Ceremonies of incantation exchange the self with the spiritual essence of the things which are the focus of the chant. In the *voodoo* cults of Africa and the New World, an object of nature can be metabolized into a *person* with the correct incantation, and that object can then be made well or ill, its spirit and that of the person being completely exchangeable in their shared spiritual essence. Recital and incantation join the reality of the human self to the reality of the world. In the primal world stories are dramatized, "acknowledging in them a special virtue which could be activated by recital."[15] The celebration of the Eucharist in many Christian churches imbeds the primal world in the everyday life of believers. The celebrant's incantation of the words of Jesus, "This is my body... this is my blood," is believed to bring the actual presence of Jesus transubstantially, "under the appearances of bread and wine," to the congregation. Primal religion is an action system on a most elemental, not to say pure, level precisely because of its metabolic exchange of the subjective with the objective in the deed. Subject and action are merged, suggested poet W.B. Yeats, when "the dancer becomes the dance." Bellah says that, "Primitive *religious action* is characterized [...] by identification, 'participation,' acting-out."[16] Modern language often fails to convey this telescopic process where space, time and action are fused. Stanner coined the term "everywhen" to describe the collapse of space into time, a time out of time, captured in the Australian aborigine's conception of "The Dreaming."[17]

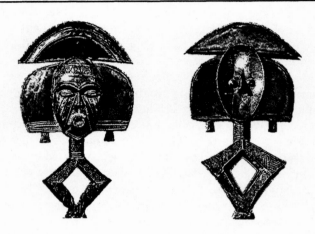

AFRICAN CARVINGS

Figure 1:1 "Abstraction by inbreeding" is a characteristic of primitive art as it seeks to reduce reality to its essential spiritual elements. Repetition and reduction of objective, representational forms over time produces powerful, but relatively unmediated abstractions, which capture the spirit of the object and render it charismatic. The figure on the right is a further abstraction of the abstract figure on the left.

Many of these elements are evidenced in primitive art, which can be characterized in a number of ways. Primitive art is undifferentiated between systems of utility and systems of symbol. These merge in individual objects. In African art a ceremonial mask is as useful as a door or a stool, and these are made in artistic forms in which content and expression are merged. Primitive art is charismatic: it invites immediate engagement and psychological reaction in relatively pure states: of awe, of fear, of rapture. Primitive art is bold: its colors and shapes are meant to initially assert and enchant. Through his art primitive man makes visible his attempts at abstraction, his attempts to create a controlled distance between himself and his environment. His artistic abstraction expresses the repetition and incremental reduction of originally representational forms, capturing their spiritual essences in what art historian

H.W. Janson called "abstraction by inbreeding," revealing "the primitive artist's concern with the otherness of the spirit world."[18] Thus, while abstraction is as intrinsic to the primal imagination as to all human imagination, it is not the highly mediated or multilayered abstraction which characterizes more advanced societies. Primitive art is ultimately spiritual, meant to bridge the distance between the viewer as subject and the art as object, and thus it is almost always contextual: it seldom exists as "art for art's sake." It is for this reason that primitive art is not usually narrative in character; it is not a means to an end, meant to convey some exterior value or capture some larger lesson. It is intrinsically tied to an action system in which the individual, the social and the spiritual cohere as one event and one substance in dynamic exchange.

Since all action is united to the spirit world, nothing which occurs is devoid of spiritual character in the primal world. Among primitive people as widely separated as those of Borneo and West Africa death or illness is never accidental, for accident implies an impersonal world where things occur because of objective laws devoid of will or personality. In the primal world the illness or death of even very elderly persons is always associated with a malevolent spirit. Illness or death from natural causes would assume a nature ungoverned by the interpenetrating spirit world which animates the totality of reality. Such an assumption would also relieve the relatives of the dead or the ill of any responsibility for retribution against those who used witchcraft against their kin. Among the descendants of escaped African slaves in contemporary Guiana, South America, the coffin of the deceased is carried around the village until it is drawn to and points at the house from which the evil spell originated. The inhabitants of that house are held responsible for the spirit-possession which caused the death. In many primitive societies death and its attendant ceremonies form a main focus for community life. In contemporary Ghana in West Africa coffin-making is a major craft industry, and even poor families always seem to find the resources to spend on elaborate funerals.

In many cases the possession of benign spirits is both sought and welcomed. Primal ritual is centered in this exchange with the spirit world. James Baldwin, in the autobiographical novel of his youth, *Go Tell It On The Mountain*, recounts a service in a Pentecostal church which is an instance of primal spirit possession in the midst of a modern city:

> And something moved in John's body which was not John. He was invaded, set at naught, possessed. This power had struck John, in the head or in the heart; and, in a moment, wholly, filling him with an anguish that he could never in his life have imagined, that he surely could not endure, that even now he could not believe, have opened him up; had cracked him open, as wood beneath the ax cracks down the middle, as rocks break up;

had ripped him and felled him in a moment, so that John had not felt the wound, but only the agony, had not felt the fall, but only the fear; and here now, helpless, screaming at the very bottom of darkness.[19]

To the degree that primal sensibilities create a fusion between the self and the spirit world, the self may also isolate itself from reality as it is experienced materially and socially, day to day. Consequently, *I-Thou* encounters should be understood at various levels of intensity and immediacy, with episodes of spirit-possession representing a very deep fusion between the self and the spiritual world, which creates, as suggested by Baldwin, a terrible solitude. In relating the meaning of the sun dance among the Plains Indians, Edward Sapir, a noted linguist and anthropologist early in this century, noted:

> The sun dance is an exceedingly elaborate ritual which lasts many days and in which each song and each step in the progress of the ceremonies is a social expression. For all that, the final validation of the sun dance, as of every other form of Plains religion, seems to rest with the individual in his introspective loneliness. The nuclear idea is the 'blessing' or 'manitou' experience, in which the individual puts himself in a relation of extreme intimacy with the world of supernatural power or 'medicine'.[20]

It is in these deeply possessed states that the "individual," in his existential isolation, experiences an interior "self."

Primal humans also see their own bodies as extensions of the natural world, and in this way no different than a tree, a rock or a stream. It is not an inert vessel which contains the spirit, but rather is one more manifestation of an encompassing spirit world. In this sense, the body is another element of nature with which spiritually to interact, especially at its boundaries: skin, hair, nose, mouth, eyes, ears, and genitals. The exchange of spirits from a dead body to a living one is something sometimes honored, but often guarded against by primitive people. Ritual cannibalism as practiced, for example, in Borneo, and associated with death rites within which the dead person's name is never again invoked, seems to be a way of incorporating the spirit of the dead. The marked tendency of primal people to tattoo, scar, pierce, braid, and paint their bodies may be another manifestation of this attempt to identify and mediate the boundaries between self and nature. The body parts are fetishized as objects-subjects of nature. One consequently not only possesses a body, one is possessed by a body.[21] The phenomenon of spirit possession, however experienced or induced, is consequently intrinsic to primal life. Beneath the surface experiences of habitual life the anarchy of potential spirit possession lurks. From this vortex a fluid and uncontrolled spirit world may reach up and carry away human consciousness. At the primal core of human subconsciousness resides the potential victim — the object to whom things "happen," and who is thus not "responsible" — and the culture of victimhood, of sacrifice, of suffering and of endurance.

The belief of primal humanity that the world of spirits is coextensive with reality itself establishes limits to which the material environment can be put. The material world is spiritually circumscribed. The lack of permanent dwellings in primal societies (even those which are sedentary) may often be connected to the fear of the seeming inertness of permanent structures, an implied lack of spirit within them. They are in a sense "dead." Structures made of relatively impermanent materials (wood, vegetation, hides, dung or mud) reflect the fluidity of natural life, and are often regarded as living beings which must be constantly refreshed or allowed to decay. Perfectly usable tools or vessels may be abandoned for new ones for the same reason, often after having been broken to insure the release of their spirits. The use of spirit houses in Micronesia, or of spirit lodges among American Indians is in part such a manifestation. The custom in traditional Celtic societies, like Ireland and Wales, to give names to houses may echo a more ancient tradition of regarding the lodge as an actual living being, possessing its own spirits. The Arthurian legends contain many of these same Celtic elements, with use objects like swords having individual names and spirits ("Excaliber"), and humans having animal names, like Merlin (raven). Cultural historian Johan Huizinga writes: "If, at the present time, ships still have names, but bells and most houses have not, the reason lies in the fact that the ship preserves a sort of personality, also expressed in the English usage of making ships feminine. In the Middle Ages this tendency to personify things was much stronger; every house and every bell had its name."[22]

Civilization, a culture based on permanent residence in permanent structures, requires humans to begin to construct essential boundaries between themselves and the world of nature. Nature, in order to be truly *used*, had to be immobilized and voided of spiritual content. Humankind had to move beyond what Bloomer and Moore termed "the body boundary" to "measure and order the world out from our own bodies."[23] The Romans ritualized this disposition of humanity into a special urban domain by digging a symbolic trench (*pomarium*) around city outskirts — but within the walls — underlining this separation between order and potential disorder. The earliest Maya cities were defined by a simple *plaza* composed of pounded lime plaster which separated the earth, and the spirits dwelling within it, from the humans walking on it.

Civilization seems to begin when the subject-object (*I-It*) dualism has sufficient strength for humans to distance themselves from nature and to regard the more permanent and shapeable materials of nature (stone, baked clay, and metals) to be relatively inert, and because they themselves are lacking in wills, subject to human will, which arranges them into permanent structures. The fact that people like ourselves, *homo sapiens*, have chosen to live all but the last six thousand or so of a 100,000-year history in uncivilized environments underlines how extraordinary this transition in basic consciousness is. Only very special circumstances seem to impel the initiation of civilization. But the intellectual consequences of urbanity are fundamental, for civilization reflects a new human understanding of self in relation to nature, and ultimately to the cosmos. That most civilized of men, and archetype of Western man, Socrates, asserted: "I have nothing to do with the trees of the field, I have to do only with the man of the city."[24]

Attendant to this process of severing the basic bonds which tie humans to nature is a breaking of blood or kinship ties. Civilized bonds are not blood ties, and indeed the prerequisite of civilization seems to be that these natural kinship ties be broken or at least fundamentally altered. In many ancient mythologies civilization begins in fratricide. Seth killed his brother Osiris, the first pharaoh, at the dawn of Egyptian civilization. Cain, the builder of the first city, killed his pastoral brother, Abel, in the Old Testament. The founding of Rome is climaxed by the murder of Remus by his twin, Romulus, who names the city for himself. Parallel Mesopotamian and Indian myths point to the same sensibility. The relations of pre-civilized human beings with one another are extraordinarily complex, and in many ways far more systematized and regulated than those of civilized people. A difference lies in the complexity of the formal institutions of civilized people — governance, religion, economy. These formal institutions, in order to function, compromise ties of blood.

NOTES TO CHAPTER ONE

1. Benjamin Whorf has suggested, for example, that the subject-verb-object structure of Indo-European languages biases them toward *things* rather than *processes*. Carroll, *op.cit.*; see, esp. "The Relation of Habitual Thought and Behavior to Language," pp. 134ff.
2. Martin Buber, I AND THOU, R.G. Smith, trans. (New York: Charles Scribner's Sons, 1958), pp. 3 - 4
3. Claude Levi-Strauss, TOTEMISM, Rodney Needham, trans. (Boston: Beacon Press, 1963), p. 21

4. Henri Frankfort, *et.al.*, BEFORE PHILOSOPHY (Baltimore: Pelican Books, 1949), p. 14
5. D.C. Holtom, "The Centrality of *Kami* in Shinto," in H. Byron Earhart, RELIGION IN THE JAPANESE EXPERIENCE (Belmont, CA: Wadsworth Publishing Company, 1974), p. 11
6. Mercea Eliade, MYTH AND REALITY (New York: Harper and Row Publishers, 1963)
7. John A. Wilson, "Egypt," in Frankfort *et.al.*, *op.cit.*
8. I have adapted the concept of "high context" and "low context" in culture from Geert Hofstede, CULTURE'S CONSEQUENCES (Beverly Hills, CA: Sage Publications, 1980)
9. Claude Levi-Strauss, TOTEMISM, *op.cit.*, p. 98
10. Bellah, *op.cit.*, p. 360; Bellah acknowledges his debt to the seminal work of Max Weber, THE SOCIOLOGY OF RELIGION, Ephraim Fischoff, trans. (Boston: Beacon Press, 1963)
11. Claude Levi-Strauss, THE SAVAGE MIND (Chicago: University of Chicago Press, 1966), p. 90 - 91
12. Walt Whitman was to become a model for the primal "counterculture" of the 'sixties, and for the "beat poets," including Allen Ginsberg.
13. W.E.H. Stanner, "The Dreaming," in William Lessa and Evon Z. Vogt, eds., READER IN CONTEMPORARY RELIGION (Evanston, Ill: Row, Peterson Publishers, 1958), p. 513
14. Levi-Strauss, THE SAVAGE MIND, *op.cit.*, p. 43
15. Frankfort, *op. cit.,* p. 16
16. Bellah, *op. cit.,* p. 363
17. Stanner, *op.cit.*, p. 514
18. H.W. Janson, HISTORY OF ART (New York: Harry N. Abrams, Inc., 1962), p. 28
19. James Baldwin, GO TELL IT ON THE MOUNTAIN (New York: Dial Press, 1963) p. 219
20. Edward Sapir, "The Meaning of Religion," in David G. Mandelbaum, ed., SELECTED WRITINGS OF EDWARD SAPIR (Berkeley: University of California Press, 1949), p. 350
21. This body-fetish phenomenon replicates itself almost exactly in contemporary "hard rock culture," which can be viewed as essentially primal in its sensibilities: its Dionysian music rooted in rhythm; hallucinatory drugs; chthonic sexuality; non-rational apprehension focused in astrology, psychic phenomena, Satanism and Eastern religion; indifference toward work and property; a fateful timelessness which courts early death. Camille Paglia says of the primal god, Dionysus: "He is not pleasure, but pleasure-pain, the tormenting bondage of our life in the body." SEXUAL PERSONAE (New York: Vintage Books, 1991), p. 94

22. J. Huizinga, THE WANING OF THE MIDDLE AGES (New York: Anchor Books, 1954), p. 227
23. Kent C. Bloomer and Charles W. Moore, BODY, MEMORY AND ARCHI-TECTURE (New Haven, CT: Yale University Press, 1977), p. 1; see also Edward T. Hall, THE SILENT LANGUAGE (Garden City, NJ: Doubleday & Co., 1959)
24. Quoted by Jose Ortega y Gasset, THE REVOLT OF THE MASSES (New York: W.W. Norton, 1932), p. 164

CHAPTER TWO

GOODS AS SOULS

The movement of goods within primal societies observes fluid social contours. Students of primitive societies have noted the absolutely central role of gift-exchange within them. The cultural habit of gift-exchange seems to be found among humanity everywhere, and to be guided by remarkably similar cultural values. In the primal world every good is thought to carry its own purposive spirit. A gift is a particular kind of good possessing its own spiritual quality, which the exchange of gifts sustains. This means, among other things, that for the spirit (which the Maoris of New Zealand call a *hau*) of a gift good to endure, it must be kept in motion. Reciprocal exchange is the vehicle by which this fluid spiritual momentum of goods is maintained in the primal world. Reciprocity is the spiritual essence that makes a gift of a good, nourishing and sustaining its gift character. A gift that is not reciprocated ceases to be a gift. "A gift that cannot move loses its gift properties," explains Lewis Hyde.[1] In this sense, gift-exchange follows the structures of totemism. A good may be consumed, but the obligations of reciprocity keeps the "spirit of the gift" in motion amid, and sustaining, many complex social relationships. Marcel Mauss, the French anthropologist whose work on gift-giving is seminal, suggested that: "This rigorous combination of symmetrical and opposed rights and duties ceases to appear contradictory once one realizes that it consists above all of a melange of spiritual bonds between things which are in some degree souls, and individuals and groups which interact in some degree as things."[2]

Once again, the dialectic of the *I-Thou* and the *I-It* is central to understanding the primal world. All exchange carries the spiritual weight not only of goods and their "souls," but of the entire social system and its complex cultural bonds. Primal exchange is consequently embedded in an extraordinary complexity of relations which no body of economic rules could begin to encompass. *Economic Man* is far too stark, calculating and materially-rational creature to function in the primal world, if indeed he can fully function in any realm, the Gordon Gekos ("Greed is good") of the world notwithstanding. In addition, primal people include in their economics a sense of distributive justice, which classical market systems in and of themselves do not. That is to say, in market economics *qua market economics* the distributive system is self-justifying. Corrections to market distribution which reflect social concerns are largely external to it. Paul Radin, one of the most imaginative anthropologists of his day, suggested that imbedded in primitive economic arrangements there is a universal standard of "the irreducible minimum." "This theory is fundamental to remember. According to it, every individual possessed an inalienable right to food, shelter and clothing. To deny anyone this irreducible minimum was equivalent to saying that a man no longer existed, that he was dead."[3]

Gift-exchange is a kind of distributive system which, among other qualities, acknowledges this "irreducible minimum." Among primal people gift-giving is a central activity, indeed the principal means by which goods transactions often take place. Bronislaw Malinowski, in his classic study of the Massin peoples of the Trobriand Islands, documents the *kula*, ceremonial exchanges in gift-giving circles with very complex rules.[4] Once again, these practices are not so remote from modern experience. To the degree that our own households and families reflect the primal world, most material transactions among members are gift exchanges, the gifts embodying the selves which are mutually given, reinforcing systems of emotional and social bonding and obligation. Among primitive people, who live in families as the near-sum of their experience, gift-giving is the near-sum of exchange.

For primitive people gift-exchange is especially important in maintaining good relations with strangers and nearby people. Hospitality is a virtue almost without equals. Among the highland people of New Guinea, a good part of tribal activity is directed toward this gift-giving. The principal source of wealth, swine, is ritually exchanged between tribes each year, one tribe receiving or giving in alternate years. Tribal headmen see their status largely in terms of the ability to return all the swine given to them plus additional swine at the next gift ceremony. This creates incentives for improving swine husbandry, and functions as a form of social saving since consumption must be moderated by the obligations entailed in returning the gift.

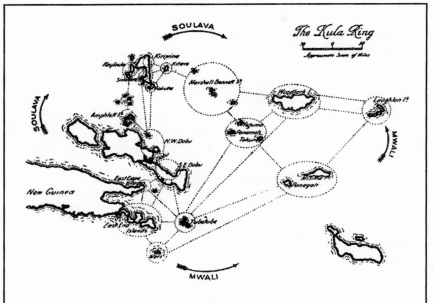

THE KULA RING

Figure 3:1 Bronislaw Malinowski documented the *kula ring*, a very complex ceremonial exchange of gifts among the Massin people, who occupy the islands around New Guinea. Two gifts lies at the heart of the gift-exchange system: necklaces, "soulava," and armshells, "mwali." The map above illustrates the connection and direction of gift cycles.

In sharing a gift, the spirit of the gift, its *hau*, remains benign. Attempts to hoard given goods and not to reciprocate them can lead to conflict. It is in the nature of the gift that it moves, or as Hyde puts it, "The gift is property that perishes."[5] As it is a kind of spiritual "chain letter," to remove a good from circulation by not reciprocating it is a kind of theft, which can only visit evil on the thief and those in contact with him. Among the Udak in Africa "any wealth transferred from one subclan to another, whether animals, grain or money, is in the nature of a gift, and should be consumed and not invested for growth." Those who hoard in this way are regarded as immoral.[6] To avoid conflict with other people, gifts are given so that spiritual reciprocity is initiated and maintained. The first colonists in seventeenth-century Massachusetts, noting that the natives who had given them goods in previous days had gathered outside their doors expecting reciprocation, coined the term "Indian giver" to describe this behavior which they did not understand.

Property, at least as understood in modern societies, does not exist in the primal world. If a gift is, as Hyde suggests, "property that perishes" a society characterized by gift-giving undermines the concept of propriety or ownership which makes property meaningful. Goods in motion cannot be truly owned, only consumed or passed on so that the spirit which animates them, giving them their purposeful character, remains benign. Ownership is itself an impediment to this ceaseless and continuous flow of goods and spirits. Paul Radin expressed the dialectic between "movement" and "property" as follows:

> In aboriginal societies, to express the matter abstractly, the recognition that "all things flow" was never lost sight of and any action or theory that denied this manifest fact had little chance of being accepted But the "flow," movement, to continue our image, may mean a number of things. It need not be "linear" or presuppose that what was once passed will never return again as the Greek philosopher, Heraclitus, who first enunciated this doctrine for Western Europe, taught. The flux could, on the contrary, be conceived as "circular" and cyclical. Property would then, for instance, pass from one person to another within a definitely circumscribed space and, after making the circuit, either return to the person, or his proxy, from whom it originally started.
> [...]
> Property is simply inextricably enmeshed in this movement of life.[7]

Since property is understood as a kind of solecism which inhibits the natural movement of goods, primal economics is inherently directed toward material poverty. The material absolute poverty of primitive people has often been noted. Dress, shelter, and food are inherently minimal. The inclination toward the "irreducible minimum" of individual subsistence in distributive relations seems inevitably to be paralleled by a reduction of all economics to minimal levels of subsistence as well. Primal economy is oriented toward the distribution of goods rather than toward their production. One could say that a bias toward distribution inhibits those cultural values, such as saving, which further a productive economic orientation. To live in a primal world is consequently to be unavoidably poor.

Given this primitive understanding of property in distributive relations one can also suggest that *theft* will have different underpinnings in the primal world. In societies where simple goods are freely available to all, possession itself is more broadly understood. Something not in immediate use by another is available for the taking, or is freely offered. It is common for modern people to note that even a simple compliment or expression of admiration for something in the possession of primitive people will result in its being offered as a gift. It is difficult for "theft" to acquire an identity in such circumstances. "Actually in a simple egalitarian society," suggests Morton H. Fried, "the taking of something before it is offered is more akin to rudeness than stealing."[8] Removing a good from common circulation may itself be a form of antisocial behavior if it is not for consumption. What we would call "saving" or capital accumulation is often understood in this negative context in the primal world. Karl Marx reflected a very ancient animus in his moral opposition to capitalism as theft. Aristotle, who lived in a market-oriented society, makes something of the same distinction in his *Politics*: "Money-making then, as we have said, is of two kinds; one is necessary and acceptable, which we may call administrative [i.e., related to household management]; the other, commercial, which depends on exchange, is justly regarded with disapproval, since it arises not from nature but from men's dealings with each other."[9]

The process of exchange is viewed here as unnatural because it undermines sociality: in gaining "unequally" from one another in exchange, men take something they have no right to. Aristotle condemns lending money for interest outright for the same reason. Lending for interest and commercial trade share the quality of taking advantage of scarcity, which is to the immediate detriment of at least one participant in this sort of "unequal" exchange, and always to the detriment of society as a whole.

The primal belief that property is a kind of theft may also justify theft as a kind of retribution, and often as an honorable exercise. Many ancient heroic tales have a Robin Hood quality which celebrates theft. Two great creation myths which have influenced the West founded mankind's autonomy in acts of theft. Prometheus stole fire from the gods so that mankind might thrive, in Greek mythology. Adam and Eve's primal act of moral autonomy is one of theft, stealing fruit from the "Tree of Knowledge of Good and Evil." The Greek god Hermes was a noted thief, and patron of thieves. Micah in the *Book of Judges* steals silver from his mother. (In the cases of Hermes and Micah the act of theft is transformed into an act of reconciliation with kin: both receive gifts of superior value for the return of the stolen good.) The famous Irish tale of Cuchulain narrates the great "cattle raid of Cooley." Homer's hero Odysseus boasts that he will sustain his voyage by raiding and pirating, in addition to the gifts his various hosts give him. Roman legend celebrated the raid in which their ancestors stole wives from a neighboring people, the famous "Rape of the Sabine Women," often depicted in art.

Theft is less an offense against property rights than an offense against individuals and their kin in the primal world. Consequently, to steal from strangers or other non-kin has a very different character than in modern, civil societies where property rights are invested by law and contract, concepts which are absent or differently formed in pre-civil societies. Property as we now understand it began to acquire a discrete identity as a right — independent of the persons who actually possess it — only when *persons* acquired the social mobility and rationality which characterize market exchange. Possession ("propriety") is only evidence of a right ("Possession is nine points of the law") in modern legal systems. Markets invest the power of motion in persons, who move *inherently immobile goods* through an act of rational will in exchange. "There is no property without an actor," posits Lewis Hyde, "and in this sense property is an expression of *the human will in things*" (my emphasis).[10]

In the primal imagination where, as Radin asserts "all things flow," the attachment of goods to persons in the form of property is difficult to sustain because persons are regarded less as willful actors than as ciphers for spirits or kinship-related obligations. The Old Testament is reflecting an ancient preference for kinship obligations over property rights when it declares: "Unto a stranger thou mayest lend upon usury: but unto thy brother thou shall not lend upon usury."[Deuteronomy 23:20] Lending money for interest ("usury") is viewed as equivalent to thievery because there is no equality in exchange: more is demanded in return than is given.[11] Thus, in this instance of Mosaic law, to "steal" from non-kin is permitted; to "steal" from kin is prohibited. Lending for interest is an offense against persons rather than property, and is permitted where that person is not a blood relative, "a stranger," because there is a net gain in wealth for the kinship group. A principle of "honor among thieves" in primitive societies often makes such distinctions between the in-group and the out-group. Anthropologist Robert Boyd confirmed this in his studies of the Machiguenga community in the forests of Peru. These itinerant slash-and-burn farmers combine hunting and gathering with fishing in isolated family units. He concludes that it is common for nomadic people such as the Machiguenga, who exchange goods primarily with kin, to feel little or no obligation to be "fair" with strangers. In contrast, "fairness saturates the give-and-take in sedentary societies, where people belong to large, economically interdependent groups."[12]

In market relations where persons are relatively free of kin ties in goods transactions, and thus more mobile in relation to one another and the material world, goods achieve the immobility necessary for them to acquire the characteristics of property. It is markets that make property of goods because it in markets that the contractual relations necessary to attach goods to willful individual actors arises. A good is both visible and usable as property within a set of exchange relations unique to the market. It is the context (or what Heidegger would call the "referential totality") of the market that transforms goods into property, because markets are arenas of actors who express their wills through goods. Alternatively, a good which is a gift becomes visible as such only in the context of the *mobile* relations of spiritual things expressed as charismatic or gift-giving. In neither case, as property nor as gift, does a good have an absolute "identity-in-itself" apart from the relations of exchange. Consequently, theft acquires its highest legal and moral sanctions as an offense against property rights in market-oriented societies. It may be that the widespread, near-institutionalization of theft ("kleptocracy") in many pre-civil societies has its roots in this primal inclination toward what modern people call "theft" as inextricable from property relations themselves. The "crony capitalism" of emerging market economies in many parts of the world, such as Nigeria, Indonesia and the Philippines, similarly reflects the contentious relations which exist between kin, or kin-like, obligations and the functional requirements of full-blown capitalism. Mature capitalism also requires, as we shall see, the subject-object dualism which is fully developed only in the civil world.

Gift-exchange rules govern primal dealings with the spirit world. Sacrifice must be given in reciprocation for the gift of the good. In the Santaria religion, which originated in what is now Nigeria and spread to the New World, food and other goods are left for the spirits to keep them benign and provident. Shinto religion in Japan is characterized by the same obligation conducted in the home at the family's shrine to its ancestors. Northwest Indians always return to the sea the first portion of the salmon catch. Returning to the god a portion of the first fruits of the harvest is an ancient custom reflected in the tradition of religious tithing — the giving of a tenth. Sometimes the first child is specially offered to the service of the god in reciprocation for this first proof of the gift of fertility.

Saving, in the sense of personal wealth-building and accumulation, is frowned on in primal societies, where it is indistinguishable from hoarding. Status depends on the generosity with which one gives gifts. The failure to give gifts, especially when it is known that one has the resources to do so, is a most profound insult requiring retribution. Among the Indians of the American Northwest *potlatching* (literally, "nourishing") was a process highly institution-alized. Tribes met to exchange gifts from the surpluses which had been accumulated in fishing, hunting, collecting and craftsmanship. What gifts were given by whom at previous potlatches were duly noted. He who was most generous had the highest praise, and goods not exchanged that could not be consumed in feasting were ritually destroyed (later as symbolic "coppers") so that their spirits, trapped by a lack of circulation, were released, causing no harm or conflict, and so that the superiority in honor of the destroyer might reveal itself. One potlatching tribe, the Haida, called their feasting, "killing wealth." H.G. Barnett summarized his understanding of the potlatch: "Virtue rests in publicly disposing of wealth, not in its mere acquisition and accumulation. Accumulation in any quantity by borrowing or otherwise, in fact, is unthinkable unless it be for the purpose of immediate redistribution."[13] The wide-spread practice of the principles which underlay potlatching in societies separated in time and space has been extensively documented. Customs exactly parallel to those of Northwest Indians have been described by Mauss, Granet and Held in Melanesia, archaic Greece and old Germanic culture, ancient China and pre-Islamic Arabia.[14]

To be sure, "killing wealth" may have distributive consequences, although that may not be its intent. The intent is essentially spiritual, to maintain the nourishing and interdependent exchange of social-goods relations, as well as to demonstrate the honor of the giver. Ritual destruction of goods at its heart is in fact a kind of distribution if it achieves the dual aim of dissolving the basis of potential conflict and releasing the spirit of the good into circulation. "The theft and even destruction of goods so common among primitive peoples in connection with funeral rites, with initiation ceremonies and on numerous other occasions, then actually serve as methods of distribution," Radin maintains. "This is particularly true in Africa and parts of Melanesia. It is absent nowhere."[15] Economic surplus never achieves a discrete identity as wealth because primal laws of motion dissolve surplus before it becomes wealth. The organic ties of all goods to people in dynamic relation subsumes goods exchanges within a matrix of social relations. As Radin asserts, "One of the most important by-products of this dominance of the social functions of wealth is to stimulate the expression of emotional-social attitudes that, on the face of things, are irrational and certainly non-utilitarian."[16] The exchange of goods in primal society thus does not accord with the norms of a classical market. The exchange of goods is so loaded with social and spiritual weight that markets cannot easily be established. Anthropologist Marshall Sahlins even generalizes that, "Markets properly so-called, competitive and price fixing, are universally absent from primitive society."[17]

❖ ❖ ❖ ❖

Anthropologists often refer to primal societies as "segmentary." Among other things, especially the structure of kinship relations, this refers to the tendency of these societies to break up into smaller groups once they have reached a certain size. Some observers have attributed this phenomenon to economic forces: once groups have reached a certain size in terms of population and available resources (including technology), the group will divide into smaller segments. It seems as likely that groups segment to avoid interpersonal conflict: the larger the group, the fewer the possibilities for interpersonal exchange and bonding, and the more likelihood there is of conflict. Groups will in fact divide even if it is economically inefficient to do so. Avoiding conflict is reinforced by communal ceremonies and the continual exchange of gifts between individuals and groups. Similarly, there is some evidence to indicate that the amount of effort groups devote to gathering food or other goods is limited by the *average* of groups in the area. Since groups have somewhat different sizes as well as different age and gender distributions, and therefore different capacities for work, individual groups work toward the norm of nearby groups, thereby avoiding consumption which might induce jealous conflict. Often, "productive intensity is inversely related to productive capacity."[18]

At the same time, the segmentary nature of primal society, its basic impulses toward preserving inner cohesion, tends to focus conflict outward. In most primitive groups adult men see much of their identity in their roles as warriors. To be sure, this does not mean incessant conflict with neighboring groups, although among some primitive people (e.g. those in Borneo) the cycle of revenge warfare is almost a way of life. But potentially conflicted relations with non-kin often means engaging in a kind of sham warfare, a playful, game-like exchange where rights are asserted and protected, without the loss of life. It may also mean on-going conflict resolution through inter-tribal marriage, trade and gift-giving. However, this internal lack of segmentation does mean that in the primal world members of the out-group are viewed in ways fundamentally different from kin. In the extreme case, among the Fiji Islanders, the word for stranger and the word for enemy is the same.

The relative lack of internal cleavages in primal groups occurs at the expense of fundamental ones with the surrounding human world. But more than this, the lack of strict internal roles, statuses, and hierarchies means that what social cleavages do exist — especially those related to age and gender — tend to be cross-cutting cleavages. That is, one's distinction from one's fellows on the basis of gender tend to be balanced with ties to them based on age. Elderly men and women have common ties which distinguish them from youth of either gender, and can prevent gender distinctions from becoming gender conflicts.

As a result primal groups do not develop the social skills which adapt them to easy communication with or flexible interaction with strangers. The etiquette of gift-exchange in some ways functions as a substitute for these more fluid social adaptations in which contention is seen as a normal part of life with people whose values and interests may be different from one's own. If one conceives of a market as a form of structured contention, as an arena purposely designed to take advantage of relative scarcities and those persons affected by them, one can understand why markets and those who would take advantage of scarcity are so avoided in the primal world.

Trading systems should be distinguished from markets. All markets are trading systems, but not all trading systems are markets. Goods may transfer among individuals through gift-giving, and among some primal groups this is the principal means by which goods are exchanged. Trading systems emerge as distance, both in terms of kinship and geography, begin to influence the movement of goods. Or as Sahlins puts it, "Reciprocity is inclined toward the generalized pole by close kinship, toward the negative extreme in proportion to kinship distance."[19] In short, trade and the principles which govern it, emerge as economic relations become distant from localized contexts.

What characterizes most of these trading systems is what goods enter or do not enter them; the basis of exchange; and who may trade. Unlike markets, which are theoretically perfect to the extent that anyone and any good can participate under conditions of complete information, and where goods exchange on the basis of competitive bargaining which sets the exchange price, primitive trading systems restrict or negate each of these. Some goods, like certain staple foods, may never enter into trade because trade in staples might violate the principles of "the irreducible minimum" of subsistence which people owe to one another. The rules of totemism may forbid the exchange of certain goods between certain people. Other valued goods may enter into trade, but only at a traditional barter price: that is, relative scarcities are not allowed to alter the terms of trade in any particular instance. If there is a shortage of one good, that will lead to a surplus of another good in terms of exchange, or the trade will clear with net creditors and debtors, who must make good the exchange at a future trade. Terms of trade may be adjusted to reflect secular surpluses or shortages over long periods, but exploiting a shortage or a surplus in any individual transaction would be regarded as anti-social and conflict-provoking.

Some anthropologists have suggested that a labor-theory of value may be at work in primal trading. To the degree that goods embody the effort of the individual who gathered or created them, those goods embody his spirit, and reflect a metabolic relationship between him and the world. To enter into an exchange relationship which does not respect the fullness of that encounter with the world by giving him less than a fair exchange (i.e. a spiritual equivalency) is considered immoral. Thus, to the degree that the scarcity of a good increases over time requiring that the traditional barter price be altered, what is being accounted for is the increased human effort required to produce it, not the changed condition of scarcity itself. Refusal to trade with traditional partners, and even with some non-traditional partners, is often regarded as hostile in primitive trading systems.

Since each person is regarded as being possessed of a spirit or spirits, the primal world is charismatic (from the Greek *charism,* "gift") in its concepts of personhood. That is, interpersonal relations, including those of influence, are a variety of gift-exchange. Here I am adapting the important concept of Max Weber, who distinguished between institutional sources of authority, and personal sources. Ceremony in the primal world in its various shamanistic manifestations is very much a charismatic arena in which spirit-possession plays a central role. Consciousness-altering substances, used in many primal cultures around the world; and activities such as ritual dancing combined with repetitive chant, are mechanisms for summoning spirits, who then take possession of individuals. Ritual dancing, often accompanied by drums, may be the means by which the spirits of the dead are summoned from the earth below. The living and the dead are regarded as bound by the same ties that bind the living. They share the same spiritual space and "possess" one another. On important occasions the spirits of the dead are thus invited to join the living. The same relationship may be shared with animals, especially those which are hunted. The dancers will adorn themselves as animals before the hunt in order to incorporate the spirits of those animals and win their favor.

Shamans are thought to be people gifted by their special access to the spirit world, which chooses to inhabit their bodies in special ways at special times. Among warriors in West Africa this inhabitation of spirits is thought to make the individual invulnerable to enemies and, since one is an instrument of this inhabiting spirit, not responsible for one's own actions individually. Spirit possession makes one a different person. During the recent bloody civil unrest in Liberia foreign reporters were astonished to see drug-using rebels garbed in wigs and dresses which they had looted from stores. These guises represented the separation these soldiers made between themselves as individuals and the roles they played in battle. In the sport of boxing in Tanzania each contestant tries to spirit-possess his rival, and outcomes are thought to rest as much upon this as upon physical skill. Thus, one is an instrument of the spirit and/or those responsible for this spirit possession. A government minister in Sierra Leone, remarking on the civil disorder and bloodshed raging in West Africa, asserted: "Here in West Africa we have a lot of superficial Islam and superficial Christianity. Western religion is undermined by animist beliefs not suitable to a moral society, because they are based on irrational spirit power. Here spirits are used to wreak vengeance by one person against another, or one group against another."[20]

There is a cultural echo of this phenomenon in post-Duvalier Haiti, one of the world's poorest countries. Many of the much-feared *tantans macoutes* denied responsibility for their murderous behavior under the fallen regime, claiming they had been bewitched by the charismatic "Papa Doc." In this primal world the person is perceived less as a willful, responsible individual than as a vessel for inhabiting spirits, often unbidden. The concept of personal agency and responsibility, so essential to both a civil, contract-based society, and rational economic exchange, are very underdeveloped or unknown. All of these elements came together in a recent Haitian ferry sinking in which hundreds of people packed on to the overloaded vessel lost their lives in a storm. A competitive ferry operator had to flee the country, with his own ferry burned and his wife almost lynched by mobs of the deceased's relatives, who accused him of "using voodoo to cause a rival ferry to sink."[21] Where kinship is primary, where there are no independent acts of nature, where the captain of the overloaded sunken ferry is not seen as personally responsible, where profiting at the expense of others in the marketplace has little legitimacy, this tragedy was bound to be attributed to evil spirits sent by a malevolent agent.

Similarly, primal leadership is accorded to those individuals who are regarded as possessing exceptional charisma. This charisma is often evidenced in the ritual use of words. Among American Indians the great chief is notable for both his dreams and visions, as was the famous Sitting Bull, and also for his words. A chief of the Blackhawk was noted for his twelve to fourteen hour declamations. Among the Hopi a "crier chief" is intimately connected to "preparing behavior," the process by which words open the way to significant rituals or concrete action central to the life of the people. Among West African tribes a "big man" is noted for being a "man of words." He is known for his "hep" (or *eye*, evidence of charisma) and his "rep" (or *speech*) which can stir a response in his listeners. These terms have entered American English from

Gullah as "hip" and "rap." A charismatic leader is "hip" (canny) and has a good "rap" (line of speech). Heroic narratives, such as the Ulster cycle of ancient Ireland, the *Beowulf* epic of early Britain, the Icelandic sagas, the Homeric ballads of archaic Greece, Congolese and plains Indian warrior myths are alike in their fusion of words and reality in incantation, words creating a truth as much as reporting a truth, with charismatic leadership.

Charismatic speech is not a vehicle of truth, it *is truth*. The manner of speech overshadows its content, which becomes a means to an end, making charisma visible. Like the dialog between the chorus and the actor in Greek drama, the charismatic speaker and his audience are gifted of the same spirit, creating through "the suspension of disbelief" the reality they act out. Audience and speaker are drawn into the same spiritual dance, which is like gift-exchange in that it keeps the shared spirit in motion. Charismatic truths have little independent existence beyond the charisma revealed through them, or the charisma of the one of whom they are spoken. All exchange expresses tensions, transpiring by overcoming degrees of resistance. Charismatic speech assumes (and is energized by) resistance in listeners, their inclination to disbelief, and thus it always seeks to convince, not simply "objectively" to relate. Among primal people exceptional charisma thus often evidences itself in self-reported stories of great courage in battle, feats of revenge, raids against enemies, valor in hunting, or superiority in giving gifts. Ruth Benedict records the boasts of a Kwakiutl Indian chief:

> I am the great chief who makes people ashamed.
> I am the great chief who makes people ashamed.
> Our chief brings shame to the faces.
> Our chief brings jealousy to the faces.
> Our chief makes people cover their faces by what he
> is continually doing in the world, giving again and
> again oil feasts to all the tribes.[22]

At the same time, the primal world and its charismatic components are, ironically, speechless. That is to say, speech in the sense of a rational and coherent representation of reality in the spoken word, does not characterize deepest communication at the primal level or in primitive societies. The mythopoetic mode is a means of communicating the ineffable. Its message is too large and too profound to be ordinarily voiced, and thus it is not "articulate" in a rhetorical sense. Speech is consequently more expressive than instrumental, and is intended to enlist the spirit of the listener and stir in him those forces of adhesion upon which charisma rests. It is a characteristic of charismatic utterance that it is accompanied by vigorous and sympathetic motion in both speaker and listener. When Christian charismatics "speak in tongues," they sway in the presence of an ultimate reality both so deeply personal and so impersonally transcendent that no pre-existing formal language can encompass it.

In primitive societies, where concepts of property are either absent or formed very differently from the modern understanding, human exchange often takes the form of language. In such exchange, words and the truths imbedded in them are themselves sources of value, and thus not regarded as "free goods." Consequently, the meanings of "true" and "false" may also differ in ways parallel to the different understandings of "property" and "theft" in the primal imagination. European travelers and anthropologists often reported that African natives routinely "lied" to one another to no obvious advantage.[23] This element of mendacity in the primal world suggests that what is true and what is false is a rather fluid matter depending upon the context and the relationship between the persons who are exchanging words. While all communication is obviously contextualized, it is more highly contextualized in the primal world. Where words are the heart (and often the substance) of human exchange, as they are in the primal world, personal truth is so valuable it must often be carefully rationed, or shielded with lies. One's "truth" defines the boundaries of an "individual self," as tentative as that self-definition may be in a primal world. Truth in the contemporary understanding, as evidenced in modern civil societies where individuality is more fully developed, has a more robust, independent and objective existence, indispensable to the myriad, often highly mediated relations of individuals in complex, mobile societies. A society can only be as extensive and complex as it is transparent to those who function within it. If primitive societies are highly segmented and localized, this is both reflected in and reinforced by the opacity of encounters with others, especially strangers. Even in more advanced societies, as in contemporary Japan, Western people are often mystified by the veil of mendacity in interpersonal relations — even in business [*cf. Part V, infra*].

Concepts of authority are central to social understandings of power. From where does power come? What makes power legitimate? Who speaks with authority? Richard Sennet asserts that, "Of authority it may be said in the most general way that it is an attempt to interpret conditions of power, to give the conditions of control and influence a meaning by defining an image of strength."[24] In the primal world where reality is confronted in relatively unmediated ways, authority is always experienced as well as perceived. No office, law or doctrine carries authority in itself. To be sure, shamanism carries about it something of the authoritative, but the shaman has no more authority than the power that is experienced through him in others. His power is transmissive, not intrinsic. There is, consequently, no office of shaman. The special gift of the chief or leader likewise must be experienced. Unless power is demonstrated on an on-going basis, authority declines, as Saddam Hussein knows so well. Charismatic leadership substitutes demonstration for office: unless followers feel moved by a leader, his authority is null. To be moved by leadership means to be connected primally in an *I-Thou* encounter with him. His will, expressed in speech-as-action and the follower's will must merge in complete sympathy. This, in turn, means that charismatic leadership is authoritative from a number of emotional sources which can include fear as well as love, repulsion as well as attraction. Because of its emotionally amorphous quality, authority in charismatic relations exists in a reality of its own where exterior facts become irrelevant. Indeed, to the extent that authority emerges from charismatic sources it must often contradict — resist — reality. The leader is believed because his personal presentation of reality sets him apart. The Nazis called this the "big lie." To sway the masses one must have a startling presentation of reality which transcends mundane facts, a "reality" which trumps reality.

It is within this context that primal exchange relations must be considered. Not only is the good filled with spirit which exchange in various ways dramatizes, plays out. The exchange relation is charismatic in the sense that a mutual offering of selves is made. Because market relations begin to impinge does not mean that the charismatic element in these relations is completely expunged. Anyone who has dealt with a talented sales person knows that bargaining is filled with these intangible qualities where the sales person is selling himself as well as a good; that the final price reflects his special grace, his value reality as well as any objective set of market relations. The authority of the final price, what makes that price fair, is a measure of the sales person's ability to draw us into his world, his reality. A visit to a bazaar in a less developed society, with its intense animation and personal encounter, demonstrates this playful blending of goods and charisma in setting the fair price, the authoritative price which enables the final exchange. In the setting of the bazaar, the asking price is only the point at which the playful dance between buyer and seller begins. A "fixed sticker price," so ubiquitous at the check-out counters in modern markets, a price which exists independently of the phenomena of individual exchange, is not understood in most traditional societies. It is held in contempt, as anyone who has accepted the initial asking price in a bazaar can testify. There can be no "truth in advertising" in the pre-modern market.

Primal people do not distinguish between labor and other activities. Perhaps that is because so little time is spent at tasks required for basic sustenance. Far from the modern myth that primitive peoples labor long hours under wretched conditions for simple food and shelter, the reality is that most primitive people spend no more than fourteen or fifteen hours each week focused on these activities; perform these activities irregularly (e.g., not every day and not to a schedule); and eat a nutritious and fairly varied diet. Such activities as gathering food are so intertwined with other activities, such as playing with children or gossip and rest that in most primitive languages there is no word for work or labor. This activity is so blended with all the other elements of day-to-day life that it has no abstracted identity of its own. According to Sahlins, "Work is accordingly unintensive: intermittent and susceptible to all manner of interruption by cultural alternatives and impediments ranging from heavy ritual to light rainfall. Economics is only a part-time activity of the primitive societies, or else it is an activity of only part of the society."[25]

No more (or less) value is placed on work than any other activity. Perhaps that is one reason why time is also regarded indifferently. The seasons are noted, along with sunrise and sunset, but one day is like another with habit and interest governing activity. Tomorrow is assumed to be like today and yesterday. Time begins to have agency when durations are more concretely segmented by the nature of activity, for example, the distance between planting and harvest. Anthropologist Edward Evans-Pritchard wrote of the Nuer people, semi-nomads of southern Sudan: "I do not think that they ever experience the same feeling of fighting against time or having to coordinate activities with an abstract passage of time, because their points of reference are mainly the activities themselves, which are generally of a leisurely character—there being no autonomous points of reference to which activities have to conform with precision."[26] Events do not occur "in time" in the primal world. Time has no independent agency, nor is it governed by individual purpose. Change is not marked by anything as neutral as time, but by wills with personalities. "When there is change, there is a cause; and a cause [...] is a will."[27] The Dakota language possesses no word to designate time, but it can express, in a number of ways, modes of being in duration. "For Dakota thought, in fact, time constitutes a duration in which measurement does not intervene; it is a limitless 'free good.'"[28] The lack of verbal tenses in other primitive languages, such as Hopi, may reflect this attitude toward time.[29]

Values and ideas such as saving require that time be imagined as something palpable — something that can be measured, scheduled, used, saved, invested, or wasted. A very common reaction of modern people to their encounters with primitive or traditional people is that they are lazy or indolent. This is, of course, a culturally-bound view which does not take into account the reality that differing societies regard time differently. By the same token less developed societies need to reflect on the consequences of these attitudes about time for economic development. Terms of modern economic thought which attempt to measure wealth-building accumulation, indeed development itself, must take into account that measures such as investment, profit, break-even point, or time-value of money are incomprehensible in imaginative systems where time is understood differently. In fact "business," from the Germanic *besich*, means "to be engaged in something requiring time." In many pre-modern countries employers find that they must pay their workers daily. Working for strangers without prompt reciprocation is not understood and resisted. Many employers find it difficult to keep workers once they have sufficient resources to quit their jobs and return to their villages. Leisure is less a reward for work than an alternative to it. The cultural connection of time to money is absent. Steven Lagerfeld summarizes: "Time is, after all, the most precious resource. An economy can be thought of as an elaborate mechanism for converting time into money, for making my 10 minutes of labor into a gallon of gasoline or a jar of mayonnaise or some other product of somebody else's labor."[30]

Concepts of space, and of motion within those spaces, have special characteristics in primal societies. We have seen how gift-exchange is closely tied to understandings of motion in which goods must be kept in circulation. In addition, in most primal societies movement is constrained to a particular geographical arena which is inhabited in highly regularized ways. On the other hand intimate relations with spirits may connect people to spaces usually inaccessible to modern humanity, such as the underground. Among migratory groups, migration is restricted to particular times and places. In this sense, most places and the events that occur within them are relatively predicable. Any variation can be disorienting. For example, among forest-dwelling people, sightlines seldom exceed a few hundred feet. Space is interpreted as enclosed and limiting. Mobility within it is habitual and cyclical. Rare encounters with broad vistas are disorienting not only because they are unfamiliar, but because they challenge concepts of motion as well. Motion is usually inhibited by heavy undergrowth, and people rarely have the experience of moving swiftly. Since animals of burden are unknown, there are strong limitations on what goods can be transported. Motion is fundamentally experienced in ways that promote psychological stasis. Thus among many forest-dwelling people, the forest is conceived as an enclosing mother, nurturing her children. Relations with it are fundamentally dependent, with goods conceived as gifts given by a mother to her children. A fundamental passivity resists change and initiative in cultural value systems.

To summarize: the primal world is characterized by its playful fluidity and the merger of the objective with the subjective. Essentially without a sense of operative time, the primal imagination conceives of causation as indistinguishable from willfulness. In a world pervaded by spirits, use-objects are neither truly objects nor truly used. Rather, the passing of things from person to person entails the obligation to understand the laws of charismatic exchange which tie people to one another and to the experienced world. Exchange is often characterized by the commerce of language, of words. It is highly localized and thus highly contextualized. In such a world there is scant room for either property or the exchange relations of genuine markets.

NOTES TO CHAPTER TWO

1. Lewis Hyde, THE GIFT (New York: Vintage Books, 1983), p. 8
2. Marcel Mauss, THE GIFT, Ian Cunnison, trans. (London: Cohen and West, 1954), p. 163
3. Paul Radin, THE WORLD OF PRIMITIVE MAN (New York: E.P. Dutton & Co., Inc., 1971), p. 15
4. Bronislaw Malinowski, ARGONAUTS OF THE WESTERN PACIFIC (London: George Routledge & Sons, 1922)
5. Lewis Hyde, *op.cit.*, p. 8
6. *Ibid.*, p. 4
7. Radin, *op.cit.*, p.124-125
8. Morton H. Fried, THE EVOLUTION OF POLITICAL SOCIETY (New York: Random House, 1967), p. 75; for the Eskimos, "A man who had made something is owner of it as long as he needs and uses it. But at a given moment someone else will need it and the owner will lend it to the former..." Geert vanden Steenhoven, RESEARCH REPORT ON CARIBOU ESKIMO LAW (Ottawa: Canadian Department of Northern Affairs, 1962), pp. 47-48
9. Aristotle, THE POLITICS, T.A. Sinclair, trans. (Baltimore: Penguin Books, 1962), p. 46. Aristotle reserves his greatest censure for the charging of interest on lent money, since it is not the product *for which money was provided*: "Hence of all ways of getting wealth this is the most contrary to nature." *ibid.*
10. Hyde, *op.cit.*, p. 94
11. The economic imagination of the market views interest differently because *time* is understood differently. Time is regarded as a *good* in itself: something which has value (e.g., in terms of its opportunity cost) and thus a price -

interest. Lending for interest is not regarded as an inherently unequal exchange, as Aristotle among others would have it, because what is given — money *plus* time — is equally exchanged for what is gotten - money *plus* interest.

12. Bower, *op.cit.*, p. 206
13. H.G. Barnett, "The Nature of the Potlatch," AMERICAN ANTHROPOLO-GIST (July/September 1938), p. 347
14. Johan Huizinga, HOMO LUDENS (Boston: Beacon Press, 1955), p. 59
15. Radin, *op.cit.,* p. 135
16. *Ibid.*, pp. 134 - 135
17. Sahlins, *op.cit.*, p. 301
18. "It confirms the deduction that the norm of livelihood does not adapt to maximum household efficiency but settles rather at a level within the reach of the majority, so wasting a certain potential among the most effective." *Ibid.*, p. 91
19. *Ibid.*, p. 196
20. Robert D. Kaplan, "The Coming Anarchy," THE ATLANTIC MONTHLY (February 1994)
21. BOSTON GLOBE, September 12, 1997, p. A13
22. Ruth Benedict, *op.cit.*, p. 190; Mohammad Ali (ne Cassius Clay), one of the most charismatic of athletes, was famous for his primal declamations: "I am the greatest. No one is greater than me. I am the most beautiful. No one is more beautiful than me."
23. Cf. Octave Mannoni, PROSPERO AND CALABAN: A STUDY OF THE PSYCHOLOGY OF COLONIZATION, Pamela Powesland, trans. (Ann Arbor: University of Michigan Press, 1990), p. 44; Eugene D. Genovese, ROLL, JORDAN ROLL: THE WORLD THE SLAVES MADE (New York: Vintage Books, 1976), p. 610; a seminal study of mendacity is Georg Simmel, "The Lie," in Kurt H. Wolff, THE SOCIOLOGY OF GEORG SIMMEL (Glencoe,Ill: The Free Press, 1950); a useful exploration of the phenomenon of mendacity as a moral issue in everyday life is Sissela Bok, LYING (New York: Vintage Books, 1999)
24. Richard Sennett, AUTHORITY, (New York: Alfred A. Knopf, 1980), p. 19
25. Sahlins, *op.cit.*, p. 86
26. Cf. Anthony Aveni, EMPIRES OF TIME: CALENDARS, CLOCKS AND CULTURES (New York: Kodansha America Publishing Co., 1989)
27. Frankfort, *op.cit.*, p. 24
28. Levi-Strauss, TOTEMISM, *op.cit.*, p. 99n
29. "Hopi may be called a timeless language." Benjamin Whorf, "Science and Linguistics," in Carroll, *op.cit.*, p. 216
30. Steven Lagerfeld, "Who Knows Where Time Goes?," THE WILSON QUARTERLY (Summer 1998), p. 60

PART II

THE TRADITIONAL WORLD

Homo mercator vix aut numquam Deo placere postest

"The merchant can scarcely or never be pleasing to God"

[Medieval Aphorism]

CHAPTER THREE

MEDIATION IN HIERARCHY

The traditional world encompasses that part of human experience which is captured in roles, rules and hierarchies. When we imagine "man" or "woman," "husband" or "wife," "son" or "daughter," "young" or "old," or other basic categories we are addressing social generalities which define expectations about roles and conduct. Each of us, at mostly unconscious levels, acts out these roles within these assumed social hierarchies. One consequence of this is that our experience is often mediated through these lenses, and consequently many more of our encounters are *I-It* experiences rather than direct *I-Thou* experiences. To the degree that a man experiences and acts out the social role of husband, he is inclined to view women other than his own wife differently, at a greater social and emotional distance. As we move from the primal to the traditional world, a cultural veil begins to descend on direct, primal experience. The formless and ludic fluidity of the primal world is increasingly obscured by the structured, balanced experience of the traditional world. The formal languages of thought and speech begin to obscure or replace the ineffability of primal experience and truth. Truth in the traditional world becomes canonized by society which transmits this truth in formal codes, and embeds it in a sense of historical time, a past which speaks to the present authoritatively. Ferdinand Tonnies captured some of this passage in his formulations of *gemeinshaft* and *gesselshaft*: the supersuccession of communal ties, the sum of playful intimacies, by corporate ties, the sum of roles and rules. Huizinga summarizes: "As a civilization becomes more complex, more variegated and overladen, and as the technique of production and social life itself become more finely organized, the old cultural soil is gradually smothered under a rank layer of ideas, systems of thought and knowledge, doctrines, rules and regulations, moralities and conventions which have lost all touch with play."[1]

The word "tradition" (from the Latin, "to speak across") itself conveys this sense of society speaking across generations to impart the rules of social order. As free as each of us might wish to believe he is of the commands and limits of tradition, there are parts of us which are tied to other people and to society by these broad patterns of expectation. While the primal ties of people to one another in kinship, and certain roles — certainly the differing expectations deriving from age and gender — are important in primitive societies, the intimate ties between small numbers of people in groups means these societies are characterized more broadly by the charisma of individuals under conditions of equality rather than formal roles within hierarchies. It is for that reason that it is in traditional society that the need for *esteem* first fully arises, and also is satisfied. As the individual person began to emerge in society so did his need for individual justification. In acting out the roles and rules which society placed before him, and in being acknowledged in various traditional ways for this decorum, the individual received the esteem of his fellows.

Traditional society is sedentary society. It comes into being when pressures on available resources make it difficult to follow the age-old pattern of segmentary society, which divides itself into smaller units as the group's size brings with it growing possibilities of conflict. In part, this is a function of the increasingly conflicted relations between economic production and consumption. We have noted the bias of primitive economics toward distributive relations, which is itself a choice to minimize productivity and the potential wealth (and conflict) which this implies. At a certain point conflict can no longer be avoided by this strategy. Traditional society turns its focus toward economic production as populations grow, which places inevitable strains on distributive relations. As population growth and density, and their demands upon resources, bring people into inevitable contact and conflict, contact and conflict are more broadly organized and institutionalized. To be sure, this strategy is found to some extent even in primitive society. Inter-tribal conflict is often controlled by such customs as reciprocal gift-giving or a kind of ritual warfare, where territory is defended or perceived wrongs righted, in sham battles where little actual damage is done. But an important paradigm shift takes place in the transition from the primal to the traditional. Population/resource pressures force a more sedentary life, in which technology and formal social organization substitute for mobility and kinship as the means for exploiting resources. Instead of the populations going to the resources in an economy of hunting and gathering, the resources are brought to the population in an economy characterized by the domestication of animals and the development of agriculture.

These developments require an important shift in attitudes toward nature. Nature now becomes more an object of human action, sedentary life in a sense immobilizing nature as well as humanity. In making nature an object, humanity makes of itself a subject. As nature is mastered in the breeding of animals for their products of consumption, and crops are planted and cultivated, the referential totality of the spiritual universe of primal society is altered. While in the totemistic primal world each plant and animal has a spirit so that use of them is expressive of this spirit, in traditional society plants and animals and other natural objects are viewed in primarily instrumental terms. The common spirituality flowing through humans and nature is no longer acknowledged in the same way. In the relative separation of humans from the all-encompassing spirit-world of the primal realm the human individual begins to take form. The individual is simultaneously abstracted from nature and begins the abstract contemplation of nature. Arnold Hauser suggests, "Consciousness of self—the general realization that I exist apart from the circumstances of the moment — marks man's first great effort of abstraction; the detachment of various spiritual activities from their function in the totality of his life and the unity of his world-view is a second abstraction."[2]

In the realm of traditional religion, gods come into being to embody the spirit world in its now more abstracted and segmented form. In such systems, says Bellah, *"religious action* takes the form of cult in which the distinction between men as subjects and gods as objects is much more definite than in primitive religion. Because the division is sharper the need for a communication system through which gods and men can interact is much more acute."[3] Discrete gods with formal characteristics emerge because denser social arrangements require degrees of organization and control which are all but impossible within the primal imagination. The opening of the subject-object gap summons the divine entities capable of bridging the space between men and their more complex environments. Individual gods thus intermediate between man and nature: they are no longer spirits coextensive with nature itself.

These mediated relations are also conceived as hierarchical, whereas in the primal world human transactions with spirits have a relatively unmediated fluidity which cannot be captured in spacial concepts of subsidiarity. Cultic action, mediated through priestly ritual, reinforces this sense of religious hierarchy. As intermediating forces gods encapsulate the qualities of humans on one hand, and of nature on the other. The roots of traditional gods in natural forces often reveal themselves in the gods having animal and human form in combination. In ancient Egypt many of the gods had human bodies and the heads of animals. These gods of traditional religion are characterized by human-like feelings, emotions and needs. In order to get good rains one must transact with the rain god, who now embodies the power and spirit of rain. Rain itself is now available to be gathered and channeled because, relatively devoid of independent spirit, it can be an object of human will. A key word here is *relatively.* Primitive people also use nature in ingenious ways. And, by contrast, even the very sophisticated and urbanized Romans used their superb engineering skills with a respect for the spirits of natural elements: since a bridge went from land to land, over water, and through air, its inauguration required that each of these elements had to be enlisted and placated through proper sacrificial ritual. One of the highest titles of Roman magistrates was *pontifex maximus* ("chief bridge-builder"), a title today borne by the Pope.

The first traditional societies emerged in the Neolithic age, ca. 7,000 BC. Settled village life based on the growing of crops and animal husbandry allowed groups numbering in the hundreds to share a common social space. A division of labor became possible, indeed became necessary, in order to sustain this concentration of populations. The rudimentary elements of a state came into existence as the old pattern of decision by consensus of family elders and leadership by charisma came to be replaced by the government of chiefs or princes, whose position in community life became institutionalized, usually through heredity and class. Hierarchy and even routine in bureaucracy began to characterize society. Leaders became more remote and impersonal, the office as important or even more important than the person holding it. This is parallel to the ritualization of a mediated religion based on transactions between the populace as a whole and state gods, conducted by a hereditary priestly class.

These first traditional, sedentary communities were established where fresh water and land for planting and grazing were available. Such communities were the most numerous on the Eurasian land mass where wild grasses (such as wheat, barley and oats) and animals (such as cattle and sheep) were also numerous, and selectively available for domestication. They also tended to concentrate where economic advances evolved in one geographical area could be easily transmitted to others through a process of cultural diffusion or of immigration.[4] As these communities grew in number a reliance on water almost always meant the concentration of populations in river valleys, where water and watered land were most abundant. Karl Wittfogel used the term "hydraulic" to define these first civilizations in order to explain the rise of complex human settlements in the Nile, Tigris and Euphrates, Hwang Ho, and Indus river valleys.[5]

Human concentration in these river valleys required an agriculture based on irrigation, and irrigation required the management of labor to build and maintain the channels bringing precious water to the crops. The dependence of large communities on the successful cultivation of one or two hybrid crops, like wheat, barley and rice, required mechanisms of community planting, harvest, storage and distribution. Wittfogel's use of the term "oriental despotism" for the authority structures which came into being to manage activities of intensive agriculture is perhaps too strong, and has been criticized by other historians, but the social shift which he points to is an important one. Egyptologist Michael A. Hoffman says: "For the acquisition and storage of surplus food to be a going concern requires a shift in attitudes, an investment in technology of food storage and redistribution, and a certain degree of centralized decision-making."[6] A rudimentary state had to come into being to manage the greatly increased possibilities of social conflict in societies where sheer population size and density confronted the necessities of a greatly enlarged food production and distribution system. As segmentary societies of the primal world were pressed together into the geographical and social propinquity of the traditional world, potential social conflict was channeled into the state where equilibrium was managed through authority structures rooted in class and hierarchy, and into markets where equilibrium was managed within the fluidity of market mechanisms themselves. If conflict is avoided in the primal world through such mechanisms as reciprocal gift-giving and segmentation, conflict is mastered in traditional societies through the institutional structures of the state and the dynamism of markets.

We have noted the resistance of primal societies to saving as a social strategy. Accumulation of surpluses which cannot be easily divided and shared is avoided. In sedentary societies where resources are brought to the population, a system of storage and distribution is necessary to provide sustenance during and after the growing season. People no longer follow the growing season into new pastures, but rather plan for scarcity by the careful husbanding of animals and storage of grain. The immediate relation between production and consumption of primal society is now replaced with a system in which present effort is directed toward future consumption. The phenomenon of "labor" comes into being. For now the focus of action is more diffuse in time; action is experienced as an imperative rooted not in reward or self-direction, but an imposition of the life-process itself. In short, labor is the burden of time, to be endured in its inevitability, as certain as birth and death. Labor represents a manifestation of action deriving from the localization of economic activity first in space, and then in time.

I suggested that most primal societies have no separate word for "labor" as a discrete activity. No such distinction is necessary when "labor," "play," "consumption" and other activities are so seamlessly blended in the course of the day. Consequently, individuals do not see themselves performing particular roles joined to discrete activities. As Talcott Parsons puts it: "Although individuals engage in a very wide variety of concrete acts [...] they do not perform these different classes of acts in *differentiated roles* in the sense true of individuals in more developed societies."[7] In traditional society, on the other hand, planning requires effort for which there is no immediate reward, and this requires a degree of institutionalization of the roles and of the social coercion which often takes the form of the state. The state may be viewed as the institutionalization of the conflict which comes into being when the immediate self-interest and motivation of individuals does not conform to the long-term interests of society as a whole. Anthony Wallace posited that the chief functional problem of society is "the replication of uniformity." "If a near-perfect correspondence between culture and individual nuclear character is assumed, the structural relation between the two becomes non-problematical..."[8] The existence of the state thus represents a failure of more advanced societies, as role differentiation becomes more pronounced, to "replicate the uniformity of nuclear character" of primitive societies, thus making the relations of individuals to their cultures more "problematical." When production and consumption are widely separated in time and space, consumption may appear to many individuals as a free good. This is particularly true because, unlike primitive hunter-gatherer societies, traditional societies require far more effort by individuals on a daily basis. In the fields of traditional societies daily labor is often required from dawn until dusk. The increased demands upon human effort, coupled with the relative remoteness of rewards in consumption, require the strictures of the state as well as society to motivate individual effort. It was appropriate that Egyptian pharaohs were depicted carrying the shepherd's crook and the peasant's flail: these represented instruments for herding flocks and beating grain from chaff, the economic basis of society. They also represented the state's capacity to lead and to punish.

Labor comes into being simultaneously with the power to command it in traditional societies. Authority must now reflect the greater distances not only between production and consumption, but also the greater distances between ruler and ruled in societies with large and scattered populations. Authority now derives not from direct, local encounters with charismatic power, but rather through indirect encounters with and through institutions. Richard Sennet calls this sort of authority "visible" and "legible." He suggests that, "The work of authority has a goal to convert power into images of strength. In doing this work, people often search for images that are clear and simple."[9] It is something of an irony that authority in the primal realm depends on the complexity of personality, emotion and encounter which is the charismatic, while in the traditional realm power becomes defined, objective and "legible." Authority is in some ways more complex in primitive societies than in more advanced ones. Authority in the traditional world derives less from process than from clearly defined roles and rules, and the symbol systems through which they are presented. The office of king is abstracted from the individual human being holding it. The office also must transcend in time the office-holder to be authoritative. To the degree that the person transcends his personality, he is identified with the authority of the office. This means the ruling prince, as suggested by Machiavelli, in some sense must empty himself of ordinary human motivations, keeping a distance between himself and the subjects of his authority. Walter Bagehot, writing of the monarchy in Britain, suggested that for its authority to endure, the light of reality must never shine upon it. Its power derives from the separation of the office from the personality holding it. The majesty of the office must overshadow the very human office-holder. A British monarch, to be successful, must be the opposite of charismatic to the great masses of his/her subjects.

Traditional art reflects this sense of hierarchy and authority. When one speaks of the "canons" of traditional art, as one does when addressing Egyptian, Chinese, Mayan or Indian monuments, what is suggested is that artistic presentation makes visible the authority of tradition. It does this by encoding in art the roles and rules which dominate the society to which it gives expression. In ancient Egyptian art these canons were evolved during the earliest dynasties, and not seriously modified in nearly 3,000 years of history. This art is characterized by a number of features. It is hierarchical in its expression. Painted wall panels and individual pieces of sculpture, for example, rigidly adhere to a doctrine of proportion and subsidiarity which sacrifices the representational to the presentational. It is frontal. Figures are meant to be addressed from one direct, head-on angle, to give authority and a feeling of awe to the encounter. Temples are laid out along a single axis, their courts, halls and chambers experienced as a linear progression, which cumulatively overwhelms the visitor. It is formulaic. The left foot precedes the right foot in standing statues. Male figures are brown-red, and female figures are white-yellow. The size of figures represent importance and rank, and so perspective and proportion serve the presentation, not the viewer. It is repetitive: whether it be an avenue lined by sphinxes leading to the great temple of Amun-Ra at Karnak; the four colossal statues of Ramases II at Abu Simbel; or the repeated registers of inscriptions on temple columns. It is narrative: it tells a story and conveys this story as a lesson or as consequential memory. In all of this it presents, above all, the authority of tradition.

Traditional art in China, India and Mezoamerica, although using different (and often more supple) canons, impart this same effect of authoritative, almost propagandistic presentation. Similarly, the canons of Soviet art, called "socialist realism," had many of the formulaic qualities associated with the ritual presentation of authority in traditional art. This propagandistic tendency in its art suggests that legitimate authority is always a problem in traditional societies. Unlike egalitarian primal societies, which are self-legitimizing, and civil societies which earn their legitimacy day to day within a complex of voluntary, consensual relations, traditional societies require on-going ritual and a very systematic and omnipresent symbol system to convey legitimacy.

An important shift in attitudes toward the spiritual world comes into being in traditional society as we have seen. A sedentary life where nature now stands at some remove, where it is now more "objective," allows spirits to take more distant and discrete form. Humans create gods in their own image because nature is at sufficient distance to allow humans to conceptualize superior beings somewhat like themselves as masters of it. In this world, where nature is now less subjective and at least partially voided of spiritual content, it can be seen to follow orderly and predictable laws. Thus in most traditional societies humans look to the global heavens in search of orderly recurrence to guide local lives and to interpret local experience. If shamanism and totemism in relation to willful, local spirits characterize primal society, astrology and ritual characterize traditional societies, where time begins to have agency, where calendars become sacred. Indeed, the word "tradition" itself implies the passing on of a system of truth, of truth as immutable process which can be captured in ritual. The movement of heavenly bodies, so useful in sedentary life where the seasons and weather must be carefully observed so that crops are properly planted and available stores conserved, now permits a view of nature in which the order of the heavens can be brought to the earth through ritual.

The first civilizations were thus associated with and centered around a presiding god or gods who were regarded as heavenly beings, separated from nature, not at one with it. It was these gods who mediated between the order of the heavens and the potentially disorderly earth. It was the will of the gods, their capacity like humans to be willful and arbitrary, which had to be placated. Traditional society is thus profoundly ambiguous in its relation to the cosmos: on one hand the recurrent, global order of experienced reality is recorded with careful observation of the heavens. Enormous effort is employed to construct elaborate astrological structures, like Stonehenge in ancient Britain or the Chaco complex in 12th century New Mexico. On the other hand, natural and other local disasters are treated as the willfulness of the gods. Confucius, the philosopher of order and etiquette *par excellence*, reflected this ambivalence of the traditional mind in dealing with this tension between global and local perspectives when he advised that men should respect the gods, but have as little to do with them as possible. It was the Chinese traditional mind that produced the extraordinary plan of Beijing, described by urbanist Edmund N. Bacon as, "Probably the greatest single work of man on the face of the earth."[10] Emeshed in ritual formulae, astronomical calculation, and esthetic canons of great beauty and subtlety, the city is a monument to social and spacial hierarchy. It is also illustrative of scale. Its basic grid form mandates that each element of the city be a microcosm of the whole at each experienced level. Human beings adapt to the formality of this grid in its myriad scales. The city, and the hierarchy of values embedded within it, not the inhabitant, is the measure of all things.

The very first cities, from which the word civilization comes, appear in Mesopotamia in what is now Iraq around 4000 BC. Each city was centered around a temple, the inhabiting god of which was thought to possess the surrounding agricultural territory and its people. The temple priesthood was responsible for both maintaining the system of agricultural production and distribution, and for performing the rituals associated with the elaborate astronomical calendar. This more complex division of labor evolved into distinct social classes with their own privileges and responsibilities as specialized knowledge was passed from father to son, mother to daughter. The existence of a relative separation of man from nature now permitted men to see objects of nature as more inert and lacking in will, and thus objects of human will, subject always, of course, to keeping human and divine will in concert through the temple establishment and its rituals.

THE PLAN OF BEIJING

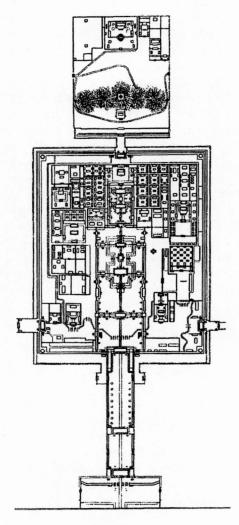

Figure 3:1

Buildings, particularly those connected with the god, his temple and its attendant structures and spaces, were built of more permanent materials such as brick, stone and stucco: the first genuine architecture. Until immortal, individual gods could be conceived, permanent buildings in which those gods presided could not be built. This intellectual transition of itself was critical for civilization to be born. But in addition to this, building permanent structures required advanced engineering skills, dependent upon an understanding of mathematics, especially geometry, and advanced forms of human organization. These in turn lead to more advanced forms of technology to serve this division of labor. For example, the potter's wheel, the high-temperature kiln, alloy metallurgy, the complex loom and the wheeled vehicle all required that space, time, motion, and natural elements such as fire be viewed in deeply instrumental rather than mostly expressive ways. They also required specialized skills available only through the complex division of labor.

Ruth White notes the absence of any evidence of markets in these earliest of Mesopotamian cities. "What was lacking in Sumerian civilization of the Early Dynastic period, or at least the early part of it, that seems so fundamental to Western urbanism today and indeed to European urbanism from the archaic Greeks onwards (but not to the civilization of the Minoans and Mycenaeans) was private enterprise."[11] The appearance of the state thus seems to precede the appearance of genuine markets, which we have noted are absent altogether, or at least very rare, in primitive societies. The early economies of Mesopotamia are thus described as forms of "theocratic socialism" in which the temple officialdom, on behalf of the proprietary god, owns, organizes and distributes all production, and all trades and skills function either within the household, or within the temple organization. Only several centuries hence during the later Sumerian dynasties do markets begin to appear and a vigorous private commerce develops.[12] By the time writing is developed (ca. 3100 BC) the evidence for substantial market activity is fairly clear. It was probably no accident that the Sumerians developed the first writing system (cuneiform) simultaneously with their development of markets, in the service of recording contracts and inventories. That market activity spread quickly and widely once it was initiated is demonstrated in surviving legal codes which, among other things, began to concern themselves more frequently with questions of indebtedness.

The same pattern emerges in the earliest Chinese urban settlements. Paul Wheatley's extensive study of the character of the first Chinese cities concludes that, "Whenever, in any of the seven regions of primary urban generation...we trace back the characteristic urban form to its beginnings we arrive not at a settlement that is dominated by commercial relations, a primordial market, or at one that is focused on a citadel, an archetypal fortress, but rather a ceremonial complex."[13] Market activity in China, sporadic and limited, is a later development. Mycenean Greece and Minoan Crete likewise offer no evidence of markets. The ceremonial centers of the Aegean island of Crete, the most famous being at Knossos, were centered about a temple-palace which combined the qualities of a shrine and of a storage and distribution center. Rodney Castleden notes: "How much political and economic activity took place outside the control of the priesthood or the king is unclear. [...] the concentration of the economy in 'royal' hands — however interpreted — leaves little margin for private enterprise."[14]

The evidence from the Greek mainland in a still later period also reveals no markets. "Kings controlled commerce early, for it was the best way of bringing in surplus income and luxury products," writes Michael Wood. "The tremendous detail of the Linear B archives at Knossos and Pylos shows that Mycenaean kings of the thirteenth century BC had precisely that control."[15] Amidst the rich complexity of human activity offered to us in Homer's *Iliad* and *Odyssey,* which recall the Mycenaean era, there is not a trace of merchants or markets. Homer's references to piracy suggests that what "private distribution" existed was indistinguishable from theft. Indeed, at the end of the Mycenaean era (c.1100 BC) when a Dark Age fell upon the Aegean, it may have been pirates and thieves who formed the core of the merchant class which was to emerge so vibrantly in later centuries. The Greek term for "merchant" and "pirate" is the same, deriving from the etymological root, *peira* ("try," "attempt").

In Egypt a variation of the same pattern emerges. The king is regarded as divine, and Egypt with all its people and resources, are regarded as his. There is no real concept of private property, since people only use the property of the god-king at his pleasure. In the Old Kingdom, in particular, the gulf between high-born and commoner was especially stark, the extraordinary effort and resources used during the "pyramid age" reflecting two very different conditions of human existence. The peasant masses achieved more dignity and autonomy only in subsequent eras, when the building of pyramid complexes ceased, and the proliferation of non-royal tombs evidenced a broader distribution of wealth. Estates and other property were in fact passed on within families, but at the death of an "owner" possession to his "heirs" had to be granted by the king, usually in the form of a state office with the official title of a functionary. Any person of status in Egypt had such a much-prized official title. The state establishment and the "officials" of the estates managed agriculture in the service of the king. They built and maintained the irrigation system which took advantage of the annual inundation of the Nile. Records were carefully kept by scribes, and a calendar coordinated with celestial events was kept by the priestly class. In a non-monetary economy, wealth was principally accumulated in agricultural products controlled by the state, and in human labor. The king's administrators were sent to the thousands of agricultural villages clustered along the Nile to conscript labor to be employed in state projects during the agricultural off-season, when the Nile was in flood. These labor gangs not only repaired and built agricultural canals, they worked in quarries and built city walls, temples, and tombs.

Talcott Parsons, in writing of ancient Egypt, parallels White's observation about ancient Mesopotamia, when he uses the word "socialism" to describe economic relations, especially during the Old Kingdom. He says of the system of draft-labor: "Service performances of Egyptian public programs were not hired from a labor force in anything like the modern sense. Rather, people served under ascribed obligations, not feudally to particular aristocratic lineages, but communally more less to a whole society which was basically differentiated only between the kingship complex and the common people. It was a kind of archaic socialism."[16] In this system the movement of most goods was in the hands of officials and of "traders," the term Egyptians used for "commercial agents for officials." "It was the job of a 'trader' to maintain the supply-demand balance of an employer by trading surplus or unwanted commodities for whatever was required."[17] It was traders who often encountered the class of thieves who used them to convert loot into other goods. There was thus a kind of Egyptian distributive hierarchy consisting of official ownership in the state, including the temples, at its apex; a semi-official system of ownership within the large landed estates, which used the even more informal class of traders, working on commission, to barter for goods; and below them a class of thieves, who seemed to play valuable roles in the recirculation of concentrated wealth — especially from looted tombs, but also from state and temple stores, with the connivance of officials and priests. Thieves were socially stigmatized and unevenly prosecuted, depending on social circumstances.

The earliest evidence of mercantile activity in India is mixed. We know the Sumerians traded in the Indus River valley c. 2,500 BC, but we know little about how or with whom they traded in India because we cannot read the language of their Indian counterparts. Following the Aryan invasions (c.1500 BC) we have Indian written sources in the form of the Vedas. There is no evidence of a regular class of merchants or markets in the earliest of the Vedas. The later Vedas mention merchants (*vaisya)* but they clearly have very low status. A passage in the *Aitareya Brahmana* describes the *vaisya* as "paying tribute to another, to be lived on by another, to be oppressed at will."[18] Only in much later Buddhist and Jainist literature do merchants begin to develop higher status, and acquire the favor and confidence of kings. Thus in India, as in most other traditional societies, markets and merchants — if they existed at all — existed at the margins of the dominant social values.

NOTES TO CHAPTER THREE

1. Johan Huinzinga, HOMO LUDENS, *op.cit.*, p. 75
2. Arnold Hauser, THE SOCIAL HISTORY OF ART (New York: Vintage Books, 1957), pp. 80-81
3. Bellah, *op. cit.*, p. 365
4. Cf. Jared Diamond, GUNS, GERMS, AND STEEL (New York: W.W. Norton & Co., 1999)
5. Karl A. Wittfogel, ORIENTAL DESPOTISM (New Haven: Yale University Press, 1957)
6. Michael A. Hoffman, EGYPT BEFORE THE PHARAOHS (New York: Dorset Press, 1979), p. 318
7. Parsons, *op.cit.*, p. 41
8. Anthony F. C. Wallace, CULTURE AND PERSONALITY (New York: Random House, 1961), pp. 26-27
9. Richard Sennett, AUTHORITY (New York: Alfred A. Knopf, 1980), p. 165
10. Edmund N. Bacon, DESIGN OF CITIES, rev.ed. (New York: Penguin Books, 1974), p. 244
11. Ruth White, THE FIRST CITIES (New York: E.P. Dutton, 1977), pp. 53-54
12. The historical period in which markets developed in Mesopotamia is a matter of contention among scholars, with Karl Polyani suggesting a late date, and H.W.F. Saggs one considerably earlier. *cf.* Parsons, *op.cit.*, p. 67n
13. Paul Wheatley, PIVOT OF THE FOUR CORNERS (Chicago: Aldine Publishing Co., 1971) , p. 225
14. Rodney Castledon, MINOANS (New York and London: Routledge, 1993), p. 110
15. Michael Wood, IN SEARCH OF THE TROJAN WAR (New York: New American Library, 1985), p. 211; "In all the Linear B documents so far known, there is not the slightest mention of merchants or their activity. Had they been an important class, it is incredible that we should not have had some indication of their existence." John Chadwick, THE MYCENAEAN WORLD (Cambridge: Cambridge University Press, 1976), p. 157.
16. Parsons, *op.cit.*, pp. 56-57; see also, Barry J. Kemp, ANCIENT EGYPT: ANATOMY OF A CIVILIZATION (New York: Routledge, 1993); and Jon

Ewbank Manship White and J. Manship White, ANCIENT EGYPT: ITS HISTORY AND CULTURE (Mineola, NY: Dover Publications, 1970)

17. Kemp, *op.cit.*, p. 244
18. A.L. Basham, THE WONDER THAT WAS INDIA (New York: Grove Press, Inc., 1959), p. 142

CHAPTER FOUR

EXCHANGE AS RITUAL

Trade, as in earliest Mesopotamia, was in dynastic Egypt largely a state monopoly. It was the function of the state to exchange surpluses from production for necessary scarce goods, like timber, imported from abroad. Trade in luxury goods such as precious stones, spices and skins appears also to have been initially largely a state monopoly. Markets thus make their first appearance in traditional societies after state patterns of production and distribution have been established. And, at least in dynastic Egypt, earlier trading systems through middle-men ended as soon as the state had sufficient strength to monopolize them, a monopoly sometimes shared with the temples and favored courtiers. Markets often appear, the later Sumerian experience being something of an exception, as a tolerated competitive alternative to the state system of exchange. Because of this markets are typically highly localized and those who participate in them subject to strict state supervision and social control.

In the traditional world the exchange of goods is closely associated with the authority of the state. The *raison d'être* of the state is that it allocates essential goods and their attendant values authoritatively. That is, since goods are now distributed more unequally, distribution is not self-validating in terms of equity as it tends to be in the primal world. It is the authority of the distributor in traditional society that makes the distribution just. This requires that the production and distribution systems be closely allied to an authoritative system of class and hierarchy, to a distributive ideology. Distribution is often systematized in ritual, with goods distributions centered in festivals and jubilees. It is also systematized in custom, such as traditional sumptuary laws: certain articles of apparel, for example, are allocated on a class basis.

In ancient Mezoamerica, home of some the most stratified traditional cultures known to history, systemization was revealed in everything from clothing to diet. Certain fabrics of certain colors could only be worn by particular classes. The classes of warrior, priest, craftsman and farmer were strictly defined. This systematization extended to warfare, which often had highly ritualistic components. The elaborate system of *chinampas* agriculture of the Valley of Mexico was perhaps the most intensive the world has yet known. "Floating islands" were produced from reclaimed lake bottoms, and carefully cultivated to support very dense population levels. This system, used at least since 100 BC, was brought to its highest levels by the Aztecs. "The whole system was so regularly laid out," writes Brian M. Fagan, "that it could only have been planned and executed under strong, centralized administrative control."[1]

In such a highly-organized system, merchants (*pochteca*) could not function "between the cracks," as they sometimes did in other traditional societies. The *pochteca* were as bound by class and ritual as other classes: "No merchant acted completely independently. The state supervised all trading activities and shared in the profits. The pochtecas' lives, like everyone else's, were bound by elaborate rituals."[2] As in other traditional societies, the social position of Aztec merchants was highly ambiguous. They played important distributive roles under strict state control, but their activities made them inherently suspect. Thus the merchants "were careful to feign humility, wearing humble clothes in public. The returning pochteca would enter the city swiftly, by canoe, at night. [...] The cargo was secretly unloaded at a friend's or relative's house before daybreak. Everything was done to avoid any impression of great wealth or any hint of conspicuous consumption."[3]

Given the resistance of traditional societies to market exchange and merchants, these seem first to appear in reaction to the inability of these societies, as material conditions become more complex, efficiently to organize the totality of production and distribution through the state. If the emergence of the state marks a kind of social failure in the passage from primal to traditional worlds, as Wallace suggests (*supra* Chap. 3), the emergence of markets mark a state failure, and to this extent the existence of markets in traditional societies undermines the authority of the state. In this respect, the former Soviet Union was very much a traditional state, its authority and legitimacy always dependent on its central role in production and allocation. But like previous traditional states it was forced by its own administrative weaknesses to rely, reluctantly, on private merchants, *biznismeny* ("business-men"), who became a shadowy part of the economic landscape. The semi-tolerated "black" and "gray" markets gave rise to *vory v zakonye* ("thieves in law") who ran the equivalent of territorial monopolies in certain kinds of trade.[4] The apparent historical origins of the merchant class in organized, semi-legitimate thievery in traditional societies seems to be replicated in contemporary Soviet/Russian experience. The "black market" may be regarded as an attempt at both a more rational division of labor and the more efficient use of economic resources, which was identified by Adam Smith as the basis for all wealth creation. Because black markets operate outside the law, their inherent capacity for wealth creation is never fully realized in the traditional societies where they arise. What in *fact* functions as "property" cannot be fully developed into an *economic asset* — something of value which can be flexibly deployed in differing contexts of opportunity — for example, in leveraging further asset accumulation.[5] Only in the civil world, where contracts and assets come into full relation, is the wealth-creation incipient in the traditional black market realized and legitimized. That legitimacy, as the word suggests, is to be found in law, and the new *conception* of law in the civil world, which rationalizes highly pluralized property relations through its focus on contracts in fully-legitimate markets.

Markets and merchants, where they exist at all in traditional societies, are never elevated in value, at least as reflected in literature or art, to a place of human dignity comparable to the state. In the numerous Egyptian tomb wall paintings produced over nearly three thousand years, which depict everything in ordinary life from duck hunting to the brewing of beer, there are no depictions of recognizable markets.[6] J.J. Janssen's path-breaking study of Egyptian village economics concluded that in this state-dominated system, prices had little self-regulatory power.[7] Genuine markets, competitive and price-fixing, are thus a very marginal phenomenon in Egyptian history. This may help to explain the fact that the markets which did exist were usually conducted by foreigners under strict state supervision. A Middle Kingdom text (ca. 1850 BC) records the fortress at Semna used to screen the traffic of Nubian merchants headed for the trading post at Iken. Other sources mention Semitic traders, later identified with the despised *Hyksos*.[8] During the New Kingdom five centuries later foreign merchants were resident in various Egyptian garrison sites from which they moved out to the markets. The northern quarter of Memphis, the delta capital, was populated by Canaanite merchants who built a temple to their god Baal there. That Egyptian markets were dominated by foreigners, principally Semites, is demonstrated by the practice of the Egyptian marketplace "to do business in the Syrian tongue," a phrase which came to mean simply, "to haggle."[9] During the Saite period (ca. 600 BC) Greek merchants (and mercenaries) were allowed to build their own town, Naukratis, in the Nile delta, the base from which they traded Aegean goods. The founding of the greatest Greek commercial city of ancient times, Alexandria, at the mouth of the Nile three centuries later only confirmed an ancient practice of private market relations dominated by foreigners, under the supervision of the Egyptian state.

The domination of markets by foreign merchants in many traditional societies represents a transitional state in which kinship relations are respected by reserving this marginalized activity for non-kin, strangers, a reflection in trade of the phenomenon we have already seen in the Mosaic distinction between kin and non-kin in lending money for interest. The almost universal phenomenon of the "foreign" merchant in traditional societies also suggests that the forces of globalization were inherent in market activity from its inception. The merchant was the means by which the localization of economic activity imposed by the traditional state and society was challenged, and ultimately overcome by the globalizing logic of enterprise. Markets in their dynamism have from the beginning sought to defeat the localized cultural boundaries imposed by contingency and the traditional state, and to replace them with an expansive economic rationalism and materialism, which became visible with the arrival on the stage of history of the first merchants. The merchant was thus from the beginning a kind of outlaw arising from the globalizing animus inherent in free markets. But the merchant also sometimes represented the localizing forces inherent in strong ties of primal kinship. It was sometimes those social groups which most insisted on maintaining a unique kinship identity within the larger society, e.g., the Jews in Europe or the Chinese in southeast Asia, which formed the merchant class. Living amid market relations sustained the relative cultural autonomy necessary to the preservation of other ties and values. Choosing the autonomy of mercantile life was consequently often as much a cause as a consequence of social marginality.

In many traditional societies, especially those lacking foreign merchants, women often play this socially-marginalized role. From West African market towns to those of Mexico, it is women who dominate small trade. In part, this is an extension of household economics. In many agricultural societies women maintain small produce gardens and yard animals, such as chickens, for household use and to trade in local markets. Women are also likely to have salable craft skills such as weaving and sewing. But the dominant role of the female trader also reflects the practice women have at complex interpersonal encounter, and especially with bargaining. In most traditional societies a woman's marriage itself is the result of a mutually-beneficial bargain between two families. Women's rights are usually highly circumscribed within marriage, especially when plural marriage or its equivalent, is prevalent. Women continue to bargain with their husbands within marriage, and with the other women in his sphere to promote their own and their children's interests. In West Africa, for example, women traders sometimes find themselves in market competition with the other women in the lives of their men, who benefit from what each woman brings to the family. Additionally, the experience of mothering requires the development of skills which promote patience and adaptability. Children can be the most skilled of bargainers in having their wants met, and it is an art in itself to deal with them day to day. The vehicles which bring women traders and their goods to African markets in places like Freetown, Accra and Lagos are called "mammy wagons," an apt description.

The dominant role of the state in the allocation of economic resources and its expression in state-sponsored foreign trade appears in the earliest of ancient historical records. In the case of Egypt we have extensive records from the monuments of the kings of state trading activity. Senefru, builder of one of the great pyramids in the Old Kingdom (ca. 2,500 BC), recorded a state-sponsored expedition to what is now Lebanon to trade for timber. Pepy, a later boy-king recorded an expedition to Kush (the present Sudan) to bring back furs, spices, ivory, gold, and a pet dwarf, lovingly depicted. An especially splendid carved panel in the funerary temple of the great female ruler, Queen Hatshepsut, in the New Kingdom (ca. 1,500 BC) recounts in detail the marine trading expedition which she sent to the land of Punt (present-day Somalia) to bring back fragrant plants to be placed in the temple of Amun-Ra in Karnak. What this monumental celebration of trade seems to effect is the Pharaoh's continuing majesty as the allocator of resources. State trade in these depictions has about it the ritual (not to say propagandistic), presentation of authority. This may explain the lack of direct evidence for what the Egyptians traded in exchange for the goods they imported.[10] We presume they traded from the abundance of grains they produced and other commodities, like gold from Nubia, turquois from Sinai, or papyrus, together with craft goods like fine linen. The monuments tell us nothing, probably for the same reason that we find so little evidence of markets and merchants: these activities were not honorable in themselves. The importation of luxury goods, especially such items as incense intended for the temples, was portrayed as tribute to the gods and to the king himself. The mundane fact that these goods were traded for Egyptian goods hardly merited recording.

In traditional China the same fundamental arrangements held. Major goods distribution was controlled by the state in important urban centers. Private property did not exist in principle, and the state felt free to transfer property (and people) as it saw fit. Major trading expeditions abroad were state-sponsored; minor trade by private merchants appears contemporaneously. The records of both Egypt and China make it clear that these state-sponsored expeditions had about them many of the characteristics of gift-exchange which we have noted in the primal world. It is clear that political bonds and relations of personal prestige are at the center of these on-going exchanges, often to the detriment of making "the best trade." Exchange was integrated into a system of tribute-giving in which inferior princes were given gifts to demonstrate the power of the superior prince. The case of traditional dynastic China is instructive here.

Gift-giving conferred status in traditional China and was central to etiquette. He who gave the biggest gifts had the highest status; or rather, he who had the highest traditional status was expected to give the best gifts. At the apex of the system, the emperor could never receive gifts of greater value than those he gave, for this would insult his supreme status. The same was true of senior mandarin officials in their dealings with inferiors. Thus China was something of a "pyramid scheme" when it came to gift-giving. By directly controlling through the state distribution system the greatest source of wealth, rice and wheat, at the base of the pyramid, the emperor was able to distribute down the pyramid gifts of greater value then those given to him directly by senior officials and client princes. When, as a political act of foreign dominion as much as a means of acquiring foreign resources, the emperor undertook "trading missions" which sent great fleets as far as the east coast of Africa, this pyramid system collapsed. Because the Chinese emperor did not have access to the base of these foreign economies to subsidize the rules of gift-giving, the emperor was in fact pouring out subsidies to foreign "trading partners" by his insistence that anything he gave must exceed the value of what he received in return. Daniel Boorstin asserts, "During the days of [fleet commander] Cheng Ho [1405-33] the Chinese practiced what they preached, with costly conse-quences. The lopsided logic of the tributary system required China to pay out more than China received. Every new tributary state worsened the imbalance of Chinese trade."[11] Torn between the desire to receive the tribute of foreigners to his celestial kingdom, and impoverishing himself in this unequal trade, the emperor finally forbade the reception of these foreign gifts and ordered that all vessels in the ocean-going fleet be sunk.

By taking this inward-looking attitude the Chinese elite, by any account the wealthiest and most sophisticated of their time, surrendered these vast areas of Asia and Africa to European princes, like the Spanish and the Portuguese, who were very willing to "receive more than they gave" (in effect to really trade) through vast commercial networks. That private overseas Chinese merchants took over some of this abandoned trade is also a direct corollary and irony of the state's abdication of it — although in the middle of the sixteenth century even the ocean-going vessels of private merchants were ordered sunk, and Chinese overseas trade degenerated into a form of smuggling. In the Confucian system private merchants were stigmatized: it was taught that peasants and craftsmen were honorable because their labor produced necessities; the Mandarin class was honorable because it was learned and connected the "Middle Kingdom" to the celestial order through its wisdom and knowledge. Merchants "produced nothing," were ignorant of the great celestial order, and were thus perceived as at best nuisances and at worst parasites indistinguishable from thieves. According to Lucian Pye, "In contrast to the rather tense closeness of gentry and officials, there was a relatively unambiguous feeling of contempt and animosity among gentry and scholars toward merchants. [...] [T]hose who ruled the empire never accorded status or recognition to the merchants."[12] When the state abandoned overseas trade private merchants were willing to undertake profitable trade, their lowly status not affected. But it also meant that almost by definition the most entrepreneurial people in China had to settle outside of China to use fully their market skills. Consequently, even today, some of the richest people in the world are Chinese living outside of China, while many of its poorest are Chinese living in China. Which is another way to say that wealth is often related to globalization, and poverty to localization. "Social values," says Pye, "were a prime reason for the failure of capitalism to develop in China."[13]

It appears to have been to facilitate the exchange of perishable, non-staple commodities and craft goods, such as pottery and utensils, and fine textiles that local markets spring up in traditional societies. In Mesopotamia the first markets appear in the great Sumerian cities at the same time as writing, ca. 3,100 BC. The state continued to monopolize trade and distribution in agricultural staples through the temple establishment. More complex private exchange required written contracts and courts to enforce them. By approximately 2,500 BC there is not only a vigorous local commerce, but Sumerian merchants are venturing by sea to profit from the goods being offered by the thriving Harappa culture of the Indus valley of India. Unlike Egypt, Mesopotamian city-states functioned within a decentralized political system where rulers did not claim divine status. The systemization of rule was thus more impersonal, with Parsons positing "a normative order almost verging on the degree of systematization and universalization found in 'historic' systems."[14] This allowed for legal systems and codes to develop a centrality that was to characterize every Mesopotamia culture from the time of the Sumerians to the time of the Chaldeans. Sabatino Moscati, a seminal thinker in the field, distinguished Mesopotamian development from the Egyptian to the greater differentiation of the secular from the religious sphere in the former as compared to the latter. Law began to develop along the lines leading to more modern and global conceptions of it because its normative character was less divinely contingent or localized in the Mesopotamian context.[15]

But private markets, even in traditional societies where they were allowed to flourish, continued to have about them those qualities which made them, like the state, something which primal peoples avoided: they were arenas of conflict. On a day-to-day basis, most people in traditional societies have little need for, or contact with, either the state or the market. The traditional village, with its kinship ties, continued very much as a self-sufficient entity. Most goods, including wooden utensils, pottery, baskets, and simple textiles were the result of household skills, passed on from generation to generation. In traditional China, for example, the village market was so rare as to be practically non-existent, and the intermittent town markets visited by no more than one peasant in five.[16] As is so often the case in appreciating the culture of traditional China, Chinese market life can be conceived in hierarchical terms. G. W. Skinner's masterful study of traditional Chinese markets disclosed that market hierarchy reflected a demographic hierarchy, which in turn moved from conditions of localization towards globalization. Closely coordinated with the cycles of the calendar, goods, tradesmen and merchants moved within an urban-rural matrix: "The city was the element which gradually became a foreign body in the local economy, looking beyond its narrow surroundings and out towards the greater movement of the outside world, receiving from it rare, precious goods unknown locally, which it sent in turn to smaller markets and shops. Small towns were embedded in peasant society, culture and economy; large towns escaped from their context."[17] Population density was central to this dynamic, with the location and hierarchy of markets closely associated with demography and geography.

CHINESE MARKET HIERARCHY

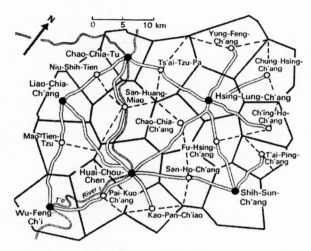

_____ Boundaries of the areas covered by principle markets

_ _ _ _ _ Boundaries of the areas covered by secondary markets

○   Principle market towns

●   Largest towns of all

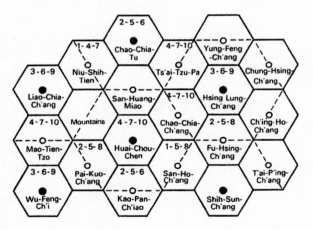

Figure 4:1

Diet in traditional societies is characterized by a heavy dependence on one or two crops as a protein source, and this is in contrast to primitive societies, where a wider variety of foods is usually gathered and hunted. The Chinese village, like its ancient Egyptian counterpart, was dependent on the state distribution system for its daily bread, especially in adverse circumstances like local drought. Regime authority is inextricably tied to its role of allocator of basic goods in traditional societies. The fall of regimes in Egypt and China was often tied to the failure of the state distribution system in adverse times. The problem of the highly centralized economy and state is that policy is indefectible: if not formed with near-perfect information and executed almost flawlessly, the whole system tends to fail either incrementally and cumulatively, or suddenly like a house of cards before unpredictable or uncontrollable circumstances. Because they lacked defectibility, these traditional regimes were "totalitarian," and economic historian Fernand Braudel even uses this word to describe the role of the state in Mandarin China.[18] It may be that the mysterious, sudden and catastrophic collapse of the Mycenean Greek state in the 12th century BC, and a similar sudden collapse in Mayan Mezoamerica in the 10th century AD were due to this inherent weakness of political-economic totalitarianism. The sudden collapse of the Soviet state can ultimately be attributed to the same basic cause.

Markets in ancient societies, often set up in regional centers on certain days, were exotic places where one occasionally went for excitement or to trade for specialty goods, such as a bronze utensil or the fine textiles produced on a complex loom. The people who ran the markets, the merchants, were usually strangers who were thought to be crafty and willing to take advantage of the naive trader. These merchants relished bargaining, using all the skills of "buying low and selling high," as anyone who has visited a bazaar in a traditional society can testify. But these professional traders were also not much admired, and often held, as they did in Aztec Mexico and traditional China and India, very low status. In the Medieval West merchants were often called "villains" because, unlike respectable people, they were to be found in towns. Indeed, merchants were often not native to the country at all, as we have seen in the case of dynastic Egypt, but rather "foreigners," like the Chinese in Southeast Asia, the Indians in East Africa, the Chechens or Armenians in Russia, the Jews in Medieval Europe, or for that matter, the Koreans in South Central Los Angeles. Merchants from Lombardy (in Italy) were so omnipresent in late Medieval European trade that "Lombard" became just another name for merchant: hence the designation *Lombard Street* found in numbers of European and American cities. In traditional society the state is remote, but sanctified by religio-cultural values and its pivotal role in the basic agricultural system.

Traditional Chinese House and Courtyards

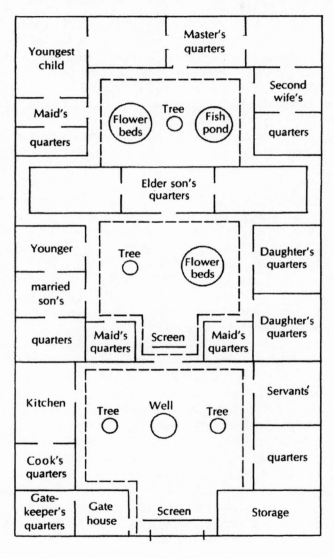

Figure 4:2

Markets are often equally remote and regarded as the arenas of exotic foreigners, often distrusted and sometimes despised. The state in traditional society thus tends to regard markets as competing and often adversarial structures to the state itself, as a challenge to state authority. Markets are sometimes encouraged, but usually tolerated, controlled and/or suppressed. It was often the case that the state blamed society's problems on merchants and foreigners, and persecuted or expelled them. The quarrel between the forces of cultural localization and of market globalization is again evidenced as a very old one.

A glance at the physical organization of a household in China, a traditional society which canonized the rules of domestic construction as it did the rules of art, religion, and etiquette illuminates some of these points. In Chinese thought, harmony with one's fellows through harmony with nature in a hierarchy of obligation is the guiding principle. The order of the heavens was mediated to humans through the emperor, "The Son of Heaven," whose own life of service was minutely regulated by astrological observation. The class of Mandarins, skilled in all the arts of knowledge, but especially in writing, served to transmit this hierarchy of values to all classes of the population. The house of a Mandarin was designed to reflect this hierarchy. On the street, closest to the hubbub of the city, and thus the furthest from the tranquil harmonies of nature, was the service area: kitchens, storage and servants quarters, arranged around a functional courtyard containing a well. Through a screened gateway issuing from this first courtyard, the visitor passed from the world of household endeavor dedicated to sustaining the basic necessities of life. Entering a second courtyard, the visitor would find the quarters of daughters, and younger sons and their wives, arranged about a shade tree and flower garden. Another secluded entrance issued into the elegant quarters of the master, his wives, his oldest son and smallest children, which included a library where volumes of the classics were studied. These rooms were arranged around a garden with an ornamental fish pool, flower garden, and a shade tree. Household harmony was reflected in this carefully balanced meeting of refined culture and encounters with nature. Its hierarchy of spaces favored family, nature and learning standing at far remove from the mundane requirements necessary to sustain life in a complex urban setting. We shall see that the *civil world*, as represented by household arrangements in Periclean Athens, dictated a very different hierarchy of domestic spaces.

❖ ❖ ❖

The market and the state are alternative and often competing methods of managing conflict in traditional societies. The state in traditional society organizes conflict by assuming a relative monopoly on the use of force to impose law and order, by confirming society's organization into a hierarchy of functions and classes, and by sustaining a parallel mythic system which unites individuals to both nature and society. The state is an essentially vertical mechanism for treating conflict. The market in traditional society organizes the contention between what is desired and those who desire it by providing access to goods on the basis of free exchange, and thus it is essentially egalitarian and non-coercive, and allows the individual relative freedom to make choices outside of traditional kinship or social loyalties, and within a democracy of information. The market is fundamentally a horizontal system for treating conflict. Markets are in this sense subversive of those values which are hierarchical, kin-oriented, and occult.

The resistance to markets in traditional societies is at least partially an attempt to protect the very nature of traditional society itself. The widespread adoption of "socialist" values among traditional elites in many emerging, less developed societies is as often a rejection of market-oriented social values as it is a realistic program for economic and social modernization. Sociologist Edward Shils asserted of Indian intellectuals, for example: "Marxism appeals to Brahmin intellectuals because it derogates the trading classes and denies their usefulness."[19] The resistance to the power of the state by civil, market-oriented societies is the other side of this equation. The development of self-governing "free cities" in late Medieval France, Germany and Italy was an expression of the emerging merchant class's desire to liberate itself from a feudal system where traditional law and hereditary privilege interfered with profitable business.

To recapitulate: The passage from primal to traditional society is marked by some important intellectual and spiritual shifts. Time, vague and amorphous in primal society, is concrete, recurrent, and central to the organization of life in traditional societies. Labor, relatively unknown as a distinct activity in primal society, is a central activity for much of the population in traditional society as the psychological distance between production and consumption widens, and the sheer size of populations to be sustained requires the effort of most adults during waking hours. Authority in the forms of hierarchy and class replaces charisma and social propinquity as a functional basis for decision and control. Leadership is based largely on office and heredity, as are the spiritual functions of the priestly class which controls and oversees ritual. A fundamental shift in attitudes toward nature in traditional societies permits the broader object-use of the natural world in the building of permanent structures, the use of more complex technologies, and the existence of markets where inert goods, almost wholly deprived of a spiritual character, are exchanged on the basis of scarcity and price. The phenomenon of globalization appears, often in the form of a foreign merchant class, as an essential impulse in market relations which challenges the localizing forces and boundaries of traditional culture.

We have noted the introduction of writing as a hallmark of the passage from primal to traditional societies, especially in conjunction with the initiation of markets. An important nexus appears here as the essentially mystical and spiritual realm associated with primal thought engages the more practical problems of production and resource allocation in traditional thought. Writing, when it first appears, has about it the synthesis of symbol and reality of magical thinking with practical thinking. For example, in Egyptian hieroglyphics, the scribes often deliberately created a discontinuous line in drawing the glyph for "snake," fearing that creating a whole, continuous line would in fact bring the venomous bite of the serpent to the writer/reader. The legs in drawings of livestock are often not attached to bodies, so the animals could not wander away. At the same time, while writing is associated with sacred texts, the most common of early documents in traditional societies are quite mundane: records, inventories, contracts. Writing thus plays a pivotal role in both reflecting and underlying a paradigm shift from the primal to the traditional worlds. Parsons even suggests that the introduction of writing is the pivotal event marking the passage from what he calls "primitive" to "archaic" society. He suggests that, "Written language, the focus of the fateful development out of primitiveness, increases the basic differentiation between the social and cultural systems and vastly extends the range and power of the latter. The principal symbolic contents of a culture can, with writing, be embodied in forms which are independent of concrete interaction contexts. This makes possible an immensely wider and more intensive cultural diffusion, both in space (i.e., relative to populations) and in time."[20] The impulses toward universality were thus incipient in the capacity for the written word, the global, abstract form distinguished from local, discrete content.

Writing both reflects and enables humanity's transformed view of itself in relation to the world. It makes possible new ideas of context and control over nature: the written word captures reality, organizes it and places it in a stream of time, now also imagined in a more palpable way as the past is related to the future through present action, the act of recording itself. Time begins to acquire an identity of its own as the mythopoetic synthesis of every element in experienced reality is unbundled. History, in the sense of an actual record of the past, embedded in the written word, comes into being and into agency as people begin to "think historically." The consequence of this for authority, especially in relation to law and institutions, is a critical one. It is also critical to the rise of commercial society. Every commercial transaction is itself a claim on history. It is the essence of contracts that they project the participants into future action. The more complex the requirements of the participants in contractual relations, the less useful is memory and the more important is a written text. The written contract is thus more than an historical document; it is a living claim of the past upon the present and the future. The movement of goods in space and time, which is the *raison d'être* of contractual relations, is thus impaired to the extent that a sense of historical time and obligation is not culturally understood and supported. The widespread use of writing may be the best evidence of a culture's full understanding of the context of commercial (contractual) relations.

NOTES TO CHAPTER FOUR

1. Brian M. Fagan, THE AZTECS (New York: W.H. Freeman and Company, 1984), p. 86
2. *ibid.*, p. 206
3. *ibid.*
4. Stephen Handelman, "The Russian 'Mafiya'," FOREIGN AFFAIRS, (March/April 1994); see also, Raymond Bonner, "Russian Gangsters Exploit Capitalism to Increase Profits," THE NEW YORK TIMES (July 25, 1999), p. 1
5. Here my argument parallels that of Hernado De Soto, THE MYSTERY OF CAPITAL (New York: Basic Books, 2000)
6. Kemp makes an interesting argument for the depiction of markets in two tomb paintings, but he also explains that because there are no texts to describe these pictures, "Our understanding of them depends on correctly interpreting the mime that the artist has used to convey the meaning." *op.cit.* , p. 253.
7. J.J. Janssen, COMMODITY PRICES FROM THE RAMESSID PERIOD (Leiden: Brill Academic Publishers, 1997)
8. William C. Hayes, "Daily Life in Ancient Egypt," in EVERYDAY LIFE IN ANCIENT TIMES (Washington, D.C.: National Geographic Society, 1951), p. 115
9. Donald B. Redford, EGYPT, CANAAN AND ISRAEL IN ANCIENT TIMES (Princeton: Princeton University Press, 1992), p. 228.
10. John Baines and Jaromir Malek, ATLAS OF ANCIENT EGYPT (New York: Facts on File Publications, 1980)

11. Daniel J. Boorstin, THE DISCOVERERS (New York: Vintage Books, 1985), p.193
12. Lucian W. Pye, CHINA: AN INTRODUCTION (Boston: Little, Brown and Company, 1972), p. 78
13. *Ibid.*
14. Parsons, *op.cit.*, p. 67
15. Sabatino Moscati, THE FACE OF THE ANCIENT ORIENT (Garden City, NY: Anchor Books, 1962)
16. Fernand Braudel, THE WHEELS OF COMMERCE, Vol. II, Sian Reynolds, trans. (New York: Harper & Row, Publishers, 1986), pp. 117
17. Braudel, *op.cit.*, pp. 117-118; G.W. Skinner, "Marketing and Social Structure in Rural China," JOURNAL OF ASIAN STUDIES (November 1964).
18. *Ibid.*, p. 588
19. Edward Shils, THE INTELLECTUAL BETWEEN TRADITION AND MODERNITY (The Hague: Mouton & Co., Publishers, 1961), p. 83
20. Parsons, *op.cit.* p. 26

PART III

THE CIVIL WORLD

Horos eimi tes agoras

"I am the boundary of the market-place"

[Inscription near the Athenian *agora*]

CHAPTER FIVE
THE EXCHANGE OF WILLS

The civil world is a realm of consensual relations. When I choose a relationship with another person or persons I enter the civil space. In primal, and even traditional, societies relationships with others spring from blood and custom. Relationships are not essentially chosen, and consequently the content of those relations is likewise not based on choice. We choose relations in order to influence their contents, to embed our personal wills within them. In a civil society the authority of everything from government to material distributive arrangements now begins to rest in consent, the mutual exchange of wills. The inclination to assert a personal will, to make choices, to predicate authority upon them, represents an important shift in human consciousness.

This shift in consciousness requires that people begin to see themselves as persons apart, possessing a unique will and having the right to such a will. In primal or traditional societies the assertion of such an autonomous self is little valued, indeed discouraged because of the conflict of wills which such an autonomy makes likely. Markets in traditional societies, for example, are marginalized and merchants along with them in part because a genuine market represents an autonomy of selves completely at odds with primal and traditional values, especially those associated with authority. Markets also require that, fundamentally, people be treated for some purposes like inert goods, just as markets come into being when material goods lose their spiritual content and thus can move according to market rules. Thus, in a historic transformation, humanity becomes the locus of both spirituality and of ethical conflict as goods (and people) are deprived of spiritual value in market exchange. Traditional ties of blood and kinship are also undermined by the very nature of markets, and to some extent, so are the ties of sympathy which kin relations express. A consciousness in which persons begin to loose their blood-specific natures, and the obligations rising from them, requires that one have the real possibility of interacting with non-kin. Primitive and traditional societies make this almost impossible because populations are scattered and relatively immobile. It is usual for people not to stray more than a few miles from their village and its web of kinship ties in a lifetime. It is not unusual for people to encounter no more than a handful of strangers in their lifetimes as well.

Thus when I enter consensual relations I become delocalized, and I enter a culture of strangers. It is likely that on a day to day basis I will encounter people whom I have not encountered before, and then with a sense of personal distance. As I drive on a crowded highway most of the persons whom I see I have not seen before, and will not see again. My attitude toward them expresses this awareness. It is awareness of others at an ultimate existential distance, an "I-It" encounter in which others compete with me for space in my lane, or at the toll booth. They serve no purpose in my life, as I am not aware of how each of them fits into the total society surrounding me, and the ways, individually, they affect my life. "Hell is other people," suggests the existentialist philosopher of the modern predicament, Jean-Paul Sartre. Nothing could be further from the experience of primal and most traditional peoples in their daily relations.

From this awareness "at a distance" comes a sense of the use-value of other human beings. Just as markets come into being in the passage from primal to traditional society as goods are understood to have a primarily instrumental character, the civil world depends in part on an evolution in which people are perceived to have use-value. That instrumentality in turn requires that I engage in a set of limited and limiting relations chosen to achieve specific ends. Contractual relations encompass these qualities, and in this context, the entire civil world is the sum of the contractual relations which it encloses. A civil world requires the emergence of relatively autonomous persons, a field of meaningful choices together with the cultural values to sustain them, and an overriding sense of the importance of contracted relationships, of a life of entwined pledges on which much of one's selfhood and livelihood, and that of others depends. The civil world is constructed as the special domain which honors these pledges and promises, covenants and contracts. Ultimately, because choices imply the autonomy to make them, the civil world is the realm of personal freedom as well. A man is free, as Nietzsche suggested, to the extent that he can make and remember promises.

The civil world is fundamentally a rational space. When ties of blood and tradition are compromised, relations between and among individuals require an alternative, more abstract common ground. Rational thought begins to rise, to become visible, on the horizon of civil relations because reason begins to provide the necessary formal abstractions, such as those of positive law, which enable exchanges among strangers. Rationality has, as a consequence, a universally-based, global character relatively detached in its practice from local and particular cultural circumstances. Reason and civility are mutually extensive: the one assumes the other. Civil society emerges with the arts of reason, and the arts of reason sustain and develop themselves within civil society as individuals are delocalized from cultural circumscription. Because the exchange of ideas and values at the level of reason requires higher and more mediated levels of abstraction, civil society rests on the formal education and acculturation of its members into civil roles. The language of civil discourse is consequently both deliberate and intimately related to the formal contexts which support the arts of rational persuasion.

Civil society, as the root of the word implies, is a world of cities. Traditional society, of course, has cities as well. But cities in traditional societies neither hold nor characterize the lives of the great mass of the population. In ancient Egypt, the capital cities of Thebes and Memphis numbered populations only in the tens of thousands. John Wilson aphorized that, "Egypt was a civilization without cities."[1] The masses of the Egyptian people lived by the millions in thousands of small agricultural villages with populations numbering in the dozens or hundreds. The same was true of most of the great civilizations of traditional China, India and the Near East.

The first inkling of civil society appears in the city-state civilization of Sumerian Mesopotamia.[2] This area was never a united country as was Egypt or China, but rather composed of dozens of independent cities, based on agriculture but tied to commerce, and in which the mass of the population appears to have lived. This decentralization of power into competing urban domains which traded with one another, warred with one another, but at the same time shared the same language, cultural values, technology and cosmology laid the basis for a civil realm which was to reach its first full flowering 2,000 years later in the world of classical Greece.

The decentralization of power into a number of competing cities made the priest-kings of Ur, Ereck, Lagash and the other cities of third millennium BC Sumeria dependent on the cooperation of all classes, including the craftsmen and the merchants, to govern their polities. And these classes were not willing to accept the arbitrary rule of priest-kings through divine right, as the peoples or Egypt or China were expected to do. The relative decentralization and pluralization of power is first seen here as one of the hallmarks of a civil society. Decentralization also furthered intellectual abstraction because variety and complexity required common ground to enable social transactions. The rise of more complex weights and measures, mathematical systems, calendars and law *codes* in Mesopotamia, the most famous being that of Hammurabi of Babylon (ca. 1800 BC), are examples reflecting growing pluralism and "democracy." The rule of law, with clearly written codes, established courts, and, above all, the concept of contracts, underlay the Sumerian social consensus. Even the gods were understood to act in concert only after discussion and voting. It is no accident that humanity's oldest examples of writing, from Sumeria, often take the form of contracts. It is also no accident that Mesopotamia was extremely short of natural resources. These constraints in the environment impelled the culture toward innovation and trade. We will see this pattern again: trade and markets flourish more in conditions of adversity than of abundance. Markets often serve as a more efficient rationalization of material, and especially human, resources under conditions of pronounced scarcity.

The prevalence of war and warfare states in Mesopotamia throughout its long history also reflected its often fragmented condition, characterized by socio-economic plurality and scarcity. Warfare, another form of organized contention which flourished in Mesopotamia, as it had not in Egypt or China during long periods of their histories, enabled the rise of a warrior class, which parallels the rise of the merchant class. Success in war as in commerce requires access to goods not generally available, a competitive advantage. That advantage often lies in advanced human organization, and the innovation and relative monopoly of certain technologies such as the horse and chariot, the compound bow, or metals such as bronze or iron.[3] The existence of a warrior class often presumes the existence of a merchant class to generate the economic surpluses necessary to supporting it, at least in the short term. The close association of a warrior class with a merchant class, and innovations in commerce with those in warfare, also suggests that successful commercial societies, from the Mesopotamians, the Greeks and the Vikings in ancient times to the Japanese and those of North America and Western Europe in our own, are often rooted in the arts of war. The collapse of the Soviet Union, whose claims to great power status were entirely rooted in its military, was ultimately tied to its failure to build the economic (and market) base necessary to sustaining a world-class war machine.

The next important civilization in which these special elements of civil culture emerge is Phoenicia, on the coast of what is now Lebanon, around 1,000 BC.[4] While the Phoenicians possessed a common language, culture and cosmology, they were never a single political entity. Rather, like the Sumerians, Phoenicians were gathered into a number of independent cities, with names like Tyre, Sidon and Biblos. The Phoenicians were the heirs of the adjacent Mesopotamian cultures, borrowing significant ideas in the realms of religion, science and law. What distinguished the Phoenicians was that their prosperity depended entirely on trade, principally by sea. Lacking a significant hinterland with good soil, the Phoenicians depended on trading high value-added manufactured goods for food and scarce raw materials. They made a choice central to the evolution of civil society: the choice to move beyond the intrinsically localized nature of an agricultural economy to a value-added market economy driven by an expansive division of labor. They took abundant local raw materials like sand and shellfish, and manufactured from them the elegant (and expensive) glass-ware and dyed textiles for which they were famous throughout the Mediterranean world. (The name "Phoenician" derives from the Greek word "purple," the expensive dye which they monopolized.) They imported inexpensive raw materials such as the papyrus plant, which they turned into paper for export. (The Greek word *biblios,* or book, from which the English word *Bible* comes, derives from the Phoenician port-city of Biblos, renowned for its exports of fine paper.) The Phoenicians established trade monopolies in essential raw materials such as tin, necessary to make bronze. The merchants and craftsmen of these cities dominated the political system, which existed largely to reflect their interests.

The development of the world's first functional alphabet by the Phoenicians, an intellectual innovation of enormous consequence, was entirely in the service of commerce, which required the easy and widespread acquisition of literacy. More importantly, the development of the alphabet raised language to higher and more subtle levels of abstraction: now reality could be captured in two dozen or so symbols almost infinitely mobile amongst themselves. The case could be made that languages, such as ancient Egyptian or Chinese, which are written in pictographic characters, never developed the subtlety of expression and imagination which advance highly abstract concepts. The case could also be made that more abstract alphabetic writing was integral to the expansive globalization of commerce, in which the Phoenicians were pioneers. Pictographic languages have a much more circumscribed, concrete, and thus localized character, and probably inhibited both Egyptian and Chinese commerce with other peoples. For all of that, the Phoenicians left few literary or philosophical texts. They were otherwise occupied accumulating material wealth by trading throughout much of the known world — buying and selling as far away as Britain, and circumnavigating Africa — to engage in such abstract speculation. But they taught everything they knew to another great seafaring and trading people, the Greeks, who vigorously built a system of abstract speculation upon it. It was within this Greek cultural system that all the elements which underlie modern, civil life developed.

Like the Sumerians and the Phoenicians before them, the Greeks were a people who shared a culture but not a single political system. A rugged, mountainous geography, with little good soil, but with an abundance of seacoast on all sides turned the Greeks toward the sea. This decentralization of power among dozens of independent city-states, together with an attachment to the sea and navigation, was to have a profound effect in the transition from traditional to civil society. Navigators must take risks and embrace contingency and change. They need to be relatively free from the intrusive power of the state, every ship's captain, in a sense, a state unto himself. Perhaps the reason the Egyptians in three thousand years of splendid history never became successful merchants, navigators or colonizers was that the basic conservatism of their cultural temper, shaped in the predictable and provident Nile river valley, and enforced by a highly centralized state, made them uncomfortable with risk and change. The commercial culture of the Greeks, based on taking risks and making adaptations to change, seems to be inextricably tied to a life in cities, relatively isolated from each other by rugged geography, but tied to the seas.

Like the Sumerians and the Phoenicians, the Greeks solved the dual problems of over-population and lacking resources through emigration and commerce. Just as the Sumerians had founded Mari on the upper Euphrates as a major colony, commercial center and source of raw materials, and as the Phoenicians had founded Carthage and other cities as trading hubs in the western Mediterranean, the Greek cities founded hundreds of colonies from Marseilles in France and Syracuse in Sicily, to the Crimea of what is now Ukraine. From colonial port cities on the edge of fertile growing areas, grain was exported to the Greek motherland. Colonizers are used to encountering other cultures and even living among them by adapting to local circumstance. But more than this, colonizers must be curious and to some degree adventurous. The Greeks were both of these. In Greek culture the forces of ethnic and city-state particularism were balanced by an outward-looking attitude that rested in the dual activities of commerce and colonization. In Greek thought, the contention of the particular with the universal, the local with the global, was to be an enduring subtext.

It was the number and scale of Greek cities which was unique and entirely new in human history. Athens at its commercial height numbered perhaps 350,000 people. Syracuse numbered almost as many. Corinth and Thebes counted populations exceeding 100,000. The great Ionian cities, such as Ephesus and Pergamum, numbered in the hundreds of thousands. In the

Hellenistic (Greco-Roman) period, the great Greek metropolises of Alexandria in Egypt and Antioch in Syria numbered almost a million inhabitants each. Commerce, and commerce alone, allowed cities on this scale to be achieved.[5] To support immense populations cereals and other goods had to be imported in vast quantities from the bread baskets of the Mediterranean world in the Rhone valley, the Nile valley, southern Russia and the Syrian plain. To pay for imports, manufactured goods and services had to be provided in return. In the case of Athens, olive oil (the petroleum of the ancient world, used for fuel, cooking, lubrication, etc.), so well produced in the rocky soil of Attica, was processed in factories for export. High quality pottery was mass produced from the excellent local clays and exported. Wine, the fruit of vines developed to thrive on hillsides, was shipped throughout the Mediterranean. Athenian metal-workers and sculptors in bronze and stone produced excellent artistic output valued throughout the known world. Athens (and later, Rhodes) became the center for the trans-shipment of goods for the eastern Mediterranean world, and drew riches from it. It was Athenian coinage, made possible by a large, state-owned silver mine, which provided the monetary liquidity that enabled complex trade.

A principle of demographic compression seems to have been at work in the emergence of civil society, as it was in the emergence of traditional society. As populations were forced into closer association in great cities, social and economic structures had to be fundamentally altered, bringing entirely new institutional arrangements with them. This localization, through intensive urbanization, of the expansive forces inherent in Mediterranean commercial culture impelled social innovation. In the Hellenic world of the sixth century BC these compressive forces required the institution of many of the social mechanisms, habits of mind, and values which characterize civil society to this day. These mechanisms and associated values required much higher degrees of intellectual abstraction than had been previously required. Density and mediated abstraction again supplemented one another.

The development of coinage represents only one of these abstractions first evidenced in civil society. It was in the Greek commercial world of the eastern Mediterranean that coinage was introduced for the first time ca. 600 BC. Any trade beyond barter required both a sophisticated banking system and a quality currency backed by the interests of a powerful state. Both of these were provided by Greek mercantile cities, but especially the city of Athens. Its navy also protected the seaways from always-lurking pirates, this protection being paid for by its allies in the Delian League. The bankers of Athens were scrupulous, and the Athenian state kept them so. A rudimentary joint-stock market provided for the pooling of risk in undertaking imports and exports by sea. A court system which efficiently and reliably enforced contracts, and which made suits possible for all citizens of whatever station, was an essential part of this civil society. Also most essential was a highly decentralized and pluralistic political system, which allowed contending economic and social interests to promote and defend themselves. For now economic relations were production-driven and market-oriented. This compares with primal economics which is characterized by a focus on distributive relations, and traditional economics where there are formal and difficult tensions between producers of wealth on one hand, and distributors of it on the other. Market societies make the wager that if the productive forces of society are allowed full reign, distributive relations will largely take care of themselves. And as every commentator from Marx to Keynes has observed, this is the fatal flaw within production-driven, market systems.

Greece was a great arena of commerce before it was an arena of "democracy." In fact, the indispensable element necessary for the rise of the first democracy in Athens were the social and individual habits inculcated by a maritime and merchant society. Only after men had become practiced in the art of negotiation and contracting and seeing their benefits in the commercial domain, did they extend them to the political domain. The marketplace had the indispensable historical role of functioning as an intermediate space between the private household and fully public life, in that it served essentially private motives in a public space. In negotiating private interests in a public space individuals became practiced in the values more generally associated with a public life, which could then be directed toward public, that is to say, common ends.

The commercial culture of Hellenic civilization was, to adopt a term from Daniel Lerner, a *mobile* culture. The movement of people and goods over wide maritime distances, together with the myriad transactions possible only in densely populated cities produced cultural habits which were "mobile" in other senses as well. Lerner summarizes: "A mobile society has to encourage rationality, for the calculus of choice shapes individual behavior and conditions its rewards. People come to see the social future as manipulable rather than ordained and their personal prospects in terms of achievement rather than heritage. Rationality is purposive: ways of thinking and acting are instruments of intention (not articles of faith); men succeed or fail by the test of what they accomplish, not what they worship."[6]

The Greeks as sea-farers, colonizers and merchants were "mobile" in Lerner's sense, but that mobility required certain institutional anchors if complex commercial relations were to be possible. Again, money played a pivotal role. The use of money lifted market exchange above the limitations of barter by providing better liquidity. As a transitory store of value between exchanges of goods money greatly increased market rationality. But money also furthered the processes of abstraction so necessary to civil society. One of the Greek words for coinage, *nomisma*, shares an etymological root with the word for law, *nomos*. Coinage was introduced into Athens in the middle of the sixth century BC after the extensive legal reforms of Solon, which laid the basis for a civil world. The introduction of coinage can thus be understood within the general context of the legal and institutional development of the Greek city-state, as Jonathan Williams suggests.[7] Once they had begun to use specie money, in the form of gold and silver coins, traders gained the confidence to use bronze coins, which had a much more fiduciary character in that their real value lay in their being guaranteed by the state issuing them. The issuing state, which accepted them in payment of taxes and debts, and mandated their use in domestic markets, also guaranteed their face value and thus had a stake in preserving the integrity of its money as an institution.

Coins began to function in markets as contracts did in law: as abstract intermediaries representing the exchange of real goods and interests. Like alphabetical language, the development of coinage reflected the globalizing impulses inherent in commercial culture in the Mediterranean world by providing a general exchange standard which could be flexibly adapted to local trading contexts. The Greek experience as merchants and colonizers required them to take risks, which in turn enabled them to build the levels of confidence in institutional devices, such as coinage, necessary for the evolution of civil society itself. Arnold Hauser proposes that,

> The capacity for abstract thought which leads to the autonomy of spiritual forms is developed not merely by the experience of colonization, but also to a very great extent by the practice of trading for money. This abstract means of exchange and its reduction of the various goods to a common denominator, the division of the original barter of goods into two separate acts of sale and purchase, is a factor accustoming men to abstract thought and making them familiar with the ideas of a common form with various contents, of a common content in various forms. Once content and form are distinguished from one another, the notion that form can subsist by itself is not far off.[8]

In this Hauser recalls Aristotle, who asserted that "money acts like a measure: it makes goods commensurable and equalizes them. For just as there is no community without exchange, there is no exchange without equality and no equality without commensurability."[9] The civil world is characterized by its "commensurablities" and its "forms." Those forms — whether reflected in writing, money, law, science, philosophy or art — receive their contents as the dialog of individuals with each other in civil life and through civil institutions alternatively fill and empty them. Edward E. Cohen's definitive work on Athenian banking makes something akin to the same point by suggesting that the "complementary opposites," which characterized Greek language and thought, both reflected and enabled the complex financial system mandated by advanced commercial relations.[10] Although the use of formal balance sheets in business was in the distant future, the idea of debits and credits required an initial, abstract commitment to a world of such dynamic symmetries. The mobility of Greek thought — raised to its highest level in the dialectics of the Socratic method experienced in Plato's writing — was energized by these symmetries, "complementarities" and leaps of imagination (social, intellectual and institutional) necessary to bring them into dynamic balance.

Greek art, which experienced an extraordinary transformation in the course of the rise of civil society in the fifth century, reflected this careful attention to abstract forms with actual, perceived contents, particularly in architecture and sculpture. The Parthenon and the other splendid structures erected on the Athenian acropolis during the age of Pericles still enchant the viewer with the subtlety and power of their expression of "complementary opposites." Doric columns on the great temple of Athena were carefully shaped to slightly bulge at their centers (*entasis*) so as to appear supple and graceful while supporting the weight of the entablatures above them. All horizontal lines appear straight (but not rigid) to the eye because the architects bowed them upward slightly toward the center so as to correct for the distortions of vision. In a similar manner, columns were slightly tilted toward the center of the facades to compensate for the appearance of a thrust outward. Sculptures on the Parthenon were placed in dynamic interactive poses, with flowing muscles or drapery, to give movement to the finely balanced but static massing. Passages of color contrast with the brilliance of the white Pantellic marble used throughout. All of this was achieved within masterful understandings of geometric proportion and perspective. Constantinos Doxiadis even proposes that important Greek ceremonial sites, such as the Athenian acropolis, were laid out *around* the individual human participant at the point at which he crosses the boundary of the sacred precinct. At this point he becomes the center of twelve, 30-degree segments of perspective focused on the defining angles of the entire architectural ensemble. Only one of these segments — that focused straight ahead on the distant landscape and horizon — is not defined by architectural elements. The individual is not only the focus of the ensemble, he places it within the larger geographical context.[11] Man has become the measure of all exchange. As one stands at the gateway (*propylaea*) of the acropolis, at this quintessential boundary, looking toward the Parthenon, one appreciates the assertion of Bloomer and Moore: "After all these centuries it is still the closest mankind has come to a building which unites the human body and the divine."[12]

Greek drama, as evidenced in such works as *The Bacchae* of Euripides, contrapuntally asserts a formal, linear, "Apollonian" order, together with a fluid, agonistic "Dionysian" reality. The other Greek arts, especially sculpture, evidenced this same exhaustive understanding of the dynamic ways in which form and content stand in tension with one other, resolved only in their appreciation by the individual eye and ear. This new perspective is to be contrasted with primitive art where form and content merge; and traditional art where either content tends to serve form, or form tends to serve content. The transformation of art meant that an aesthetic attitude itself became fully possible, and could begin to sustain a higher human need. For artistic imagination was now the articulation of individuals; and the work of art, like the individual, could begin to exist for its own sake — an extension of the quest for self-realization. Artists, as the West came to understand them, thus emerge in the civil culture of Greece for the first time.

As a more mobile society, the Greeks, albeit to different degrees in different cities (and the real exception of Sparta, land-locked and agricultural), rid themselves of the rigidities of monarchical and aristocratic power, based on class and heredity, when they saw that commercial rights in property were inextricable from political rights in democratic institutions. The rule of law based not on tradition or religious sanction, but on self-interest and social interest negotiated through rational discourse required building a culture of civility which had never fully existed before in human history. The structures of authority in civil culture draw from the primal world those elements of charisma centered in speech and persuasion, and from the traditional world those elements centered in a respect for abstract rules and roles found in institutions. Their further abstraction as rational, contractual discourse underlay evolving civility in the classical world. The special requirements of civility prompted a paradigm shift from the world of the traditional to the civil as important as the paradigm shift from the primal to the traditional.

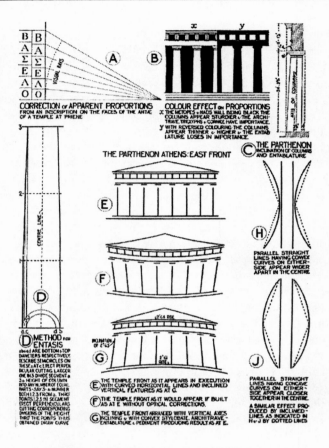

DYNAMIC BALANCE IN GREEK ARCHITECTURE

Figure 5:1 The tension between form and content, reality and perception — a characteristic of Greek culture and of civil society — is resolved only in individual appreciation. The Parthenon is an archetype of this resolution. The search for dynamic balance in art reflects a mobile, commercial society, every credit the "complementary opposite" of every debit.

THE ACROPOLIS: MAN IS THE MEASURE

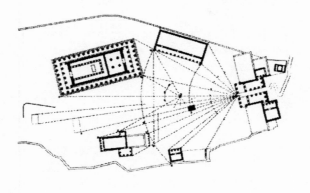

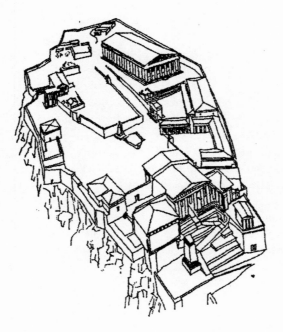

Figure 5:2

The culture of civility was shaped by some fundamental attitudes which had grown out of commercial culture. The first is that the building of wealth and its wide-spread distribution among the citizenry were indispensable elements of republican freedom. "An imbalance between rich and poor is the oldest and most fatal ailment of all republics," wrote Plutarch, echoing Aristotle. If conflict comes from the building of personal wealth by some while others remain poor, the solution is not the abolition of wealth (the primal solution); nor its centralized accumulation in a small, divinely-sanctioned elite in an authoritarian society (the traditional solution); but rather the vast increase and distribution of wealth through a vigorous expansion of markets, and the sharp reduction of the role of the state in production and distribution. It also meant the continual extension of the rights of citizenship. The history of both Greece and Rome (as of later civil societies such as the US and Britain) is the history of the expansion of civil and political rights (and with them better access to material resources) to more of the population in order to maintain social stability.

In the classical world of Greece, and for a time in its successor, Rome, the state was reduced to an economic referee in what were essentially market-driven economic systems: it policed the arteries of commerce; it guaranteed the coinage; it protected private property; it established a relatively efficient and incorrupt court system; and it promoted representative government. The Athenian government, for example, owned no major economic resources directly, except for the silver mine at Laurion necessary to supply the public mint. But it provided regulation of markets so that, for example, critical grain reserves would always be on hand in spite of incentives for private grain merchants to take advantage of shortages and higher prices elsewhere. Lionel Casson notes that, "The grain trade of Athens was too vital to the city's well-being to be left completely in the hands of private businessmen. Yet the government had neither the administrative machinery nor the desire to take over any part of the actual operations. It did the next best thing: it exercised careful control."[13]

This unprecedented legitimization of the marketplace required that the public spaces of the state and the private spaces of the market remain relatively separate. To the degree that markets become "public," or the state becomes "private," the basis of civil society is undermined. The anchor of civil society becomes the citizen himself, for he mediates in his own life the tension at the boundaries between the public and the private. The citizen emerges for the first time as an autonomous being because the civic realm now exists in a space designed for discourse concerning public things. Indeed, the Latin *res publica,* "public things," distinguished a republic from competing, essentially private modes of governance: aristocratic or monarchical rule resting on heredity and modeled in family and household organization. In classical civilization public life took precedence over private life because it was in public that a man's highest nature as a reasoned citizen could be demonstrated. The word "public" derives from the Latin root *pubes* (adult) suggesting that public life was the reward for those sufficiently mature to function outside domestic spaces. Democracy as the highest expression of public life is characterized by its *visibility*, made possible because equal citizens are figuratively, and often literally, in sight of each other as decisions are made. A forum is a place "outside" (from the Latin *fori)* enclosed spaces. It is in public places that equality began to replace hierarchy in relations, for as Aristotle suggested, there is no exchange without equality. As property became fully possible and visible in the referential totality of the market, the citizen became fully possible and visible within the referential totality of the public space.

The private realm, on the other hand, as characterized by the household, was largely invisible and lower-order. To spend time there was, literally, to "be deprived" (from the Latin, *privare*: to separate, to deprive). The private household was neither visible, nor a place of equals, but rather a system of necessary hierarchies based on gender, age and condition of servitude. Its traditional organization required that the householder had to leave it to find his equals in the freedom of public spaces. In terms of Maslow's hierarchy of needs we have moved from the realm of safety and nourishment of the primal, to the realm of the company and esteem of others of the traditional, to the realm of self-esteem in the civil world. Political theorist William Riker has argued: "Democracy is self respect for everybody. Within this simple phrase is all that is and ought to be the democratic ideal. Man's respect is an understanding of his dignity. It is the value he sets on his own full development, the condition and result of his self-realization. It is his recognition, with neither pride nor groveling, of his indispensability to society and his insignificance in the universe. Most of all, within the limits society allows, its is a function of his self-direction and self-control, of the choice and living of the life he thinks best."[14] Greek democracy was not for "everybody." But for those who shared in it, the first intimations of self-esteem as the result of participation based on choice became obvious. Civil society had enabled and sustained this higher human capacity and need as neither primal nor traditional society could.

The focus of Greek, more particularly Athenian, education on the arts of rational persuasion in rhetoric and philosophy was the corollary of the Greek focus on the public life of the *polis* as the highest good. When Aristotle asserted that "Man is a political animal," what he meant was that human beings achieve their ultimate self-realization in reasoned discourse only in the political domain of civil life. In a word, civil bonds, unlike those of kinship and/or religion, are those which are freely and rationally chosen. The bonds that unite the free citizens of the *polis* are those of the laws adopted democratically after open exchange within which the arts of reason are fully articulated. An open, democratic system which respected freedom and law is the one Pericles emphasized in his famous "funeral speech" [ca. 431 BC]: "Our constitution is named a democracy, because it is in the hands not of the few but of the many. But our laws secure justice for all in their private disputes, and our public opinion welcomes and honours talent in every branch of achievement, not for sectional reasons but on grounds of excellence alone. [...] Open and friendly in our private intercourse, in our public acts we keep within the control of law."[15] If the market is a place of private self-interest, the *polis* is a place of the public interest. "Our citizens attend both to public and private duties, and do not allow absorption in their own various affairs to interfere with their knowledge of the city's," says Pericles.[16]

The public and the private are understood to stand in dynamic relation. Aristotle compared the constitutions of the major Greek cities precisely to differentiate and categorize them on the basis of geographic, demographic and economic similarities and differences, the global form of the *polis* understood as a vessel for local content. These were, in turn, postulated to generate differing interests and institutions to resolve conflicts deriving from them. It was Aristotle's view that a principal function of public life in the *polis* was to transform these merely private interests into policies for the public good by devising appropriate institutions.

The civil world is characterized by the number and relative density of its social and institutional boundaries. There is a seeming paradox here. If a mobile society comes about in the process of overcoming the boundaries of space, time and blood, why should other boundaries characterize it? *Chosen*, dynamic boundaries, culturally conceived to enhance the interactions of strangers, to enhance civility, differ from traditional boundaries which are rigid, inherited and unquestioned. Civility is, in a basic sense, a powerful etiquette:

an iteration of boundaries as useful, rational tools of human conviviality, rather than as absolute moral standards. The primal world shuns boundaries: the relative absence of class, status, or property lines is a deliberate strategy for reducing social conflict by avoiding interior social segmentation in favor of external segmentation. Parsons asserts that, "a lack of boundedness seems to be an important mark of a society's primitiveness."[17] The traditional world creates boundaries between and within markets and the state, but the great mass of people have little direct contact with either the market or the state, and experience life in largely primal modes. The civil world, on the other hand, embraces the possibilities of social conflict and institutionalizes them, because all citizens directly participate in both the market and the state. Conflict cannot be treated in mobile societies through avoidance mechanisms, but must be confronted through more flexible, adaptable institutions which channel conflict into, at the very least, non-destructive modes, and optimally into socially useful mechanisms of change. Just as important, the individual household in the emerging civil society of Greece now had to define appropriate boundaries for itself as it participated, through the householding citizen, in both public life and the domain of the marketplace with their myriad contractual transactions.

The household in primal society is coterminous with society itself; its boundaries are society's boundaries. Household tasks are shared by the wider kinship group, as are childbearing and decision-making. At the level of the communal village, these practices continue in traditional society, with the domains of the market and the state largely foreign to day-to-day social practice. The village is, in fact, the world for the villager: its boundaries are his boundaries. The traditional Russian word *mir*, used to describe the rural commune connotes all: it means, simultaneously, community, world and peace. The household in a civil society, such as classical Greece, is reduced in size because it is reduced in economic extent. In many cases it is a nuclear family of mother, father, and children and perhaps one or two other related adults. A wealthier household would include servants and employees. Even if it is an extended household of several generations within a single kinship system, the household of civil society is very different in kind than that characterized by the village or the tribal clan. Because it is an urban household, the division of labor is more marked. That individuation in practice has important conse-quences for self-perception. One household might specialize in making bronze utensils, while another produced linen cloth. In the first great urban complexes, to be sure, families continued to make much of their own clothing, prepared (and even grew) some of their own food from basic ingredients, and provided basic services such as gathering water, for themselves. Yet, this complexity of civil society necessitates boundaries precisely to manage the greater possibilities of conflict when so great a number of people, confined to an urban space, interact so intensely in so many kinds of relationships.

NOTES TO CHAPTER FIVE

1. John Wilson, "Egypt," in Henri Frankfort *et.al.*, *op.cit.*
2. Cf. Harriet Crawford, SUMER AND THE SUMERIANS (Cambridge: Cambridge University Press, 1991); and Samuel Noah Kramer, THE SUMERIANS (Chicago: University of Chicago Press, 1971)
3. Cf. John Keegan, A HISTORY OF WARFARE (New York: Alfred A. Knopf, 1993), esp. p. 228
4. Cf. Maria Eugenia Aubet, THE PHOENICIANS AND THE WEST (Cambridge: Cambridge University Press, 1996); and Sabatino Moscati, THE WORLD OF THE PHOENICIANS (New York: Frederick A. Praeger, 1968)
5. An excellent overview of commerce in the eastern Mediterranean during the Hellenistic period is F.E. Peters, THE HARVEST OF HELLENISM (New York: Simon and Schuster, 1970)
6. Lerner, *op.cit.*, pp. 48-49
7. Jonathan Williams, ed., MONEY: A HISTORY (New York: St. Martin's Press, 1997), p. 29
8. Hauser, *op.cit.*, p. 81
9. Aristotle, NICOMACHEAN ETHICS, Martin Ostwald, trans. (New York: Macmillan Publishing Company, 1962), p. 127
10. Edward E. Cohen, ATHENIAN ECONOMY AND SOCIETY (Princeton: Princeton University Press, 1992)
11. Constantinos A. Doxiadis, ARCHITECTURAL SPACE IN ANCIENT GREECE (Cambridge, MA: The M.I.T. Press, 1972)
12. Bloomer and Moore, *op.cit.*, p. 110
13. Lionel Casson, THE ANCIENT MARINERS, 2nd ed. (Princeton: Princeton University Press, 1991) p. 109
14. William H. Riker, DEMOCRACY IN THE UNITED STATES (New York: The Macmillan Company, 1953), p. 19
15. Thucydides, HISTORY, II 37 A.E. Zimmern, trans. (Oxford: Clarendon Press, 1911), p. 197
16. *Ibid.*
17. Parsons, *op.cit.*, p. 38

CHAPTER SIX

COMMERCE AND BOUNDARIES

The delineation of boundaries within civil society helps us to understand the character of the civil world itself. First, there is the boundary between public and private. In pre-civil society the very idea of "privacy" is unknown since no one exists apart from a common space in which all activity takes place. In a clan or a village everyone knows everyone else's business and almost all of life is shared. The first fully developed civil society, that of the Greeks for which Athens was exemplary, defined a boundary between public and private to maintain the coherence of households in large cities. Because it was possible that one shared little in common with the household directly adjacent (there being no necessary ties of kinship, or direct economic interdependence) the market and the state were the two essential arenas which brought individuals (and their households) into direct conversation. If both state and market were to sustain themselves it was essential that old boundaries marked by kinship be obliterated, or at least muted. One cannot enforce a public contract if the judge favors his own kin. One cannot maximize the value of markets if kin relations fundamentally determine the conditions of exchange. Civility required the evolution of a stranger-friendly culture.

When the law-giver Kleisthenese of Athens abolished the traditional clan groups at the end of sixth century BC, and assigned people to artificial *demes* for public purposes, he was acknowledging that the household, the state and the market could exist only if other claims on loyalty were lessened, and also that the household, the market and the state are distinct elements in a civil society. The equivalents of these *deme* associations were also a hallmark of all fully-functional civil societies in subsequent eras. They were the indispensable intermediating groups which made institutional democracy work, because they were the practical lines of transmission between the diverse interests of citizens and government decisions. Nicholas F. Jones says that a major consequence of these intermediating groups was that "the Athenian citizen body as whole must have been highly conscious of its potential for participation in constitutional functions."[1] Classical Athens represents a good model of a fundamentally civil society which has influenced the shape of every civil society after it down to our own day.

The household in Athens was carefully separated from the external or public world. Athenian houses were inward-directed, organized around a courtyard.[2] There were no windows facing the public street, the law in Athens forbidding them. When one entered the door of an Athenian house, one passed a post called a *hermes*, named for the god Hermes, the protector of boundaries. Its presence signaled the importance of the boundary that was being crossed in moving from the public to a private space. Within the house itself there were other clear boundaries. There was the office or shop within which the family plied its specialized trade. The office/shop was enclosed within the household, but could be entered only from the street, its functions and the other functions of the household sharply differentiated. Within the household, the men's quarters and the women's quarter's were carefully separated. A *hermes,* with an erect phallus (the penis itself conceived as a boundary which both separates and unites men and women), was sometimes placed in the courtyard to protect this border, which distinguished the world of women, centered in children and domestic tasks such as cooking and weaving, from the men's quarters, which had more direct access to the public spaces of the street. There was a *symposium* or entertaining room to which only the male guests of the male adults of the household were admitted.

This boundary within the household was reflected outside it. Women were seldom permitted to leave the house, and then only heavily veiled and accompanied by an adult male. Only men were permitted a public life in the markets, the theater, gymnasium and other public venues. This hierarchy of domestic spaces found its philosophical expression in Plato, who made a similar division of the human body on the basis of the higher, distinctly human functions, the breast and head (representing courage and reason), and the lower, animal functions, the stomach and genitals. Hannah Arendt, citing Jaeger, summarizes the animus of this separation of the Greek household from the public world of the *polis*:

According to Greek thought, the human capacity for political organization is not only different from but stands in direct opposition to that natural association whose center is the home (*oikia*) and the family. The rise of the city-state meant that man received "besides his private life a sort of second life, his *bios politikos*. Now every citizen belongs to two orders of existence; and there is a sharp distinction in his life between what is his own (*idion*) and what is communal (*koinon*)."[3]

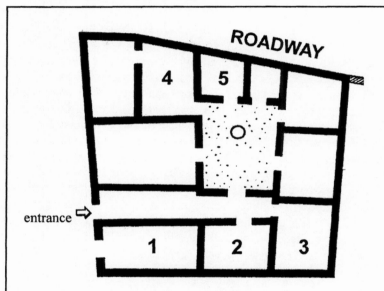

A HOUSE IN 5TH CENTURY ATHENS

Figure 6:1 This house in the industrial quarter of Athens, near the *agora*, refines clear boundaries between public and private functions. The office/shop [1] is enclosed with the boundaries of the house, but is accessible only from outside. The symposium or entertaining room [2] and the master's room [3] have direct access to the public streets. The women's quarters [4] and the service rooms [5] are secluded beyond the court, carefully separating the world of men and their focus in public life outside the household from the world of women, children and slaves with their focus in the private world within it. The entrance, as the border between public and private spaces, was marked with a post called a *hermes*, named for the protecting deity of boundaries.

The contrast between a Greek house, shaped by the requirements of a civil society, and a Chinese house, shaped by the values of a traditional society is stark. While the Chinese house reserves its most privileged spaces at far remove from the street, the Greek house places its privileged spaces closest to the public world of the streets. Where the Chinese idea of repose and serenity is represented by the master's quarters, with its fish pools, gardens and shade tree, enjoyed in the company of wives and children, the Greek house separates men from women and children — its most privileged room being the *symposium*, a place for the social interaction of men, most of whom come to it from the public world outside the household, and where vigorous debate, such as that recorded in Plato's *Symposium*, was a favored diversion. In addition, the house of a wealthy Chinese would be elegantly and abundantly furnished; while a Greek house, even that of a wealthy man, was sparsely decorated because the "higher life" was spent largely outside the house in public spaces. The house of a wealthy Chinese is also characterized by its geometric hierarchies, and regularities — the right angle being its sovereign *trop*, reflecting the carefully planned urban context. Athenian houses are often irregular in shape, reflecting the fluid adaptation of architecture to more organic private property lines, and to the kinetic evolution of cities themselves in a mercantile society. The contrast of these Chinese and Greek houses with the shelters used in primal societies (temporary, often open on the sides, with no real distinction between indoor and outdoor use of space), is even more stark.

The *agora*, or public place, was an ancient fixture of Athens, and existed before its use as a market. The boundary stones around the *agora*, which functioned as *hermes* defining it, are suggestive of its special character and its relation to this god. Wherever dissimilar things meet there is the possibility of confusion, and, indeed, Hermes was known as the god of confusion and consternation. He is thus the pre-eminent deity of markets and merchants, those words deriving from his Roman name, Mercury (Mercator). Markets are structured as (mercurial) places of uncertainty and change, and thus in the Greek imagination required a special presiding god.

Hermes is also the protector of other boundaries: he is a god of medicine, separating the ill from the healthy; the god of learning, separating knowledge from ignorance; the escort of the dead to the afterlife, separating the living from the deceased; the god of travelers, who cross boundaries as a matter of course; the god of communications since he crossed the boundaries separating men from the gods, whom he served as messenger; the god of rhetoric because persuasion brings ideas across boundaries of contention; and, finally, the god of thieves, who cross every boundary to make a livelihood. That the Greeks had one protecting god for both merchants and thieves suggests the ways in which the two were connected in ancient imagination. The evolution of Greek theogony was well advanced by the time commercial society came into being. Pre-commercial society in Greece as elsewhere was conservative, hierarchical and aristocratic. The authoritative distribution of goods was intrinsic to the legitimacy of state power. Redistribution by intermediates was always a challenge to this authority. "Private" property and trading in property, to the extent that they transpired, were nearly indistinguishable from thievery, which we have seen often functions as a subset of distributive relations in the primal world. Thieves, as a consequence of their primal origins, experienced a kind of tolerance in traditional society which commercial, civil society rooted in contracts and property by its very premises had to deny them. Merchants entered the socio-economic niche vacated by thieves as redistributors, and inherited their presiding god.

The process through which property and markets in conjunction acquire intelligibility by coming into relation with one another — but at the expense of their identity with other cultural values — can be summarized in the passage from theft to markets. This is a process in which distributive relations evolve from initial conditions of social localization and economic marginalization, characterized by deliberate economic subsistence, minimal economic activity, and absolute poverty. In primitive societies, such as those found in the highlands of Borneo, decentered, kin-based segmentation in effect marginalizes all distribution to the peripheries, where theft in the form of raids on the gardens or livestock of neighbors is culturally institutionalized (cf. Radin, *supra* Chap. 2) as one manifestation of this fluid localization in the movement of goods. In traditional societies only those subgroups which remain marginalized at the periphery of the social system (e.g., Gypsies in many parts of Europe), as others are mobilized into more pervasive and centralized economic relations, perform this now despised but also useful service of theft-based distribution. In Italy, for example, tourists are advised to be on guard against Gypsies in the train stations, museums and elsewhere, but also discover the "informal" markets where such things as cameras can be obtained at a bargain price. In mature civil societies the plurality and mobility of individuals in principle free both economic relations and subgroups from the periphery. Everyone is mobilized into the fluidity of social relations based in the centrality of markets and contracts. Since no one in principle exists at the economic periphery of society, theft as a means of distribution loses any justification or accommodation. Now only law and markets legitimize the possession and transmission of goods. The globalizing impulses of markets finally defeat the localizing impulses of kin-based tradition.

In civil society property moves because of the will of the contracted possessor; property is literally that which is "one's own" (from the Latin, *propius*) as distinguished from that which is another's or in communal use. Consequently, it is not only that contracts in relation to property are weak in pre-civil societies. In many ways, the concept of property-as-contract is neither culturally understood nor supported in societies where the more pronounced immobility of persons is supplemented by the more pronounced mobility of goods. The market in civil societies is the legitimate means by which goods transfer among individuals through their willful surrender of possession. The market requires that goods be immobile unless willed by their owners into movement. It thus also requires that individuals be more mobile and rational in relation to goods. Precivil conceptions of property, certainly primal ones, assume the relatively independent mobility of goods — enabled by spirituality and thievery as well as the dynamics of gift-giving and trade. Thus when one speaks of widespread thievery in precivil culture as some sort of institutional weakness that can be corrected with better laws and law enforcement one is speaking from a civil bias: one assumes the *a priori* legitimacy of "property" and the illegitimacy of "theft," which law only reflects and instrumentalizes.

But even at the height of Greek commercial culture poets and philosophers favored the more ancient pre-civil values to the newer "bourgeois" ones. We have seen how Aristotle compared honorable "household economics" to dishonorable "retail trade." Hauser says, "The poets and the philosophers had little sympathy for the bourgeoisie, whether wealthy or poor; they supported the nobility even when they themselves were of bourgeois origins."[4] This was a pattern to be repeated often in subsequent eras. In the midst of vibrant commercial cultures the intellectual class often aligned itself with values which were fundamentally anti-commercial, often anti-democratic, and in many ways elitist and reactionary. There appear to be two basic explanations for this. On one hand intellectuals as a class of priests and scribes attached to the traditional state were being displaced, at least in influence, by the newer class of merchants. On the other, the free market is motivated by its own self-contained values, distributive outcomes being relatively independent of some external system of valuation. Markets by their nature thus tend to devalue the importance of intellectuals as the ultimate voice of social ethics. Perhaps this is why attempts at full-fledged socialism have had their greatest success in traditional societies, like Russia or China. "Socialism" is the rule of intellectual elites and their basic, pre-civil values in the face of Western civil societies and their ascendant commercial elites

The dependence of civil life on distinct spheres and multiple boundaries negotiated by individual citizens required new definitions of the human self. Civil society requires that individuals contemporaneously play different roles, depending on the world in which they find themselves: husband, father, master, son, citizen, soldier, merchant. Indeed, the word *person* (from the Latin *persona*, "mask") evolved from this multiplicity of roles in civil society. To the degree that boundaries represent *stasis*, fixing relations to locations, persons had to be mobile, moving across multiple boundaries. A "person" is an artificial and abstract construct, composed of a number of roles, or relations, which an individual might play in various theaters of civil life. This cultural abstraction, initially evolved in Greek drama, was perhaps the greatest legacy of Greece to Rome. The Roman construction of civil law, which became the norm in the West, is based on the separation of real, biological individuals from their legal personalities. All citizens become equal under law because the subjects of the laws are not "real" (and thus unequal) individuals at all, but rather legal persons, who have equal rights and responsibilities as citizens. The identical white *togas* (from the Latin *tegere*, "to cover") which the Roman citizen wore in public was the emblem of this equality. Their intent was to cover private identities (and inequalities) in public, civil spaces. The *toga* was a uniform of citizenship.

As the Roman empire expanded across the Mediterranean world and beyond, rights of citizenship were selectively extended to those not of Latin blood. St. Paul, a Greek-speaking Jew from the city of Tarsus in Asia Minor, invoked his rights as a Roman citizen. In order to facilitate the bringing of so many diverse peoples with differing customs into the sphere of one law, the Romans began to distinguish between *ius gens* (the law of peoples), that is, particular bodies of law applicable to the needs of certain groups (such as the *Torah* of the Jews), and *ius naturae* (the law of nature), that law common to all humanity issuing from the shared "nature" of human beings themselves. This was a leap the Greeks, at least not until Alexander's pan-Hellenism, were never able to make. The boundary between barbarian and Greek was, to them, unbridgeable. The Roman universalistic conception of a law governing all humanity, arising from that humanity, was to have far-reaching effects in subsequent centuries. It was to have important implications for conceptions of authority as well. It was the Romans who firmly established in the West the intellectual and legal basis for conceptions of popular sovereignty, *vox populi*. On the standards of Roman legions and on public monuments the letters "S.P.Q.R." were inscribed: *Senatus Populesque Romanus: the Senate and the Roman People*. Authority is solidly embedded in law, constitutionally created by the Roman Senate and the Roman people. Pan-Hellenism and Roman universalism were also reflected in the globalization of art, architecture and other cultural forms in the Mediterranean world. The artistic forms originally developed in Greece had by the Third Century BC become the first "international style." From Alexandria in Egypt, to Antioch in Syria; from Carthage in Africa to Rome in Europe, the temples and the gods were in Greek dress. *Koine*, the Greek commercial tongue, was the *lingua franca* spoken everywhere.

As a result of these globalizing tendencies rooted in commerce, and the important abstractions and constructions which arose from them, the concept of "contract" took on new dimensions. A contract became enforceable in civil law as the agreement between two or more legal persons. Who the kin of these persons are, or the circumstances of their birth, are deliberately irrelevant because the contract establishes its own sphere of rights and obligations within the larger construct of civil law. In taking this critical step from traditional to civil concepts of law, a further step becomes possible. If a person is an abstract entity created by law, not biology, then it is possible for these artificial "persons" to be composed of more than one biological individual, i.e. a number of individuals might be given a single body in law ("incorporated"). The corporation, so essential to any modern complex economy, is not possible without the civil society which created the intellectual terms of its existence: the possibility for institutional ties not based on kinship, and a system of law which regulates abstracted rather than biological individuals.

This has had very concrete consequences in the development of complex business societies. The traditional Asian trading house, as an instance, has functioned without a fully-evolved civil society and civil conceptions of contract and law. As a consequence, it has been limited in scale and in its capacity to grow by the number of male relatives available to do the firm's business.[5] Taiwan's economy is characterized by the lack of large firms; numerous medium and small firms dominate. Even larger, more complex industrial organizations, such as Korea's *chaebol,* are owned by a single family with kin relationships to other *chaebol.* "Nepotistic capitalism" is not restricted to the countries of Asia, or even to the developing world. Italy, too, is characterized by small family-owned firms, and weak civil institutions, especially at the national level. But a kin-oriented, nepotistic business system is likely to be more prevalent in traditional societies, or even modal, because civil, contractual relations within the public sphere are underdeveloped or completely unknown. As barter had limited exchange relations in goods, the introduction of coinage had enlarged them in the Greco-Roman world. In Hauser's terms, an abstract "form" had mediated *liquidity* in market relations, which increased their scope and complexity. A parallel phenomenon occurred in law. The abstract legal "person" created the fungibility in relations among real individuals necessary to the more complex associations of a civil society and a globalizing environment.

Civil society, based on the negotiation and enforcement of free contractual relations among persons, individual and corporate, stands at the heart of the principles of civil liberty and the rule of law. In carefully defining and protecting multiple boundaries within which persons function as rightful entities civil society differentiates itself from both the primal and the traditional worlds. The primal and the traditional, with their roots in kinship, the world of spirits, and an externally-imposed authority, needed to be transcended if the civil world was to come into existence. It was also necessary if concepts of justice were to move from revenge and retribution to higher ethical levels. Huizinga asserts: "We moderns cannot conceive justice apart from abstract righteousness, however feeble our conception of it may be. For us, the lawsuit is primarily a dispute about right and wrong; winning and losing take only a second place. Now it is precisely this preoccupation with ethical values that we must abandon if we are to understand archaic justice."[6]

In Aeschylus' great play-cycle, *The Oresteia*, this transition from the "archaic" to the "modern" is marked in the drama of classical Athens. These plays tell the story of the family of Agamemnon, a leading figure in Homer's narratives. Agamemnon, king of Mycenae, sacrificed his daughter to the sea god to achieve fair winds for the voyage with his army to Troy. Agamemnon's wife, Clytemnestra, fulfilled the "law of blood" and avenged her daughter's spirit by killing her husband upon his return, since she owed more to her daughter, whose blood she shared, than to her husband, whose blood she did not share. Orestes, the son of Agamemnon and Clytemnestra, subsequently killed his mother to avenge his father's spirit, because a son owes more to his father's blood than to his mother's. The spirits of hell were sent by Clytemnestra's spirit to torment Orestes for this matricide. Fleeing the Furies to Athens, Orestes sought judgment from its virgin goddess, Athena (who was not born of a mother, springing full-grown from the forehead of her father, Zeus). Athena gave judgment in favor of Orestes, since she herself was neither a mother, nor of a mother. But Athena went further. Realizing that this blood revenge cycle will never end unless the primal source which fed it is transcended, she decreed that henceforth in Athens judgment will no longer be divine. Rather, free and equal men would make and enforce the law, under the protection of the Furies, now transformed into the benevolent Eumenides. The rule of law and not of blood, of reason and not of gods, would take the form of a human court to meet on the Hill of Ares.

> Let our wars rage on abroad
> With all their force
> To satisfy our powerful lust for fame
> But as for the bird that fights at home
> My curse on civil war[7]

The spiritual and intellectual journey which Aeschylus charts in the *Oresteia* describes the evolution of the civil world itself. He also marks a fundamental shift in the idea of authority. Authority no longer exists in either charismatic individuals as in the primal realm, or in the hierarchy of roles and rules of traditional society, but in the *process* of human reason and judgment. As Athena exclaims, "I am in my glory! Yes, I love Persuasion!"[8]

There is an irony in this separation of men from the gods in the progress of Greek civil life, because what characterized classical religion and differentiated it from the religions of Egypt or Mesopotamia were the more intimate relations between humans and gods. Pindar asserted, "Of one race, one only, are men and gods." Not only did Greek divinities take completely human form with completely human emotions, gods and humans came into close physical contact, with humans sometimes born of a union between a god and a human. In at least one case a god, Herakles, was born of a human mother. Since human form and motives were now ascribed to gods, the arbitrariness of divine will became less satisfactory to the Greek mind. The *Orestia* is one manifestation of this important spiritual shift. Another is philosophical discourse, where Aristotle, using the term "God," makes reason and justice coterminous with the divine; and where Plato condemns as pernicious myths stories about the gods which depict them as engaging in activities, such as rape, forbidden to humans.

The inevitable secularization of human thought which issued from this merge between the human and the divine makes it possible for the modern student to read Greek scientific and philosophical texts with little reference to Greek religious thought or practice. The Greek invention of scientific inquiry as we know it required this final, radical separation from the world of external wills infusing the material environment. Nature had now become completely inert, moved only by laws understood through empirical observation and rational measurement. When the great physicist and engineer, Archimedes of Syracuse, claimed that, given a correctly placed fulcrum and a lever of proper length, he could move the world, he expressed a humanist view of nature at radical odds to that of primal or traditional peoples. As a consequence we observe in the civil world a further evolution in human spiritual life. What began as a continuation in the merge between the distinctly human and the distinctly divine ultimately uncovered the contingency of the divine. It is the human locus in relation to the divine which begins to shape religious imagination. Bellah describes what he calls "historic" forms of religion in terms of "salvation." Each such religion (e.g. Judaism, Christianity, Islam, Buddhism) takes its central meaning from what it has to say about the ultimate destiny of mankind. Man thus emerges, and becomes visible, on this horizon of religious evolution. "That is to say," says Bellah, "that it is for the first time possible to conceive of man as such."[9] Human beings are now capable of functioning outside of highly localized and contingent cultural contexts and to define themselves in relation to larger, more abstract and more universal principles. They have become *individuals*.

It has sometimes been asserted that the Greeks were the "first individuals." The Greek emphasis on autonomous reason and judgment is partially responsible for this association. What is also implied is that in initiating the idea of *personae* — the multiple masks which people use to function in the various arenas defined by complex civil boundaries — something irreducibly real had to function behind these masks to provide a coherent identity, or unhealthy schizophrenia could result. In modern civil societies the difficulties individuals experience in managing the competing role claims made upon them does sometimes produce mental breakdown. The individual (literally, the "undivided" and hence "unmasked") human being developed as a defense against the fragmented nature of a mobile, changing society. Classicist H.D.F. Kitto alludes to this underlying reality when he asserts that, "The instinct for seeing things as a whole is the source of the essential sanity of Greek life."[10] Seeing things "as a whole" is by itself evidence of the *delocalized* human being called into existence by the globalized environment into which Greek commercial culture had been impelled by its expansive nature.

The Greek passion for truth and authenticity in thought and imagination; the Greeks' radical curiosity about the world; and their insistence on rational clarity, were based on the evolution of "the individual." To be sure, this is not the only possible response to the imperatives of multiple roles and the identity issues which rise as a consequence. Another response is to abandon the world in which such conflicting claims are made. The response of Gautama Buddha to his experience of life as both prince and pauper was to reject worldliness in order to achieve the ultimate integrity of *nirvana.* The response of Confucius in China was to so imbed the "individual" in the world, and a hierachy of roles, that the individual surrendered to the situational. A critical departure of the West from the East was initiated in the so-called "Axial Age," [ca. 500 BC] when Buddha, Confucius and the Greek philosophers were active. The West choose to embrace a dynamic, ultimately unresolved tension between "the individual" and "the world," where the East choose either to lose the individual in the world, or remove him entirely from it. It is this distinction which powers some of the differences between the traditional and the civil worlds.

The findings of social psychology confirm these broad cultural differences between the East and the West. In a series of studies comparing European Americans to East Asians, conducted by Richard Nisbett, Easterners were found to think more holistically, paying greater attention to context and relationship, relying more on experience-based knowledge than abstract logic, and having higher tolerance for contradiction. They were thus less likely to recognize discontinuities between themselves and their environments and more likely to accommodate as a personal response. Westerners, on the other hand, were more "analytic," tending to detach objects from their context, to avoid contradiction, and to rely more heavily on formal logic, and thus more willing to actively seek to resolve the tensions between themselves and their world.[11] This relative detachment of the judging, willing consciousness from its surrounding world constitutes the basis of Western individualism.

The individual emerged from the development of those elements of personality which have been given a number of names by theorists and clinicians. They revolve around an evolution from object-centeredness to subject-centeredness, from lower-order psychological needs to higher-order needs. Schactel, for example, distinguishes between the "allocentric" (other-centered) and the "autocentric" (self-centered) in personality. Similarly, Guilford's experiments described "convergent" versus "divergent" thought. Physiological psychologists separate "right brain" cognition from "left brain"

cognition. De Laszlo, writing from a Jungian perspective, distinguishes between "extraversion" and "introversion": "The life of the extravert is lived mainly through his direct attention, frequently to the point of identification, to the object of his interest. The life of the introvert derives its value from his internal assimilation of whatever material enters his experience. The dynamics of both types are, therefore, opposite and compensatory. This is not to say that any given person reacts exclusively in one or the other fashion, but rather that the possibility exists for anyone to observe the predominance of one reaction pattern over the other in large numbers of persons as well as within himself."[12]

The allocentric, or other-directed nature of extraversion is tied to its alliance with lower-order needs, such as those for security and sustenance. These needs and the impediments to satisfying them are largely to be found in the exterior, material environment. Primal modes are centered in this field-dependent, high-context sensibility. *I-Thou* encounters represent moving out in a process of unmediated assimilation into the environment. The inner-directedness of introversion, on the other hand, comes about only after lower-order needs are satisfied. The hierarchy of needs then moves toward the higher-order satisfactions such as self-esteem and self-actualization. These are largely achieved within the interior spaces of the self, the spiritual environment defined at a distance from the material world. In autocentric modes the external world is assimilated and ordered to the interior self and, now perceived and manipulated at a distance, the material world is largely perceived as *I-It*. The scientific method, first achieved as modern people understand it among the Greeks, represents a moving *out* toward the inert natural environment which is engaged, observed and measured in order that it may be drawn *into* those interior spaces of the mind which make abstract judgments about reality, and model them intellectually.

The multilayered complexity of a civil society requires that the individual be both "outer-directed" and "inner-directed;" the first because functioning in such a dynamic and changing environment requires strong adaptive or "mobile" skills; the second because personal integrity places a premium on the inner processes of assimilation and meaning-creation. If this is the case, we might describe a spectrum which runs from the primal, through the traditional, into the civil worlds. The dominantly *I-Thou* character of primal relations promotes a merge of the self into the world, an allocentric mode in which the self is captured in constant response to and accommodation of the external world, which, in effect, abolishes interiority. In primal modes there is no independently existing self, and life is characterized by reaction rather than action. As one moves along the spectrum into traditional modes, more *I-It* experiences come to dominate life as the world is mediated through the formal relations of institutions and roles. Establishing the correct relationship between the self and the world situationally is a dominant concern in the "wisdom literature" of traditional thought and ethics, Confucianism being the sovereign example.

As one moves into civil life, the autocentric begins to emerge in advanced thought and experience. Socrates proclaimed that, "The unexamined life is not worth living." Diogenes walked the streets of Athens in broad daylight with a lamp, "seeking an honest man." The authentic self and its particular satisfactions as the seat of judgment and will emerges in final subjectivity. And thus the Hellenized Jew, Paul, promises: "For now we see through a glass, darkly; but then face to face: now I shall know in part; but then shall I know even as also I am known." [I Cor. 13:12] Self-actualization in transcendence now becomes an urgent possibility for a portion of the population. The individual becomes increasingly normative.

The individual becomes more normative in civil society in two senses. Individuals increase in number to the point where "the individual" and the values especially associated with individualism command public discourse and practice: reason, judgment, law and freedom. And process becomes central rather than ends, as the individual becomes an end in himself within a civil society. This sharply distinguishes the civil world from the traditional world with its focus in hierarchy, authority, obedience and some communal definition of the "good life," be it religious or secular, in which all not only should share but must share. What has characterized civil society down to our own day, especially in its democratic expressions, and distinguishes it from traditional society (which in modern times often appears in socialist dress), is the denial that there can ultimately a be a communal "good life." A good life is an individual aspiration, never a social achievement. What constitutes a good life in the final analysis is a function of individual judgment. As Michael Ignatieff has phrased it, "Civil society may be a flawed ideal, but in one central aspect there is no gulf between promise and performance. In a civil society, no paradise beckons."[13]

NOTES TO CHAPTER SIX

1. Nicholas F. Jones, THE ASSOCIATIONS OF ATHENS (New York: Oxford University Press, 1999), p. 49; on the development of the Athenian polity, see Raphael Sealey, A HISTORY OF THE GREEK CITY STATES 700-338 B.C. (Berkeley: University of California Press, 1976)
2. I owe this understanding of the Athenian house to Eva C. Keuls, THE REIGN OF THE PHALLUS (New York: Harper & Row, Publishers, 1985)
3. Arendt, *op.cit.,* pp. 24-25

4. Hauser, *op.cit.,* p. 83
5. Cf. Martin King Whyte, "The Chinese Family and Economic Development: Obstacle or Engine," ECONOMIC DEVELOPMENT AND CULTURAL CHANGE (October 1996)
6. Johan Huizinga, HOMO LUDENS (Boston: Beacon Press, 1950), p. 78
7. Aeschylus, THE ORESTEIA, Robert Fagles, trans. (New York: Penguin Books, 1979), p. 269
8. *Ibid.,* p. 274
9. Bellah, *op.cit.,* p. 366
10. H.D.F. Kitto, THE GREEKS (New York: Penguin Books, 1957), p. 176
11. Erica Goode, "How Culture Molds Habits of Thought," *Science Times*, THE NEW YORK TIMES (August 8, 2000), p. D1
12. Violet S. de Laszlo, "Introduction" to THE BASIC WRITINGS OF C.J. JUNG (New York: The Modern Library, 1959), p. xiv; see also, J.P. Guilford, "A Revised Structure of Intellect," REPORTS FROM THE PSYCHOLOGI-CAL LABORATORY, No. 19, pp. 6, 7 and 9; E.G. Shactel, METAMORPHO-SIS: ON THE DEVELOPMENT OF AFFECT, PERCEPTION, ATTEN-TION, AND MEMORY (New York: Basic Books, 1959), p. 83
13. Michael Ignatieff, "On Civil Society," FOREIGN AFFAIRS (March/April) 1995, p. 129

CHAPTER SEVEN

HOMO FABER

The formation of the normative individual was associated with the elevation of human action as work, rather than as labor. We noted that in traditional society the phenomenon of labor arose in relation to the continuity of production, and from the separation of action from its fruition in consumption. The word "labor" (from the Latin, "to endure, to suffer") suggests the sense of burden which labor brought with it. Labor was also a collective experience, done like, or in the company of one's fellows. Labor carries with it a sense of passive inevitability. Its inevitability reflects the necessity of labor to sustain biological life. Inevitability also fuses with futility because labor is a sisyphean activity which must be endlessly repeated, every harvest giving way to another planting. The sense of futility surrounding labor reflects the fact that the fruits of labor are not only consumed and therefore must be replaced, but labor in a sense also "uses up" in a metabolic way the bodies and spirits of those who do it. And thus labor never ends except in death.

The repetitive, futile cycle of labor is essential to its connotations of endurance and suffering. It was this animus of labor as suffering in which the worker "reified" himself in his effort only to have his product expropriated by property relations that motivated the moral outrage of Karl Marx. In traditional society labor itself is respected because it is necessary. But it confers no honor on those who do it. On the contrary, in traditional society class is largely determined by one's distance from labor. To have servants who perform labor on one's behalf is the essence of nobility. In Mesopotamian belief the gods created men precisely to relieve themselves of the labor necessary to their subsistence. As Thorkild Jacobsen puts it, man "was created to relieve the gods of toil, to work on the gods' estates."[1] In Egypt the dead were buried with miniature models of servants (called *ushabtis* or "answerers") to labor for them in the hereafter. Sir Alan Gardiner writes, "If agriculture was the common lot

of the peasant, such employment could not fail to be abhorrent to the wealthy."[2]
To be a gentleman — a person of "gentle birth" — meant that one did not have
to exert in labor to sustain one's physical existence.

Traditional society is disinclined to change or innovate because the sense
of time is cyclical — nothing truly *new* ever appears under the sun. It is also
disinclined toward change because thought tends to be more separated from
action. That is, the world of action, including the processes by which the
products of nature are rendered through labor into objects of human use and
consumption, is widely separated from the processes of creative imagination.
In traditional China the Mandarin class was signified by its distance from toil.
The exquisitely soft and manicured hand of the Mandarin official was the
symbol of his freedom from the personal degradation of labor. In the caste
system of India the higher castes are marked by the distance from labor of their
social functions. In ancient Egyptian society young men were urged to become
scribes or clerks: "Put writing in thy heart, so that thou mayest protect thine
own person from any (kind of) labor and be a respected official," while the
scribe "...is the one who directs the work of everybody (else)."[3] Thus the
Egyptian mind, like the traditional Chinese and Indian minds, while marked by
its capacity for the canonization of ideas, seldom speculated or applied this
speculation to material invention. Similarly, wheels were found on children's
pull-toys among the Maya, whose priests focused on the stellar heavens, but the
wheel never appeared in practical use on vehicles. Explosive powder appeared
in ritual fire-works in China with no thought to its practical applications in
activities such as mining or warfare.

The traditional mind is conseqently more pragmatic than empirical. The
Chinese were capable of astonishing feats of technical ingenuity in the midst
of a pervasive conservatism, which resisted innovation. But pragmatism is not
empiricism, which is a more generalized abstraction of the pragmatic attitude.
Empiricism is pragmatism *plus curiosity*. For if the Chinese were the most
pragmatic of people (and Confucius the most pragmatic of philosophers) they
were also the least curious. There was thus never a sustained integration into
theoretical structures of what was learned in practice. Practices were codified
with an astonishing (to the Western mind) indifference to the larger principles
of theory which characterizes an empirical bent. In short, there was a lack of
discernment. Innovation was never extended or sustained programmatically in
the ways which have characterized science and engineering in Western
societies beginning in the late Hellenistic period, but especially since the
seventeenth century.

❖ ❖ ❖ ❖

The civil society of the Greeks impelled purposive action and theoretical speculation to be joined, at first weakly and not systematically, but by the Hellenistic period very vigorously in intellectual centers like Alexandria. The coming into being of "the individual" made this transition possible. Because it was a commercial society, the business elites propelled the process by which the ideas deriving from mathematics, geography, and physics were given practical form in the marvels of ship-building, navigation, and engineering which made large commercial cities and the transportation networks which sustained them possible. The elites made it possible for purposive action, work, to have a connotation which labor does not. The word "work" derives from a Germanic root meaning "to shape, to give form." Thus in English, as in Latin, there are two words with different roots to describe these two very different activities, work and labor.

Work, unlike labor, is the purposive action which shapes and forms the objects of nature, and is characterized by the evidence which it leaves in its wake. Work becomes visible and thus "public" in a way that labor never does. Hannah Arendt suggests, "Unlike the *animal laborans*, whose social life is worldless and herdlike, and who therefore is incapable of building and inhabiting a public, worldly realm, *homo faber* is fully capable of having a public realm of his own, even though it may not be a political realm, properly speaking. It is the exchange market, where he can show the products of his hand and receive the esteem that is due him."[4] Through work the genius of the creative mind takes obvious and often useful form. And thus work is a means by which "the individual" becomes visible in the world, the uniqueness of the product of individual work giving evidence of his existence. "I" come into full being when my unique self-hood can be made public by acts which can be judged, measured, and authenticated. My work becomes actual evidence of my unique existence in the world. My work and its evidence in the free exchange market become the basis from which I gain both the esteem of others and my own self-regard.

First in the marketplace and subsequently in the political realm civil spaces were created where the basic need for esteem and self-esteem could be sustained in exchange: initially through material goods, and subsequently through ideas and values. *Homo mercator* (the merchant) is a variety of *homo faber* (the worker), and could come into his social dignity only when work itself was dignified. Work achieved its maturity in the life of the market because it is in free exchange that work becomes visible and is authenticated. Individuals create themselves as well as goods through the exchange relations of the marketplace. The capacity for discernment, for the measured and judging distance, is the base from which *homo faber* creates his world. And thus *homo faber* is a supreme expression of *homo sapiens* (the discerner). To bring an end to markets is to diminish work as well, and thus the possibilities for the individual to distinguish himself in creative effort. Economic systems which minimize markets inevitably minimize individuals. What replaces work is the futile and mindless burden of labor, diminishing the humans who do it. Only in the fantasies of socialist theory do individuals become free through collective ownership and collective effort combined with economic planning. Anyone who dealt with laborer or functionary in the now-gone communist systems of eastern Europe, these unsmiling, unmotivated pieces in a mindless, unproductive apparatus, understood that in these "workers societies," the one thing that could not exist was "work."

In elevating work, the Greeks elevated art. The first important artists whom we know by name were Greek poets, sculptors and architects. The Greek artist became more than simply a craftsman because the work of art now embodied and authenticated a unique individual and his individual aesthetic. According to tradition Socrates, the pre-eminent model of the "public man," was a sculptor in "private life": it took a Greek sensibility to blend the work of the hand and the mind in such an artful way. In the transformation of work into art there is an important parallel transformation of that primal human habit: the giving of gifts. On one level the artist retreats into his irreducible, individual self to find his talent, his genius. He is quintessentially private, inhabiting a personal "Bohemia" apart from the world. When he gives his art for the world to see, he moves into a quintessentially public world — to be seen gives the final life to the creative process: the work cannot be in any sense "real" until it is validated by an audience. The work of art begins the process of circulation which sustains its life.

The Greek word for the inner genius of a person is *daemon,* and what finally made each man individual was the unique *daemon* which represented his irreducible authenticity. It was said of Socrates that his *daemon* would "speak to him" when he was about to act in a way that did not accord with this authentic, inner nature. The artist, in making his *daemon* public, is in fact giving his inner self to the world, a gift. According to Lewis Hyde, the material poverty which often accompanies the artist is intrinsic to this process by which he empties himself in order to make his gift. The reciprocation is that the gift is appreciated and the spirit of the gift is kept in circulation by the succession of audiences who see it and validate it. The artist achieves an immortality as his gifts continue to circulate and be sustained in life after he himself has died.

❖ ❖ ❖

When classicist Edith Hamilton asserted that the "Greeks were the first people in the world to play," she was epigramatically referring to the enormous importance the Greeks gave to sport in their lives and in the great festivals like the Olympic games.[5] The classical Greeks reserved their greatest works of sculpture for gods and athletes because in their minds the great athlete was god-like. Champions were given the title, "immortal," laurels which they shared with the gods. In the act of play before an audience, one's *arete,* excellence, could be revealed. The individual self is displayed to the world in a form fully understood, the sport or game at which one has achieved mastery. Pindar wrote odes to athletes which have no parallel in any other culture of antiquity:

> He who wins, of a sudden, some noble prize
> In the rich years of youth
> Is raised high with hope; his manhood takes wings;
> He has in his heart what is better than wealth.[6]

It is the nature of play itself that placed games at the heart of classical Greek civilization. Huizinga defines play as, "a voluntary activity or occupation executed within certain fixed limits of time and place, according to rules freely accepted but absolutely binding, having its aim in itself and accompanied by feelings of tension, joy and the consciousness that it is 'different' from 'ordinary' life."[7] Playing a game thus has all the characteristics which underlie contractual relations. Games were the summit of a system of play within Greek society, which found its expression in various forms, *inter alia,* in political debate, the theater, and the market. Market exchange has all the elements of play for the dedicated business person, and these ludic elements associated the world's first great commercial culture with the sensibility which created the Olympic contests. Thus play also became the paradigm for another globalizing element in the classical world: the great athletic games which attracted contestants from throughout the Mediterranean world. A common set of rules engaged in a competitive environment, focused in particular places and times reflected and modeled globalized commerce itself.

The companion of play is not labor, which uses up human substance and makes one just like one's companions in effort. The companion of play is work, for work leaves concrete evidence of our individual selves in the world. But this happens only if one triumphs. As one works for evidence of gain, one plays to win. The Greek sense of play carried with it none of the modern notion of competition for its own sake. Perhaps that is why team sports were so little a part of Greek games. The point of participation in the games was to win so that one's individual superiority could be acknowledged. The evidence of play lasts as long as play itself and the legend which celebrates the victor in song and memory. The evidence of work, the shaping of the world with lasting results, gives it a kind of immortality too, and thus in creative individuals work and play begin to merge into one transaction. Anyone who has watched a child at play appreciates the purity of concentration in effort and imagination of work-play. Greek commercial culture, with its worldliness, its values of empiricism and productive effort, and its emphasis on competition and personal gain — combined with a sensibility which elevated forms — was essential to developing this sense of work as play, and play as work. That sport achieved such status in the world's first great commercial society is probably thus not accidental. Sport, like commerce, involves taking risks for gain. Perhaps that is why "prize" and "price" share an etymological root, *pretium*. Work-play is a means of proving to oneself and others one's individual worth in a society where hereditary privilege no longer carries the same weight as in the traditional world. The intimate connection between the man of commerce, who in the modern phrase "works hard and plays hard," and the athlete was forged in the classical world. It should not be surprising that only with the full recovery of commercial, urban civilization in the nineteenth century did sports again begin to achieve in egalitarian, mass society the centrality they had in the classical world.

It is a characteristic of the classical world that as work and play were elevated to positions of dignity in thought and practice, the position of labor became increasingly degraded. For what characterizes society and economy in the Mediterranean world from the fifth century BC onward is an unequaled expansion of the institution of slavery. To be sure, most traditional societies (and even some primal ones) knew slavery. It was a common practice known not only in Egypt, Mesopotamia and China, but in the Old Testament as well. But slavery was, while often important, a peripheral element in these agricultural societies. The near-slavery of various forms of serfdom was not unknown, but agriculture was usually based on a free peasantry resident in thousands of villages scattered throughout the countryside. Craftsmen and other workers were usually not legally in bondage.

Beginning with the world of classical Greece this changes abruptly. It is estimated that half the population of Athens were slaves. The increasingly integrated economy of the Mediterranean world and its security requirements came to depend upon slavery as a function of its mercantile character. The vast sea trade in grains and other commodities required more and larger vessels to achieve economies of scale so necessary for trade in low value-added products. This was paralleled by the number and greatly increased size of naval vessels. These vessels required ever larger crews laboring in ever more confined and degrading conditions. This was labor few free man would do unless paid a wage that would have made the voyages unfeasible. The rise of a class of maritime slaves was the result. The integration of commodity markets by widely expanded maritime trade made agriculture increasingly unprofitable for the small and medium farmer, who was driven from business by the large estates which used economies of scale, and increasingly, slave labor to maintain profitability. Similar trends appeared in mining and construction. Reliance on slave labor, together with new technologies, was spurred by the construction of the ports, aqueducts, roads, and large buildings which characterized an economy linking populous cities to the agricultural hinterland. Labor, often complained of and regretted in traditional societies but also respected, lost its status as a dignified necessity as it increasingly assumed the character of slavery.

The pervasiveness of slavery in the Mediterranean world of the Greco-Roman era also demonstrates the action of another principle — the declining ability of animate sources of power to sustain complex civilization. Marion J. Levy, Jr., an important theorist of modernization, distinguishes between relatively modernized and relatively non-modernized societies on the basis of their dependence on inanimate or animate sources of power. He says, "I conceive each of these two elements as the basis of a continuum. A society will be considered more or less modernized to the extent that its members use inanimate sources of power and/or use tools to multiply the effects of these efforts. Neither of these elements is either totally absent from or exclusively present in any society."[8] Primal societies use human animate power in combination with simple tools to multiply effort. Traditional societies add to these domesticated animal power, and inanimate sources of power deriving from water and wind. The first civil societies of the ancient classical era depended increasingly on human slavery as highly urbanized and mercantile environments placed ever increasing demands on traditional sources of power — and thus planted one of the seeds of social disequilibrium which would end classical civilization itself. Only in the civil societies of the West, beginning late in the eighteenth century, were new and massive sources of inanimate power (the steam engine and electricity) available to supplement traditional sources. The decline of legal slavery (and its equivalents, like serfdom) in modern complex civilizations was made possible, at least in part, by the extraordinary rise in sources of inanimate power and the industrial proletariat associated with it.

We have noted that the initiation of the civil realm is associated with the multiplication of I-It encounters in the human world. The use-value of people (what Marxists call "commodification") begins to parallel the use-value of things as markets become central to the experience of humanity inhabiting a culture of strangers. Slavery, which in many of its dimensions is to see fellow humans as ultimate strangers (indeed, even to doubt whether the slave is really human at all) is in this sense to be organically associated with the civil space as much as is personal freedom. The dehumanization of the slave (and as we shall see, of women) was a result of confining full "humanity" to life in the public realm, the realm of the adult, free male. In modern industrial societies this problem may take different forms, given the abolition of legal slavery and female emancipation. But the underlying dynamic is the same. People objectified as *things* to be used and manipulated — as consumers, employees, voters, or "celebrities" — carries some of the same moral burden as does slavery. The decline of public, civil life in the twentieth century, and the rise of mass society was paralleled by the rise of persons as ciphers for things, and to the new discipline called *statistics*. As Stalin, the ultimate statistician responsible for the deliberate death of millions, so felicitously put it, "The death of a single person is a tragedy; the death of a million is a statistic."

A parallel phenomenon of the classical age was the increasingly lower status of women. Greek women of the archaic period appear to have had more status and rights than those several centuries later in classical Athens. It might be that as men gained more control over their own lives in commercial civilization, they developed a new consciousness which valued freedom from nature in civil life. Women, because of their associations with a life of child-bearing, came to be regarded less as companions in life than as reminders of the human past circumscribed by the relentless demands of nature. Radin asserts that, "Viewed psychologically, it might be contended that the history of civilization is largely the account of the attempts of man to forget his transformation from an animal into a human being."[9] The pervasive misogyny of Periclean Athens seems to have had deep roots in a fear of "the feminine" as destructive of the forms and values of rational, civilized life. The Jungian analyst Florida Scott-Maxwell makes such a hypothesis about civilization: "The taut bow and pointed arrow of the masculine principle were needed if civilizations were to be born, and life was to move forward. Perhaps man's greatest need was to separate himself from the feminine, the maternal oneness. In order to create himself he had to discriminate the masculine from the feminine, to discriminate against the feminine, knowing its formlessness to be his greatest enemy."[10] That which we often most admire about classical Greek civilization — its spirit of curiosity and play, its dedication to rational discourse and artistic beauty, its commitment to public life and popular governance — were achieved at the expense of the diminishing private household: the realm of women, children and slaves. In the household was confined, in the Greek mind, the primal fluidity of the pre-rational and the pre-civilized, inescapable, but rigorously subordinated to the higher order of public life.

In Greek life and thought we witness once again the forces of localization contending with those of globalization. The universalism of science contends with the particularism of religion; the economic globalization of markets is contradicted by the economic localism of the household; the universalism of philosophy is in contention with the particularism of gender roles and slavery.

Work, unlike labor, is directed toward gain, and thus usually encapsulates a *linear* concept of time within which something both new and permanent comes into the world through the action of work. From gainful work comes surplus without which saving and investment are not possible. And thus work shares with play another element: perceived virtue. Max Weber's "Protestant Work Ethic" doesn't require that one be Protestant or even Christian to fully embrace this aspect of commercial culture. But it does require that human effort be freed from the stigma of the unremitting cycle of labor, to which Christian thinkers like Augustine had consigned it as a sign of God's punishment for original sin. It required that human spirit and intelligence be positively connected to the material world and the transformation of that world as evidence of the encounter. The world seen as an arena of human purpose, will, judgment and action is indispensable to the "work ethic." It is essential to commercial culture that work be seen as related to accumulation-as-virtue. The evidence of the business person's action in the world is the wealth he accumulates not only for consumption, but as evidence of his success in work.

The first Greek philosophers evidenced an attitude of "virtue in worldliness." Cicero reminds his readers that these earliest thinkers were "public men," that is, practical men of the world. The thought of these men did not arise from traditional cosmology or religious speculation, from kinship relations or spirits circulating throughout nature. Theirs was an imagination rooted in experience with and curiosity about the material world. That classical Greece was a commercial culture tied to the sea must have played a powerful formative role in shaping this sort of thought. The earliest Greek philosophers, the so-called "Seven Sages," were well-traveled, experienced men. The first of these, Thales of Miletus (c.600 BC) was a merchant and had traveled throughout the eastern Mediterranean. He was, in the words of Kitto, "the first who expressed his ideas in logical and not mythological terms."[11] Anaximander, his intellectual successor, was also a well-traveled man who served merchants as a map-maker.

These first philosophers lived in the great Greek seaport cities of Ionia, with their contacts with all the known world. Their philosophical endeavors sought not origins, as had the great mythic cosmologies of Egypt or Mesopotamia, but first causes, causes rooted not in the heavens, but in the world, in matter. Thales identifies water as the first cause; Heraclitus identifies fire; and Anaximenes identifies air. Each of these elements is devoid of divine or spiritual animation. What was being sought were basic essences or *principles*. It was this quality which identified the Greeks most centrally, according to Kitto: "A sense of the wholeness of things is perhaps the most typical feature of the Greek mind."[12] The Pythagoreans abstracted still further and evolved a cosmology based on the mathematical principles of geometry. The focus of explanation had shifted decisively from nature toward humankind, and the distinctly human powers of apprehension, abstraction and judgment. In a fundamental sense these first men of science, as we understand it, become judges of the world, of all truths and values, and ultimately of the gods themselves. What all this points to is a new attitude: one of a basic optimism about the capacities of human beings to direct their own lives through the direction of the material environment.

To be sure, standing in tension with this optimism was a powerful underlying sense of tragedy, of mortality, of humanity fated to be destroyed by its own aspirations to self-direction, the *hubris* of reaching too far and flying too high. But the sense of linear time, what was to become a sense of historical time in the modern understanding in the writings of chroniclers like Herodotus and Thucidides, intimated purpose and direction. And with these were associated a temper of dominion. Commercial culture has always required this sense of dominion because without it, and the confidence it brings, there can be no sustained embracing of risk. Traditional society is risk-averse. Innovation, even when its advantages are clear in the short-run, is shunned in traditional society because of the long-term risks which are associated with change, as Daniel Lerner has so skillfully documented. He writes: "Traditional society is nonparticipant — it deploys people by kinship into communities isolated from each other and from a center; without an urban rural division of labor, it develops few needs requiring economic interdependence; lacking the bonds of interdependence, people's horizons are limited by locale and their decisions involve only other known people in known situations."[13]

In Lerner's view, mobility is, as we have seen, also central to innovative, risk-taking values. He describes the "mobile person" as "distinguished by a high capacity for identification with new aspects of his environment; he comes equipped with the mechanisms needed to incorporate new demands upon himself that arise outside his habitual experience."[14] As gain and risk became associated with the fundamental optimism generated by all aspects of a vibrant commercial culture, a new autocentric attitude toward the world came to dominate the societies of the West, which were the successors of Greece and Rome. Could it be that this fundamentally cultural attitude is so indispensable that it explains that, with the possible exception of Japan (an exception that may not be truly exceptional as we shall see) the only fully achieved pluralistic, technological, commercial societies remain those of Western Europe and their North American offspring?

Understanding the conditions under which civil culture can be eclipsed is illustrative of the foundations of the civil realm. It also may offer insight into the modern civil culture which has held sway in the Western world for two centuries. The decline of the classical world, first in Greece and subsequently in Rome, was a gradual and complex process. But in terms of our argument several trends appear critical. Civil culture required the management of social conflict through the widespread distribution of economic benefits in the market. In a basic sense, civil society embraces the market as a better means of avoiding conflict than primal society which avoids both economic surplus and markets, or the traditional society with its hierarchical distribution of power in the state and the economy.

Having committed itself to pluralistic and republican institutions as a means of both encouraging and managing a market-oriented society, the civil realm also brought with it greater possibilities of social disequilibrium which could not be controlled. In the case of Athens, the popular governments and the economic prosperity upon which they depended came at the expense of an enormous slave class and the decline in the rights and status of women. It also required that Athens build a powerful military machine, principally a navy in this maritime society, and to tax its allies in the Delian League to pay for it. The integration of commodity markets in the Mediterranean world made possible the supply of great populations in the cities at low prices, but it also impoverished small and medium farmers, and encouraged the depopulation of the countryside upon which the cities depended for the sale of goods. As the dispossessed used their increasing presence as an urban under-class to make their demands heard, cycles of popular dictatorship, aristocratic tyranny, and foreign war to keep the maritime empire intact, undermined popular institutions. The decline and eventual collapse of the Athenian polity associated with the Peloponesian War was, in part, the result of these underlying disequilibria.

The decline of Rome demonstrates these same trends. Republican institutions were undermined as the economic integration of the Empire dispossessed the yeoman farmer, always the economic basis of Roman republican virtue. Rome was supplied with cheaper grain imported from the great breadbaskets of the Empire, especially Egypt, with which the Italian farmer could not compete. Service in the Roman army with payment in booty distributed by popular, winning generals became the basis of a constantly expanding warfare state. Rome's population swelled with mostly-idle people entitled to free grain, wine and oil distributed from public warehouses, and to public entertainments paid for by ambitious politicians.[15] The cities of the empire, of which Rome was paradigmatic, were increasingly administrative in character and economically parasitic, absorbing resources without providing value in return. As technically advanced as classical civilization was, it ultimately rested on an agricultural system which, in spite of innovation, produced relatively small surpluses upon which expanding commercial cities depended.

By the time conquest had extended the empire to all of the Mediterranean world and northwest Europe, much of the countryside not only in Italy but elsewhere had been depopulated as the army, slavery, the administrative bureaucracy, and then the urban dole absorbed the displaced populations. In such an environment social tensions overwhelmed republican institutions and almost continual civil war throughout the first century BC finally put an end to them. Demagoguery, military dictatorship, and finally imperial-bureaucratic rule sought to deal with social and economic dislocation. When imperial expansion and annexation could no longer fuel this inherently unstable system, the forces of disequilibrium and decay prevailed. Government by assassination typified Roman institutions as each emperor was replaced by yet another general in the course of the third century. The price system became increasingly inflationary as stagnant or declining economic resources were overwhelmed by the demands of underproductive and idle populations, especially in the swollen cities.

Finally, at the end of the third century, the Emperor Diocletian imposed price and wage controls. Craftsmen were forbidden to abandon their professions, sons being required to follow the trades of their fathers. Farmers were forbidden to leave the land where, debt-ridden, they became functional serfs. The unity of the empire itself was dissolved by Diocletian's decision to decentralize it into East and West, each with its own *augustus*, and to further divide these halves, each headed by a *caesar*. The essential elements of the highly localized feudal system, which was to replace the collapsing Roman Empire in Europe, were being foreshadowed. As civil servants (*curiales*) abandoned the unstable, violence-ridden cities for secured villas in the countryside (*suburbes*), civil life began to disappear altogether. By the end of the fifth century urban culture had collapsed completely in the Western portion of the empire, which now fell under the rule of Goths, Franks, Lombards, Vandals and other invading peoples.

The localizing forces which were to characterize Medieval society and economy had defeated the globalizing forces which had extended the boundaries of the Roman Empire to much of the known world. But it was not localization in economic and social relations which brought into being the conditions which sustained Medieval life. Rather, it was *delocalization*. That is, the integrative economic forces which came to dominate the Mediterranean world in the Greco-Roman period were characterized by a growing asymmetry. As wealth production elsewhere dispossessed the small farmer, craftsman and trader, there was no corresponding localization of other economic activities. The depopulation of rural areas and the flight of populations to the cities was the demographic reflection of these delocalizing economic forces. Globalization always brings with it the possibilities, even probabilities, of an asymmetric relation between the economics of localization and those of delocalization. In our own day, from Mexico to West Africa, the delocalization of economic activity (especially the production of agricultural commodities in rural areas) without a corresponding localization of other economic activity produces demographic dislocation, characterized by the movements of large portions of the population, nationally and internationally, especially to "mega-cities" like Los Angeles and Lagos, in search of livelihood.

The civil world was from its initiation based on values and institutions in which consent and exchange are abiding and central. As ties of blood and tradition are transcended within civil society, persons become highly mobile, and their complex pledges to one another are shaped by the values of rational persuasion and positive law. Market exchange was the basis for the inception of civil life, and to its continued existence, as market values modeled rational exchange and the normative centrality of personal lives based in contracts. Life in the civil world is consequently mediated by highly abstract forms of thought and value formation from which the individual emerges, and becomes the focus of high culture and of moral imagination. But it is also in the civil world, driven as it is by the globalizing tendencies inherent in markets, that the disequilibrium between localizing and delocalizing trends evidences itself most powerfully.

The civil world is consequently shaped, for better and for worse, as a culture of strangers.

NOTES TO CHAPTER SEVEN

1. Thorkild Jacobsen, "Mesopotamia," in Franfort, et.all, *op.cit.*, p. 186
2. Sir Alan Gardiner, EGYPT OF THE PHAROAHS (New York: Oxford University Press, 1964), p. 32
3. John A. Wilson, "Egypt," in Frankfort, *et.al. op.cit.*, p. 97
4. Arendt, *op.cit.*, pp. 140-141
5. Edith Hamilton, THE GREAT AGE OF GREEK LITERATURE (New York: W.W. Norton and Company, 1930)
6. Kitto, *op.cit.*, p. 174
7. Huinzinga, HOMO LUDENS, *op.cit.*, p. 28
8. Marion J. Levy, Jr., MODERNIZATION AND THE STRUCTURE OF SOCIETIES (Princeton: Princeton University Press, 1969), p. 11. Thus, the presence of a large slave class should not presume the idleness of the citizen or free men in places like Athens. Slavery *supplemented* the animate power of the non-slave economic sector. "There was on the contrary not a sector of material production in which they [citizens and free men] were not present in one capacity or another." Yvon Garlan, SLAVERY IN ANCIENT GREECE, Janet Lloyd, trans. (Ithaca, NY: Cornell University Press, 1988), p. 141
9. Radin, *op.cit.*, p. 3
10. Florida Scott-Maxwell, WOMEN AND SOMETIMES MEN (New York: Harper & Row, Publishers 1971), p. 39
11. Kitto, *op.cit.*, p. 177
12. *Ibid.*, p. 169
13. Lerner, *op.cit.*, p. 50
14. *Ibid.*, p. 49
15. This phenomenon of *euergetism* (civil philanthropy) was a dominant feature of classical society, definitively treated by Paul Veyne, BREAD AND CIRCUSES, Brian Pearce, trans. (New York: Penguin Books, 1990)

PART IV

THE INDIVIDUAL WORLD

It is more basically a sense of *truth*, a sense of having reached the ground of one's being (or, if you prefer, of one's "nothingness") in the crucial realization that one is completely defectible, that one is "he who is not" in the presence of "him who is."

— *Thomas Merton*

CHAPTER EIGHT

THE INEXCHANGEABLE SELF

The civil world is not a world of individuals, strictly speaking. It is a world of free and equal persons — citizens — related to one another by choice and under law. It is the fungibility of persons, their essential interchangeability (what Aristotle termed "comeasurability") in the civil world, which gives civility its egalitarian and democratic character. In Greek thought the pursuit of excellence and esteem in the public space implied that anyone could be judged by a common, that is to say communal, body of standards and rules. The world of sport reflected this social attitude. As a result, to do things peculiar to oneself (*idiotes*) was in the Greek view quite literally "idiotic;" that is, to be a "private" person. It is the character of individuals, however, that they are peculiar to themselves; that they lack interchangeability. At the highest level of functioning, humanity resides in an inexchangeable human being who is unique, and thus ultimately a stranger to every other individual. The individual is humanity compressed to its final density, its ultimate abstraction. It is this capacity for definitive individuality which sets humankind apart from other animals, and which determines our species being. It is this final abstraction and uniqueness which often contradicts the impulse of public life toward a common discourse, a common set of values, a common set of appreciations. The affirmation of an individual self simultaneously rises out of public life — for it is in fullest exchange with one's fellows that one's differences from them emerge — as it rejects public life as the ultimate arena within which the individual self, irreducible and inexchangeable, can function.

The emergence of the normative individual raised another irony in consciousness. The subject-object duality, almost completely absent at the primal base of the developmental pyramid, begins to achieve near-sovereign status in the civil world. This duality made science and philosophy, as well as market relations and politics as modern people understand them, possible because it enabled fundamental and dynamic distinctions between form and content. At the same time, this duality stands at odds with the quest for holistic integrity, where form and content merge, which characterizes the individual. This feature of individuality had inherent in it the bases for contention of the individual with his surroundings, including his society, and ultimately with himself. Bellah suggests that it is this issue which characterizes modern religion. "The central feature of the change is the collapse of the dualism that was so crucial to all historic religions," he suggests. "In the world view that has emerged from the tremendous intellectual advances of the last two centuries there is simply no room for the hierarchic dualistic religious symbol system of the classical historical type."[1]

The individual began his self-discovery in the public life of the *polis,* but he could not realize it there. When Socrates chose death rather than exile from public life he exemplified the dilemma of the individual who must be both authentic and social, living day to day at the highest levels of human communication, without surrendering *daemon,* the unique interiority which makes each of us what he is. This tension is reflected in Heidegger's term *Dasein,* which he devised to express life as it is lived and experienced individually. *Dasein* means "being there," (*da,* "there" plus *sein,* "being"). Individuals are both "existent" and "located;" which means each human being has a world, something experienced globally, in its fullness beyond time and space; what Romain Rolland called "the oceanic," and Freudians call "Ego." Simultaneously, that world is experienced from a unique location. No two human beings occupy the same existential space because each of us comes into his own world at different times, in different social settings, and from different circumstances — all of which locate us in different temporal, cultural, and moral settings. Thus, as Augustine suggested, each of us is ultimately "a problem" (*questio*) for himself, the quest which is a fully human life. This existential problem lies in the tension between the "is-ness" and the "thereness" inherent in an individual life experienced within the stream of time, conditioned in natality and mortality.

The anxiety and alienation of which existentialists speak derive from the awareness that while we attempt to experience our worlds as totalities, unlimited in time and space, as *Being,* we are constantly made aware that because of our "there-ness," our location in space-time, in fact what we experience is *being,* specific, individual lives lived between birth and death. We sometimes become aware of this existential tension and anxiety in the experience of romantic love. The power of romantic love transforms every part of us as our sentiency is refracted through it into immortal intimations. The experience of the fusion between ourselves and our beloved is so powerful that when we become aware that this fusion is in fact not complete, especially if our affection is not reciprocated, feelings of anxiety and ultimate aloneness overwhelm us. We experience what phenomenologists call a "break." We and our beloved, once experienced as a global and singular "is," are in fact individual "*theres*," located in different *Daseins*. It is the certainty of death which all humans share, regardless of their individual *Daseins*, which essentially propels the search for ultimate Being, dislocated from mortal space-time. When we are "in love" we feel free from, or at least reprieved from, this mortal certainty; we intimate the immortality of religious rapture.

When I ask a friend how things are going in "his world," or when we discuss "the world of computer programming" we are acknowledging that reality coheres in ways reflecting different realms of total experience. We also acknowledge that reality for each of us begins with what Heidegger called "everydayness" (*Alltaglichkeit*). Our worlds are built up incrementally and dialectically as we engage our lives day to day, at all levels of detail, practice and abstraction — achieving what Nietzsche called "a country of my own, a soil of my own, an entire discrete, thriving, flourishing world..."[2] We in fact never fully stand apart from reality as rational individuals, assessing and behaving within a completely abstracted, objective, "I-It" situation.

Our belief in a determinative "mind-body" split is as old as the Greeks, and was recalled to Western philosophy in very influential ways by Descartes and Kant. But in the end this stance has failed to satisfy the quest for a life-meaning. Existential understanding, beginning and ending in *Dasein* and the everydayness of life, constitutes individual being, an attempted, alternative questing. Being is not understood as a property of people or things. But rather people and things have an existence unified with the experience of them. For Heidegger, "Self and world belong together in the single entity *Dasein*. Self and world are not two beings, like subject and object," but rather "self and world are the basic determination of Dasein in the unity of the structure of being-in-the-world." Being comes into thought in *time*, as a *temporal event,* as a "movement into presence." "It is the event (*Ereignis*) of disclosedness in which entities come to be appropriated into intelligibility."[3]

In my previous formulations of important elements of commercial life, such as property, I have suggested that these should not be conceived as "things-in-themselves." Rather, entities such as property come into being as a function of the collective experiences of the individual human beings who constitute a society at any point in time. Thus property becomes fully intelligible in the social experience of the market. The market is the horizon on which property becomes visible, is first fully experienced by individuals and groups, and comes into use and thus into meaning for them. Using Heidegger's familiar image of the hammer which has full meaning only in relation to nails, objects of economic life have their fullest meanings in their dynamic cultural contexts. Thus for primal peoples, goods move principally in the context, the referential totality, of the charismatic, gift-giving. In the traditional realm goods move in terms of exchange relations intelligible within the context of hierarchical authority. Property discloses itself fully in the dynamic experience of market relations in the civil world.

The transition from the civil to the individual is marked by a shift from the essential worldliness of the civil to the otherworldliness of the contemplative, interior self. As we have seen this shift can be identified with the autocentric and convergent in personality development. It is enabled by the development of ideas and cultural values related to the transcendant, which is to say dialectical engagement of life at the highest levels without abandoning the real, material world. To be an individual is thus to live in irony, as the existentialists always remind us. This irony of the human condition flows from our simultaneous "is-ness" and "there-ness," our consciousness that we live in the tension between being existent and being located. This transcendent consciousness which characterizes our individuality is linked to the need for each of us, as individuals, to have a world of his own, a world whose animus is to sustain human life as it is experienced and actualized individually. The individual becomes fully intelligible only within the individual world, which combines both the interiority of the other-worldly, with the concrete everydayness of the material and social worlds.

In the primal world, spirit and matter are nearly one, their interpenetration making the passage from one state to the other a completely fluid process. There is only a weak independent sense of self because the *I-Thou* mode of being encapsulates the self in an "other." The primal mode is thus not a moral mode to the extent that morality is the result of individual conscience and judgment. Allocentric sensibilities in their essential reactivity and other-directedness do not possess the inner-based grounds of individual morality. To be sure, primitive societies have standards of behavior, but these are not essentially moral standards because they are enforced not by individual conscience and judgment, but rather by habit and the many informal mechanisms available to relatively small, close-knit groups. The mechanism of shame, by which people "lose face" before their fellows through the discovery of an infraction, is not an essentially interior moral mechanism governing conduct. Because of its inextricable ties to the spirit world, primal personality is not responsible in any modern sense: it does not independently think, judge or act. Rather, primal humanity reacts to circumstance, including the all-pervasive spirit world which may take possession at any time, governing actions. Concepts of primitive justice centered in retribution, "an eye for an eye," reflect this reactivity.

In the traditional world spirituality is mediated by the gods through formal religion and ritual. The opening of the subject-object gap now permits an alterity in which humanity is seen to exist in a material world over which there is now a degree of dominion, provided the forces of nature are enlisted by respecting the gods and giving them their due. But the traditional world is also not an essentially moral one because the codes of behavior in a religion-based society are concerned with maintaining social order and authority, and are thus either no different than those of the primal realm, or are inclined toward respecting the special prerogatives of the gods and their legitimate representatives. Acting right obviates being right. Behavior which rises from *obedience* (from a Latin root, "to hear" and thus "to submit to instruction") lacks the self-direction of genuine morality. When Abraham responds to the command to sacrifice his son it is from obedience, not morality, that he acts. Thus, the books of Leviticus and Deuteronomy in the Old Testament do not contain genuinely moral imperatives. They are catalogs of "shalls" and "shall nots," taboos, prescriptions, prohibitions, and exhortations with roots that are socially totemistic rather than individually conscientious. Consequently, it is not unusual, as in the case of traditional China or Japan, to have religious values with no moral content strictly speaking. Indeed, to the extent that Confucianism is a social etiquette or code, it is not a religion at all. Confucius himself has nothing to say about specifically religious observance. Robert S. Elegant has suggested that the Confucian system has in fact more to do with *manners* than with morals, placing "a premium upon appearance — rather than the reality — of rectitude"[4] It is this social appearance, not the individual reality, of rectitude which characterizes the traditional world.

In the civil world material reality is understood in terms of abstract thought and rational inquiry, which appear to give humans mastery. The gods and the spirit world which they mediate shift further into the background, with Cicero and Marcus Aurelius being representative of many of the thoughtful Romans of their day in doubting the existence of the gods, but seeing belief in them to be useful for most people in enforcing social codes of behavior. Morality, in the sense of an individual basis for thinking, judging and acting, required the existence of the personal to bring it into being. What Nietzsche called the "sovereign individual" is characterized by "his own independent, protracted will and the *right to make promises...*"[5] For it is the individual person, relatively separated from the all-encompassing demands of kinship and functioning within complex environments which make competing role demands, who becomes the locus of moral imagination and choice. It is the promises and pledges which he makes and honors which attach him to civil life and to the mutually dependent spheres of personal freedom and moral choice. And, as we have seen, it took the special character of the civil world to achieve and secure the reality of the personal, and to make this value central, visible and usable in judgment settings.

Personal ethics, in this sense, is a redundancy: all ethics in the meaning of humans making moral judgments on the basis of individual reflection are inherently personal. It was the initial decline in kinship identifications with their focus in retribution, and then of specifically religious thinking with its focus in obedience and a hierarchy of obligations, that brought about the philosophical and ethical thinking which summoned mature morality into existence. My argument closely parallels that of Piaget, Erickson and especially Kohlberg in their work on the development of the moral senses. Lawrence Kohlberg's *Moral Judgment Scale* describes a developmental process for individuals initiated with a focus in obedience and punishment, through a conformist or mechanical "law and order" orientation, to a moral maturity centered in a respect for the consent of others, and judgments reposing in individual conscience.[6]

What makes an individual world possible is the development of the values associated with transcendence experienced at its highest level; the belief that the material world lacks ultimate and meaningful substance in itself. It is the sensibility that begins to occur as human beings rise through the hierarchy of needs to its summit in self-actualization. As lower order needs are satisfied in *I-Thou* encounters, and the world is mastered in *I-It* encounters at the upper end of the needs hierarchy, the world and worldliness lose their capacity to arrest the questing self. The experienced environment is demystified and, voided of intrinsic meaning, becomes in existential terms "absurd." The quest for ultimate reality and ultimate meaning, as that search nears the pinnacle of the needs hierarchy, turns inward toward the world of the self. As the traditional and civil worlds came into existence through the social dynamic of demographic compression, a final compression frees the individual from his environment altogether. The autonomous self emerges, extruded from a material and social world of such complex density that the individual can find ultimate meaning only outside of it, within himself.

The search for ultimate, meaningful reality begins to find its focus in a single, all-pervading, and perfectly spiritual substance or essence which can be identified with transcendent being. This being stands apart from the material world, which is now utterly inert, normatively empty, the more-detached object of human scrutiny and will. This being also stands apart from the facts of daily life, whether experienced in private or public spaces. The first individuals came into being as an act of separation of persons from both contemporary society and the natural world. They were engaged in a sort of *I-Thou* exchange, that between individual self and ultimate being, but an exchange in which neither the *I* nor the *Thou* absorbs the other. Thus, this unresolved *I-Thou* exchange is not a return to the animistic monism of primal spirituality. Primal life is experienced, in Stanner's phrase, as "a one possibility thing"[*supra* Chap. 1]. Individual life is experienced, in Bellah's phrase, as "an infinite possibility thing."[7] It is this intimation of the "all-in-all" that is encountered in deeply meditative and contemplative states, as described by the Trappist monk Thomas Merton: "It is more basically a sense of truth, a sense of having reached the ground of one's being (or, if you prefer, of one's 'nothingness') in the crucial realization that one is completely defectible, that one is 'he who is not' in the presence of 'him who is'."[8]

In contemplating infinite possibility, the self confronts an ineffable "other." The essence of human exchange in the individual world is the creative actualization of this other, potential self by proposing a "him who is," to a "him who is not." The individual emerges and defines himself ultimately as an autonomous being as he mediates exchange at this final of experienced boundaries, that separating the potential from the actual self. And the agent of this exchange is the individual will to create meaning. Paul Tillich asserted that, "Man is able to ask because he is separated *from*, while participating *in*, what he is asking about. [...] Ontic and spiritual self-affirmation must be distinguished but they cannot be separated. Man's being includes his relation to meanings. He is human only by understanding and shaping reality, both his world and himself, according to meanings and values. His being is spiritual even in the most primitive expressions of the most primitive human being. In the 'first' meaningful sentence all the richness of man's spiritual life is present."[9] These "meaningful sentences" which form the basis for a spiritual identity recall Buber's assertion about the radically distinct nature of humanity as it takes "its stand" in "the word" (and thus the world) through dialectical exchange with it. Hannah Arendt's formulation, "Whatever touches or enters into a sustained relationship with human life immediately assumes the character of a condition of human existence,"[10] likewise posits meaning-creation from every encounter as the substance of humanity. At the heart of all of individual human life as exchange is ultimate existential questing, the search for the "meaningful sentences" which creatively actualize an individual life. Augustine summarized his own spiritual journey into self-knowledge as a prayer for healing, for wholeness: "Have pity on me and heal me, for you see I have become a problem to myself, and this is the ailment from which I suffer."[11]

Those widely separated near-contemporaries, Diogenes the Greek and Job the Jew, may conveniently mark the point in history where this process began its most powerful expression. Ultimate meaning was the contemplative quest of both men. The masterful internal exchange of the Book of Job poses those quintessential questions of meaning which have faced the individual since he made his appearance in the late classical era in the Western world.

> My soul is weary of my life; I will leave my complaint upon myself; I will speak in the bitterness of my soul.
> I will say unto God, Do not condemn me; shew me wherefore thou contendest with me.
> Is it good unto thee that thou shouldest oppress, that thou should despise the work of thine hands, and shine upon the counsel of the wicked?
> Hast thou eyes of flesh? or seest thou as man seeth?
> Are thy days as the days of man? are thy years as man's days,
> That thou enquirist after mine iniquity, and searchest after my sin? [Job 10: 1-6]

It is the existential loneliness of Diogenes and Job — Diogenes living naked in a barrel, and Job in desolation on his dung heap — that mark them as individuals. This alienation and isolation is the essence of the self-referential. It is young Socrates standing, on the eve of battle as a soldier in the Persian war, in absolute silence for hours in contemplation. It is also Augustine wrapped into a fetal position, weeping in his garden. It is the initial ground from which the search for all knowledge, meaning, and action as understood by modern individuals begins. Kafka and Beckett in our own era understood Job and Diogenes completely, and in a way are their modern expressions. Later Greek thought in the form of the Platonists, the Cynics and the Stoics came very close to this concept of the individual, and Socrates was a model. But in the end even Socrates could not imagine a fully human life outside the *polis*, the special community of men. In India the Buddha achieved the ultimate in self-hood, but through the abnegation of reality, which was defined as suffering, rather than through its transcendence. It was in the Christian tradition that the final elements needed to produce the autonomous "individual" came into being.

It has been suggested that Christianity can be understood as a form of Hellenized Judaism, and that Paul, a Jew immersed in the Hellenistic world of the eastern Mediterranean, fundamentally shaped what came to be Christianity in Greek terms. Robert Payne says, "In a hundred ways Greece left its imprint on the young religion which was still uncertain of its destination," to which A.N. Wilson adds, "Paul thought in Greek. He wrote in Greek. Together with Philo of Alexandria, he is the great conduit through which Jewish concepts and stories and patterns of thought came to the Gentile world."[12] Paul combined in his life and thought the suffering, questioning Job of later Jewish thought with the detached, questioning Diogenes of later Greek thought. In his confrontation of being and his self-affirmation within it, Paul expressed his individuality: "But by the grace of God, I am what I am." [I Cor. 15:10]

From Judaism Paul took the idea of the ultimately transcendent single God, who stands apart from the universe which he created. He is "formless" precisely to distinguish himself from the world of forms which he created. The pinnacle of that creation was humankind, for he made them "in his own image and likeness," essentially spiritual, not material. Thus creation is no longer just an explanation of reality, but a vindication of it. God's covenant and promise of salvation from the contingencies of the mortal condition — want, conflict, injustice and death — is a collective one with the Jewish people. Man's essential being, entirely spiritual, is now separated from nature by a difference which distinguishes him from all else in creation. But their shared spiritual origin joins men collectively in a brotherhood of historical destiny, within which the Jewish people have special responsibility because of their covenant with God.

Paul joined this Jewish view with an historically delocalized concept of covenant: now the promise is a global one, made to all humanity in all eras through Christ. But at the same time, the covenant is realized only individually as each soul makes its faith commitment to God through his son, Jesus. In the Christian view each human being is radically distinct and inexchangeably individual. Consequently, salvation is no longer understood to be collective, but individual. The contingent world is overcome through a radical act of individual faith. All boundaries within the material world, especially those defining kinship, gender and social station, are transcended within faith. Paul asserts, "There is neither Jew nor Greek, there is neither bond nor free, there is neither male nor female: for ye are all one in Christ Jesus."[Galatians 3:28] Each human being stands as an individual in relation to a fully transcendent divine reality. "For there is no respect of persons with God." [Romans 2:11]

Which is to say that God is no respector of masks, of roles, of clans or genders, of identities which are not completely authentic in their self-understanding in relation to ultimate being. Human "is-ness" and "there-ness" are finally reconciled in this faith relation with what St. John called *Logos,* the "Word," which is identical with reality "moved into presence" and into intelligibility. "In the beginning was the Word, and the Word was with God, and the Word was God." [John 1:1]

These ideas were potential in the work of the early Greek thinkers in their search for single, explanatory essences in the material world, which later Greek thinkers (and Hellenized Jews, such as Philo) tried to reduce to entirely abstract principles of order. When Aristotle speaks of "God" he means truth as the ultimate ground of being. The Platonists denied the ultimate reality of the material world altogether, "The Good" being a perfectly ideal state. These ideas, together with others from what Karl Jaspers called the "Axial Age," such as the Persian Zoroastrians who saw reality as a struggle between a principle of Good (a single, creator god), represented by fire, and Evil (a devilish anti-god), represented by darkness, came together in Jewish monotheism during the period of Exile (ca. 500 BC) to produce a single God, transcending nature, with a special relation to humans who are distinguished from nature in their unique dialogue with this single divinity.[13] Jews, who as merchants populated every major center of the Mediterranean world, critically affected later classical thought in its most influential form, the great Judeo-Hellenistic synthesis that became Christianity. The Jewish interpretation of this transcendent reality never denied the ultimate reality and eternity of the material world. The covenant between men and God promised the bringing of the celestial kingdom to earth, the heavenly order of God's will becoming the earthly order with the coming of the promised savior. Jewish thought never sought to transcend the world, sacrificing worldliness for otherworldliness.

The Christian variation of these themes viewed the savior not as God's agent in bringing the celestial order to Earth, but rather an end to "the world" as the "Son of God" through his sacrifice, opened the celestial kingdom to men through his act of reconciliation. Reflecting advanced Greek thought, especially in the gospel of John and the epistles of Paul, early Christianity identified God with spiritual essences. God is at one with *logos,* the rationality and intelligibility of the universe; his word brings it into being. God is also love (*agape*), the encompassing principle of adhesion which unifies creation, and also unites humans to God. "God is a Spirit: they that worship him must worship him in spirit and truth." [John 4:24] Jesus Christ, himself identical with God, represents the instrument of man's reconciliation to God because he embodies the pinnacle of spiritual exchange. This is "he who is not" in the presence of "him who is" in Christ's passion at Gethsemane and on the cross, where the fully human encounters the fully divine self. Life for the individual Christian means embracing this human/divine passion to overcome the "thereness" of the world.

Christian thought thus evolved a sense of action in which mankind is at once the passive recipient of the gift of God's love, and the active agent of grace through faith. Unable to save himself he gives himself in suffering to a suffering God who redeems him from the material world. The central act of the Christian is an act of faith, and it is an individual act utterly devoid of a collective character. The Christian may live in community, especially that of his fellows who are likewise "saved," but as a consequence of his act of faith the Christian is cosmically alone, an individual *in* the world but not *of* the world. It is this irreducible, inexchangeable self, an individual, who ultimately thinks, judges and acts. Denis De Rougemont asserts, "The new man — more fully set free than the Greek individual, more fully committed than the Roman citizen, but set free by the very faith that has committed him — is the archetype of the nascent West: he is the person."[14] The universe of this "new man," this individual person, required a space of its own, an individual world

The realm of the individual and its otherworldliness was closely associated from its inception with the concept of guilt. To be sure, shame has probably existed as long as the human race. But shame and guilt are not identical. To feel shame, as we have seen, is to feel diminished, to "lose face," in the eyes of those whose esteem one values. Shame is an allocentric mechanism of behavior control, and in many traditional societies, such as those of China and Japan, a central one. Guilt, by contrast, is an interior sense of inadequacy which comes from feeling diminished in one's own eyes. Guilt is a function of the individual in a state of self-alienation, and thus presumes a "self" as a condition of its existence. The spiritual expression of guilt is sin (which Tillich described as identical with separation), a defining element in the evolution of Western consciousness. For awareness of sin is, ironically, a powerful impulse to action, to the process of creative interaction with the material environment.[15] The existentially guilty individual is either paralyzed by guilt, or liberated by it in acts of creation in which the self is renewed and transformed, or in Christian terms, "born again." The creative act issues from an existential dissatisfaction with the located self, a self-in-the-world as is. It is "he who is not," exchanged for "him who is." The very otherworldliness of the origins of the individual acknowledges both rejection of the world, and engagement of the world. The guilty exchange between engagement of the world and withdrawal from it defines much of Western humanity's character since the initiation of the Christian era.

In one sense, the evidence of the creative self in the world is evidence of a reconciliation with the divine. Work in this meaning is an act of creative reconciliation. "To work is to pray," affirms the Benedictine credo, "and to pray is to work." When the Christian mystic St. Therese (the "little flower") said she left her hours of prayer to work in the kitchen, and there saw "Our Lord in the pots and pans," she was simultaneously affirming a life of *individual* purposive action, withdrawal from the "higher rewards" of the world, and the incarnation itself: the reconciliation of this world with the next in the person of the Man-God Jesus. It was the Christian sect of the most unremitting existential guilt, Calvinism, that later energized those most unremitting business societies of the Dutch, the Swiss and the Scots because of its emphasis on the redemptive evidence of work in wealth; of the world both engaged and transformed in action; business ("busy-ness") as an individual calling.

The ascendance of the individual world, as well as the eclipse of the civil world, was marked at the end of the Roman Empire in the West in the thought of Augustine. Writing to explain the meaning of the great catastrophe of this time, the sack of Rome by the barbarians in 410 AD, Augustine posited that man's true nature was not expressed in the "earthly city" represented by the civil culture of Rome. In this he only echoed the Church Father Tertullian's assertion two centuries earlier that "no matter is more alien to us than what matters publicly."[16] Rather, Augustine asserted, man's spiritual nature was realized in the transcendent "City of God." The material world, hopelessly compromised by the disobedience of Adam, transmitted as original sin to his descendants, could only be a place of suffering. Man's location in the material world, the "City of Man" — the world of sickness, violence and ceaseless toil to stave off the certainty of a mortal end — could be overcome only by embracing the God whose own overcoming of the material world in death and resurrection made it possible for individuals, through faith, to achieve eternity in the City of God. The loss of Rome, and the *idea* of Rome in earthly citizenship and public virtue, was in fact no loss at all in the Augustinian teaching. Instead the Christian found in the community of the faithful "an outpost of heaven."

The conceptualization of "sin," as it has been understood in the West since Augustine pronounced it, was also vital to the conceptualization of "will." In classical thought rational inquiry itself produced the sense of right, which was actualized by public duty. That is, right conduct was thought to flow automatically from the knowledge of right and the citizen's internalized obligation to submit himself to the highest standards of conduct in public life. In the Christian view, the public world of civil conversation no longer impels duty, and reason alone no longer evidences what is right. Because sin is evidence of man's separation from the will of God, only man's will to choose righteousness as an act of faith overcomes sin. As it was an act of willfulness which originated Adam's sin, it is an autonomous act of individual will by his descendant which impels righteousness, the *free will* to choose good rather than evil as integral to salvation. Willfulness and sinfulness were thus conceived and born as twins in Western consciousness. This defining individual willfulness became an important element in the cultural inheritance of Western civilization. In substituting will for duty, Christianity promoted a new understanding of the human person, the individual defined by his freedom to choose.

The negation of the ultimate importance of the transitory material world meant the end of community in the civil sense. Because salvation was irreducibly individual and not collective, persons now stood in spiritual isolation before their God. The only material community of any value was the transitory community of believers through which souls passed on their way to the celestial City of God. The collapse of the economic and social bases of the civil world at the end of the Roman empire produced a fundamental bifurcation in life-consciousness, which was to endure for centuries in the West during the Middle Ages. The culture of cities based on commerce had ended; and the civil values which supported that culture faded, meaning on one level a return to traditional society in the Medieval period. The great mass of people again lived by agriculture in Europe. A small, land-owning elite controlled both the economy and the rudiments of public authority left in the feudal system. Hierarchy, kinship, class, and ritual religion in a non-literate rural society was the reality for most people. With the rudimentary state most people had little contact. The few markets and market towns had little influence on the lives of the great majority of the population.

At the same time, however, the great traditions of civil life and thought endured, albeit in altered form, in the church and especially the monasteries. These were the respositories of the globalizing forces inherent in merchant societies, and thus the real source of economic dynamism during the early Middle Ages.

NOTES TO CHAPTER EIGHT

1. Bellah, *op.cit.*, p. 371
2. Friedrich Nietzsche, THE GENEALOGY OF MORALS, Walter Kaufmann, trans. (New York: Vintage Books, 1989), p. 17
3. Charles B. Guignon, "Introduction," HEIDEGGER, Charles B. Guignon, ed. (Cambridge: Cambridge University Press, 1993), p. 13
4. Robert S. Elegant, THE CENTER OF THE WORLD, 2nd ed. rev. (New York: Funk & Wagnalls, 1968), pp. 43-44n
5. Nietzsche, *op.cit.*, p. 59
6. Lawrence Kohlberg, THE PHILOSOPHY OF MORAL DEVELOPMENT (San Francisco: Harper & Row, 1981); see also, Jean Piaget, THE MORAL JUDGEMENT OF THE CHILD, Marie Gabain, trans., (Glencoe, Ill.: The Free Press, 1948); Erik H. Erikson, CHILDHOOD AND SOCIETY (New York: W.W. Norton, 1985)
7. Bellah, *op.cit.*, p. 371; the relation of the "primal" to the "spiritual" is a very complex problem, with which we cannot deal fully here. There are those who locate the ultimately spiritual impulses in the unmediated experiences of the "primitive." Soren Kierkegaard viewed Christian faith in these terms: "All profane, temporal, worldly intelligence has relation to destroying one's primitivity. Christianity has relation to developing one's primitivity." Peter Rohde, ed., THE DIARY OF SOREN KIERKEGAARD (New York: Carol Publishing Group, 1993), p. 159
8. Thomas Merton, CONTEMPLATION IN A WORLD OF ACTION (Garden City, NY: Doubleday & Co., 1971), p. 286.
9. Paul Tillich, THE COURAGE TO BE (New Haven: Yale University Press, 1952), pp. 48 and 51
10. Arendt, *op.cit.*, p. 11
11. Augustine, CONFESSIONS, R.S. Pine-Coffin, trans. (New York: Penguin Books, 1961), p. 239
12. Robert Payne, THE MAKING OF THE CHRISTIAN WORLD (New York: Dorset Press, 1966), p. 59; A.N. Wilson, PAUL: THE MIND OF THE APOSTLE (New York: W.W. Norton & Co., Inc. 1997), p. 28
13. John Van Seters is prominent among a number of Biblical historians who locate the origins of the essential elements of Judaism within the period of the pre-Exile and the Persian era of the seventh century and later. IN SEARCH OF HISTORY (New Haven, Conn.: Yale University Press, 1983); from an archeological point of view, the same stance is supported in Isreal Finkelstein

and Neil Asher Silberman, THE BIBLE UNEARTHED (New York: The Free Press, 2000)

14. Denis de Rougemont, MAN'S WESTERN QUEST, Montgomery Belgion, trans. (New York: Harper & Brothers, Publishers, 1957) p. 28
15. Cf. Helen Merrill Lynd, ON SHAME AND THE SEARCH FOR IDENTITY (New York: Harcourt, Brace & Co., 1958); studies of creativity in individuals have in fact demonstrated the correlation between guilt and creation in creative people. Cf. Jacob W. Getzels and Philip W. Jackson, CREATIVITY AND INTELLIGENCE (New York: John Wiley & Sons, 1962)
16 . Arendt, *op.cit.*, p. 65

CHAPTER NINE

WORK AS PRAYER

The church, and the monasteries in particular, became the repositories of civil virtue during the Medieval period. They embodied all the special elements we have identified with the civil world. Membership in them was in principle voluntary, a matter of contract among free, equal and individual persons. Monastic office was elective; decisions made "in chapter." Breaking one's ties to kin was a central condition of monastic life, and taking a new name symbolized this break. As the word "monastery" (solitary) implies, this was a community of individual selves, *individual lives* being led side by side in separated cells, altars and choir stalls. The Rule of St. Benedict (ca. 550 AD), named for the father of monasticism in the West, had as it purpose to seal off the community of contemplation, work and prayer from the decayed world outside the monastery walls. Norman Cantor compared life in the Benedictine monastery to that on a space ship in its self-sufficiency and isolation. This life of contemplation was by its very nature inarticulate, non-communicating, solitary. Some monastic orders took vows of silence. Observing the "Grand Silence" for some period each day was part of the observance of many monasteries. At the same time, learning, inquiry and reason were never entirely replaced by faith and contemplation in monastic life. Almost all of the leading thinkers and writers of the Medieval period were members of religious orders. The life of European monasteries was lived in the spiritual exchange between the individual and his community; between men both brothers and strangers; between inner-directedness and outer-directedness; between faith and intellect. Paul had voiced this spiritual reconciliation between civility and individuality before monasticism gave actual expression to it. "Now therefore ye are no more strangers and foreigners, but fellowcitizens with the saints, and of the household of God."[Ephesians 2:19]

The monastic orders recognized no political borders; were to various degrees independent of local princes; and, being the almost-sole repositories of literacy, communicated in a universal language, Latin. A life of work/contemplation in a monastery captured an earthly version of the heavenly household of God. "Sit in your cell as in paradise," exhorted the 11th century monk, St. Romuald. In fact, the careful orchestration of monastery life to "The Hours" was intended set its life apart from worldly ("secular") time. The mechanical clock, a monastic invention, was devised to time action to a regime higher than nature, unbounded by the sunrise or the sunset. Time was abstracted from nature. This conception of time was entirely new in human experience, and critical to the full development of commercial civilization. For now time became the possession of individuals, and thus part of the calculus of rational, individual choice — which inevitably involves alternative models of the productive uses of time in relation to other resources, such as capital and labor. The process by which men moved from clocks to personal time-pieces, watches, to govern their use of time in the development of full, commercial civilization in the sixteenth century consequently represents more than an efficiency. It represents a development, begun in the monasteries, by which time itself became encapsulated in conceptions of individual personality.

The civil cultures of Greece and Rome had never evolved this sense of the temporal or attached it to their concepts of persons. Time in the Medieval, monastic context acquired independent agency. A schedule which one makes and one keeps is fundamentally different from a calendar to which one is bound. The creation of wealth in the abstract sense in which we have been discussing it, wealth understood as inextricable from individual worth, can happen only when time is understood as it began to be understood by monks observing the canonical hours. Each modern person models abstracted time in his or her own life by seeing time as central to individual, *willful* purpose and enterprise. Using time in this individual sense to measure reward in wealth-building is thus a cultural artifact unique to the Western world. We will see that time in many other societies has a far less robust and palpable sense. Where Western people often believe that "time is money," business people in non-Western societies often affirm a more casual attitude, expressed as, "We work to live, we don't live to work," as they linger over long lunches. This abstracted and individualized sense of time in the West is also central to the development of the concept of a *career*.

The word "career" (from the French *carriere*, "roadway" or "race course") combines elements of competition, goals, gains, and pace all related to points in time. What distinguishes the evolving concepts of personal action in the Western world, at least since the monastic experience, is the value of individuals tied to a "course" with a goal to be achieved in scheduled time, indeed to be measured in time. The runners one sees early each morning on suburban roads run a personal course, the omnipresent running watch used to measure a "personal best." The life of work-play, which was first fully understood by the Greeks, receives this new dimension in the Christian experience of time and vocation in monasteries. In its various guises it continues to animate Western commercial culture.

In monastic life the secular world, with its ties to the transitory and mute powers of nature, was transcended in the association of free men in a life of prayer and study, as well as individual and cooperative work. Just as the civil realm of the classical world came into existence when humanity felt free enough from nature to assert dominion over it, monastic piety freed humans from the claims of nature, and of society as it had been previously understood. This freedom allowed more mastery of the material and social worlds than the ordinary run of Medieval people. For one thing, monastic life was in principle open to all, and many from the nobility were drawn to it. Social class and kinship barriers were broken down to allow within monastic life a more efficient division of labor based on ability. Hauser says,

> It is known that aristocrats were in a majority in the early medieval monasteries; certain monasteries were, in fact, almost exclusively reserved for them. Thus people who could otherwise probably never have handled a smeary paint-brush, a chisel or a trowel came into direct touch with arts and crafts. It is true that the contempt for manual labour remains widespread even in the Middle Ages, and the idea of power still continues to be associated with that of an idle existence, but it is unmistakably evident that now, in contrast to classical antiquity, alongside the life of the seigneur, which is associated with unlimited leisure, the industrious life acquires a more positive evaluation and this new relationship to work is connected amongst other things, with the popularity of monastic life.[1]

The material world was consequently not to be entirely denied in monastic life; it was to be affirmed in entirely new ways. The very absorption of individuals in a prayerful life empowered them to deal with the material world. This encounter of the world was mediated through vows of poverty and chastity, and supported by vows of obedience to monastic rules designed to liberate men from the claims of materiality. The pledge of chastity institutionalized the severing of kinship or other ties so essential to this form of sociality. The pledge of poverty also had the extraordinary effect of freeing individuals to encounter the world in special ways: the motivation for producing goods was now not primarily for individual consumption or for sale for personal profit. As work had been liberated from labor in the civil realm in the context of property and free exchange, work as wealth-creation was fundamentally liberated from consumption and profit, and became a value in its own right. This distance of monastic life from the world and secular time permitted these to be engaged and mastered through work in a special way. Each monk acted out the words of Paul: "...work out your own salvation with fear and trembling. For it is God which worketh in you both to will and to do of his good pleasure." [II Phil., 13-14]. Work and prayer had merged.

The single most important source of many of the improvements in agriculture, crafts and technology in the Medieval period was the monastery. The Benedictine monk Theophilus listed in his *Schedula diversarum artium*, written at the end of the eleventh century, a series of monastic inventions from glass-making to chemical production of dyes.[2] Monasteries were often also the centers for local industry in such activities as brewing and milling. Monastic relations to trade in many crafts were essential to keeping rudimentary commerce alive. Because the religious orders had establishments all over Europe, these skills were transmitted by peripatetic monks. In many ways monasteries in the Middle Ages functioned like transnational corporations do today. Owing little allegiance to the polities in which they were located, resources, including ideas and personnel, were freely deployed from one unit to another. After the founding of the Cluniac Order within the Benedictine stream of monasticism in the early 10th Century all of these impulses toward an ordered economic existence quickly spread throughout Europe. The permission of greater influence by lay members in economic matters further rationalized the division of labor, and lessened distinctions between clergy and laity in general.

What is remarkable about monasticism was that the globalizing force which propelled it lacked a real center. To be sure, monasteries had mother houses and systems of authority. But in Medieval society the lack of modern roads and communications structures meant that the unity of the system had to be embedded *in the system itself.* In this sense it was like the great proliferation of Greek merchant cities around the Mediterranean centuries before. Like this expansive Hellenic system in which cities founding colonies, which then founded cities of their own, the monastic system arose like a great branched tree of enterprise as monastery founded monastery, its unity embedded in a common *Rule* and the inherent dynamism of the system itself.

The efficient management of these complex operations by the monastic orders was perhaps the greatest source of concentrated wealth in the Middle Ages. Double-entry book-keeping was consequently another monastic development. The business enterprise as it was understood in the classical world lacked a full sense of the individual person functioning within it. Quite apart from the fact that most businesses were held within families in antiquity, they lacked the dynamism of the modern corporation because they did not articulate, certainly not formally, the idea of the business career. Public life had great legitimacy in the Greco-Roman world and made claims of duty on the individual citizen, denying him the single focus of a "career" in any modern sense. The career as a vocation as well as an occupation required the final abstraction and internalization of time and work on an individual basis that was first experienced in the Medieval monastery.

The discipline of monastic life organized around a "Rule" set the stage for some of the most prominent elements of modern business life. By mandating uniform standards of dress, grooming and hygiene it created a life of habit, as indeed monastic dress was called. The emphasis on punctuality and order so evident in modern civil societies (and so lacking in many others) was reflected in the identical garments each monk wore, their colors of brown, black, white and gray radiating sobriety and seriousness as life was led in step with "The Hours." Monastic furniture was produced from standard patterns. Among the innovations in furniture was the drawer, designed for the orderly storage of documents. Monasteries themselves were built to a standard plan, the common inhabitation of numerous individuals requiring careful design solutions which, once accomplished, were repeated in subsequent structures. In some religious orders these plans were part of the Rule itself. Witold Rybcznski writes: "The Rule described work schedules in detail as well as the layout of buildings, which followed a standardized plan, like businessmen's hotels today. It has been said that a blind monk could enter any of the more than seven hundred Cistercian monasteries and not get lost."[3] The extraordinary legacy of centuries of monastic life to modern business civilization cannot be overestimated. But its principal legacy was to preserve the essence of the civil world inherited from classical antiquity, and to pass it on to the modern era.

The rebirth of the civil world as the dominant mode of life in western Europe at the end of the Middle Ages has many of those characteristics identified with the passing of traditional society. The first of these was the rise of cities tied to one another in commerce. In the north of Italy in the twelfth century, Venice, Siena, Verona, Florence, Pisa, Milan and Genoa flourished. At about the same time the Hansa cities of the Baltic, with names like Danzig, Lubeck and Hamburg developed a vigorous maritime commerce. This was paralleled by the blossoming of the great Flemish commercial cities in the low countries: Brughes, Ghent, Liege, and Antwerp. Each city was marked by its freedom from the dominant feudal system, with its heredity rights, and its hierarchies of kings and princes. Significantly, all of these late Medieval commercial cities were connected to important waterways, and maritime commerce. These cities were also chiefly characterized by republican forms of government based on the equal citizenship under a common charter of rights of its dominant property-owners and merchants. These mercantile republics looked self-consciously to ancient models of classical civilization, which soon blossomed into the intellectual and artistic revolution of the Renaissance.

Venice is a good example of the merchant republic which rose at the end of the Medieval period. It began as a island city, protected by its lagoons from the disorder on the mainland at the end of the Roman Empire. Initially Venice was little more than a depot, importing raw materials from the interior, and then re-exporting them to the East, especially to Constantinople. Its citizens came to see that wealth lay not in the export of raw materials, but in the value-added enterprise of manufacturing. Soon Venice was manufacturing goods which it sent to its interior suppliers. A developmental chain reaction was set in motion, described by Jane Jacobs:

> But Venice, the pioneer city of the European economy, did not remain a mere supply depot. By diversifying its own production, starting with a base in salt and timber, it proceeded to develop and, thereby to provide a Venetian city market for depot settlements of the north and west — which then built up city production of their own, each in its turn. As the cities of Europe, passing the spark of creative economic life from one to another, multiplied, they also drew into their trade the subsistence life about them and transformed it.[4]

The bankers of Venice became famous for their skill and prudence. The vast commercial fleet was protected by an effective navy. Its republican government was dominated by wealthy merchants whose names were enrolled in the famous "Golden Book," and its civil life marked by a respect for freedom unknown in feudal Europe. Edward Muir suggests that, "Venice became the most famous living example in early modern Europe of the advantages gained from government by a thoughtful few. Admiration for the Venetian republic largely took two forms, in praise either for the wisdom embodied in Venice's political institutions or for the devoted civic virtue practiced by the patrician rulers."[5]

Florence soon followed the Venetian model. Freeing itself from dependence on its agricultural hinterland, it began to manufacture high quality textiles and leather goods, using local hides and high quality imported fibers, especially wool from England. These commercial trades were financed by local bankers, of whom the Medici became the most powerful. The republican government of the city guaranteed these trades with its own coinage, which became a standard of liquidity in Europe. Important intellectual shifts accompanied this change. The essentially secular arguments for government in Dante's *De Monarchia* published in the fourteenth century were reinforced by others, most prominently Machiavelli's *Discourses* and *Il Principe* at the end of the fifteenth century.

These trends toward urbanization and commerce within a secular context were, ironically, aided by one of the greatest disasters in European history, the "Black Death" of 1348-1352. In this brief span of years up to one-third of Europe's population perished from bubonic plague. The horror of this event, so vividly detailed in the *Decameron* of Boccachio, had profound implications for the intellectual and social life of Europe. Realism and social fluidity began to pervade European thought and practice as the conditions of human life were deeply altered.[6] At the same time, the value of individual human life was elevated as the cost of labor rose greatly. The acute labor shortages which Europe experienced in the wake of the plague encouraged an exodus from agricultural work to the towns and cities where a better living could be made. The trade guilds, once closed and hereditary, now opened themselves to ambition and talent to replenish their memberships.

The breaking up of the extended family, the clan and its associations, may have been the single most important impact of the Black Death. As individuals were released from traditional kinship ties they were free to associate and innovate in many new ways, giving rise to the marked entrepreneurialism which was to characterize Europe for generations to come. The plague was in fact a form of instant saving and accumulation. There was a huge automatic infusion of capital into the European economy as wealth per capita sharply rose with this near instant decimation of the population. In an environment where capital was freed up simultaneously with an increase in the cost of labor, there were great incentives for technological innovation and risk-taking in commercial ventures. The century following the upheaval of the Black Death was one of urbanization, commercialization, and discovery. The invention of the printing press, coupling growing literacy with the voyages of discovery culminating in Columbus' 1492 venture, laid the basis for the global commercial civilization which began to blossom in the fifteenth century. But these also greatly enlarged the European imagination with important intellectual and social consequences. The infusion of New World precious metals, gold and silver, into the European economy united enlarged imagination with enlarged resources.

The rise of humanistic values in the context of an urbanizing, commercial culture provoked a turning away from the basic bifurcation of human consciousness of the Middle Ages, which was characterized by the traditional, non-urban life of the great majority on one hand, and the highly concentrated (but inherently expansive), organized and enterprising life of the monasteries on the other. A renewal of worldly values required the substantial changes in Christian organization and practice which took place during the Reformation. Medieval notions of hierarchy and authority conflicted with the values growing among an educated, commercial middle class, which had sprung up outside the feudal system. The Protestant Reformation created an alternative fusion of the individual and the civil realms in the writing of thinkers such as Luther and Calvin.

Luther's abandonment of Augustinian monasticism for a life in the world was united with a respect for the earthly order and earthly princes. Luther's tract *On the Babylonian Captivity of the Church* is as much an economic and political argument as a religious one as it attempted to win the support of Germany's merchant class. It was Luther who underlined the great paradox of Christian faith in its relations to action: that action itself, "works," was the expression, and not the basis of a life of faith. That the Christian was to obey God's law *because he had been set free from it*: "It is clear, then, that a Christian has all that he needs in faith and needs no works to justify him; and if he has no need of works, he has no need of the law; and if he has no need of the law, surely he is free from the law."[7] The man of faith is thus a man of works and righteousness, but he stands in a dynamic tension with them, lest they make claims from which his faith has freed him. The Christian must live in the world, not apart from it. But this means he lives in the presence of compromises he is not permitted to make. "With the acceptance of the world not as it is," says Bellah, "but as a valid arena in which to work out the divine command, with the acceptance of the self as capable of faith in spite of sin, the Reformation made it possible to turn away from world rejection in a way not possible in the historic religions."[8]

The great Erasmus was in himself a "compromise," a bargain of the worldly with the otherworldly: both a priest and the illegitimate son of a priest. An extensive traveler, he was a confidant of great figures like Thomas More. Thus when Erasmus emerged from the retreat of the monastic life he had led at Steyn, he encouraged the mastery of the world with its attendant risks to spiritual life. He extolled a special kind of courageous "Christian Knight." Simon Schama says: "Going into the world, the better to master its vanities, was the quotidian ordeal to which Erasmian humanists subjected themselves. The awful risk that in so doing the things of the world might master them was ever present, especially for men like [Thomas] More, who accepted high office, but it was a risk from which they were not permitted to abstain."[9] There is consequently a fundamental ambivalence built into the rediscovery of public, civil life in the Renaissance and Reformation. The individual was born from the moral strands which began to emerge in late antiquity and was solidified in the life of religion during the Medieval period. The emergence of the individual into the life of "the World" in the fourteenth and fifteenth centuries carried this ambivalence with it. In a sense, the great dynamism which powered Western cultural values, and made them globally ascendant from the seventeenth century on, was a product of this dialogue between unreconciled spiritual values resting in individuals, and material values resting in the world.

The Reformation in general, and Erasmian humanism in particular, consequently placed individual conscience and piety at the very center of Christian belief in the "priesthood of all believers." The new man of faith was an individual confident of his ability to live in the world as he prepared for the next. The Calvinist burghers who gaze out at us from the Dutch portraits of the seventeenth century are men confident in both their rectitude and their obvious prosperity. Dressed simply in black and the other subdued tones which remind us of monastic garb, their starched collars are their only obvious indulgence, and in fact highlight their moral seriousness. As we look at these men gathered in group portraits, unrelated by blood, starkly and identically attired, free members of a voluntary corporation designed to create wealth in the context of a stern, shared faith, we realize that we are looking at a transformed version of the monastery. The modern corporation may have been born in the Netherlands of the early seventeenth century, but its incubator was the Medieval cloister. Rybczynski summarizes the Dutch commercial ascendancy:

> All these circumstances produced a people who admired saving, frowned on conspicuous spending, and naturally evolved conservative manners. The simplicity of the Dutch bourgeois expressed itself in many ways. The dress of the Dutch male, for instance, was plain. The doublet and trousers were the seventeenth century equivalent of the modern businessman's three-piece suit, and like it they were unaffected by fashion, the quality of the cloth might vary but the style remained unchanged for generations. The favorite colors were dark: black, violet or brown. The officials of the clothmaker's guild, in Rembrandt's famous group portrait, were prosperous (as their lace [sic] collars and amply cut cassocks indicate) but somber to the point of drabness.[10]

These portraits as well as the secular landscapes which were so common in Dutch art in the period also tell us something about the new conditions of artistic patronage. Wealth was now sufficiently distributed in society for a large class of artists to make their livings from the well-to-do middle classes. Amsterdam alone supported hundreds of artists, and it took this sort of critical mass for a number of individual geniuses like Hals and Van Dyke, and above all Rembrandt, to emerge. Unlike aristocratic and religious patrons of previous eras with quite different agendas in making artistic commissions, the new merchant classes sought more private pleasures in pictures of favorite pastures and townscapes; of animals and still-lifes; of loved ones. These pictures are sentimental in the best way: intimate, humane, deeply personal — full of individual meaning.

If individual wealth is God's way of demonstrating to his elect that they are in fact saved by grace and faith, ostentatious shows of wealth approached blasphemy in the eyes of these Dutch merchants. In the Erasmian sense, the world is demonstrably engaged and mastered without a spiritual surrender. But there was *spiritual risk* in this tension between the goods of this world and the goods of the next. In the Erasmian bargain with the world there is always the specter of "The Fall." Indeed, carved over the door of the Bankruptcy Court in Amsterdam's seventeenth century city hall is a figure of Icarus, dropping out of the sky because he had risked flying too high. These dual themes of faith and risk were to become a dominant paradigm in the religion of Protestant Europe.

Nowhere was it better presented than in the great nineteenth century Lutheran theologian, Soren Kierkegaard, who extolled the *Knight of Faith*, who "belongs to the world, no Philistine more so. He takes delight in everything, and whenever one sees him taking part in a particular pleasure, he does it with the persistence which is the mark of the earthly man whose soul is absorbed in such things. He tends to his work. So when one looks at him one might suppose that he was a clerk who had lost his soul in an intricate system of bookkeeping, so precise is he. [...] The stranger leaves him with the thought that he certainly is a capitalist, while my admired knight thinks, 'Yes, if the money were needed, I dare say I could get it'."[11] Kierkegaard's confident "knight of faith" does "not do the least thing except by virtue of the absurd." And for Kierkegaard "absurdity" is "living simultaneously in the infinite and the finite."

Capitalism as a sort of worldly otherworldliness has become a faith, totally absorbing the individual without annihilating him. His wealth-getting is the embrace of risk *as risk*, for the essence of the life of faith is the risk inherent in it. The individual stands at the heart of existential risk itself. "After the individual has given up every effort to find himself outside himself in existence, in relation to his surroundings," Kierkegaard wrote, "and when after that shipwreck he turns toward the highest things, the absolute, coming after such emptiness, bursts upon him not only in all its fullness, but in the responsibility he feels. Had I to carve an inscription on my grave, I would ask for none other than 'the individual'."[12] This "absurd" passion for accumulating wealth without consuming it (or being consumed by it) is a measure of the tension the man of spiritual integrity maintains with the material domain. It is also one definition of the capitalist temper. The capitalist is less a person who accumulates to consume than a person who accumulates in order to invest (risk) in further accumulation. Wealth-building is a means of keeping score, of measuring one's ultimate worth in the scheme of things. It is the measure of a successful career.

The world's first publicly-traded corporation was the Dutch East India Company, chartered in 1604. All the intellectual bases for this new sort of enterprise were laid, in a legal sense, in antiquity with the evolution of the notion of a legal person as an artificial product of civil law. What makes its appearance important lay in another direction. Beginning in the Netherlands in the late Renaissance period business experienced the acceleration of a trend that began in the late Middle Ages: the separation of business from household activity. The intellectual and social distinction between these two sorts of economies was, of course, known to the Greeks. But it was the Dutch who substantially removed major portions of business activity from the household to specially dedicated spaces: the shop, office, warehouse, bank and exchange. The Amsterdam Stock Exchange, the world's first and oldest, was only an extension of a trend where houses of business were entirely freed from household and kin associations. This resulted in the dignifying of business activity to an unprecedented extent.

The practical but nonetheless elegant buildings which characterize the public architecture of the towns and cities of the low countries during the Dutch ascendancy were to set the precedent for the modern city and its skyline of commercial structures. Public life and business life were blended in the world's first completely bourgeois culture. Amsterdam, Europe's largest and richest city in the seventeenth century, was punctuated by the gables of business establishments, the towering parapets of the Exchange and the spires of the churches addressing each other. Amsterdam represents the apotheosis of a trend in urban life and design that can be traced to the late Medieval market town, of which Culemborg is typical. Unlike the great cities of antiquity these towns were not established as ceremonial centers, strongholds or as the residences of princes.

The market town in the low countries is characterized by what urban historian Edmund N. Bacon calls "a never-ceasing series of kinetic sensations."[13]

CULEMBORG (1648)

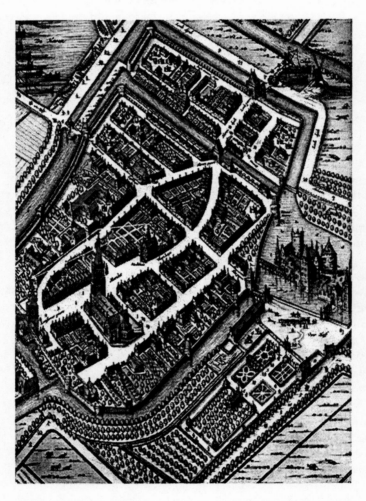

Figure 9:1 A typical European market town during the Dutch ascendancy, its central organizing element is the market space. Like the merchant society to which it gives expression, no plan is imposed. Rather, a "kinetic" order evolves from use over time.

At the center of the urban experience was the marketplace, shaped over decades by practical use. It was surrounded by streets and buildings which achieved their dynamic unity only in their counterpoint to one another. It is a unity achieved only gradually over decades and centuries of pragmatic evolution, as builders had to give practical and esthetic expression to their work in both individual and social terms. There are none of the grand axes of traditional design, imposing an order on urban experience. Rather, like the commercial society to which they gave expression, these towns have a utilitarian scale and a dynamic humanism as streets flow into one another, and into the country-side they dominate. These towns and cities are as unplanned, energetic, and "kinetic," as their merchant citizens.

The removal of important business activity from the household into its own dedicated spaces meant a parallel transformation of the household. A principal consequence of this removal was that the man of business now often set forth from his house during the day to engage in commerce. The house that was left behind became something familiar to the modern imagination: a *home*. The word "home" is itself significant: it comes from a Germanic root *heim*, meaning "to lie, to rest." A house becomes a "home" when it grants comfort from the public world of business to those who dwell in it. The character of this home was inextricably tied to the transformed role of those left in charge of it: wives. Rybczynski suggests that the "feminization of the home in seventeenth-century Holland was one of the most important events in the evolution of the domestic interior."[14]

This was probably the first time in history when women had in fact a domain of their own. Everything about the Dutch house indicated that it was planned for and by the women who were the masters of it. And this mastery was strikingly institutionalized. All visitors to Holland noted the obsessive cleanliness of Dutch houses. Dutch cities themselves were not particularly clean, the canals used to dispose of wastes. The Dutch had no standards of personal hygiene different from others of their time. The extraordinary cleanliness of Dutch houses had a different significance. According to Rybcznyski, "When visitors were required to take off their shoes or put on slippers, it was not immediately on entering the house - the lower floor was still considered to be part of the public street - but on going upstairs. That was where the public realm stopped and the home began. This boundary was a new idea, and the order and tidiness of the household were evidence neither of fastidiousness nor of a particular cleanliness, but instead a desire to define the home as a separate, special place."[15]

The resulting change in the status of women, especially compared to that of women in the commercial society of classical Greece, was extraordinary and its evidences numerous. Women had widespread protection under Dutch law, and the instrument of the marriage contract was there to re-enforce those protections. Ordinary women were celebrated in Dutch art as never before in history, and they were usually presented in domestic environments — "at home," with children, pets, musical instruments. The room which most characterized their domestic functions, the kitchen, became, in the words of Paul Zumthor, a place of "fantastic dignity" and "something between a temple and a museum."[16] The location of the kitchen was central to the Dutch house. It was beautifully appointed with cupboards and sideboards displaying china, silver and linens. The large hearth and chimney piece, covered with elaborate decorative tiles, was the focus of the room and a center for family life and entertainment. But more than this, the dignity of the kitchen demonstrated that Dutch women, including those with wealthy husbands, did most of their own housework, even when assisted by servants. When an envoy of the Prince of Orange came to pay his condolences to the widow of the Grand Admiral of the Dutch fleet, she could not rise to greet him. She had injured herself while hanging laundry.

Women were the masters (or mistresses) of a domestic economy of near-equal rank with the public lives of their husbands. The new genre of art for which the Dutch were to become so justifiably famous, the art of family and domesticity as seen especially in Vermeer, is a tribute to the new status of women in bourgeois life. What is notable is that this elevated status took place not in woman's emancipation from domesticity, but rather in her rule over it. It also underlined a reality which was to become more obvious in the following centuries. Women were in fact becoming the companions of men in the making of business culture. Family, understood in the domesticity of the home, was the bedrock upon which fortunes were being built and sustained. Kinship, in an entirely new sense of the *intimate* nuclear family, became the foundation of a business career.

Finally, "home" became the basis from which women began to develop a special emotional, intellectual and social perspective. In the course of the eighteenth century, the "at home" became the social means by which talented and witty bourgeois women engaged the world outside. Largely excluded from the public life of business and politics on account of gender, and from royal court circles by the lack of aristocratic birth, the wives and daughters of wealthy merchants in France, England and Germany — women like Mme. de

Stael in Paris, or Rahel Varnhagen in Berlin — held *salons* to which the brightest stars of wit and creative talent were invited. Women even found their own public creative medium — the novel. The growth of a large and literate middle class produced an audience for the kind insight, wit and wry observation which only those completely at home in domestic spaces could provide. From Jane Austen to Edith Wharton, the great woman novelist was the master of a genre of writing centered in the complexity of human feelings and relationships; of broad themes found in enclosed spaces; the romance of the meticulously observed drawing room and boudoir, garden and ball room. The next step could not be far behind. Women of the caliber of Mary Wolstonecroft began to argue for the full inclusion of women in the rights of public life, including education. And soon after, men of the stature of John Stuart Mill began to support them.

The industrial revolution magnified these realities: not only did the absolute numbers of wealthy people grow, wealth could now be accumulated on a scale heretofore unimaginable. Keeping score and demonstrating one's election through building a vast personal fortune, now usually completely devoid of its original religious character, became the moral necessity of the modern age. Success in business had become a supreme moral imperative, and the "man of business" the exemplar of personal and civil virtue. Andrew Carnegie penned an essay entitled *The Gospel of Wealth*, and gave almost all of his vast fortune away, keeping his own end of the Erasmian bargain. John D. Rockefeller sang in the church choir every Sunday while he ruthlessly built Standard Oil, but gave $500 million to charity, and passed out shiny new dimes to all who asked for them.

The civil world had taken on a different character. It now began to exist to provide the context for individual goods rather than social goods. Or rather, individual goods and social goods became more indistinguishable. The civil world of the classical age was designed to support a collective good, the place where private interests could be subsumed to the public interest. Adam Smith posited an "invisible hand" by which the public good and private interests converged, at least partially, in the free market. Eighteenth, and especially nineteenth, century liberalism was inclined to see civil society as a neutral forum, almost a referee, within which individual, private careers could be conducted. The utilitarian thought of Bentham and Mill, which was unable to see the social contract as much more than a relative weighing of individual interests — "the greatest good of the greatest number" — perfectly expressed the temper of modern business societies.

But it was not only the business enterprise that provided sustenance to the individual, although it was clearly here that the animus remained. The industrial revolution brought with it massive population growth, urbanization on a gigantic scale, and entirely new levels of communication. Mass society was born, and with it modernity itself. Modernity and mass society are closely related in that the essence of the modern temper was to radically assert the individual in the midst of the assaults on individuality which the compression of populations in mass society brought with it. As the term suggests, mass society was the articulation of individuals. It was after all characterized by great numbers of individual people located within an atomized whole. In contemporary mass society (which Vance Packard characterized as "the lonely crowd") individuals could become the worst enemies of individuality, becoming "herdlike" as Nietzsche suggested, when the traditional intermediating structures of society — family, church, polity — were dissolved in a rapid and widespread mobility of people, values and associations. As a consequence, some theorists, like Stuart Hall, seem to have given up on "the individual" altogether, suggesting that, "We can no longer conceive of the 'individual' in terms of a whole, centered, stable and completed Ego."[17]

"Modernism" as an intellectual and cultural movement arising from the experience of mass society achieved its discrete identity at the end of the nineteenth century, and was characterized, according to Norman Cantor, by its, "ahistorical, non-narrative or 'synchronic' ways of thinking; the microcosmic, small-scale dimension; self-referentiality; and moral relativism."[18] Modernism looked at the world from the inside out, always from a disconnected distance, from the vantage of "the self." Charles Taylor suggests that, "Our modern notion of the self is related to, one might say constituted by, a sense (or perhaps a family of senses) of inwardness."[19] The phenomenology of *alienation* which was to characterize the arts, literature and philosophical trends of the twentieth century, with profound implications for society and politics, is the organic articulation of mass society. New forms of corporate organization (and reorganization) were summoned into existence to give individuals the possibility to identify themselves in meaningful ways in mass society. The trade union, the political party, and the artistic or intellectual movement were some of the means for forming a coherent identity amidst the demands of rapid change. An "age of ideology" — socialism, fascism, nationalism and their variants — sought to bring individuals and ideas together in ways both persuasive and adhesive. The decline of both ideology and organizational commitment at the millennium's end left open the question of the means to a purposeful identity in post-industrial society.

The world of the individual was initiated in the classical age but fulfilled only in the Christian era. The function of public life in the classical age was to give men the opportunity to realize themselves apart from the necessities of the traditional household — bound up as it was with life as it is lived at the base of the needs hierarchy. In a public life the citizen had the possibility to use the higher human powers of reason and appreciation in the realms of law, art, sport and science. In the market-place he could make himself visible in exchange through the products of his work. In a public life of equal exchange relationships he could overcome the inequalities of household organization with their roots in the primal and traditional past. But in the end, the realm of public life, as important as it was to esteem and ultimately self-esteem, could not satisfy a yet higher need: the need for an authentic, inexchangeable, *transcendent* self.

In Christian thought, and more especially in Christian organization — the church and the monastery — a new realm was born. Corporate organization shared an essential characteristic of public life in that it was personally and not kinship based, yet it was as demanding in personal loyalty. But unlike public life, corporate life was deeply concerned with individual meanings and rewards. Corporate life was best reflected in the monastery, which was both a household, and thus concerned with the necessities of elemental human sustenance, but also a spiritual space where the individual sought and perfected meanings. In the post-Medieval world the corporation, especially the business corporation, increasingly became the instrument through which individuals sought both the esteem and self-esteem of public life, and the satisfactions of a purposeful identity and existence. Household, *polis,* and monastery combined, the corporation — the business enterprise, the university, the academy, the party, the union or intellectual movement — became the arena in which individuals sought self-actualization. As corporate life itself was called into question at the millennium's end the individual was increasingly left with a naked self, a life with little organized social context in which to define meaning.

NOTES TO CHAPTER NINE

1. Hauser, *op.cit.*, p. 171
2. *Ibid.,* p. 172
3. Witold Rybczynski, HOME: A SHORT HISTORY OF AN IDEA (New York: Penguin Books, 1986), p. 29
4. Jane Jacobs, CITIES AND THE WEALTH OF NATIONS (New York: Random House, 1984), p. 133

5. Edward Muir, CIVIC RITUAL IN RENAISSANCE VENICE (Princeton: Princeton University Press, 1981), p. 19
6. David Herlihy, THE BLACK DEATH AND THE TRANSFORMATION OF THE WEST (Cambridge: Harvard University Press, 1997)
7. Martin Luther, CHRISTIAN LIBERTY, W.A. Lambert, trans. (Philadelphia: Fortress Press, 1957), p. 12
8. Bellah, *op. cit.*, p. 369
9. Simon Schama, THE EMBARRASSMENT OF RICHES (New York: Alfred A. Knopf, 1987), p. 326
10. Rybczynski, *op. cit.*, p. 54-55
11. Soren Kierkegaard, "The Knight of Faith and the Knight of Infinite Resignation," in A KIERKEGAARD ANTHOLOGY, Robert Bretall, ed. (New York: The Modern Library, 1946), pp. 119-120
12. _____, "The Present Age: A Literary Review," in A KIERKEGAARD ANTHOLOGY, *op. cit.*, p. 258
13. Bacon, *op. cit.*, p. 164
14. Rybcznski, *op. cit.*, p. 72
15. *Ibid.*, p. 66
16. Paul Zumthor, DAILY LIFE IN REMBRANDT'S HOLLAND, S.W. Taylor, trans. (New York: Macmillan and Company, Publishers, 1963), p. 41
17. David Morley and Kuan-Hsing Chen, eds., STUART HALL: CRITICAL DIALOGUES ON CULTURE (London: Routledge, 1996), p. 226
18. Norman Cantor, TWENTIETH-CENTURY CULTURE (New York: Peter Lang Publishing, 1988), p. 20
19. Charles Taylor, SOURCES OF THE SELF (Cambridge, MA: Harvard University Press, 1989), p. 111

PART V

WORLDS IN TRANSITION: THE CASE OF JAPAN

We must not, in this progressive reform movement, simply adopt the externals of Western
customs; we must go further and reform people's minds as well.

— *Kozaki Hiromichi [1887]*

CHAPTER TEN

SELFLESS CAPITALISM?

The last century is characterized by accelerating globalization. The coming of modern technology, especially the steam engine and electricity, linked the world's societies and economies into a communications network which began to challenge all human values and institutions. This was in fact a second cultural globalization. The first, initiated during the age of discovery beginning at the end of the fifteenth century, and culminating in the rapid transformations of the seventeenth century, left few parts of the globe untouched. In the Americas, great empires fell, and whole populations were decimated, principally by diseases to which indigenous peoples had no immunity. More than 80% of the native population of Mexico perished in the years following the conquest by Cortez in 1519. The indigenous people of the Caribbean basin, including what became Cuba and Puerto Rico, disappeared entirely. The African slave trade, intimately tied to the need to replenish the working population in the Americas, caused the death of millions and fundamentally affected social structures throughout the continent. This first globalization was thus characterized by an extreme asymmetry between localizing and delocalizing impulses as indigenous cultures encountered the West. In the New World even the most advanced civilizations had not passed much beyond the stone age. Tools were simple; the wheel, the plow, and animals of burden were unknown; and these societies depended entirely on raw human labor to build and maintain their impressive cities. Under these circumstances little syncretism was possible as the forces of globalization thrust civilizations with very different technical and economic substrates together. The indigenous cultures were thus almost completely delocalized. Even their biologies were delocalized owing to the inability of native immune systems to adapt to the very different bacteria and viruses which the Europeans brought with them.

But the part of the globe which first felt these momentous changes most directly was Europe. New sources of wealth, especially in precious metals, impelled an economic revolution of enormous dimensions. The "second globalization" of the nineteenth century, based on integrative technology, speeded up a process which had been taking place for more than two centuries. These new technologies, first widely assimilated in Europe, and growing demographic pressures also furthered a continent-wide process of political and social transformation which created new states and eliminated old ones, especially in Germany and Italy. The struggle of the European political system to accommodate this rapid change issued in two disastrous world wars, in which tens of millions of people died, and convulsive cultural and social changes resulted. If Europe, the source of many of these changes, equipped with some knowledge and resources to deal with them, fared so badly on its way to global adjustment, the impact on countries like Japan was all the greater. The assault of global forces on this traditional society forced an internal economic transformation unparalleled in any country. Palmer and Colton conclude that the Meiji revolution in Japan, launched in 1868 "still stands as the most remarkable transformation ever undergone by any people in so short a time."[1] The human costs in social displacement and war were equivalent to those suffered by Europe.

Japan is often the case in point for those who wish to argue that it is possible to be a fully modern society, without being "Western." The argument is made that Japan is a highly urbanized and educated, technological, market economy with the full array of modern civil institutions, including democratic government. And yet it is claimed, Japan in so many ways is more "Asian" than "Western." In some important ways Japan has been different in its history and development than other traditional societies. Like some of the early civil societies we have noted, Japan is a land-poor nation, tied to the sea. Its mountainous geography distributed over a number of islands made centralized government difficult, and the Japanese feudal period had many of those characteristics of decentralized government and economy which have existed in the West. Commerce by sea was necessary between the Japanese islands and with the Asian mainland. Because of the scarcity of good agricultural land, Japan was much more urbanized than any Asian society: during the Shoganate, the capital city of Edo (modern Tokyo) numbered over one million in 1700, making it the world's most populous city. The Japanese capacity for the quick adoption of elements of foreign cultures has been noted often, and this relative flexibility is probably related to both the maritime and urban traditions which made the Japanese less adverse to at least superficial change. Japan was not only more highly urbanized than most traditional societies, it was as a consequence much more highly literate. At the time of the Meiji Restoration, about 60% of the population could read and write this difficult language.

Because of Japan's self-enforced, rigid seclusion from the world for two centuries until its encounters with the West in the middle of the nineteenth century, certain distortions in its social evolution occurred. For example, the military or *samurai* class was numerous, but also relatively idle. Their status required that they be supported in a style equivalent to their high social rank. Given Japan's isolation from foreign sources of wealth through trade, a native merchant class grew almost as a symmetrical necessity. We have seen this in other military states: markets and mercantile innovation are propelled by the pressures of pronounced scarcity which supporting a military class brings with it, especially if that class is idle, as the *samurai* largely were. Although traditionally despised, and subject to death with impunity for even disrespectful language to *samurai*, the *chonin* (or townsmen) came to control much of the country's liquid wealth. Unlike enterprising Chinese merchants, who often emigrated, Japan's mercantile class remained and grew in influence.

Japan's ancient military tradition sets it apart from countries like China where Confucian values denigrated the military. This is significant because in many ways the medieval Japanese *samurai* tradition parallels the monastic tradition of the West, which we have identified as a precursor to the modern corporate economy. The *samurai* lived as a "class apart" with their own rules and traditions, even a separate court system. Their sense of ascetic discipline had many monastic elements about it. In military organization the Japanese learned the dual self-discipline and mastery of the world which monastic organization modeled for Europe, and the geographic mobility. But where European monastic values placed spiritual integrity and self-knowledge at the heart of "the Rule," Japanese militarism held as its ideal selflessness in absolute loyalty and obedience. Thus while Japan's militaristic feudal past is in many ways reflected in *kaisha*, Japanese corporate organization and culture, it carried with it the ultimate values of duty and discipline rather than those of individual actualization.

Fernand Braudel has made an important distinction between *capitalism* and a *market system* in attempting to understand the rise of modern Japan. In China there was market activity, but it was highly localized as a manifestation of an economic order centrally controlled by the state. "In a system like this, accumulation could only be achieved by the state and the state apparatus."[2] No such centralized economic system was possible in Japan since the 14th century

Ashikaga period generated the many independent and competing economic and social forces which characterized feudalism. The lack of a centralized state meant that the pluralist accumulation which characterizes capitalism could take place within *the economic system as whole*, not only in one of its parts. And thus the values and incentives of the market sector shaped capital accumulation itself. This is another parallel to the pluralized accumulation of wealth (especially in the monastic system) in the West.

The Buddhist tradition, together with Confucianism, shaped much of the formal belief systems of Japan. Buddhism, in particular because of its focus in purely spiritual concerns, left its mark in a way that "secular" Confucianism did not. For Buddhism is a spiritual discipline which seeks the ultimate negation of the world, which is viewed as transitory and a place of suffering. De Rougemont has used the term "excarnation" to describe the spiritual impulses of Buddhism, and contrasts these with the "incarnation" which formed the focus of spiritual life in Europe since the Christian era. Jesus Christ and Gautama Buddha become alternative models of the individual: "The Son of God, uncreated, transcendent, enters into immanence and History, makes Himself into a material body, flesh of a poor child - all in order to speak to men in their own language, in terms of their existence, and to save them where they are, by sole faith in the act of forgiveness, and the love and grace of God. The son of the king of this world leaves his princely palace to enter upon the most destitute solitude, and there discovers that the way of salvation is to reject the world, the body, and suffering in order to rise to transcendent Nothingness."[3] If De Rougemont is right that the incarnation dignified the world and the flesh, then a powerful tension is created between transcending the world and the immanence of the world. "The Individual" was formed in this tension in the West. In Japan the individual was not valued "in the world," but rather in his escape from it through spiritual discipline. Lacking this tension, Japanese culture never produced the existential guilt which has powered the creative imagination in the West. Rather, it produced shame, a means of confirming the immanent condition itself.

Japan emerged into the modern world in the middle of the nineteenth century after more than two centuries in isolation during the Tokugawa period. A deep cultural xenophobia had confined the Japanese to their home islands and rigorously excluded foreigners and their values. A basic impulse had confirmed a historical value system in which the Japanese had always made clear distinctions between themselves and other peoples, making this society one noted for being closed to outsiders. Japan emerged from this cocoon with great reluctance, and only in response to the displays of Western power in Asia, which was being reduced to colonial or semi-colonial status. Its rapid industrialization and adoption of Western ways was designed to protect the Japanese traditional core. Japan's wholesale adoption of the German civil code, British naval and French army organization, and American industrial methods was a thin skin, drawn over immemorial custom. Thus Japan remained essentially a traditional society and has yet to demonstrate that it is a civil society as I have described it. At the same time, the unique configuration of cultural elements in Japanese history and society made possible a more symmetrical balance between localizing and delocalizing impulses as Japan began to fully confront globalization in the middle of the nineteenth century. Indeed, in no other contemporary society is the dynamic between localizing and delocalizing forces so pronounced at every level of experience.

Primal modes continue to be dominant, as in any traditional society, for the mass of people in Japan. But all primal impulses are also tightly structured within traditional boundaries of behavior, which may appear to the outsider as a kind of personal rigidity, as a pervasive thwarting of a deeper, more spontaneous primal personality. In describing Japanese communication Ray T. Donahue, who has lived and taught in Japan over an extended period, posits a Japanese "traditional style characterized by emotionless facial and vocal expressions, reticence, serious demeanor, and an unremitting sameness of routine."[4] An almost obsessive formality implies a primal self always on a leash, fearful of a lack of functional social boundaries. This is probably related to the Japanese awareness of the relative newness of their national culture, especially as compared to that of China, to which Japan owes a fundamental cultural debt. The Chinese, confident of the great antiquity and originality of their splendid traditions, seem more comfortable within their cultural skin, and consequently less rigid and more assured in their individual self-presentations.

As in other traditional societies, genuine markets and the state are also peripheral elements in the life of most people. Ancestor veneration and maintaining correct relations to the spirit world are still very important to most households, regardless of class or education. Household shrines where food is offered to the spirits of the dead are still central to much Japanese piety. Religious observance in connection with public and private functions, including business, has its parallel perhaps only in the United States among contemporary industrial societies. Japan's ethnic and cultural homogeneity has been achieved by making, as do primal societies, fundamental distinctions between "insiders" and "outsiders" (*uchi-soto*), "kin" and "strangers," overcoming internal social cleavages by establishing basic ones with the rest of the world.

If one looks closely at Japanese religious practice, one quickly discovers that is exactly what it is, "practice." Students of religion have often been perplexed by the Japanese habit of protesting that they do not "believe" in religion, while simultaneously being quite observant in practice. Ian Reader, who spent much time teaching in Japan, notes that his students, while almost unanimously denying that they have religious beliefs, acknowledge widespread practices, like making visits to Shinto shrines to make offerings to *kami* before important exams. Likewise, Japanese professionals almost to a person deny that they are religious. But Reader noted a conversation between two of his Japanese colleagues in which one asked the other to which sect of Buddhism his family belonged. The reply was: "I don't know; no one in my family has died yet." Since nearly all Japanese have Buddhist funerals, regardless of their other religious observances, it was being suggested that he had no need to know what sort of Buddhist he was until it was useful to know. Reader summarizes: "The Japanese do not live in a system which demands full-blooded, belief-oriented and exclusive commitment that precludes any other. Rather, their orientations are situational and complementary: the necessity of dealing with the problem of death demands one set of responses and orientations while the time of year or the birth of a child requires another."[5]

What this implies is that much of Japanese consciousness is shaped by the allocentric modes of primal thought. In Bellah's terms, Japanese religion is an action system, directed outward through practice, in which "belief" and "deed" are merged. The wide-spread use of ritual drums (*taiko*) and vigorous movement in commerce with the spirit world of Shinto recalls primal ceremony in other cultures. The lack of religious "conviction" in the face of very widespread religious practice announces a basic other-directedness which obviates the individual self. It is the individual self that is the seat of faith and the sort of spiritual integrity which Westerners would connect to religion. Religion in Japan resides in a very different consciousness, the spirit world of primal relations. The wide-spread veneration of *kami* (things, events, places, and persons which are mysterious, awesome, sacred) rests firmly in primal allocentrism, and in a sense requires self-abnegation as the price of this encounter. The Japanese inclination to ritual and *action* similarly requires forms of self-denial (or at least self-discipline) which can be seen at every level of Japanese society, not least of all the Japanese economy.

✧ ✧ ✧

The Japanese inclination to undervalue individuality has often been noted. The saying, *deru kugi ga utareru,* "the nail that sticks out is beaten down," reflects a rigid cultural mode which distrusts non-comforming individualism. This can be seen in a number of ways culturally. The first is the notion of the human body as a machine. In the martial arts of Japan the mind must discipline itself through practice to the point where it becomes an instrument of the body's mechanics. The practice of *karate* requires that the individual mind be emptied so that it can be instantly and reflexively available to the commands of the body in combat. The Japanese fascination with robotics seems to share the same roots. Japan does not own the great majority of the world's industrial robots only because of a shortage of labor or a need for efficiency. Rather, efficiency itself is an ideal of which the totally disciplined body is the model. The recent craze in Japanese toys for "morphing" carries this ideal to its extreme: a human figure can be metamorphosed into a space ship, or a race car, and vice versa. The boundary between human and machine is obliterated completely.

Japanese life is also saturated with *manga,* "cartoon books" which are read by everyone from university students to business executives. This focus on the visual augmentation of language suggests both the limits in subtlety of pictographic languages, and the pervasive contextualization of the written and spoken word in Japan. *Manga* are not at all "comic," and some of the most pervasive themes are sex and violence, in a society famous for decorum and order. Japan is also a great source of animated art, much of which appears on American television. This also includes video games such as Nintendo, again evidencing a fascination with two-dimensional images, lacking individual "depth," but focused in action. Psychiatrist Takeo Doi says that, "To be born a Japanese is to know that everything has a front and a back."[6] *Omote,* the "front" of something, invariably has a reverse *ura* or "back." This constitutive orientation toward the two-dimensional may explain the central roles of *paper* and *wrapping* in Japanese culture.

The British social anthropologist Joy Hendry has developed a theory of "wrapping" to understand Japanese culture.[7] The Japanese are famous for the art of gift-giving, and central to this pervasive practice is the wrapping of the gift in several layers of beautiful paper. The container is as important, and in some cases, more important than the gift itself. It is interesting to note that the Japanese word for "paper" is *kami,* the same word, though written with different characters, as is used for that amorphous concept concerning the mysterious world of spirits and gods. In a sense the paper wrapping itself is spiritual, and the gift is wrapped in layers of spirits, which are being kept in motion, recalling the gift-cycles of primal life. The widespread use of paper for lanterns, screens, doors and windows in Japanese houses has the same connotation: the household is enveloped in spirits, the house is a spiritual entity. This layered wrapping is found everywhere from dress (where some traditional costumes have a dozen separate layers) to business practices (where a letter will often be folded into a blank piece of paper, which is in turn inserted into an envelope, itself enclosed in an outer envelope). *Origami,* "paper-folding," is an art in its own right, taught to children at an early age.

There is a close cultural connection between two-dimensionality and the creation of three-dimensional forms that occurs as more than a metaphor in much Japanese experience. The mask, an omnipresent image in Japan, is an instance of the two-dimensional appearing as three-dimensional. One recalls the importance of putting on the "right face" in Japanese sociality as the essence of decorum. Practices such as *origami* underline the relations between "present" and "presentation," the former wrapped in the latter. A social etiquette such as the Japanese, based in such putting on of "faces," is central to notions of social role and hierarchy as well as of individual personality. Between the *omote* and the *uri* is an undisclosed, and not easily discloseable self. Doi locates one of the essential elements of Japanese personality in this hidden self. He describes a "double standard" of *tatemae* (what is expected) and *honne* (one's true feeling or intention): "For the Japanese themselves, there is nothing ambiguous about the double standard or *tatemae* and *honne*. As a matter of fact, this is a measure of maturity in the Japanese sense: that people have the knowledge and existence of a double standard and adjust their lives accordingly."[8] This element of primal mendacity in Japanese sociality places little value on sincerity, but rather acknowleges those skills which help persons to function situationally with a measure of control. "Putting on the right face" (nearly equivalent to "being cool" in American slang) suggests not hypocrisy, as it does in the West where individual integrity is often an ultimate value, but rather the more fluid mechanisms rising from the charismatic, the art of controlled self-presentation in a highly localized context.

Japanese culture is often described as "high-context."[9] Behavior, particularly speech, is closely associated with the total social context within which it takes place. This means that presentation is more indirect, diffuse and holistic: one has to be especially sensitive to non-verbal cues as in all primal communication. The subject-object-verb word order of Japanese syntax reflects and facilitates this indirectness in expression. So does the use of ellipsis, omissions in expression, which can be recovered by the listener only through his experience with individual speakers, their context. Skillful listening is consequently more assumed and valued in Japanese communication than in other, less high-context cultures such as ours in America. In practical terms this means that communication with strangers, even other Japanese, is inhibited by the nature of the language itself, and that there is a bias toward the sorts of on-going, long-term relationships, especially in business, which will promote the holistic context within which communications are most advantageously conducted. Japanese culture, as a high context culture, is consequently also highly localized in its animus and opaque ("wrapped") in its expression — and thus an element inhibiting Japan's global incorporation.

In important ways, everything in Japan is wrapped for presentation, encoded in a hierarchy of explicit and implicit meanings, of which the Japanese language and its uses are themselves models. This gives at least superficial flexibility to a system famous for its ability to adopt with relative ease the surface features, or faces, of other cultures. Consequently, one will find no more fashion-conscious consumer in Paris or New York than the Japanese woman in Tokyo. And yet she remains, in spite of her education and surface sophistication, remarkably traditional and thus subservient in social relations with men. All of Japan's institutions and practices conspire in this. Peter Tasker, one of the most astute Western observers of Japan even asserts, "In behaviour, speech and outlook, Japanese men and women are so far apart that they seem to belong to different races."[10] The double-standard, the two faces, the *omote* and the *ura* trace the path into Japanese selflessness.

The Japanese cultural value system requires that the individual be self-less, that is, "without a self." Japan's major contribution to the world's great spiritual systems, Zen Buddhism, is animated by the same focus on utter self-discipline within which the self is enveloped in a totality which abolishes otherness. In abolishing otherness this spiritual discipline of course abolishes self as well. D.T. Suzuki, the great teacher of Zen to the West, says:

> I am in Nature and Nature is in me. Not mere participation in each other, but there is a fundamental identity between the two. [...] Identity belongs in spacial terminology. In terms of time, it is timelessness. But mere timelessness does not mean anything. When Nature is seen as confronting me, there is already time, and timelessness now turns itself into time. But time-serialism has its sense only when it goes on in the field of timelessness which is the Buddhist conception of *sunyata* ('emptiness').[11]

"Emptiness" as a value has its expression in Japanese esthetic minimalism: the grace of utterly simple flower arranging; the presentation of *sushi*; the subtle understatement of a Japanese rock garden; the elegant social symmetry of the tea ceremony; the stark beauty of calligraphy and *haiku* poetry. In contemporary Japanese film, exemplified by the mastery of Kurosawa, silence — the absence of speech — plays an important role, as it does in everyday life where, for example, in business meetings periods of silence are not the source of awkwardness that they are in the West. In traditional Japanese domestic architecture emptiness as a value is seen in the preference for voids and undesignated spaces. Static "rooms" as such are absent in traditional design and replaced with fluid spaces which merge imperceptibly into one another. Often completely unfurnished, but exquisitely appointed, spaces are separated only by mobile screens and *fusuma* sliding doors. The "individual" is an intrusion in such spaces, almost a violation of their spacial integrity. Hendry says of traditional Japanese houses:

> However, the house is designed in such a way that the inner areas appear quite distant from the outer ones, and the sliding doors appear to wrap the inner areas and protect them from the outside. Just as with language, layers of polite formality conceal (and occasionally reveal) an inner sanctum, and the nearer the outside one finds oneself, the more formal is the expected behaviour. The same applies to the formality of garments, the food consumed, and the gifts exchanged.[12]

The Japanese have a great tradition of miniaturization. The *bonsai* tree and miniature carp ("gold fish") are the best known in the West, together with miniaturized electronic products like the Sony Walkman. Another is the doll. The ancient Japanese art of doll-making has very little to do with children, though children are often given these beautiful figures as gifts. Rather, each doll is a miniature person, perfect in every detail, a model of control and self-control. As one interacts with the best of Japanese miniatures one feels empowered, and that is perhaps why toys are so popular with all children: they are one area where the child can feel in control amidst adult hierarchies. The *ura* of this sensibility of the miniature is that, like "The Incredible Shrinking Man," the ultimate fate of progressing smallness is to disappear altogether, to become ultimately self-less and "empty."

Systems which devalue individual selves tend to emphasize maintaining the esteem of others. All social systems in Japan from the family to the business enterprise promote intense interpersonal interaction and bonding. There is a great emphasis on group loyalty and solidarity, and with these values comes the possibility of the ultimate failure of those who find themselves isolated socially and psychologically. The pressures for conformity can be intense. Suicide, the ultimate self-abnegation, is a persistent problem for Japan, especially among adolescents for whom "losing face" is particularly painful. Bullying in school of youth considered outsiders for whatever reason is the often-noted reason for rising rates of juvenile suicide. Recently a number of businessmen and leading government figures died in a rash of suicides connected to the national financial crisis. The Health and Welfare Ministry reported a sharp increase of suicides among middle-aged men in 1998. 27,102 suicides in the first 10 months of 1998 represented a 38% rise over the previous year.[13]

THE HOUSE OF A JAPANESE NOBLEMAN

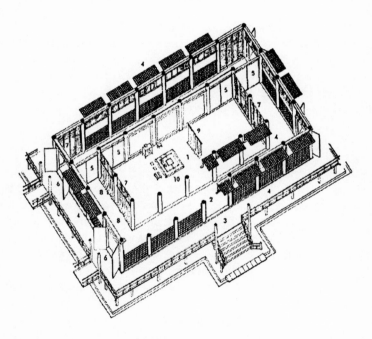

Figure 10:1 The house of a Japanese nobleman (shinden) illustrates the centrality of "wrapping," or layering which pervades Japanese culture. In this hierarchy of spaces, #1 is the principal room, or "moya," #2 is the verandah, or "hisashi," #3 is the open verandah, or "sunoko," #4 is the rail, or "shitomido." As one moves from the interior spaces to the exterior spaces, presentation becomes more formal. Interior spaces are masked by layers of screening. In all of this a process of social decoding is central to understanding various levels of openness in presentation.

Ritual suicide, *seppuku*, has an honorable history in Japanese life, making it that much more difficult a problem to address. Ironically, suicide may be the means by which the hidden and potential individual self discloses that individuality as a final act, an ultimate unwrapping. One does not have to be a Freudian to accept the notion that suicide is an essentially aggressive act, directed outward in punishment of a disrespecting world. Nothing else affects family and colleagues is such a devastating way. The death by public suicide of Japan's most famous modern novelist, Yoshio Mishima in 1970, was the end of a writing career obsessed with hidden beauty and violence, and the loss of Japanese identity in Western ways. The title of his most famous novel, *The Confessions of a Mask*, sums up both an individual life and the culture that has little place for lives lived individually. The incipient individual exists in Japan as the individual exists in human nature. Unlike the West which has provided the realm within which the individual can be actualized, Japan has provided instead the culture of suicide, which fully acknowledges the individual only in this abdication of both society and life.

One of the elements which most characterizes Japan as a traditional society is the strong role of all social hierarchies. Those based on kinship, age and gender are the most immediately obvious to an outside observer, but also to those who examine Japanese business systems. Hierarchy begins in families where the young are clearly subject to the old, women to men, and all to family obligations, especially those involving ancestors. Respect for and veneration of ancestors is a central part of filial piety, for the dead and the living are regarded as sharing the same household. Each family will have a home shrine, *butsudan,* and a neighborhood shrine, *bodaiji*, where ancestors are venerated. Family outings and other recreation are often blended with these ritual observances. During *o-ban*, that time of year when the ancestral spirits are thought to visit their kin, ritual observance is especially intense. Priests from the *bodaiji* are also continuously active elsewhere: no business would commence without its new quarters being blessed by the neighborhood *kami.*

These cultural values have deep consequences. Divorce rates, by far the lowest in the industrial world (less than 2%), reflect not happy marriages (rates of dissatisfaction within marriage are among the highest in the industrial world), but rather the strength of families, and the low status of women. Women, even those with good educations, have scarce opportunities outside the home, and there are few women in management or the higher professions. The great popularity of *manga,* especially pornographic magazines read openly, for example, by white-collar workers on the subway, with no sense of shame, indicates the depth of the casual disregard of women as full partners. That rape is one of the most persistent themes of these omnipresent sex "comics," the final sexual expression of bodies as machines, is even more disturbing to many observers. Lasker makes the following troubled appraisal of Japanese popular culture: "The fact remains that there is a huge market in Japan for images of human damage and defilement. There is even a goulish genre of popular movie which specializes in the compilation of documentary footage of executions, torture and air crashes."[14] The *ura* of this *omote* is that actual levels of violence, and crime in general, are low in Japan. The streets of big cities are safe and the use of private security guards is rare. The Japanese emphasis on discipline, order and subjection of the self to the social good make Japan's urban context livable, especially for women, in a way it is not, for example, in many American cities.

Contemporary Japanese cities are not really cities at all. Rather, they are layered accretions of overlapping kin-based neighborhoods, where people live for generations in highly localized settings. Housing is crowded, often cheaply built, and infrastructure such as sewage and utilities astonishingly primitive for "modern" cities. The often-haphazard plans of Japanese cities; the irrational system for numbering addresses; their twisted, congested streets; their lack of zoning and garish impression demonstrate a fundamental indifference to urban values approached in the West only in newer cities like Houston. In these urban villages it is not unusual for a Japanese family to have a dozen relatives within five minutes walk of the family shrine. Most goods are bought from local retailers in very small family-owned stores, which have strong followings. Everything from municipal swimming pools to subway cars is densely, almost claustrophobically crowded.

Interpersonal relations are central to all of life at every level in Japan. But Japan is far from a "mobile" society in Lerner's terms. Not only do people live in the same neighborhoods for a life-time, shopping at the same stores, attending the same schools and seeing the same neighbors, Japanese typically also work in the same environments for life with the same employer. During the medieval period, Japan was characterized by *han*, systems of loyalty in which a lord and his castle(s) were self-sufficient economies of farmers, craftsmen and warriors. (Interestingly, the Japanese character for "han" is the same as the Chinese character for "mandarin," underlining the mandarin-samurai parallel.) The modern counterpart of the *han* is the *keiretsu*.

❖ ❖ ❖ ❖

The *keiretsu* is a system of corporate organization which is simultaneously a business and a social system. Kuniyasu Sakai says that, "*Keiretsu* are the ultimate force in Japanese industry."[15] Centered around a bank or banks which hold controlling shares in an array of companies, which in turn hold shares in each other, this system of industrial feudalism is hierarchical and role conscious. Each person and each firm knows its place in what is really a tributary hierarchy. The very formal (and very important) practice of exchanging business cards before meetings, and exchanging beautifully-wrapped gifts afterward, are just two of the means of confirming role and status upon which the whole system depends. They symbolize the *system* of gift-giving at the heart of Japanese social relations. Business cards do not identify individuals, they identify role and position in a hierarchy of relations: who reports to the person and to whom he reports. Gifts symbolize the on-going system of mutuality which business relations bring into being. Ian Reader says, "This matrix of reciprocity, of creating obligations, receiving benevolence and responding with gratitude mirrors standard social relationships within Japanese society in general, where gift-giving and the creation and repayment of obligations have long been important."[16]

The role of contractors and sub-contractors in this system of interwoven business relationships is typically Japanese. A firm which is a member of a *keiretsu* is expected to be loyal. It will buy and sell only within the *keiretsu* organization. It will pay higher prices if necessary to deal with a fellow *keiretsu* supplier. If one of its buyers needs to be supplied at lower profit margins (or in some cases, no profit) so that its own prices can be kept low in competitive markets, it is expected to be accommodated. Sakai asserts: "From the day a subcontractor accepts the first contract — probably from a small subsidiary of one of the giant companies — it has given up its freedom. It is told what to make, when to put it on line, and how much it will get for it on delivery."[17] These critical intercompany sales have all the characteristics of primal gift-giving. They are intended to reduce risks, competition and conflict; to build long-term ties of kin-like loyalty and interdependence; and to ensure the prosperity of the group as a whole. This system of hierarchy in which the individual is subordinated to his firm and his firm subordinated to its industrial "clan" reflects classically traditional modes of thought and practice. It is yet another form of organizational "wrapping."

These tradition-based economic relationships mean that the typical Japanese almost never encounters a real market. Often the house in which he lives has been passed on for generations, or his apartment is provided/subsidized by his employer as a reward for life-time loyalty. He and his family may be treated in a company clinic, and his children may attend a company school. Many companies arrange social dating and marriages for employees, and supervisors are honored attendees at weddings. If a Japanese owns a car he is usually expected to buy from a firm affiliated with his *kieretsu*, and many firms do not allow competitive brands in their parking lots. Only goods produced within the *kieretsu* are served at his company's functions.

When he goes to his local shops, the prices will reflect an elaborate system of distribution in which each level adds its own mark-up to the price. There are 1.62 million "mom-and-pop" shops and small distributors in Japan employing 6 million people. Shops with one or two employees account for 57% of all retail outlets. The law gives neighborhood shopkeepers a veto over new stores of more than 500 square metres.[18] Goods circulate largely through these "gift circles" in which one deals only with certain suppliers and in turn is assured of a regular supply of goods to sell at a mark-up. The large number of distribution levels (and mark-ups) a good may have to pass through before it reaches the customer is no measure of efficiency, let alone of competitive markets, but rather of the great value the system puts on solidarity, including full-employment, within hierarchical relations.

As a sort of "selfless capitalism" the Japanese distribution system is yet another example of complex wrapping or layering, the retail sale a final wrapping of an elaborate system of gift-giving. The price of food staples is influenced by these same principles, which attach legitimacy to distributive relations to the degree that everyone benefits from them. Rice, the Japanese protein staple, sells at ten times the world price because foreign rice cannot be imported. Similar restrictions are placed on beef and fruit imports. The Japanese state sees its legitimacy and prestige to be intimately tied to the distribution of food staples: a well-publicized event each year is the planting of the first rice of the season in a paddy of the Imperial Palace by the Emperor himself. Consumers thus pay prices which reflect not competition but cooperation, and the government sees its role as the guarantor of the food supply (and the livelihood of farmers) to be central, as in any traditional society. Japanese consumer products typically cost much more in Japanese stores, where competition is strongly muted, than in American stores where prices usually reflect competition. Japanese tourists in Hawaii, for example, typically spend a good part of their stay buying Japanese-made gifts in local stores where they sell at a fraction of their prices in Japan. As in any traditional society there are deep and formal tensions between the producers of wealth and its distributors.

Finally, the place of "kleptocracy," which we have noted often occupies a semi-legitimate status in pre-modern societies, should be especially noted. Organized crime is pervasive and plays a role in Japan comparable to that of the

Mafia in some big American cities, which with their poor and immigrant populations are in their own ways "pre-civil." Construction, the largest industry in Japan, is suffused with "corruption." The line between legitimate business and what is really crime is often a hazy one in Japan precisely because civil institutions are both weak and formal. The Japanese term *sodenoshita* is rooted in the ancient practices of extortion and bribery, which go back to the era of the Shogunate. The public and private spheres, distinguished by law and civil institutions in the West, are indistinguishable in Japan, and thus "corruption" — both "public" and "private" — is a way of life, made all the more compatible because of the importance of gift-giving in traditional sociality. The fluidity of goods supplements the immobility of people as in all pre-modern societies.

NOTES TO CHAPTER TEN

1. Quoted in Kenneth B. Pyle, THE NEW GENERATION IN MEIJI JAPAN (Stanford: Stanford University Press, 1969), p. 31
2. Fernand Braudel, THE WHEELS OF COMMERCE, Vol. 2, Sian Reynolds, trans. (New York: Harper & Row, 1986), p. 588
3. de Rougemont, *op.cit.*, p. 11
4. Ray T. Donahue, JAPANESE CULTURE AND COMMUNICATION (Lanham, MD: University Press of America, 1998), p. 298
5. Ian Reader, RELIGION IN CONTEMPORARY JAPAN (Honolulu: University of Hawaii Press, 1991), p. 16; Robert N. Bellah has discussed this situational practice element of Japanese religion and its parallels to the Western Protestant "work ethic" in TOKUGAWA RELIGION (New York: The Free Press, 1985)
6. Peter Tasker, THE JAPANESE (New York: E.P. Dutton, 1988), p. 66
7. Joy Hendry, WRAPPING CULTURE (Oxford: Clarendon Press, 1995)
8. Doi Takeo, "Dependency in Human Relationships," in Daniel I. Okimoto and Thomas P. Rohlen, INSIDE THE JAPANESE SYSTEM (Stanford: Stanford University Press, 1988), pp. 22-23
9. Cf. Donahue, *op.cit.*, p. 14 ff; and Geert T. Hofstede, CULTURE'S CONSEQUENCES (Beverly Hills, CA: Sage Publications, 1980).
10. Tasker, *op.cit.*, p. 100
11. Daisetz T. Suzuki, "The Role of Nature in Zen Buddhism," in H. Byron Earhart, RELIGION IN THE JAPANESE EXPERIENCE (Belmont: Wadsworth Publishing Company, 1974) pp. 133-134
12. Hendry, *op.cit.*, p. 100
13. "Japanese Suicides Rise Dramatically," SAN FRANCISCO EXAMINER (March 18, 1999), p. B12
14. Tasker, *op.cit.*, p. 120

15. Kuniyasu Sakai, "The Feudal World of Japanese Manufacturing," HARVARD BUSINESS REVIEW (November-December 1990), p. 8
16. Reader, *op.cit.*, p. 27
17. Sakai, *op.cit.*, p. 6
18. Liam T. Ziemba and Sandra L. Schwartz, POWER JAPAN (Chicago: Probus Publishing, 1992), p. 342. Recently the American warehouse store, Toys R Us, took advantage of deregulation to build a number of giant stores, which quickly eliminated all small toy retailers in their areas.

CHAPTER ELEVEN

THE WAY OF *WA*

Japanese management practices reflect the traditional world I have described. The *kaisha* (company) functions less as a corporate entity and more as a family. Nakane Chie, a social anthropologist, says, "The term *kaisha* (company) symbolizes the expression of group consciousness. *Kaisha* does not mean that individuals are bound by contractual relationships into a corporate enterprise, while still thinking of themselves as separate entities; rather, kaisha is "my" or "our" company, the community to which one belongs primarily and which is all-important in one's life. Thus, in most cases, the company provides the whole social context of a person and has authority over all aspects of his life; he is deeply emotionally involved in the association."[1]

The *kaisha* may function in many ways like a family, but its source lies in another direction. The family as a kin group, and the *house* as a "name" group were distinguished in Japan. *Koseki-ho*, or Law of House registration of the Meiji period, reflected this ancient distinction between "blood" and "name." G. B. Sansom describes the *house* as "composed of the head of the House and of members who are subject to his authority. Those members may include not only his kindred by relationship of blood, but also persons, male and female, who are not his blood relations and who enter the House with his consent. The House is in fact a name group and not a blood group, and its purpose is the continuation of ancestor worship."[2] A central functional aspect of Japanese practice, ancestor veneration, became the basis for functional organization, the house, which often sustained itself by admitting new members, "strangers."

Property rights in this system were vested in the house and its head, not in individuals. In this sense, Japan's conceptions were like those of many other traditional societies in Asia, wealth being understood in a collective rather than individual manner. Property relations and interpersonal relations were seamlessly blended in house organization. At the same time, because the house had an artificial element (recall the *demes* of Kleisthenes' Athens) similar to the evolution of Western corporate culture (*supra* Chap. 6) it could be more flexible in its organization than, for example, the kin-based trading house elsewhere in Asia. It was possible to more easily layer Western concepts of law and of the individual person upon such a system. Thus, when new law codes were introduced in the Meiji period, the institutionalization of private property rights in individuals, so important to the development of a modern market economy, was an easier step for the Japanese to take. But there was an added tension between the individual and his group in such arrangements arising from the adoption of Western concepts. And thus perhaps the most notable feature of the new Civil Code was "that while in matters of function it made no significant changes in the prevailing family system, in regard to property it was obliged to approach very closely to Western practices."[3] The Japanese emphasis on *wa* (harmony) in management practices recognizes these tensions, as does the emphasis on putting on the "right face," adaptive behavior suitable to the situation.

Employment in Japan is typically for life, and most people begin employment with a firm — their house — in their youth and stay until retirement. Dismissal is almost unheard of, expelling someone from his job being the equivalent of expelling someone from his family or his village. The Japanese adhere to Radin's definition of primal livelihood: "the irreducible minimum." Unproductive employees become "window men;" they are not fired but shifted to the side to spend their time in relative idleness, staring out the window and enduring the shame associated with their situation. As in traditional societies in general, labor is known in a way that work is not. Japanese white-collar workers evidence a level of stress and job dissatisfaction which is among the highest in the industrial world. Employees are expected to arrive at work early and stay late. Working conditions are relatively primitive. Surprisingly, there are few personal computers, and desks are typically piled high with papers (*kami*). Managers are expected to work overtime as a matter of course, and not to use fully vacation time. Many white collar workers visit home only on weekends. On weeknights they stay in "capsule" hotels, which are little more than layered sleeping cells. The term "salary man" (*sarariiman*) suggests a kind of futile managerial serfdom in Japan where there are few opportunities for creative, innovative challenges in diverse environments.

What exists is rigidity within a low-risk and secure environment, as in any traditional labor force. In industrial environments and in many service environments (like department stores) all workers wear company uniforms. Workers bow deeply to supervisors, and in factories the day begins with regimented physical exercises and the singing of the company song. Even in corporate environments group exercise breaks are not unusual. Labor unions typically function as adjuncts to management; contention between workers and management, seen as normal and even healthy in the US, is regarded as a threat to harmony in Japan. But there is also a dark underside to this social cohesion as it confronts the realities of global competition. Unable to abandon the cultural commitment to life-time employment, employers have begun to use psychological and social pressure to force resignations. *Chinmoku no kotoba*, or "silent language," is used more frequently to bully employees to leave their jobs on their own. This includes such tactics as sending employees to remote sites far from their families, to being deliberately ignored by fellow workers, to disconnecting their telephones. In one case, the human resources officer of a major software company hanged himself because he could not bear the bullying any longer. He had resisted the laying off of workers he considered competent and loyal. When his daughter filed a law-suit against her father's employer, her husband gathered all the relatives, including the widow, to pressure his wife to drop the case. Psychiatrist Keizo Takagi says that managers know that bullying is unethical, but do not know of any other way to get workers to resign, given the constraints of the lifetime employment system.[4]

Whatever stigma the mercantile world may have in Japan is so encased in traditional *samurai* concepts of hierarchy, loyalty and collective exertion that it is muted indeed. Thus the typical Japanese manager does not have a career in the sense that many in the West do. He has few individual goals, and little of the mobility necessary to achieve them. His time and life-goals are not scheduled to an agenda which reflects his own desire for a "personal best." His advancement, keyed to age and seniority and based on his performance in a group, ties him to both a calendar and a hierarchy which have little in common with most Western corporations. Indeed, the Japanese firm has about it all the qualities usually associated with the military.

Even Japanese business schools, a relatively new and not widespread phenomenon, begin their training of managers with the classics of military strategy. Phrases like "frontal attack" and "encirclement" characterize published Japanese business strategy papers. It was in fact the *samurai*, the traditional warrior class, who founded the post-1868 economy, and it is this which may account for its character and scale. The small, traditional commercial class in Japan was notoriously fractured among themselves when modernization began. The *samurai*, more mobile, with commanding values of duty and loyalty, and used to functioning within non-kin hierarchies, largely displaced the original merchant class and its petty values, applying military values to industrial organization. The military class never played such a pivotal role in the development of other national economies. Some of the greatest names in Japanese industry are those of *samurai* families.

Because stocks in major companies are largely held within individual business groups, Japanese companies, including banks, have not been much interested in maximizing profits, which of course is a more risky strategy. The very high debt loads in both the Japanese public and private sectors are consequently less reflective of risk-taking than of kin-like mutual confidence between and among people who pursue long-term business goals. Leveraging represents solidarity as much as any weighing of the "debt-equity decision." Building market-share is consequently the typical strategy of the Japanese firm in entering or competing in markets. Market-share strategies emphasize the maximization of revenues rather than profits, and indeed, it is not surprising that in recent decades Japanese firms have had the lowest return on investment (ROI) among major industrial countries. But they have had the largest growth in market-share. Market share is a measure of power: to the degree that a firm controls markets it begins to control other actors within them, like suppliers and their prices, retailers and their mark-ups, as well as prevailing payable and receivable terms and banking relations. When a Japanese manager asks another about the market share in the industry his firm holds, he is asking a question parallel to that of a *samurai* who wishes to know how many castles another's master has: these are measures of power. Market-share strategies are also risk-avoiding strategies: ways in which to avoid unpredictable competition on an on-going basis.

It should be noted that Japanese concepts of strategy are significantly different than those found in the West. The primal allocentrism of Japanese thought makes the abstract and linear concepts of strategy so often found in the West nearly incomprehensible. Richard T. Pascale has asserted that, "The Japanese have particular discomfort with strategic concepts." Rather, Japanese management concepts emphasize the pragmatic, situational and intuitive, with "peripheral vision" as "essential to discerning changes in the customer."[5] This means that Japanese firms are much more comfortable with pursuing what might seem like inconsistent policies, pragmatically learning and adapting as they go, in contrast to Western firms which tend to favor rationality and consistency. In short, the Japanese do not *mediate* the environment in formal organizational ways to the degree that Westerners do, and view intuitive encounter, especially interpersonally, in business matters as both useful and culturally congenial.

The conservatism of the Japanese cultural temper also affects individual motivation. In turn for security and fewer personal risks, individuals are expected to be loyal and to be paid on the basis of seniority rather than performance. Japanese pay scales place the individual worker within a system where, for instance, a CEO is typically paid only seventeen times as much as a skilled worker. This is about one tenth the discrepancy in the United States. Interactions with one's fellows emphasize the group. Promotion, like compensation, is based on age. It would be unthinkable for an older man to report to a younger man. Retirement at age fifty-five is typical precisely because age-inappropriate supervisory situations become a greater possibility as longer service and a tapering management pyramid have their effects. All of these elements, from the flattened salary pyramid to the role of seniority have their parallels in military systems in the West.

There are few private offices in Japan. Managers sit side by side at desks and tables in large rooms without partitions. Everyone is in the sight of everyone else. There is no privacy, and in fact the indigenous Japanese language lacked a word for it: *praibashii* was adopted directly from English. Japanese meetings can seem interminably long because decision is by consensus. The role of a manager is to bring about this consensus through long discussions at work, and many hours of socializing three or four nights a week after work. The language of meetings is high-context and indirect, or "wrapped." One would never say "no" because this both creates tension and tends to assert individuals. The sovereignty of *wa* is ever present. Issues are discussed and rediscussed, each level of discussion subtly, almost inadvertently unwrapping dissent or agreement which must be addressed. Shintaro Ishihara says, "For many cultural reasons, Japanese are not used to free-wheeling debate. Uncomfortable in confrontational situations, we try to avoid a clash of opinions."[6] A *ringi* document is circulated in working groups to which each member assents with his personal character stamp only when consensus has been reached. The circulation of *ringi* documents on *kami* (paper/spirit) once again recalls the spiritual bonding of gift-giving. This process means that decisions may take a long time to reach, but once they are reached individuals are disinclined to interfere with their execution.

It is consequently a system that does not promote innovation. Where Japanese products have been successful in world markets it is largely in those areas where technology and ideas are borrowed from abroad, and then incrementally improved, or wrapped, through superior quality control in manufacturing. Thus Japan produces excellent computer hard-ware, but has not been nearly as competitive in soft-ware development, where innovation and rapid adaptation to changed conditions is essential. Similarly, Japan is highly successful in the production of automobiles, but lags in pharmaceuticals. If one conceives of manufacturing as a process of layering, and superior manufacturing as exceptional skill at enfolding components within one another, one can appreciate the cultural bases of Japanese manufacturing excellence. But if one thinks of creativity as the processes by which dissimilar elements are brought into tension with each other, the playful element necessary to experimental success, one can understand why Japanese culture does not support genuine creativity. It has been noted that Japanese baseball players and musicians have a similar problem — they over-practice, developing rote skill levels far in advance of individual levels of creative performance. The creativity which we have identified with the playful element in human consciousness is always tied to the embrace of risk: whether in performance or intellectual inquiry. Conservative, risk-averse strategies such as rote learning or the obsessive perfection of technique tend to undermine creativity.

As in other traditional societies, roles are more important than individuals. Japanese corporate leaders are noted for being colorless. They achieve their positions by standing out not as individuals with ideas, but as careful consensus builders who are rigorous in their observance of formality and decorum. Like the Mandarin or military leader, they are masters of a system to which they have belonged since initiating their employment. They sit rigidly upright in armchairs at meetings, like hereditary princes upon their thrones, impressive not because of what they say, because they say little, but because of the way they embody the legitimacy of the system. Important business decisions are initiated at the middle levels of this "ringi" system: it is here that all the influences which shape the system converge. This also separates the top leadership from responsibility for the results of conflict or failure. In a system of life-time tenure in the firm, the top leadership is protected, as it must be because in the hierarchy full responsibility rests at the top. When hundreds of people were killed a few years ago in a plane crash, the president of the airline took full responsibility, resigned his position, and spent the following year visiting the families of the deceased personally to apologize.

The Japanese economic system thus has more in common with a traditional society than a contemporary Western one. The most competitive markets in which they engage are not Japanese, but global markets. And they are often successful in these markets by strategies such as "dumping" goods at below cost prices to achieve market share and drive out competition. One result of this is that Japan has very large and persistent imbalances of trade with every area in which it trades. In a sense, in an echo of traditional China, Japan gives more than it receives. Like a traditional Confucian tributary system, the Japanese send more goods than they receive in return as the price for domination of markets. Japanese leadership is often proud to the point of arrogance that they dominate markets and sell to the world more than they buy. Japanese consumers are penalized for this imbalance because, in return for economic security, they pay very high domestic prices to subsidize this tributary system. This system has not yet collapsed, like the ancient Chinese one, because global trading has something the fifteenth century did not: fiduciary money. Japan can fund these huge and persistent outflows of wealth by accumulating wealth in foreign currencies like the dollar (principally in low-risk bond and real estate purchases) to balance the ledger, at least on paper, at least in the short run. But in the long run, precisely because the very values of traditional Japanese society hinder its full incorporation into the global economic system, Japan may not be able to function without a basic cultural transformation. The bursting of this "bubble economy" in the late 'eighties has caused major economic dislocations which have persisted, but which have not yet even begun to undercut the cultural bases of the system.

If the Japanese are typical of traditional societies in living remotely from real markets, they are also remote from the state, which is powerful in its role in providing economic security for society as a whole. The organs of government, especially the Ministry of Finance, the Ministry of International Trade and Industry, and the Bank of Japan have played critical roles in Japan's industrial policy. These organs of government are in turn closely allied with business centers through organizations like the Keidanren (Federation of Economic Organizations) and the ruling Liberal Democratic Party. The Japanese term *kokutai*, which translates as "imperial polity," summarizes a hierarchy, or layering of relationships public and private with the Emperor at the top. It suggests that Japan is one extended kinship system, a great family, whose global economic expression is "Japan, Inc."

Japan is formally a democracy and apparently a civil society. There are elections within a constitutional framework, a legislature, and there are independent courts, and organs of opinion are free and there are numerous corporate organizations. But these accouterments of civility are primarily superficial. Civil society is only the surface, two-dimensional wrapping of an underlying system dominated by primal and traditional modes. "For over a quarter of a century," asserts Karel von Wolferen, of the Institute for Independent Japanese Studies, "informed Japanese and foreigners alike have readily expressed doubts about the authenticity of Japanese democracy."[7] The same political party effectively always wins elections and has been in power since the end of the American occupation in 1951. The press is remarkably unanimous, and through "press clubs" often serves as a mouthpiece for the political and economic establishment. Real power lies in the bureaucracy, which is not elected at all. Courts exist, but people hesitate to use them because they violate *wa*, and to sue is to lose face. Tanaka Hideo asserts, "Put simply, many matters in Western nations that are dealt with within the framework of the regular machinery of law are left in Japan to work themselves out outside this machinery. This peculiarity has been pointed out time and again by lawyers from foreign countries while visiting in Japan."[8]

The number of civil suits per capita in Japan is about 5% the rate in the United States. There are only about ten thousand practicing lawyers in Japan, fewer than in a large American city. Contracts are formal, and suits over them are rare. In Japan, as in any traditional society, what is important is personal interface and social connection — on-going context. Carolyn Hotchkiss summarizes: "To Westerners, contracts define rights and duties of the parties; to Japanese, contracts express the nature of the business relationship."[9] Japanese firms prefer to deal exclusively with their own suppliers, even at higher prices, because bonds of trust have been carefully built and cultivated with them. The American firm which hopes to penetrate Japan's dense layering as a supplier, feeling a superior product at a good price and an "iron-clad" contract is sufficient, soon realizes the Japanese play to a very different script.

Japanese modernity is more apparent than real. It was not even apparent in terms of standards of living only a generation ago. In this respect the historical precedent of Russia is instructive. Visitors to Russia in the early nineteenth century were amazed at the beauty and luxury of the capital, St.Petersburg. Some described this city, founded by the modernizer Peter the Great as a "window on the West," as the most magnificent city in Europe. Its formal boulevards and great squares lined with Italianate palaces and cathedrals designed by some of Europe's great architects and planners gave Russian life a most contemporary appearance. Its fashionable elite spoke exquisite French and cultivated cosmopolitan tastes. Yet below the surface of this contemporaneity was a backward, traditional society rooted in the conservative countryside. Similarly, in the nineteen sixties some commentators, impressed by such accomplishments as the Soviet space program, said that Russia, under communism, was evolving into a pre-eminent world superpower, even evolving toward a form of social democracy. Yet, as events have proven, the underbelly of Russia was the same backward system of primitive markets and an authoritarian state as had prevailed for centuries under different guises.

Having failed to make the critical transitions to civil society which is the irreducible basis for modernity, the USSR superficially mimicked the West with meaningless parliaments and elections, empty constitutions and courts, and a patina of sophistication only inches deep. Russia's isolation from the world throughout most of its history, with occasional "revolutions from above" motivated by the desire to "catch up" with the West for reasons of national security, undermined its ability to adapt to contemporary circumstances. Whenever it even approached a true cultural transformation, it returned, after a period of turbulence, to a closed, traditional character. Immemorial cultural responses invariably reasserted themselves. In many ways Japan is as isolated from the world as Russia has been historically. Japan has paid for that xenophobic isolation by first building a highly militarized and aggressive state, and when that failed in the ashes of World War II, with an economic tributary system which really doesn't integrate the Japanese economy fully into the global one, but in fact keeps the world at a distance.

The case of Japan is interesting because it highlights the important role of intellectuals in bringing about or resisting cultural change. Intellectuals in most societies have functioned at the boundaries of cultural value systems with their underlying forces in the realms of economics, politics and technology. As societies face change it has historically been the role of intellectuals to guide social values in the direction of various degrees of accommodation or resistance to change. Edgar Morin states: "The intellectual emerges from a cultural base and with a socio-political role (cultural in this context is defined as a self-conscious concern with cultural dimensions).... Thus the intellectual can be defined from a triple set of dimensions: (1) a profession that is culturally validated, (2) a role that is socio-political, (3) a consciousness that relates to universals."[10] It is this self-conception in relation to universals that poses the critical issue for intellectuals in relation to change. Any change to a relatively coherent system of cultural values poses the problem of relativization. To what extent can norms be modified without undermining a normative system's integrity? In the field of religion, for example, to what degree can the findings of science be allowed to affect doctrinal teaching? The responses can range from "fundamentalist": a denial of the truth or relevance of the scientific finding, to "reformed": science may be accommodated in various degrees by altering or even abolishing particular doctrines. The danger of the fundamentalist position is that adherents may become more isolated from the mainstream of a changing society. The danger of the reformed position is that values may become so diluted over time that they are indistinguishable from other modes of thought.

Intellectuals often have a personal and institutional interest in maintaining the *status quo*. Particularly in traditional societies where intellectuals have functioned as priests/scribes in close association with other centers of power, a challenge to prevailing values becomes, in effect, a challenge to the distribution of material and symbolic goods, including those flowing to intellectuals themselves. And more subtlely, challenges to prevailing intellectual values can be a challenge to intellect itself, its importance and its value to society. When values which have their origins in commerce, for example, begin to affect society, they may begin to undermine values which have their origins in speculation. Commercial values which emphasize pragmatism, material reward and risk-taking, what we have called "the mobile imagination," can result in a kind of philistinism which mocks the abstract, the formal or the artful. Thus, anti-intellectualism can result from the very nature of a commercially-oriented society. This conflict between intellect and practice in commercial societies is as old as the Greeks. We have seen how, with few exceptions, whatever other differences most Greek thinkers had among themselves, they shared a distaste for "trade" and the values coming from it. They tended to support the aristocratic values of traditional society.

Shils has described what he calls a "constitutive orientation...toward the sacred," among intellectuals.[11] Richard Hofstadter associates intellectuals with "piety."[12] This infers the intellectual's traditional functions as priest, scribe and prophet. But it points to something else as well. It is in the "I-Thou" modes that we have located the spiritual and the sacred. Intellect is in this dimension rooted in the primal sensibilities, and in this sense every "primitive" is a kind of intellectual in his fundamental disposition toward the world as a place of wonder, infused with the spiritual. As the primal and traditional realms where shaman and priest play central roles are eclipsed by civil society, intellect itself is torn in two directions. One direction affirms the past with its focus on the sacred and the communal, while another, more empirical strand emerges to rationally engage the world, always risking what has been formulated in order to find more complete answers.

The modern intellectual often finds that he must make choices between what are, in effect, reactionary and revolutionary elements in his temper. These choices are hard to make because it is often difficult to distinguish between what is revolutionary and what is reactionary. Was Karl Marx a revolutionary in his insistence on a "scientific" view of society, which must inevitably be radically altered into historically new forms? Or was Marx in fact only a traditional intellectual, protesting in an ancient manner against commercial society, and calling for a return to a normative order where essentially non-material values would reign? The case could be made that revolutions led by intellectuals like Lenin or Mao, Castro or Khomeini inevitably return society to a kind of traditional order ruled by a new class of Mandarins, suspicious of change and insistent on doctrinal orthodoxy. Peter Nettl's dictum, "As modernity advances, the intellectual retreats,"[13] seems to apply. This may explain why modernization in the West, and to a limited extent in Japan, took the forms that it did.

The feudal period in Europe fragmented political power, even when the vision of a "Holy Roman Empire" attempted to reassert universalism. Secular power and spiritual power were likewise fragmented, with various degrees of tension and conflict between the universal Catholic church and local, political authorities in Europe. During the Reformation even this universal spiritual power was fragmented between Catholics and Protestants, and within the various sects of Protestantism. The result was that at the end of the Middle Ages traditional intellectual elites in Europe, almost exclusively clerical in nature, faced increasing competition from ideas and values coming from other social classes, and associated with contending sources of political and economic power. It is thus probably not accidental that the emerging commercial culture of Europe reached its highest flowering in northern Europe. It was here that the universal church was most weakened, and that political power was most fragmented. The emerging commercial classes were able to evolve a counterculture to the aristocratic, hierarchical order which characterized Medieval thought and practice. Lay intellectuals, often closely associated with the needs of merchant societies, attached themselves to more pragmatic, empirical paradigms which ushered in the "scientific revolution" of the seventeenth century.

The seventeenth-century Netherlands, divided between Catholics and Protestants, the Empire and local princes, aristocrats and merchants, and dispersed into a number of semi-independent cities, was an incubator of the kind of tolerance within which intellectual civility could thrive. In the course of the seventeenth and eighteenth centuries, many of these same factors underlay the rise of the intellectual civility we associate with figures like

Newton, Locke, Smith and Mill in Britain. Standing at further remove from traditional aristocratic elites, intellectuals in northern Europe had to strike out on their own. More separated from both religious and secular power (and thus able to criticize them), they also enjoyed their own institutions (particularly the university and the scientific academy) and the patronage of a commercial elite. In short, unlike intellectual elites in societies like China, which merged their institutions and those of the states they dominated, western intellectuals created a civil culture of their own, apart from, but in dialogue with the larger society. Within that civil culture they created an environment of inquiry and debate relatively open to new ideas, which then could be instrumentalized in the larger culture. Adam Smith and his colleagues played this role in the momentous events associated with the industrial revolution in Britain. Elsewhere in Europe, intellectuals were often either coopted by the state, or were alienated from it, as in eighteenth century France, and their thought tended to have a Platonic, disengaged quality more interested in abstract principle than in actual practice, and consequently more subject to polemical rhetoric.[14]

The experience of Japanese intellectuals more closely parallels that of intellectuals in northern Europe than that of intellectuals in places like traditional Egypt, China or India. Japanese formulations of social thought, particularly in its religious dimension, were never as universalistic as in, for example, China. The Chinese Mandarins had evolved a highly systematized and universalistic conception of humanity in its relations to society as a whole. The Confucian canons were never seriously doubted or even significantly altered to fit changing circumstances. The lack of an empirical bent was the Confucian intellectual's sovereign trait. Joseph R. Levenson says: "If Chinese in modern times have been forced to wonder where science belongs in their heritage, it is not because their forbearers were constitutionally unable to nurture a growing tradition in science, but because they did not care to; early Ch'ing empiricists were not aiming at science and falling short, but living out the values of their culture. There can be no presumptuous western question of 'failure' in Chinese civilization — only recognition of a Chinese taste for a style of culture not the style of the modern West, nor of modern China."[15]

It was precisely the elegant degree of integration which Confucian thought had achieved in many centuries of superb civilization which made it difficult to change without the attendant risk of ultimate disintegration. The Mandarin class saw its social role as inextricably tied to an unalterable conservatism in thought and practice. The tragedy of Chinese history over the past two centuries can be tied to the canonized harmony of this deeply conservative tradition which chose deliberately to ignore the global threats to China's very existence. "A whole pattern of cultural preferences held together," asserts Levenson, "all appropriate to one another and to a specific social order, which was to fall into jeopardy soon."[16]

Japan's history of feudalism and various degrees of isolation never produced a class of intellectuals standing at the apex of a unified social system as in China. In Japan the *samurai* class was the "class apart" with its own privileges. They served not only the national regime, but regional lords as well. The military was one of the four officially recognized classes in Tokugowa times, and these *samurai* had to value discipline and loyalty more than intellectual purity if they were to serve various masters. Japanese thought thus had a pragmatism about it quite different from the experience of China, from which many Confucian ideals were borrowed. Japanese intellectual arts, such as poetry and theater, were inseparable from the *samurai* code of discipline, with its fundamentally pragmatic outlook. Nor did Japan ever fully develop a universalistic religio-philosophical system such as Confucianism. Rather, Japanese thought and experience were more pragmatically influenced by a number of spiritual and intellectual systems, of which Buddhism and Confucianism, introduced from China, were only two.

This proliferation of "useful" cults is something which characterizes Japan even today. *Nicheren Shoshu*, one of the cults founded in this century which has gained adherents in the United States, requires no formal "belief." Rather, adherents chant for desired real goods, like romance or money, the reward for correct practice. The various priesthoods, Shinto and Buddhist, in Japan were more connected to individual religious sites and practices than to any formal dogma, and individual Japanese, whether at home or at other shrines, have felt able to function without priestly services. Deeply personal and pragmatic in these matters, Japanese have not depended on authoritative sources. Unlike the traditions of Egypt and China, which moved beyond direct, primal modes of religious expression into institutionalized traditional modes, Japanese piety has remained essential primal. And at some important levels, Japanese piety is deeply personal and existential: various modes of Buddhist spirituality such as *Zen* demonstrate that and separate Japanese experience from Chinese experience in this important aspect. Thus, the distinctly priestly or scribal sources of traditional intellect never developed fully in Japan. "The Japanese religious world is not separate from the general flow of life, but an intrinsic part thereof, upholding, strengthening and giving sustenance to it."[17]

Because there was no unified intellectual class in Japan in the same senses as in Egypt or China, institutionalized and closely associated with a centralized system of power, there was not the same resistance to change. Change could occur in Japan, at least formally, without impinging on sacred doctrines or the privileges of a class of *literati* charged with preserving them. Japanese intellectuals, most from *samurai* or even merchant backgrounds, from the time of the Meiji Restoration at the end of the nineteenth century were able, to various degrees, integrate elements of Western intellectual achievement, such as the civil law code, into Japanese practice. This in turn only illustrates what Parsons has defined as "the widespread, intensive and extensive specialization" in cultural matters which has defined the modern West.[18]

Unlike intellectuality in pre-modern cultures, such as China, where scholars were defined by their focus in a body of wisdom literature, modern Western thinkers used scientific inquiry as the basis for economic, legal, linguistic, anthropological and other sorts of knowledge. The relatively late development of a centralized civil service in Japan, at the same time as western-style universities in the post-1868 period, placed the modern Japanese intellectual in a context where he was associated with modernization itself, and all the sorts of intellectual enterprises connected with it. Indeed, to the degree the Japanese were very aware of their important national enterprise, catching up with the West, numbers of intellectuals tended to *identify* themselves with change as essential to national renewal. In this way their experience paralleled to some extent that of their Western counterparts in the seventeenth and eighteenth centuries, who often saw themselves in the *avant garde* of social change.

This was not without its ambiguities. As in Russia during the same period, intellectuals sometimes divided them selves into "Westerners" and "Slavophiles," or in the case of Japanese intellectuals into "Westerners" and "Nipponophiles." Was it possible for Japan to modernize without losing its cultural soul? How they answered this question was often a function of what Andrew Barshay has called "insider" or "outsider" status. The insider was a "new man," who combined in himself a transformed psychology and a technological orientation. The intellectual technocrat was a *shi* (or samurai) whose character made him fit to rule on the basis of his superior expertise. Barshay summarizes: "The West never ceased to be the bearer of models of power and of culture to modern Japan. But, as we have seen, the development of national institutions for the training of experts and the dissemination of their knowledge brought with it a sense of distinction between insider and outsider in public questions."[19] Among intellectual insiders embracing a "Western" consciousness was given concrete form in the ability to affect decisions of public consequence, and thus was valued. Among outsiders, Western culture was often viewed and embraced, if at all, with suspicion and a sense of personal and cultural disenfranchisement. Once again, the two faces of Japan confront the outside observer: the *ura* and the *omote*.

✧ ✧ ✧ ✧

Since the Meiji Restoration in 1868 Japan has been concerned with the conflicted relations between the West and its own culture. Its response to the powerful forces of globalization which overwhelmed its Asian neighbors was to initiate a process of modernization which avoided the essence of modernity. Rather, using its traditional pattern of "putting on faces," the Japanese adapted Western technology and, usually superficially, Western institutions to its primal and traditional structures. This strategy of wrapping Japan in Western paper has had its costs. The militarization of Japanese society which eventuated in the disastrous defeat of World War II left deeps scars on the Japanese psyche, but did not alter basic orientations. Substituting economic might for military power, Japan since 1950 has developed an export-driven tributary state, which for its maintenance requires Japan to develop large surpluses in its trade with other nations, precisely to deny outsiders access to its markets — and thus to its homogeneous social and cultural structures. This tributary system in turn requires that global trading and banking structures, not to mention Japan's trading partners, be compliant. For example, the Japanese consumer, unable to purchase what his own effort produces, has almost a third of the world's savings, equivalent to a year's American GDP, sitting in savings accounts earning, on average, less than one per cent interest because Japan's financial institutions are largely closed to outside competition. In addition to providing Japanese firms with cheap sources of investment capital, these savings could potentially undermine the world financial system should they suddenly flow out of or into Western financial institutions.

In all of this, Japan's trading partners have been compliant. In the short run, this compliance has been forthcoming because it has suited its principal trading partners, especially the United States, which enjoy an abundance of sophisticated Japanese goods at low prices. The Japanese people, who subsidize this gift-giving with hard work and the lack of inexpensive consumer products (not to mention such amenities as adequate housing), have tolerated this because of their traditional concern for security, social cohesion and hierarchy. Japan's current economic difficulties would be even deeper except for the massive deficit spending the Japanese government has maintained to cushion their effects — spending that cannot be maintained indefinitely. With uncharacteristic bluntness the Minister of Finance declared early in 2001 that the financial situation was "catastrophic."[20] In the long-run, this immunity from global forces will be difficult for Japan to sustain. The trade deficits of its principal trading partners cannot be indefinitely sustained, either. The system can be maintained only as long as deficit countries can be lent the money to pay for these trade imbalances. One scenario was suggested by Lester Thurow:

At some point, whatever the Japanese do, foreigners outside of Japan will become nervous about the value of their dollar holdings and want to exchange them for assets denominated in yen or marks. At that point Japan basically has to be willing to absorb an enormous number of dollars in a short period of time — a sum many times that of the United States annual trade deficit. As it absorbs those dollars, the dollar will be declining in value in Japan and someone (the government) will be absorbing enormous financial losses.[21]

Japan represents an interesting case of a society's attempt to manage globalizing economic forces without introducing the asymmetry between localization and delocalization which is inherent in this process. It has successfully industrialized itself, and become a global economic superpower without the disruptive delocalizing of any significant portion of its economy. This means that small, inefficient farms; small low-technology manufacturing; and labor-intensive retailing and financial businesses subsist side by side with some of the most efficient, technologically advanced firms in the galaxy of global firms. Only Japan's ability to close these inefficient sectors to global competition, and its use of great amounts of financial leveraging, have kept the localizing/delocalizing forces inherent in globalization from having the disruptive affects — at least in the short-run — they have had elsewhere. As the Japanese case illustrates, a society may resist all but the most superficial elements of Western modernity. Japan's outer wrapping of civility conceals layers of defense against fundamental social change which the globalization of the Japanese economy has initiated. The on-going "ordeal of civility" which Japan faces is to integrate itself into the structures of global modernity, or to disintegrate because of a failure to do so.

This is not a matter of "if" but "when." Because of its ideology of free trade, and Japan's strategic importance in Asia in the context of the Cold War, the United States has been willing to endure decades of massive trade deficits in its relations with Japan's closed markets, based on a closed society. The Japanese know that maintaining critical elements of the Japanese social consensus, including high levels of general welfare, general economic equality and full employment, they must structure their economy in ways which places the burdens of global economic adjustment on other societies. The generally unchallenged position of the Japanese elite rests on this bargain. Thurow argues that, "Japan's markets are not open, but at the same time there is no reason why Japan should change its habits, culture, or traditional business methods to satisfy American demands. The Japanese way of doing business makes for a more inclusive egalitarian society." In contrast, "The American way leads to a large degree of inequality and the Japanese have every right to reject it. They have a right to defend the Japanese way. At the same time, the United States does not have to accept a big trade deficit simply because Japanese culture is different."[22]

There is, in short, a fundamental cultural divide between the United States and Japan — one that is the result not of market forces, but of failed international institutions — principally the trading and banking regimes, which permit the Japanese neo-mercantilist tributary system to endure, and of a failed ideology, near-*laissez-faire* capitalism, which has been ascendant in the United States for a generation. This cultural divide is really a global fault line, because it separates the world's two largest economies, and because the situation is not tenable forever. As Thurow puts it, "But let no one doubt that this earthquake will happen. No one knows when, but the forces on each side of the fault are enormous."[23] Japan's resistance to fundamental social and cultural change is not evidence, as some would suggest, that it is possible to pick and choose from those elements of modernity which globalization presents, but rather indicative of the powerful resistance to basic change inherent in all cultures — a resistance that cannot be forever postponed.

J.W. Burton, arguing from a systems view, says, "It is probably not accidental that abilities to adjust diminish with the acquisition of abilities to change the environment. The latter is likely to be preferred as causing less hardship to members of the system concerned. [...] In this sense the ability to adapt is limited in practice by whatever ability there is to alter the environment."[24] In the relative short run, the past thirty years, Japan has skillfully played upon the Western, especially American focus on its strategic position versus China and the Soviet Union in Asia; and with "free trade," an extension of the ideology of free markets. It has found that, with the exception of Ronald Reagan, who was the most ideologically committed to market principles, no American president or administration or related trade policy endures for more than a few years, and thus it has not had to take seriously any American attempts to dissuade it from keeping its markets (and its society) closed. In addition, Japanese officials have found that the American political system is remarkably pliant to influence by well-financed lobbies, and they have built one of the most powerful lobbies in Washington, staffed with many former high U.S. government trade officials, to deflect the pressure on Japan's economic policies.[25]

The principle here is universal: at some point any society as a relatively coherent system of cultural values must either reject intrusive elements which threaten that coherence, or assimilate them and reconfigure into new patterns of coherence and equilibrium. Unlike most other traditional societies, Japan has superficially adapted enough of those elements, or "wrapped" itself within them, necessary for contact with the outside world, without fundamentally changing its social values. The primal strategy of defending component social systems by reducing internal segmentation in favor of external segmentation seems to be at work here. The Japanese have managed to draw clear boundaries between themselves and the international system, and to force systemic change upon the rest of the world, including Americans workers, who have seen high-paying jobs in industries like autos and electronic products transferred to Japan, and upon Third World countries which are used as raw material sources and cheap-labor export platforms.

A key differentiating feature of Japan, as compared to other traditional societies, is its political system. At this level of abstraction a political system represents those decision processes which confront and channel forces of change. Alfred Diamant describes political development in terms of the "increased capacity to sustain successfully and continuously new types of goals and demands" through the production of "new types of organizations."[26] Japan's historical experience with organizational complexity and flexibility — a result, in part, of its *samurai* heritage and *han* traditions — has permitted the creation of a political system more nimble than those of most traditional societies, especially in dealing with the modern West. Other traditional societies have weak or non-existent political institutions, and depend on a combination of charismatic authoritarianism, and hierarchical and kin-based social structures.

Japan is very much the test case for those who believe it is possible to be both "modern" and yet not "Western." If the forces of economic and technolog-ical change which are sweeping the world are issuing from sources deep within the transformations characterizing Western societies during recent centuries, can Japan truly adapt to them without fundamentally reconfiguring its society and its culture? Murray Sayle, an Australian writer who has lived with his family in Japan for many years thinks not. Describing Japan as a "pre-modern society," Sayle contends that, "Japan is hostage to American prosperity, and America is hostage to Japanese frugality. Ethno-economics has locked the two nations in a loveless embrace, and smaller Asian economies into a sumo wrestler's hug by Japan. Something has to give. But what?" The logic of globalization suggests that no amount of tinkering with ingrained, highly localized economic policy or traditional institutional devices will make much difference in the long run. Japan needs a social and cultural revolution, one that it has postponed for more than a century since its first encounters with the forces of change unleashed from the West. Japan's population is the oldest in the industrial world and, with a declining birthrate and almost no immigration, not replacing itself. Societies increasingly composed of older people are the least likely to embrace the dynamic and far-reaching process of *sustained* social and cultural change. "Today's aging Japanese," says Sayle, "formed by an antiquated, inward-looking, ultimately self-defeating system, have no idea how to change it — or whether they even want to."[27]

NOTES TO CHAPTER ELEVEN

1. Nakane Chie, "Hierarchy in Japanese Society," in Okimoto and Rohlen, *op.cit.*, pp. 8-9
2. G. B. Sansom, THE WESTERN WORLD AND JAPAN (New York: Alfred A. Knopf, 1968), p. 448
3. *ibid.*, p. 449
4. Catherine Makino, "Japan Bullies Unwanted Employees," SAN FRANCISCO CHRONICLE (March 19, 1999), p. A10.
5. Richard T. Pascale, "Perspectives on Strategy: The Real Story Behind Honda's Success," CALIFORNIA MANAGEMENT REVIEW, Vol. XXVI, No. 3, Spring 1984, p. 48
6. Shintaro Ishihara, THE JAPAN THAT CAN SAY NO, Frank Baldwin, trans. (New York: Simon & Schuster, 1989), p. 13; This fluidity is reflective of the relative lack of a *moral* basis for the formation of values in traditional Japanese thought: things are either wise or foolish, not right or wrong. Hirona Seki, a historian of ideas, says: "Moral leadership is a very hard thing for Japan to understand. In Japan we don't have this [Western] religious tradition. [...] If we are to establish political leadership, we must learn a new tradition." Nicholas D. Kristov, "A Man With a Plan? Japanese Prefer Premiers Who Speak Softly and Hold a Lot of Meetings," THE NEW YORK TIMES, July 20, 1998.
7. Karel Van Wolferen, "Japan's Non-Revolution," FOREIGN AFFAIRS (September-October 1993), p. 55
8. Tanaka Hideo, "The Role of Law and Lawyers in Japanese Society," in Okimoto and Rohlen, *op.cit.*, p. 194
9. Carolyn Hotchkiss, INTERNATIONAL LAW FOR BUSINESS (New York: McGraw-Hill, Inc., 1994), p. 86

10. Edgar Morin, "Ideas, Intellectuals, and Structures of Dissent," in Philip Rieff, ed., ON INTELLECTUALS (New York: Doubleday & Company, Inc., 1970), p. 88

11. Edward Shils, "The Intellectual and the Powers," in Philip Rieff, *op.cit.,* p.27

12. Richard Hofstadter, ANTI-INTELLECTUALISM IN AMERICAN LIFE (New York: Vintage Books,1966), p. 28

13. Peter Nettl, "Power and Intellectuals," in Conor Cruise O'Brien and William Dean Vanech, eds., POWER AND CONSCIOUSNESS (New York: New York University Press, 1969), p. 25

14. Cf. Lewis A. Coser, MEN OF IDEAS (New York: The Free Press, 1965)

15. Joseph R. Levenson, MODERN CHINA AND ITS CONFUCIAN PAST (New York: Doubleday & Company, Inc., 1964), p. 17

16. *Ibid.*, pp. 17-18

17. Reader, *op.cit.*, p. 54

18. Talcott Parsons, "'The Intellectual': A Social Role Category," in Rieff, *op.cit.*, p. 12

19. Andrew E. Barshay, STATE AND INTELLECTUAL IN IMPERIAL JAPAN (Berkeley: University of California Press, 1988), pp. 18-19

20. Typical of this continuing buffering, in spite of campaigns for the reform of Japan's financial institutions, is the recent attempt by the government to neutralize rule changes which would have forced banks to value their stock holdings at current market prices instead of the prices they paid for these securities. Banks have been unloading these cross-holdings to avoid recognizing losses on them when the accounting rules change in 2001, driving stock prices even lower. The proposed policy would allow the government to sell bonds and use the proceeds to buy this avalanche of stocks, which would be sold back to the banks when business conditions and stock prices improve. In December 2000 the Posts and Telecommunications Ministry—which controls the postal savings bank, the largest in Japan — announced it would buy $2 trillion in stocks over the next five years. Stephanie Strom, "Japan Struggles to Bolster Stocks and Perhaps Banks, Too." THE NEW YORK TIMES (December 29, 2000), p. W1

21. Lester Thurow, THE FUTURE OF CAPITALISM (New York: Penguin Books, 1996), p. 201

22. *Ibid.*, p. 208

23. *Ibid.*, p. 205

24. Burton, *op.cit.*, p. 19

25. Cf. Pat Choat, AGENTS OF INFLUENCE (New York: Alfred A. Knopf, Publishers, 1990)

26. Alfred Diamant, "The Nature of Political Development," in Jason L. Finkle and Richard W. Gable, eds., POLITICAL DEVELOPMENT AND SOCIAL CHANGE (New York: John Wiley and Sons, 1966), p. 92

27. Murray Sayle, "The Social Contradictions of Japanese Capitalism," THE ATLANTIC MONTHLY (June 1998), p. 94

PART VI

WORLDS IN CONTENTION: THE CULTURE WAR

... a coalition of Marxists, Africanists, feminists, gay propagandists, and deconstructionists who were united by their hatred of American society and all its works, and intellectually by their rejection of the belief in scholarly or aesthetic standards and objective truth.

— *Norman Podhoretz*

CHAPTER TWELVE

THE PRIMAL CONFRONTS THE CIVIL

Japan represents a relatively unique demographic situation among contemporary nations. Its very large population is remarkably homogeneous. With the exception of a few Caucasoid aboriginals (*Ainu*) on the northern island, and several hundred thousand Koreans, who in spite of having lived in the nation for generations remain very much at the margins of society, Japan's population is characterized by its lack of demographic diversity. Its cultural values are widely shared over the great mass of the population, regardless of social class or geographic origins. Japan's isolation from the world during the centuries of the Shogunate and lack of significant immigration for many centuries before that has much to do with this cultural uniformity. Japan is thus a good example of an entire national culture facing the forces of change within globalization. Some societies, on the other hand, are characterized by the coexistence of a number of differing cultures within their social matrix. This complexity presents a different series of issues as each cultural segment faces both the forces of global change and the consequences of these changes for their relations with other cultural segments. The United States offers an interesting example of each of four cultural worlds coexisting, often uneasily, within the same society.

The history of the United States in the substantial form in which we have it begins in the seventeenth century with the arrival of the first English colonists in North America. As such its cultural influences were situated within those great forces giving birth to civil society in Europe contemporaneously. Nation-building, and the values associated with it, were in the forefront of English life and thought during the seventeenth century, a century characterized by civil war and revolution, and the influence of thinkers like Thomas Hobbes, who popularized the theory of the "social contract." The first settlers, in Virginia and subsequently Massachusetts, arrived under the auspices of the commercial trading companies which promoted colonial activity not just from Britain, but from other major trading nations of the era, including the Dutch and the French. When the first New England colonists touched land at Cape Cod in 1620 they signed the famous *Mayflower Compact*, a covenant defining the conditions under which they would governed themselves as a "civil body politic," before disembarking. Their first printed document was a pledge: *The Oath of a Freeman.* They saw society as a contract, and thus the first British colonies were governed under charters, corporate and/or royal, signifying the civil bases of these new societies.

This was a pattern to be repeated throughout American history. The *Declaration of Independence* and *Constitution* of the later American common-wealth subsequently confirmed many generations of these covenantially-conceived politics within civil understandings of society. America was settled within this intellectual framework, defining the proper relations between individuals within society, and was reinforced by the shared ethnic and social origins of the earliest settlers. Most importantly, the traditional, Medieval conceptions of society based on social class and hierarchy were never successfully transplanted to the New World, always excepting the South where the institution of slavery carried with it at least pseudo-aristocratic social connotations. The majority of the settlers came from Britain, and others such as the Dutch in New York were soon assimilated to English colonial culture. Most settlers came from the middle classes of craftsmen, independent farmers and tradesmen. The rich had no need to come to America, and the poor lacked the means to do so.

Thus America during the first several centuries of its existence was characterized by a population that was largely British, Protestant, English-speaking and drawn from the middle classes of society. The presence within this population of increasing numbers of African slaves, and of aboriginal Indian peoples, did little to modify a situation of remarkable uniformity — and equality. This equality of station and situation was the characteristic which most captured the imagination of foreign visitors, including the most famous observer, Alexis de Tocqueville. The ability of the original thirteen colonies to establish first their independence and subsequently their nationhood was certainly enabled by the social values they shared, regardless of geographic or economic differences. America was always at its historical core a civil society.

Civil society from its remote beginnings in the ancient Middle East has been characterized by the forces of resource scarcity and socio-economic pluralism. We have observed these forces shaping emerging commercial, civil societies in places as diverse as classical Greece and the Netherlands in the seventeenth century. America, from its beginnings, lacked the most essential of all economic resources: human population. The number of aboriginal people was small north of the Rio Grande, and Indian peoples were sparsely settled. The population of the American colonies was scattered and overwhelming rural, with 90% of the people living outside of towns and cities at the time of the War for Independence (1775-1781). The existence of the frontier, with its vast untapped natural resources, also contributed to the mobility of this population. Americans could move in search of opportunity in ways that were usually not possible for farmers and craftsmen in Europe. America (again, always excepting the slave-based society of the South) never had a class of rural "peasants," characterized by their passivity, immobility and lack of opportunity. This meant that most individual Americans had a kind of economic power wielded by few in other societies. Their labor was valuable and they could demand much in return for it because they had the mobility provided by options. Shortages of skilled labor also furthered technological innovation and made America a society of pragmatic and talented tinkerers, inventors, and engineers.

The paradox of wide-spread slavery in parts of the American polity can also be partly explained accordingly: in a society so mobile, characterized by the ability of individuals to go to the expanding frontiers in search of opportunities, only slavery could produce the submissive and immobile work force necessary to plantation agriculture. The corollary of the independent and mobile yeoman farmer in a land of labor scarcity was the totally subjugated slave. The fact that America was hugely endowed with all the other resources necessary for creating wealth only increased the value of the individual person required for exploiting them. This continued to be true during those many formative generations before large-scale immigration and a closing frontier tipped the scales in favor of employers of labor. Americans have consequently been culturally shaped as individuals since the beginnings of European settlement. If trends within European, especially British, thought had not so advanced the rise of civil culture in North America, these socio-economic forces promoting individuality certainly would have. In a reversal of the classical pattern, in which civil society created individuals, in America it was individuals who created civil society. Ultimately, the individual requires a civil society, social arrangements which are contract-based and which formalize the individual wills of individual persons. Americans experienced their lives and their values in individualistic terms.

Pluralistic governance presumes a civil society, but is not identical to it. The processes of civil governance share many of the bases of civil society, certainly their roots in individual and willful consent, but differ from them as well. It is useful to distinguish between civil *government* and civil *society*. Civil society may be defined as lacking any element of explicit coercion. Individuals are free to participate in or withdraw from the processes of civil society as it suits them. This is never true of government, pluralistic or otherwise: there we are ultimately bound by law regardless of our feelings or interests in any particular case. For that reason, civil society is often seen as an alternative means to government in reconciling individual and social conflict. Indeed, civil society is often to be preferred to government because it is more flexible in seeking solutions to social problems outside of the formalities of law and administration. Robert D. Kaplan (in a variation of a thesis advanced by Robert Dahl) proposes this when he suggests that democracy is most possible in societies where government deals with secondary issues. Primary issues — especially who gets how much of what; who is to be basically advantaged — is left to the more fluid mechanisms of civil society because material abundance allows the relative inefficiencies of such mechanisms. He says, "And because what is argued about is likely to be secondary than something to fight and die for, democracy has evolved as the lowest common denominator of practical wisdom for a nation of individuals, most of whom prefer to be left alone to make money."[1]

Democracy has always presumed growing material abundance and its fairly widespread distribution within the population in order that civil society can resolve conflict within its boundaries. Lester Thurow suggests that as a society approaches a "zero-sum game" (the gain of one person being the loss of another) government tends to grid-lock and fail as an on-going mechanism of conflict resolution.[2] Government consequently functions as a kind of "damage control" in its relations to civil society. Only to the extent that the more informal mechanisms of civil society cannot resolve conflict does government use its monopoly of law-making (and ultimately its monopoly in the legitimate use of force) to resolve conflict. As resources become more scarce conflict is likely to grow both in scale and intensity, and government is likely to be called upon to resolve issues which civil society is no longer able to do. The decline of civil society as the dominant means of conflict resolution is also a measure of the stresses which pluralistic government, always limited in its power, will begin to experience as greater demands are made upon it. The capacity of Americans to organize themselves within civil society to promote common goals and to resolve various conflicts is thus a hallmark of the American cultural character. Alexis de Tocqueville, that early nineteenth century French visitor to America, was acutely perceptive in this regard, as in so many others. He wrote in his *Democracy in America* [1835-1840]: "Americans of all ages, all conditions, and all dispositions, constantly form associations. [...] and I have often admired the extreme skill with which the inhabitants of the United States succeed in proposing a common object to the exertions of a great many men, and in getting them voluntarily to pursue it.[3]

The United States as a society evolved governmental arrangements from a most unique set of circumstances. European nation-states began their formation as the sovereign form of human governmental arrangement in the seventeenth century in response to two basic dynamics. First, revolutions in technology, especially the technology of warfare, made the smaller polities which characterized the Middle Ages unviable. What John Hertz called "the gun-power revolution" made the fortified strongpoint or castle defended by a small group of soldiers obsolete.[4] Now required were extended, fortified frontiers — rivers, mountains, coastlines — and large standing armies and navies to defend them. These in turn required a large economic base and the state machinery to extract from it the resources needed to maintain a sophisticated war machine. The growth of large, centralized states in Europe beginning in the seventeenth century is in part the story of building large, economically sustainable armed forces within a defended geography. What Hertz defined as "defensibility" became an imperative of statecraft.

Second, rapid population growth in Europe required more sophisticated technology and socio-economic arrangements, especially in supporting the expanding cities. Establishing uniform currency, tax and commercial laws was essential. So was promoting the colonial settlement of burgeoning populations. The nation-state evolved in inextricable relation to the more complex problems of both expanding and distributing economic resources. The great trading companies, such as the Dutch East India Company, Hudson's Bay Company, and the Virginia Company, were mechanisms for generating an expanding base of wealth from which the state could derive needed revenue. The colonial enterprises which brought settlers to the New World were intimately related to the wealth-creating pressures which the new states of the Old World faced. Consequently, strong, centralizing trends in government were vital to the state-building enterprise in Europe.

In America, neither of these imperatives was especially salient. Economic resources — rich soil, fish and wildlife, timber, minerals, water — were nearly unlimited and relatively easily accessed. America also had no real frontiers to defend militarily, having thousands of miles of oceans between it and possible enemies to the east and to the west; and weak, small states to the north and to the south. There was no peacetime military regime until 1947. In 1940, a full year after World War II had broken out in Europe, the United States armed forces globally ranked 22nd in numbers of personnel, between Greece and Portugal. The renewal of a military draft, introduced in 1940, passed the House of Representatives by a single vote just months before Pearl Harbor in 1941. Americans built a polity without the commanding motivations of their European brethren. It seldom seemed odd to us that the national state was expected to play only intermittent and marginal roles in defense and in economic production and allocation. Only with the 1930's Depression, World War II, and the subsequent Cold War, did Americans grudgingly begin to accept — and never fully — what other mature polities had long known: the state is a central and necessary instrument supplementing the activities of civil society, including the market economy. It is this resistance to government per se which may explain a long-noted characteristic of American political leadership: its failure to attract the most talented. Nineteenth Century British statesman James Bryce, whose *The American Commonwealth* is a classic of social observation, suggested that, because there were so many other opportunities for achievement and advancement in an expanding America, careers in a diminished form of government held few attractions for ambitious talent.

The dominant civil norms which have stood at the center of American society since its inception in the seventeenth century are being challenged by three other sets of cultural values which inhabit the primal, traditional and individual worlds. These worlds are in contention with America's civil culture, and with one another, where the incompatibility is, if anything, even greater.

Primal America is most fully evidenced in America's black "underclass." This term was first used by Gunnar Myerdahl, the Swedish social scientist whose ground-breaking work, *The American Dilemma* [1944] is seminal. It was Myerdahl who recognized that World War II was radically changing the economy of the South, were most of America's black poor had lived in highly localized and immobilized circumstances. The transformation of Southern agriculture during the war through rapid mechanization, and the movement of millions of poor blacks to large Northern cities to take jobs now open to them because of labor shortages, would fundamentally transform American society, he argued. In subsequent work, he used the term "underclass" to distinguish these poor black people inhabiting America's cities in such large numbers from other urban immigrants, most of whom had traditional working-class characteristics. Deeply structural transformations of the American economy, especially those reducing the need for unskilled manual labor, would impact members of the black underclass in special ways tied to their historical experience.[5] This special experience, unlike that of most other poor immigrants to America's cities, placed them outside the usual structures of socio-economic class.

Leon Dash, a journalist whose Pulitzer Prize newspaper series about a black underclass family was made into a much-praised television documentary, uses The Urban Institute's definition of *underclass*: "...a family belongs to the underclass if [...] it's headed by a single female and its members are welfare dependent, marginally educated, chronically unemployed, and engaged in repeated patterns of criminal deviance."[6] I am making this case because of the visibility of the black underclass, as well as its numbers. There is a large, mostly rural and small-town, white underclass in America as well; but it tends to be less visible. As one wanders backroads in Appalachia; the scrub pine area of northern New England (especially Maine and New Hampshire); up-state New York, and many remote areas of the South, Middle West and the Mountain States one sees all the elements of primal life visible in the black ghettos of the big cities and the rural South: material poverty; fluid family structures, including widespread illegitimacy and female-headed households; low educational achievement; substance abuse; idleness and violence.

Black primal life, expressed either in the rural South or the urban ghetto, is like all primal experience a reactive life of unmediated engagement. It is the life characterized by Stanner as a "one possibility thing." Life unfolds with an inevitability which obviates a sense of time and purpose. Life is experienced by individuals and endured day to day with little sense of a past or of a future. Allocentric psychological modes absorb individuals into their environments without much abstraction or reflection. Stimulus-response mechanisms hold a sovereign immediacy in the lives of individuals whose attitude toward the world is often an essentially playful acting-out. Daily life is experienced as the satisfaction of "deprivation" needs: those pressing, lower-order "scarcity pleasures" (eating, sex, affection, etc.) which seek to avoid pain. This often means casual and disordered social and sexual relationships; food and substance abuse; unplanned pregnancies and deserting fathers; disorderly children; outbreaks of violence; and schemes gone wrong, leading to encounters with police and other authorities. Such behavior is regarded by most students of the phenomena of social deviancy, especially habitual criminality, as a pattern of subcultural behavior. These patterns demonstrate, in the words of Ferrell and Sanders, that "cultural and criminal processes continually interweave along a continuum of marginality, illegality and public display." At the margins of the dominant civil society, individuals cohere into groups which constitute networks "of symbols, meaning, and knowledge" constituting a "collective way of life."[7]

Students of social deviancy have also noted the lack of impulse control which characterizes the core of sociopathy in many deviant individuals. Primal culture, as an unmediated, reactive culture, by its nature places few controls on impulsive behavior and creates time-horizons which are so "present-oriented" as to be unable to capture the longer-term consequences of immediate action.[8] And in many ways the primal world in fact furthers such impulsivity in individuals because it lacks the complex, inhibiting boundaries and symbol structures of more advanced societies. In primitive societies such impulsivity in individuals has fewer negative social consequences because populations are scattered and immobile, strangers are few, and pervasive kinship bonds moderate all behavior. Enclosing routine and habit limit impulsive possibilities and impose an implicit (but external) structure on individual lives. But in mobile and dense urban environments where social relations, especially those related to property, are very complex, and where interpersonal encounters with strangers require more formality and discipline, the lack of self-restraint in individuals may have very negative consequences. The basic incivility which pervades under-class life thus constitutes a significant barrier to successful functioning in a modern society, a culture of strangers.

Civil society is ultimately possible because individuals are self-disciplined and self-directed, and thus capable of functioning within the many abstracted and institutional contexts which a mobile culture presents. Where the sense of "self" is unformed, and social contexts are weakened, individuals have neither the internal nor external constraints necessary to civil life. Nicholas Lemann has documented such primal lives in his insightful investigation, *The Promised Land*, which explores the experiences of former sharecroppers from Clarksdale, Mississippi, who made the great trek north to Chicago during and after World War II.[9] Common to the biographies of most of these men and women is the almost complete lack of purposeful self-possession in their lives: life just happens. There is a pervasive ethos of victimhood. A liaison or marriage here; a birth or death there; a sudden "call from the Lord;" crises caused by children or lovers; constant movements of locale; and various addictions come and go as does any money accumulated. That "all things flow" is a hallmark of the primal, as Radin has suggested [*supra* Chap. 2]. Perhaps that is why rivers are such a pervasive metaphor, captured in gospel songs like "Roll, Jordan, Roll," or Percy Mayfield's "The River's Invitation," in the world of the black underclass. And such a world, one that is playfully experienced more than it is rationally known, mitigates against a self-directed life.

The quest for the esteem of others is compelling in a primal life lived in a modern setting because it is the need always on the horizon in an existence spent toward the bottom of the needs hierarchy. In a life of intrinsically limited possibility, lived in a more possible environment, the need for a sense of self is a constant urgency. James Baldwin entitled a collection of his essays, *Nobody Knows My Name*. This is the powerful theme, each in its own way, of Lorraine Hansberry's play, "A Raisin in the Sun," and Richard Wright's novel, *Native Son*. The sense of identity which recognition brings is an imperative often pursued with expressive passion. It is reflected in the gang life of black boys, with its socio-dramatic display and self-presentation, and the motherhood of black girls, with its animus of adult maturity and status within a matriarchal community. It is nowhere better seen than in the dedicated fanaticism of young, inner-city basketball players pursuing their elusive "hoop dreams," to be stars in the NBA. In a world where esteem is so urgently compelling, losing face, to be *disted* ("disrespected") is the primal offense not to go unanswered.

A number of these points can be illustrated from black English, sometimes called "ebonics," the *patois* of the black underclass.[10] As a primal language, black English serves less to mediate between subjective thought and objective reality than as an expressive fusion of word and reality. Urbanologist Lee Rainwater used the phrase "the expressive life-style" in describing inner-city black values.[11] The expressiveness of black underclass life lies in its objectivity, the modes through which it moves into presence and into reality only in the eyes of an audience, and derives it vitality from these encounters. Exotic dress, grooming, carriage and speech are often integral to this playful self-presentation. *I am seen and heard, therefore I am.* Black English is expressive (more than instrumental) in that it is a deeply mythopoetic language intimately tied to a dynamic, immediate relation to the experienced world. Black language is a form of self-presentation, a way of being in the world, a way of becoming existentially visible, which I have identified with the charismatic. Black speech has been the conceit which made meaningful exchange possible among a people who had been denied property (indeed, who themselves had been property). Lacking property and thus lacking markets, poor black people often enter the visible world of exchange through the dynamics of language. Ralph Ellison, author of the fiction masterpiece, *Invisible Man*, brilliantly discloses the passion for visibility located within language. "Without light I am not only invisible," he wrote, "but formless as well; and to be unaware of one's form is to live a death. I myself after existing some twenty years, did not become alive until I discovered my invisibility."[12]

The "form" of which Ellison speaks is the form of language, the means by which his words brought him into the world of "light," of appearances. He makes the same point in his meditations on the ways language is shaped by people precisely to give them form. Black people, he suggests, were quintessentially American in contributing to the creation of a language which would validate their own lives and experiences. Like other Americans, "to become themselves," he said, "they had to revamp their concept and use of the English language."[13] Language attempted the empowerment of black people existentially in ways parallel to property and markets for the middle classes of civil society. As such black English is an action language, doing by saying. "Walk it like you talk it." Words inspire responses; they move; they have power. Thomas Kochman, in his insightful analysis of "rapping," the speech of the black ghetto, suggests: "The prestige norms which influence black speech behavior are those which have been successful in manipulating and controlling people and situations."[14] In a world where esteem is the compelling need, persuasive speech becomes the dominant instrument of self-presentation. Street rapper or preacher, prestige in the ghetto is the intimate companion of artful and playful speech. Truth is not understood as something which stands objectively apart from speech. Rather, speech and truth create one another in the artful "rap." "Rap" and its attendant "Hip-Hop" lifestyle are mythopoetical at their primal cores.

The phenomenon of creative truth-making in mutual exchange is to be noted in the speech pattern of call and response so pervasive in all black vocal expression. An omnipresent vocal form in West Africa, the chant or song is characterized by a principal vocalizer, who sounds a call which evokes a response, rather like the lead singer with backup singers in American popular music, which had much of its origin in the musical idioms of the black church. Jazz, perhaps America's greatest contribution to music, is characterized by the distinct voice of each instrumentalist as he extemporaneously innovates in response to a shared bass line and the other players' voices. As a kind of primal art, jazz is a quintessential example of "abstraction by inbreeding," of a process of mutuality and variation which reduces musical ideas to their simplest, purist, most powerful forms through extraordinary musicianiship. A "jam session" is nothing so much as a rich, musical conversation, soul to soul with no inhibitions; unmediated, without a conductor or a written score. The musician becomes the music. Similarly, in black churches the skilled preacher summons spontaneous reactions from his listeners ("That's right!;" "Amen!"). Even in casual conversation black speech often invites ("See what I'm sayin'?") interjecting reactions of agreement. In movie houses it is common for black patrons to talk back to the actors on screen. In this way truth is gathered, accumulated, and *experienced* as artifice in mutual exchange. Truth is consequently understood in ways that are focused in personality and expression. It is the power of personality and its presentation in speech which makes the word (and thus the world) what it is. Truth hardly exists outside the charisma of verbal presentation.

Black English is also characterized by its lack of focus in time and tense. This does not mean that past and future have no identity, but it does mean that they are very diffusely understood.[15] Like Hopi, Dakota and a number of other primal languages, black English is extemporaneous, "without time." Verbal tenses do not exist as they do in standard English, especially for the basic verb form "to be." For example, the expression, "He be coming," only implies tense within context. Context in fact replaces specific focus in time and tense. Similarly, pronoun forms are often invariant. "He" can sometimes represent either gender and the possessive pronoun. "They" is used both nominatively and possessively: "The womens they in they house." (The use of coupled nominatives is common; pluralization is almost invariably achieved by adding an "s," even to collective nouns, and does not require verbal agreement; the verb is unstated and understood.) This lack of grammatical subtlety and more mediated abstraction through such devices as inflection reveals the relative rejection of mediation itself in the language, and accounts for some of the directness and liveliness of vocabulary: one is not "depressed;" one is "down," "low," or "blue"; something is not "exciting;" it is "hot" or it "rocks;" one doesn't "relax," one "chills." Mediated abstraction requires a strong sense of duration, of things lasting as forms in time.

In a world in which past and future are more indifferently understood, mediated abstraction is less imperative. Indeed, to the extent that language is charismatic, attaching real persons to one another in present speech, abstraction is a barrier to interpersonal encounter, and its inherent relations of influence. For black English is a spoken language which personalizes and reveals the speaker. Understanding is strongly contextual, aided by the expressiveness of the speaker, his tone, his gestures. Reality is not "out there" in ways which characterize written language, intended for more diverse and unknown readers across time, and therefore more objective and abstract in its expression. Black English presumes a specific, present audience, addressed by a particular speaker who is making himself visible in speech. And always to persuade, not simply to relate. Charismatic speech thus pervades all relations of influence. The preacher has played wide leadership roles in the black community in part because of his command of charismatic speech, and the power inherent in it.

Illiteracy is pervasive within the black underclass. This is usually ascribed to poor schools with bad or indifferent teachers, and to fluid, disorganized families. What is seldom noted is that black underclass life and its associated primal values intrinsically avoid the abstract mediation of the environment which the ability to read and to write represents. We have noted the critical relationship between the written word and the passage from the primal world, which Parsons [*supra*, Chap. 4] and others have suggested. A world interpreted abstractly through written symbols is almost completely absent in the life of an underclass child. Books, newspapers and magazines are few, and children seldom witness adults, themselves usually illiterate, reading. Worship in some black churches is almost entirely focused in singing and preaching, with no readings from scripture. In underclass households the always-on television, radio or stereo are the ludic and reactive means through which the world is encountered. By the time a child goes to school he has already largely rejected abstract, highly mediated modes of interacting with the world. His capacity for written language, which must develop in the early years of life, may never be remediated. Any instruction he receives at school is not only unsupported in his home environment, it is continuously challenged by primal forms of unmediated, reactive experience. Without a growing command of written language advanced education itself becomes difficult and unrewarding, resulting in the large drop-out rates in inner-city schools, and making legitimate work increasingly unlikely. In prison environments, one of the most pervasive characteristics is the inability of inmates to read or to write.

Concepts of time as they evolved among the black underclass were reinforced by concepts of action, particularly work. The slave experience, where willful work was by definition excluded, attached the burden of labor to a sense of time devoid of individual purpose. Primal concepts of time originating in Africa supported this sensibility. "The black [work] ethic represented at once a defense against an enforced system of economic exploitation and an autonomous assertion of values generally associated with preindustrial peoples."[16] says Eugene D. Genovese. The "lazy Negro" so often complained of on the Southern plantation, as either slave or sharecropper, derived in part from concepts of work typical of primal and traditional peoples. After the end of slavery it was a common puzzlement of abolitionists, who had always insisted that freed slaves would be vigorous workers once given personal and economic incentives, that black workers remained relatively idle and underproductive.

What these observers failed to note was that the entire Southern economic system, including the relatively leisured life of white landowners, was underproductive and pre-civil in its sense of work. Freed black workers brought traditional African values to their concepts of work, but also the values of the planter class. During Reconstruction David Marcie suggested: "It was part of the teachings of slavery that a gentleman was one who lived without working. Is it wonderful that some of the Negroes, who want now to be gentlemen, should have thought of trying this as the easiest way."[17] The continuing poverty and socio-economic backwardness of those deep South states (e.g., Mississippi and Alabama) which had built their economies on large-scale plantation slavery and sharecropping only evidence the depth of these cultural values. Observers have repeatedly noted, then as now, that free black workers continued to work to subsistence levels. This is an echo of primal values, intrinsically oriented toward non-accumulation and material poverty. But it is also intimately related to both slavery and sharecropping.

Under slavery the quotidian theft of their very lives was obvious to the black underclass, and justified to them with the social trappings of legitimacy. Under the sharecropping system legal slavery was abolished, but what replaced it was in many ways worse. The black farmer and his family were completely vulnerable to the arbitrariness of the system of economic rewards, without the paternalistic protections which the master had afforded his valuable property under slavery. "The settle," the end of harvest time when landowners settled accounts with their sharecropping tenants, was so manifestly abusive that many sharecroppers ended the growing year even further in debt to their sharecropping "partners" than when they planted. Poverty was an inevitable fact in spite of skill or effort. And the resulting sense of injustice was pervasive and irremediable. Nicholas Lemann says: "There was no break on dishonest behavior by a planter toward a sharecropper. For a sharecropper to sue a planter was unthinkable. Even to ask for a more detailed accounting was known to be an action with the potential to endanger your life. The most established plantations were literally above the law where black people were concerned."[18]

The system of slavery was a system of total exploitation, a social as well as an economic system. As such it furthered a culture of mendacity on the part of master and slave alike. It pervaded all Southern culture, black and white, and continues to this day: Southern culture was literally a story-telling culture. It was not in Virginia, the oldest state, where at least a tiny portion of the planter class with names like Carter, Randolph and Lee could credibly affect aristocratic origins, but rather among the entirely *parvenu* planter class in places like Alabama and Mississippi that one finds the pretentious, Greek-colonnaded "manor houses" with the fanciful names (*Belle Reeve; Halcyon*), and the airs of aristocracy. Slavery was reinforced by the systematic propaganda of "Southern gentility," of false manners and sentimental custom, largely invented from whole cloth.

In such a system, the slave and later the sharecropper created a mendacity of his own. The cultural norm of "gettin' over," a subtle but pervasive web of taking and dissembling, was partially a response to the systematic theft and lies of the white owner and his overseers. After the Civil War, in the days of "Jim

Crow," mendacity became an omnipresent way of life in the South, with "separate but equal" accommodations, "literacy tests" for voting, the "white primary" and all the other false facades of an ever-present *apartheid* negotiated by both races over a psychological distance that belied propinquity. But some of this phenomenon also had primal African origins where, as Genovese suggests, "Africans considered lying — or what Europeans and white Americans understood as lying — an ingredient of courtesy. European travelers as well as anthropologists reported that Africans repeatedly 'lied' to each other in matters of no importance when they had nothing to gain."[19] The artful lie, still evidenced in the false compliment in our contemporary culture, was part of a more pervasive system of self-presentation in Africa. The black English word "jive" describes skill in artful untruth-telling (like an actor on stage) and often has complementary connotations. In the South, the practice of telling exaggerated "tall tales" became culturally institutionalized and created a literature, including Joel Chandler Harris's stories of "Uncle Remus" and Mark Twain's stories of "Huckleberry Finn." The black ghetto reflects this uncivil Southern past.

In the black ghetto lying is inextricably tied to expressive self-presentation, to being "cool" (in control, hip, aloof), especially in dealing with strangers. Sociologist David. A. Schultz asserts in his study of a black, underclass community: "Learning to lie effectively is central to the notion of 'cool' and the expressive life style. Children are taught early that it does not pay to tell the truth, particularly to strangers, who might be bill collectors, plain clothes 'fuzz,' or simply someone who is interested in some personal and immediate gratification."[20] Theft also has normative roots in primitive societies, where concepts of property are weakly formed, as we have seen. The pervasive practice of lying and stealing by slaves was noted by masters and slaves alike, and by sympathetic historians like Herbert Aptheker and Kenneth M. Stamp.[21] Lies and theft were rooted in a sense of deprivation and retribution among slaves, and their sharecropping descendants, but also in primal concepts of truth and property which were *sui generis*.

Truth as it is understood in the civil world requires the subject/object duality. Formal logic, the philosophical expression of this separation, postulates that for "A" to be "A," it cannot be "B." We noted the rise of science as modern people understand it within this formulation. Truth acquires its own identity in a formal language functioning between subject and object, as mathematics does in science. The objectivity of reality takes form in the abstraction of the descriptive language. In the primal world the object/subject separation is weak or unknown. We have noted this mendacity in Japanese culture, for example, where *honne* (one's true feeling or intent) is distinguished from *tatemae* (what is pleasing to others, or what they expect). Within the black underclass, and within Southern culture generally (e.g., the *belle*, which every "lady" was expected to be), concepts of truth never achieved an objective, civil character. "I tell what ought to be true," says Blanche DuBois, Tennessee Williams' archetypal voice of the South. Mythopoetic modes of truth-making in charismatic relations achieved sovereign status. It is probably no accident that Mississippi has had more *Miss Americas* than any other state, and that the South continues to dominate these exercises in mythopoetic play. The South is also the principal locus of the hundreds of children's beauty pageants that teach little girls like JonBenet Ramsey the arts of mendacity at an early age. This element of Southern culture was brought to the North by poor black people.

The culture of mendacity, of jive and hustling, and the arts of charisma became almost indistinguishable in the black underclass in matters of love as well as money. "Livin' sweet" was the phrase used by men to describe a life of living off a woman through the arts of seduction and trickery. The blues songs of such great lyric artists as Billie Holiday and Bessie Smith form a whole corpus of musical lament, of being "done wrong" under the spells of lying and unfaithful lovers. The art of the "scam," ubiquitous on the streets of the ghetto in the schemes of the hustler in his various presentations, thrived even during relative prosperity when jobs were plentiful. From street pimp to street preacher, the life of the hustler is one of seamless reaction, as described by Malcolm X:

> Right now, in every big city ghetto, tens of thousands of yesterday's and today's dropouts are keeping body and soul together by some form of hustling in the same way I did. [...] Full-time hustlers never can relax to appraise what they are doing and where they are bound. As is the case in any jungle, the hustler's every waking hour is lived with both the practical and the subconscious knowledge that if he ever relaxes, if he ever slows down, the other hungry, restless foxes, ferrets, wolves and vultures out there with him won't hesitate to make him their prey.[22]

We have noted that the lack of boundedness is a pervasive characteristic of the black primal world. The proliferation of exotic cults and political movements, with their costumed leadership, is a case in point. Black identity groups, from Marcus Garvey's *Back To Africa* movement [UNIA] to Black Panther nationalism, as well as secret societies and sects, of which Louis Farrakhan's *Nation of Islam* is only the most prominent, have been widespread historically within the underclass black community, and characterize lives actually lived within the illusory world of dress-up play-acting. Ralph Ellison wrote that the black experience in America "throws up personalities as fluid and changeable as molten metal rendered iridescent from the effect of cooling air.":

> Sometimes in responding to the conflict between their place in life as Negroes and the opportunities of America which are denied them, these personalities act out their wildest fantasies; they assume many guises without too much social opposition (Father Divine becomes God) first because within the Negro world the necessities of existence, those compromises men must make in order to survive, are such that they do not allow for too rigid defining of value or personality (only the lower-class Negroes create their own values, the middle class seeks to live up to those of the whites); second because whites tend to regard Negroes in the spirit of the old song, "All Coons Look Alike to Me," seldom looking past the abstraction, "Negro" to the specific "man." [23]

In a life of extravagant self-presentation, the disguise of the imaginary "somebody" covers the nakedness of the social "nobody."

Participation in modern market societies requires attitudes toward the experienced environment which enable its transformation into a personal, operative world. Success within this world depends on culturally-acquired values, especially those related to time, action and exchange. Among the black underclass, whose cultural values are closely associated with the primal world, successful participation in civil society, including the market economy, presents fundamental difficulties. In the first instance, it is the lack of functional boundaries within the black underclass which most inhibits the insertion of the self into a civil world. These boundaries, such as those which define and realize discrete property and objective, instrumental knowledge, simultaneously structure the world and enhance human mobility within it. These are indispensable elements of civil society and of market relations, of the successful negotiation of a culture of strangers, rather than one of brothers and sisters. They make it possible to segment and use time. They make it possible for work to emerge as purposive action. They make it possible to accumulate and to use wealth, and to separate it from consumption. In fact, these boundaries advance a world which is dominated by the values of production, rather than those of consumption.

The accumulation of primal cultural values in the black underclass makes wealth-building and its associated values all but impossible. Concepts of work, of structured relations with an economy, of property, all conspire against success in a market economy. Instead, the individual is immersed in a body of individual, social and material relationships characterized by the fluidity of things and people. The intimate nuclear family is weak, and thus the tightly focused families within which middle class wealth is initially built and measured are also weakly formed. The modal family unit of the black underclass, recalling some African patterns, is the extended matriarchy. The family is centered in a number of related women and their children. In Africa, where polygamy and its equivalents were dominant, women often advanced their interests and those of their children within their own female kinship system of mothers and grandmothers, sisters and aunts. Descent was often matrilineal, reckoned through the mother. The world of men was often a world apart.[24]

This system endures among the black underclass in various mutations. Men often function, if at all, at the peripheries, and usually contribute little or nothing to the family's finances or security. Currently, up to one-third of inner-city black men are either in prison or on parole/probation. As Parsons has noted, the status of men in their families is usually a localized reflection of their status in the surrounding world.[25] In the economy of sharecropping, and later the urban ghetto, women could usually find such employment as domestic service, where they often won the respect and affection of their employers. In addition to the steady cash income which she brought to her family, the black woman could build ties to the surrounding white world which she could draw upon when needed. Black men, usually only semi-employed and often not for cash (but for "credit"), were of little financial support to their families, and they offered few bridges to, or defenses against, an often-hostile environment.

The conflicted relations between the sexes in poor black communities has very deep roots in this past. Psychiatrists William H. Grier and Price M. Cobbs argue that "black men develop considerable hostility to black women as the inhibiting instrument of an oppressive system. The woman has more power, more accessibility into the system, and therefore she is more feared, while at the same time envied."[26] In current "gangsta rap," as in the older verbal exchanges called "the dozens," vulgar and hostile attitudes toward women characterize the values of many ghetto youths. Children are more or less raised ("come up") within this conflicted matriarchal matrix, it being common to children's biographies to live, at different times, with various female relatives other than the mother. Day to day sustenance is usually a function of the activities of this web of female kin, each managing a subsistence economy focused in the individual household. This is an economic system of primal localization, a variety of the "domestic mode of production" which characterizes primitive economics, described by Marshall Sahlins as a "species of anarchy": "The domestic mode anticipates no social or material relations between households except that they are alike. It offers society only a constituted disorganization, a mechanical solidarity set across the grain of a segmentary decomposition. The social economy is fragmented into a thousand petty existences, each organized to proceed independently of the others and each dedicated to the homebred principle of looking out for itself."[27]

I am describing a system directed toward goods distribution rather than goods production, which reflects a classical primal economy. If primitive economics is "anarchic" in its modes of production, it becomes more social and more organized in its system of distribution, which is characterized by its remoteness from productivity. In mature market economies the focus of human endeavor is production and productive relations, and these are intimately related to the system of distribution. The firm, the owner, the manager, the employee and his household evolve self-definitions focused in productivity and its rewards in distributive consequences. This is also the historical weakness of capitalism. By assuming that distributive relations will take care of themselves, underconsumption and uneven distribution in consumption create tensions within the system that lead to periods of economic stagnation and contraction. Distribution is thus an intrusive problem of a system biased toward production incentives. In a system focused in consumption and distribution, on the other hand, such as is found in classical socialist systems, production and productivity are relatively ignored, and thus the problem is to establish effective productive relations. Production is the intrusive problem in a system biased by consumption and distribution.

The economic system in which American blacks, especially those of the underclass, find themselves supports patterns of consumption and distribution widely separated from the productive engines of economic relations, which are highly segmentary, localized and minimalized in their expressions among the black poor. W.E.B. Du Bois, America's first great black scholar, wrote in 1940: "The American Negro is primarily a consumer in the sense that his place and power in the industrial process is low and small."[28] As a primal system focused in distribution, the economy of the black underclass is a system of gift-giving. Goods, and people themselves, circulate within kin and kin-like relations of reciprocation and dependency. Carol Stack's study, *All Our Kin: Strategies for Survival in a Black Community*, explores this issue as it relates to "The Flats," a community in south Chicago. She reports a typical instance of the intrinsic fluidity of money (and consequent lack of saving and capital formation in black communities), in the family of Magnolia Waters. Waters received a $1,500 inheritance, which was intended for the purchase of a house. However, word of her good fortune spread quickly within her kinship network, and one by one each of Waters' relatives appeared at her door with a need — a burial expense;

an unpaid phone bill; a broken TV set, etc. — which she met by taking money from her inheritance. Within six weeks her $1,500 was gone, dissolved in gift-giving consumption. To have saved for a down-payment on a house, to have invested her capital by refusing to give to her kin, Waters would have had to stop "participating in the sharing and mutual aid" of her kinship system.[29]

Relations with others, focused in kin, but also including church, public housing, health, education and welfare officials, are an extension of a system of matriarchal economic distribution and dependence which takes the form of gift-giving — in economic terms, "transfer payments." The public welfare system, which employs a substantial (usually female) black middle-class, and the welfare recipient are united in symbiotic relations of exchange separated from productivity. Throughout the rural South and within the northern ghettos productive employment on a day to day basis, always problematic in any case, has been in steep decline for a generation. Sociologist William Julius Wilson reports that in the Chicago inner city most adults do not work during a typical week.[30] This pattern is repeated in other urban ghettos and in towns like Clarksdale, Mississippi where almost the entire black population is on government assistance or pensions, and those who are employed work in the public and social service sector. The system of production is one of paper and forms, cash and coupons, appointments and qualifications, services and entitlements, and of a ritual, bureaucratic oversight focused in economically isolated households. Government payments as salary, pensions and public assistance, in the forms of SSI, aid to dependent children, food stamps and Section 8 public housing form the income basis for most individuals and families. These highly localized units of production have little relation to each other; only to the ultimately remote and common system of public (and sometimes private) distribution and redistribution of which they are a part. This seeming order deriving from a common distributive system barely conceals the incipient anarchy beneath. In describing the "domestic mode of production" among primitive peoples, Sahlins says: "And if in the end anarchy is banished from the surface of things, it is not definitely exiled. It continues, a persistent disarray lurking in the background, so long as the household remains in charge of production."[31] And because the domestic system "entertains limited economic goals, qualitatively defined in the terms of a way of living rather than quantitatively as an abstract wealth,"[32] to live in a primal world is always to be intrinsically oriented toward material poverty. "Geared to the production of livihood, it is endowed with the tendency to come to a halt at that point."[33]

From the end of the nineteenth century on, commentators — including Du Bois — have noted the waste and spend-thrift habits of the black poor, and attributed them to slave values where there was no benefit to individuals in conserving anything: goods are "free" when people are not. But this view neglects a deeper, primal value system where wealth-building is not culturally understood and actually discouraged. In an examination of money flows within the black underclass community, the primal roots of poverty reveal themselves. Almost all money flows are forms of consumption which remove money from the community before there are the significant multiplier effects which build and sustain community income, and before capital can be accumulated.

The black church has historically absorbed major resources, and the black preacher was always something of an entrepreneur. In addition to mainline black churches, the variety of "store-front" churches, with their self-ordained clergy, is evident on every street in the ghetto, as are shamanistic psychic advisers, mediums and card readers. The black ghetto of Miami, for example, houses more than three hundred and fifty churches. Unlike the Catholic church in inner cities, which provided such invaluable resources as schools, colleges, hospitals, and service organizations to its immigrant members, black churches have relatively little to show for the resources they absorb. Such groups as the Association of Nurses and Ushers (which ministers to congregants who "fall out" during worship in episodes of spirit possession) absorb resources without providing tangible, long-term benefits.

The black church has also supported a pervasive "culture of death" within the underclass community, where dramatic funeral ceremonies are a central aspect of spiritual life. This may reflect the central role of animistic death rites in West Africa. The economics of death and burial have historically supported a large class of burial insurance salesmen, funeral homes, and related enterprises such as florists and casket sales. Often the only form of insurance which the ghetto and rural poor have is burial insurance. Poverty-stricken families sometimes make the biggest purchases of their lives by spending on what will only fade, decay or end up under the ground. In one case a family paid $311 each month in burial insurance premiums from a $1,030 income.[34] The wealthiest member of a black community is often, as a consequence, the local undertaker.

Vanity items, such as grooming products, jewelry, watches, hats, wigs, sports shoes, and expensive automobiles draw billions of dollars out of poor, black communities. Of special interest is the "church hat." Black women spend millions of dollars each year on extravagant hats to express "hattitude," especially when attending church.[35] The hat shop, which has all but disappeared in the rest of America, is a fixture in black neighborhoods. According to the Boston Initiative for a Competitive Inner City, while the average American spends $1,508 each year on clothing, inner city blacks spend $2,440 in support of the expressive life-style.[36] Entertainment, gambling, liquor, and drugs are also a constant and often destructive drain on resources. Hugh Price, President of the National Urban League, has complained that, "The reality is, no matter how great incomes become for individual blacks, our wealth is not sustained because we have very few assets that can be passed on from generation to generation."[37] What small surpluses accumulate in these communities are dissolved in consumption and waste. The truly wealthy in the black community, usually sports or entertainment figures, do little to raise the living standards of other blacks because what they do is so completely tied to the "expressive life-style," to personal expression and self-presentation. They often do not model the habits of education, discipline, thrift and personal character which build and sustain wealth. They in fact reinforce attitudes which shun the abstract and the formal, and stigmatize those, especially young men, who show intellectual interests ("act white"). John Hoberman, James McWhorter and others have noted a pervasive anti-intellectualism within portions of the black community, which often denigrates academic achievement, and which is especially damaging in an economy increasingly rewarding the capacity for highly mediated abstraction.[38]

A disproportionate part of the black middle class works in the public or not-for-profit sector as teachers, clerical workers and administrators, police officers and firefighters, postal workers and clergymen. None of these are routes to sustained wealth-building for the community as a whole. Business formation within the black middle and working-class communities, a route to sustainable wealth-building and employment for other black people, remains underdeveloped. This contrasts with groups such as the Jews, the Koreans or the Italians, whose prosperity and participation in the larger economy and culture centered in the development of small businesses within their own neighborhoods, but also within black communities where such entrepreneurship was often lacking. As in other pre-civil societies, "foreign" merchants play an important but conflicted role in localizing the larger economy. While black entrepreneurs complain about discrimination by banking institutions in lending, other groups have circumvented the banks and built kin or community-based modes of saving and investing. Thus, as some minority groups are character-ized by kin-based modes of saving and investing, the black minority has been characterized by kin-based modes of consumption and distribution, and a dependence upon the public sector or external private sources for investment.

These realities have meant that the forces of economic globalization disproportionately affect the black community, especially the black poor, because there are so few cultural buffers to adverse change. The economic and social basis of life for poor black people, marginal at best in the passing industrial economy of the North and the passing agricultural economy of the

South, was almost completely delocalized by the global forces transforming American society.

It may be useful to look at the role cultural values played in advancing one of these other minority communities, the Jews, because groups like the Black Muslims have often simultaneously vilified and envied Jewish success. Traditional Jewish culture is by its nature primarily instrumental rather than expressive. It has been a culture centered in *The Law*, its myriad abstract interpretations, and its practical applications. The rabbis meditated about, and mediated between, principle and practice. Werner Sombart asserted that Jews were called to live according to the Law in this world, not the next, making Judaism a *this-worldly asceticism*: "Holiness is the rationalization of life."[39] Every Jew is in this sense a member of a religious order which, while hardly monastic, imposes a "Rule," a system of discipline, of enclosure and of boundaries inextricable from a day-to-day world of covenants and negotiations, themselves symbolic of Jewish self-interpretation and experience. So inseparable were culture and commerce in some Jewish communities that the honor of holding up or rolling up the *Torah* scrolls was sold to the highest bidder.

Unlike black English which is spoken, but seldom read or written, Hebrew is a language which is read, but seldom written or spoken. It is also characterized by the multiplicity of its tense forms. Growth into Jewish maturity, symbolized by a boy's confirmation, or *bar mizvah*, is associated with the mastery of an unspoken, tense-oriented language in its abstract form, the *Torah*. This assumes an analytical distance from the world, mediated and reflective, not immediate and spontaneous. To be a Jew, suggested novelist and critic Cynthia Ozick, is to "make distinctions." Among other things, to be Jewish has traditionally meant making distinctions between what is permitted or forbidden; what is true or false; and what is valuable and what is not. A Jewish life is lived among complex intellectual and social boundaries which master the fluidity of ideas, values and experience. Culturally, a Jew is raised to be deeply social (in understanding his reciprocal relations and obligations with others in his community), and a critic; and it is this capacity for critical thinking, making distinctions, which has served the Jewish immigrant so well in advancing himself in a civil society, in business and the professions.

While charismatic leadership in the black community is typically centered in ministers who need to produce little of material value to achieve positions of influence, leadership in the Jewish community has rested in the more pragmatic business and professional classes, which could be described as the opposite of charismatic. When one thinks of black leadership, individual names and personalities dominate: Thurgood Marshall and the NAACP; Martin Luther King and the SCLC; Malcolm X and the Black Muslims; Jesse Jackson and the Rainbow-Push Coalition. Jews have achieved extraordinary influence and prosperity within an often-hostile American society. And yet it would be difficult to identify any particular leaders or personalities (with the possible exception of Stephen Wise two generations ago) associated with that success. This is an instance of leader-centered groups, versus group-centered leaders, the former largely expressive, the latter largely instrumental.[40]

This important difference in leadership styles between blacks and Jews has cultural roots, and demonstrates the handicap that primal cultural modes bring to effective change in a civil society. In practical terms, it has meant that in the few generations since their large scale immigration to America's large cities, Jews have advanced, in spite of prejudice, from the menial and industrial jobs first available to them to the businesses and professions which advance success in an information-based society. These same factors may also explain the relative success of Asian immigrants. This has not happened to nearly the same extent to the many black immigrants who came to America's big cities. That these problems of the black poor are cultural, and thus more intractable, is evidenced in the distance that black leaders, like Jesse Jackson, have put between themselves and the underclass. Don Rose, a former Jackson associate, has observed: "There are problems in the black community for which he has no solution. Drugs, crime, not just unemployment but unemployability — that's a pretty gritty level to deal on, and no one has any programmatic answer. Jesse doesn't. Trickle-down isn't going to change that. The sociopathy of the ghetto is hard core."[41]

The forces of globalized competition have greatly reduced the number of unskilled jobs in factories, warehouses, and construction, especially in the inner cities. There has thus been a delocalization of a large part of the economy in which American black people have earned their livelihoods, as unskilled agricultural and urban workers. While all working-class people have been negatively affected by these trends, inner-city blacks have been disproportionately impacted because they are largely separated from the social networks that provide the best access to available work, and because the removal of many industrial jobs to the suburbs has widely separated work from available black housing, which is concentrated in inner cities. Cost-cutting to meet foreign competition has caused American firms to reduce expenses through intensive applications of technology, and the out-sourcing of low-skill jobs to Third World countries. The reduction in growth of public sector jobs, especially in the military, is closing a traditional door of mobility out of the ghetto and the countryside for many underclass blacks (and whites).

But more fundamentally, unskilled jobs place the fewest burdens on primal sensibilities, and conflict least with the total constellation of cultural values and attitudes which poor black people brought with them from the South. It is characteristic of unskilled jobs that they are based in reactive modes, where the worker is really an extension of the tasks he does and the tools he uses. His world of work is a world of stimulus-response. The work is thus relatively unmediated, a process of habit rather than of thought or judgment. Repetition with some degree of strength and agility is all that is required to master such work. In a reversal of the Marxist notion, that being an object of one's work and one's tools leads to alienation from one's subjective self, the unskilled worker ironically preserves his autonomy and his cultural values precisely because his work does not absorb him. Its allocentrism cannot challenge his values, as may the skilled, problem-solving and judgment-based job of the educated worker. The disappearance of unskilled jobs consequently threatens the cultural base as well as the livelihood of many black people. Conversely, the biases of underclass culture increasingly conspire against the possibilities of finding work and earning a living in a dynamic, rapidly changing, increasingly abstracted and globalized environment. Only within the playful (but very lucrative) world of professional sports, and to some extent popular entertainment, does the reactive and unmediated allocentrism of black underclass life find continuing cultural support.[42]

NOTES TO CHAPTER TWELVE

1. Robert D. Kaplan, "Travels into America's Future," THE ATLANTIC MONTHLY (July 1998), p. 67

2. Lester Thurow, THE ZERO-SUM SOCIETY (New York: Penguin Books, 1981)

3. Alexis de Tocqueville, DEMOCRACY IN AMERICA, Henry Reeves, trans. (New York: Oxford University Press, 1947), p. 319

4. John H. Hertz, INTERNATIONAL POLITICS IN THE ATOMIC AGE (New York: Columbia University Press, 1962)

5. Gunnar Myerdahl, AN AMERICAN DILEMMA (New York: Harper & Brothers, 1944); also A CHALLENGE TO AFFLUENCE (New York: Pantheon Books, 1962), esp. p. 34

6. Leon Dash, ROSA LEE: A MOTHER AND HER FAMILY IN URBAN AMERICA (New York: Plume, 1996), p. 4; see also, Elijah Anderson, CODE OF THE STREETS (New York: W.W.Norton & Company, 1999) on black

underclass life in Philadephia; Frank McCourt's autobiographical ANGELA'S ASHES (New York: Charles Scribner's Sons, 1996) documents a primal, underclass life in Ireland.

7. Jeff Ferrell and Clinton R. Sanders, "Culture, Crime and Criminology," in Jeff Ferrell and Clinton R. Sanders, eds., CULTURAL CRIMINOLOGY (Boston: Northeastern University Press, 1995), pp. 3 and 4

8. Cf. James Q. Wilson and Richard J. Herrnstein, CRIME AND HUMAN NATURE (New York: Simon and Schuster, 1985), esp. pp. 416ff.

9. Nicholas Lemann, THE PROMISED LAND (New York: Vintage Books, 1992); an insightful parallel analysis of poor white immigrants to Cincinnati from Appalacia is: Greg Jaffe, "Appalachian Trails," THE WALL STREET JOURNAL, (April 8, 1999), p. 1; an interesting cross-cultural analysis is that of Susan Abbott, "Gender, Status, and Values among Kikuyu and Appalachian Adolescents," in Thomas S. Weisner, Candice Bradley, and Philip L. Kilbride, eds., AFRICAN FAMILIES AND THE CRISIS OF SOCIAL CHANGE, (Westport, CT: Bergin and Garvey, 1997)

10. Cf. J.L. Dillard, BLACK ENGLISH (New York: Random House, 1972)

11. Lee Rainwater, "Work and Identity in the Lower Class," in Sam H. Warner, ed., PLANNING FOR A NATION OF CITIES (Cambridge, Mass.: MIT Press, 1967)

12. Ralph Ellison, INVISIBLE MAN, 2nd ed. (New York: Vintage Books, 1995), p. 7

13. John F. Callahan, ed., THE COLLECTED ESSAYS OF RALPH ELLISON (New York: The Modern Library, 1995), pp. 452-453

14. Thomas Kochman, "Rapping in the Ghetto," in Lee Rainwater, ed., SOUL (Chicago: Aldine Publishing Co., 1970), p. 74

15. Cf. John Horton, "Time and Cool People," in Rainwater, *ibid.*

16. Eugene D. Genovese, ROLL, JORDAN, ROLL , *op.cit.*, p. 286

17. *Ibid.*, 297

18. Lemann, *op.cit.*, p. 19; see also, Pete Daniel, THE SHADOW OF SLAVERY (Urbana, Ill: University of Illinois Press, 1990)

19. Genovese, *op.cit.*, p. 610

20. David A. Schulz, COMING UP BLACK (Englewood Cliffs, N.J.: Prentice-Hall, Inc., 1969), p. 78; Ellison notes that "lie" is "an Afro-American term for an improvised story." *Introduction* to INVISIBLE MAN, *op.cit.,* p. xxii.

21. Herbert Aptheker, AMERICAN NEGRO SLAVE REVOLTS (New York: International Publishing Co. 1993); and Kenneth M. Stampp, THE PECULIAR INSTITUTION (New York: Random House, 1990)

22. Malcolm X (with Alex Haley), THE AUTOBIOGRAPHY OF MALCOLM X (New York: Ballantine Books, 1964), pp. 111-112

23. Callahan, *op.cit.*, p. 343. This fluidity of boundaries within a culture of mendacity may have disastrous consequences for public policy. The AIDS

epidemic in the black community resists control, in part, because of cultural denial. In a Centers for Disease Control study of 8,780 HIV-positive men who said they were infected by having sex with another man, one-fourth of the black respondents described themselves as "heterosexual," as compared to only six per cent of white men. Linda Villarosa, "AIDS Education Is Aimed 'Down Low'," THE NEW YORK TIMES (April 3, 2001), p. D5

24. Anthropologist Jane Guyer distinguishes between women's "lineal strategies" of advancing their interests through their children, while men pursue "lateral" strategies through acquiring more women. "Lineal Identifies and Lateral Networks: the Logic of Polyandrous Motherhood," in Caroline Bledsoe and Gilles Pison, eds., NUPTUALITY IN SUB-SAHARAN AFRICA (Oxford: Clarendon Press, 1994); see also Jack R. Goody, ed., THE CHARACTER OF KINSHIP (Cambridge: Cambridge University Press, 1973), esp. Jack R. Goody, "Polygyny, Economy and the Role of Women."

25. Talcott Parsons and Robert Bales, FAMILY SOCIALIZATION PROCESS AND INTERACTION PROCESS (New York: The Free Press, 1955)

26. William H. Grier & Price M. Cobbs, BLACK RAGE (New York: Bantam Books, 1968), pp. 52-53

27. Sahlins, *op.cit.*, p. 95

28. W.E.B. DuBois, DUSK OF DAWN ESSAYS (New York: The Library of America, 1986), p. 707

29. Carol B. Stack, ALL OUR KIN: STRATEGIES FOR SURVIVAL IN A BLACK COMMUNITY (New York: Harper & Row, 1974), esp. pp. 105-107

30. William J. Wilson, WHEN JOBS DISAPPEAR (New York: Random House, 1996)

31. Sahlins, *op.cit.*, p. 96

32. *Ibid.*, p. 86

33. *Ibid.*.

34. Scot J. Paltrow, "In Relic of '50s and '60s, Blacks Still Pay More For a Type of Insurance," THE WALL STREET JOURNAL (April 27, 2000); see also Dan Morse, "Shirts for the Dead Are the New Rage In Some Inner Cities," THE WALL STREET JOURNAL, (February 4, 1999); Samuel R. Delaney, the noted science-fiction writer, came from the family of a prosperous Harlem mortician; see his biography, THE MOTION OF LIGHT ON WATER (New York: New American Library, 1988); Michael Espy, Secretary of Agriculture in the Clinton cabinet, came from a wealthy family of Mississippi undertakers, as have a number of other Southern black political figures.

35. Cf. Michael Cunningham, *et.al.*, CROWNS: PORTRAITS OF BLACK WOMEN IN CHURCH HATS (New York: Doubleday, 2000)

36. Cf. "Harper's Index," HARPER'S (July 1999), p. 17

37. "Urban League Targets Prosperity," THE BOSTON GLOBE (July 31, 1998), p. A13

38. John Hoberman, DARWIN'S ATHLETES (New York: Houghton-Mifflin, 1996); John McWhorter, LOSING THE RACE (New York: Basic Books, 2000)
39. Werner Sombart, THE JEWS AND MODERN CAPITALISM, Mordecai Epstein, trans. (New Brunswick, NJ: Rutgers University Press, 1982), pp. 225-226
40. Manning Marable, BLACK LEADERSHIP (New York: Columbia University Press, 1998), pp. xvi-xv; typical of this expressive leadership have been the "million man" marches, with their dramatic display and rhetorical flourishes - accomplishing little in the way of tangible benefits. Charismatic leadership, to be viable, must be on constant display, hence its intense media focus.
41. George Packer, "Trickle-Down Civil Rights," THE NEW YORK TIMES MAGAZINE (December 12, 1999)
42. In the world of professional basketball an interesting shift has occurred as black players have come to dominate the game (currently, over 80% of NBA players are black). It has become less a tactical team sport engaged across the court, than a game of reactive skill played tightly under the basket, spotlighting charismatic (often flamboyant) individual players. Conversely, white players out-score black players at the free-throw line, where concentration and focused timing at a distance from the basket are rewarded. Cf. Donal E. Carlson, "An Environmental Explanation for Race Differences in Basketball Performance," JOURNAL OF SPORT AND SOCIAL ISSUES 7, (Summer/Autumn 1983)

CHAPTER THIRTEEN

THE PSEUDOPRIMAL AND THE PSEUDOTRADITIONAL

The rise of youth culture at the beginning of the twentieth century was one consequence of a global industrial revolution. For the first time, large numbers of young people faced a world radically different from that of their elders. This meant that the traditional values of elders and their authority were less relevant. More than this, adolescence was invented.[1] Before the nineteenth century, children had abbreviated childhoods, and began to live fully as adults by ages thirteen or fourteen, or even before. The coming of a more technological, urban culture now required more education, and began to delay adult responsibilities among the growing middle class. It is not unusual in our own day for people to be well into their twenties before they begin to live independently and make their own livings. This protracted pre-adulthood was heightened in the United States because in a highly mobile, immigrant culture children were likely to have even less in common with the values of their parents. The rise of an autonomous American youth culture, and its final ascendancy as popular culture on a global scale, was to have a profound affect on values.

It should not be surprising that as American youth culture began early in this century the language and music of the black underclass became its models. As disengaged and often rebellious outsiders, young people saw in the spontaneity of expression of the black underclass an example of apparent non-conformity and freedom. By the 1920's substantial parts of the white middle class were adopting, through its youth, the idioms of speech and music of the black ghetto. A "pseudoprimal" element began to infuse middle-class white culture. First, as Jazz and Ragtime, then as the Blues, Swing and Rock, black musical experience and its related slang — introduced by such black-influenced culture heroes as Elvis Presley — began to affect American attitudes toward the world. This was true especially of the worlds of expression and pleasure, sexuality and gender manners, style and fashion, religion and spirituality, family structure and child-rearing, and of drugs and alcohol.

By the 1960's there was not a major branch of American popular culture which had not been affected by these trends rooted in the experience of the black poor. Indeed, in fields like fashion, the direction of traditional influence was often reversed. Styles that used to begin among the white upper classes, who took their cues from Paris, and then spread them sequentially to the middle classes and to adult-conscious youth, now originated among the black underclass. By the 'seventies the streets of the ghetto were where many important fashion statements began, were quickly adapted by white youth, who were then emulated by their elders. Danny Hoch's wonderfully funny portrait of a white youth trying to emulate a black kid from the ghetto was recently achieved on screen in "Whiteboyz." One of these "wiggers" (the black term of opprobrium for these white cross-overs) is William Wimsatt, the only child of a University of Chicago professor. Growing up on Chicago's south side, surrounded by discipline, order and as much excitement as PBS programming could provide, he longed for the life of the black kids around him. Black youth seemed "to roam freely," like their rap, their graffiti tagging and their music. His book, *Bomb the Suburbs*, was the 1990's version of a trend in adversary American culture which had begun in the 1940's with the "beat" writers.

The role of the "beat" writers and artists in this absorption of black culture by the white middle class was central. During the 1940's and 1950's a group of writers began to create what was to become a "counterculture" (the term is Theodore Roszak's) to that of middle-class white America. All of these artists were outsiders in American life because of their life experiences, especially those relating to sexuality and/or ethnicity. Jack Kerouac, "the king of the beats," did not begin to speak English until he went to school, was bisexual, and always felt like a stranger in his world.[2] The social disruptions and fluidities of World War II had also detached this group of writers from stable community anchors. As outsiders they turned to the ultimate outsider as the model of the new, alternative America which they envisioned.

The basis of this beat counterculture was drawn almost entirely from the experience of the black underclass. Norman Mailer, an intimate of the beats during this period, proposed this in his influential essay, "The White Negro"[1957]. "In such places as Greenwich Village," he wrote, "a manage-a-trios was completed — the bohemian and the juvenile delinquent came face to face with the Negro, and the hipster was a fact in American life. If marijuana was the wedding ring, the child was the language of Hip for its argot gave expression to abstract states which all could share, at least all who were Hip. And in this wedding it was the Negro who brought the cultural dowry."[3] The beat writers — Kerouac, Allan Ginsberg, Gregory Corso, William Burroughs and the others — created a new sensibility with a jazz beat and a total rejection of conventional boundaries, including those of "respectable" language. Jack Kerouac's best-selling *On the Road* [1956], the clarion call of the "beat generation," was quite literally without boundaries. The original manuscript was composed on a roll of continuous teletype paper with no pages or conventional punctuation. Kerouac claimed to have written it in an improvisational jazz style, which he called "spontaneous prose," with no editing, in a pure stream of consciousness, aided by generous doses of drugs and alcohol. He chronicled his life on the road, transversing America, disregarding the traditional constraints of work, responsibility and conventional morality. It was a celebration of primal fluidity. To this the beat writers added elements of Eastern mysticism — especially Buddhism, which Kerouac celebrated as the life of liberated detachment in his novel, *The Dharma Bums*. By the late 'fifties the mass media were saturated with accounts of the beat generation, as "beatnik" and "hippie" entered English vocabulary.

Easy sex and drugs; a rejection of the habits and values of work; of families and responsibilities, found an ear in the enormous "baby boom" generation coming of age in the 'sixties. The Vietnam War and near race-war in the US made it possible for millions of middle class white youths to question conventional authority and the values on which it was based. Becoming a responsible adult is always a challenge in any case, but sheer proportionate numbers (and an abundance of leisure time on college campuses) gave this generation of young people the power to challenge their elders and maturity itself. "Don't trust anyone over thirty" (a slogan first coined during the Berkeley "Free Speech" movement) became the motto of a generation. Among the major reflections of this mood outside of popular culture, especially music, were the universities, which became increasingly in style and substance places of self-discovery and personal relevance, rejecting formal educational patterns, and such "authoritarian" devices as lectures, grades and graduation requirements. The rise of feminism, environmentalism, gay liberation and various identity movements made their marks as well, and represented to some commentators, among them Charles Reich, whose *The Greening of America* became a best-seller, nothing less than a new age of human consciousness. The greatest musical phenomenon of the century, The Beatles, represented the institutionalization (not to say canonization) of this new consciousness, as beat and rock culture became central to the lives of middle-class youths and many of their parents. The staid *Times of London* declared the release of the Beatles' "Sargeant Pepper's Lonely Hearts Club Band" as nothing less than a "defining moment in Western civilization."

What distinguished this growing counterculture was not only its lack of elitism, but its *anti-elitism*. As Gertrude Himmelfarb (following Adam Smith) suggests in *One Nation, Two Cultures*, there had long been two competing cultural strains in middle-class, market societies. One strain was vigorously enterprising, frugal, family-oriented, work-respecting, and self-disciplined within a socially moral orientation. The other strain was pleasure-oriented; inclined toward sensual and material consumption; individualistic, intuitive and ironic rather than rational; and indifferent toward traditional morality, including religion. In class-based societies, such as Britain, the pleasure class saw the benefits of bourgeois morality in producing the goods and the stability necessary to their lives of leisure and consumption. Oscar Wilde and the *decadents* at the end of the nineteenth century, and the *Bloomsbury* set at the beginning of the twentieth century, had no interest in spreading their values to the middle classes, let alone to the masses, toward whom their attitudes ranged from patronizing to contemptuous. Egalitarian America lacked this class consciousness. The counterculture had no desire to co-exist with middle class values, which it viewed as the enemy. It sought to revolutionize American society by promoting a Whitmanesque "New Age" — transcending bourgeois, competitive "elitism" in all of its presentations ("materialism," "racism," "sexism," "intellectualism," etc.), while it celebrated popular culture, the values of "the people." In attempting to transform America from a civil culture of strangers into a primal culture of brothers and sisters, the counterculture challenged the meaning of citizenship, and the civil world itself.

The globalization of American popular culture, with its beat and rock underpinnings, was made possible because, as an ultimately primal expression, its esthetic was easily shared. Popular culture lacks a specific focus in any tradition, in any particular language. Its elementary beats and rhythms, even its language of presentation, requires little interpretation. It can be assimilated whole, without much cultural mediation. In this sense the ascendancy of American popular musical culture was like the ascendancy of American commercial culture. Its presentation became standardized, reduced to a few, powerful, easily comprehended symbols and uniform products — like the "golden arches" of McDonald's and the youth-based, fast-food phenomenon which has swept the world from Moscow to Buenos Aires. The qualitative leaps in communications technology which came of age in the 'sixties, especially jet travel and satellite communications, created what Marshall McLuhan called the "global village." The insatiable media created their own messages to feed themselves — and often the media became the message. Popular culture became form without content, in the sense that the form is the content. "What you see is what you get," animates primal art. But for all of that, popular culture has a *punch*, an immediate connection to individual consumers and audiences. This is the essence of its style.

The rise of style as a social phenomenon is closely tied to the rise of the commercial middle classes in Western society. If one looks at the history of fashion, it is in the late eighteenth century that one can locate the rise of style. Style is closely related to the need for self-presentation, to making oneself visible in the world. The class-based societies of traditional culture are focused not in style, but in costume: that is, in custom. One's dress, one's self-presentation, was a branch of social etiquette. In the royal courts of Europe, this etiquette was carefully controlled. Articles of apparel were subtlety regulated, and what was being asserted in all this was the legitimacy of tradition. The new was a threat to this ordered world. The rise of the wealthy bourgeoisie thus created a problem. How was the person of means and accomplishment to present himself in this world of aristocratic custom? He found himself with models of dress, for example, but would he not appear ridiculous affecting a costume unsuited to his place in the overall social etiquette? Moliere's masterful comedy, "The Bourgeois Nobleman," both embodies and mocks the dilemma faced by the *nouveaux riches* becoming so visible in French society. As aristocratic ideals declined during the Enlightenment, and the new merchant class and its interests become more ascendant in Europe, style as a means of self-presentation arose as a cultural response.

Style encapsulates two qualities simultaneously. On one hand, style is by its nature transitory. To be "in style" or "out of style" suggests that the presentation *in itself* has little value. What has value is currency, being *a la mode*, "with it;" having the individual sense of taste which makes one fashionable. To be aristocratic was to be appropriately costumed; it had a giveness tied to birth and tradition. On the other hand, to be bourgeois meant to be sylish, to have an individual quality made manifest in one's presentation. This quality was thus closely tied to sincerity, the authentic self-expression by which an individual person becomes visible, moves into presence, in the world. In speaking of artistic style, W. H. Janson asserts: "Of a thing that has style, then, we expect that it must not be inconsistent within itself, that it must have an inner coherence or unity; a sense of wholeness, of being all of a piece. This is the quality we admire in things that have style, for it has a way of impressing itself upon us even if we do not know what particular kind of style is involved."[4] What had been a characteristic of art, style, began to define the characters of persons in bourgeois society.

In style two contrary energies are reconciled only in individual presentation: permanent sincerity and transitory artifice. Style, as both a phenomenon and as an esthetic, rose in response to the inherent mobility of people within commercial culture. It provides a language of identity and presentation, and it furthers commerce because each style replaces another style. The "creative destruction" of capitalism, asserted by Schumpeter, is nowhere so vividly demonstrated as in the realm of popular culture with its rise and fall of styles, each presentation creatively destroyed by the succession of yet another style. Style is consequently central to the consumer culture of modern capitalism.

The contempt of many intellectuals for the bourgeoisie, and its styles, is often tied to their self-conception as members of an elite, as aristocrats charged with the conservation and presentation of immortal truths and values. The rise of commercial society tended to erode the social position of intellectuals, especially in their roles as priests and prophets — the companions of princes — and it eroded the very belief in the eternal verities which were the basis of traditional intellectual life. To the extent that they have come to terms with bourgeois culture, many intellectuals have often come to regard it as their role to "raise the consciousness" of ordinary folk to these immutable higher truths, the standards, being eroded by the mobility of commercial society. This essential elitism of intellectuals as connoisseurs and teachers often attracted them to socialism because the latter undermined commercial culture, while it simultaneously preserved the role of intellectuals as guardians and interpreters of higher human values. More recently in America, that elitism has attracted some intellectuals to conservative politics because of its supposed support of higher standards and values.

Amidst the massive assault on social convention which the ascendancy of "New Age" beat and rock culture represented in the 1960's, a second trend appeared simultaneously. After World War II unprecedented economic prosperity, coupled to such transformative legislation as the GI Bill of Rights (guaranteeing veterans a college education and home ownership) created a large, new middle class. It was a middle class unlike that of other societies in that it was so proportionately large, and defined by extremes of geographic mobility and economic opportunity, with no adequate role models. In the South and the West, in particular, large population growth through immigration, and very significant increases in family income (much of it generated from the expanding military-industrial complex of the Cold War) created particular disorientations.[5] World War II had in fact promoted an industrial revolution in these regions, transforming economic and social relations, and producing a kind of belated Victorianism reminiscent of an earlier era's attempts to deal with new wealth, social mobility and the stresses which came with them. A pastel, neo-Victorian world of chrome and *kitsch* promoted a culture of plastic conformity and denial. The enormously popular *Paint by Numbers*, introduced in 1951, reflected the prosperity and leisure of a new class of consumers uncomfortable with functioning outside given borders. How were these millions of economically secure families, often with immigrant, working-class backgrounds, to live, to behave, sometimes hundreds of miles from where they were born?

The rapidly expanding popular media, especially television, were there to instruct. The "middle-class" American family became the family of Ward and June Cleaver, of Ozzie and Harriet Nelson, of Donna Reed and of "Father Knows Best." They were always white, and they lived in *ersatz* colonial houses on neat, shaded, suburban streets. Kids did cute and troublesome things, but were lovingly obedient. Mother wore pearls and pumps while she did the housework — and she was a fanatic with a sponge, devoid of mercy toward "ring around the collar," or "yellow waxy buildup," which she attacked with an array of "new and improved" household products. Post-war consumer culture was intimately tied to the creation of insatiable buyers anxious to demonstrate their "good life," their achievement of the "American Dream."[6]

Everything was orderly and secure in this imagined world, where "life" and "style" merged to produce a "lifestyle." All of life's most important questions had been answered and encoded in an unquestioned American Way of Life. Joseph Epstein eulogized over this middle-class America as "a time of prosperity, tranquility, and extraordinary optimism about the future."[7] This was, of course, a mostly fanciful version of the real lives of the middle classes. But it was a powerful body of images and a secure goal for people of immigrant or blue-collar background, new to affluence and economic security — and to social insecurity. This neo-Victorian world of the middle classes had hardly been secured when it came under attack by the values of the "hipster" and the counterculture. At the same time, American cities began to look increasingly black — and disordered. What Patrick Buchanan was to call the "culture war" was about to begin. The style of "pop," of a liberated life of self-realization within the higher consciousness of "hip" culture, collided with the style of "pap," the antiseptic, bland, conformist and insecure values of the new middle class.

America is a land without genuine tradition, as Louis Harz, Walter Lippmann, Lionel Trilling and so many others have noted, and in this sense has always been a land of style, of perpetual renewal, of "liberal imagination." This, perhaps more than anything else, defines the American character, the character of what Crevecoeur called this "New Man," this American. American cultural optimism rises from this sense of the new as a defining element in history. *Novus Ordo Seclorum* — "a new order for the ages" — is the national motto, which appears on every dollar bill. British observer Charles Handy wrote that, for Americans, "History is seen not as a nightmare from which we cannot awake, as it often is in Europe, but as something to be transcended, to be fashioned anew."[8] All attempts to create tradition in its basic sense of a hierarchy of roles and rules sanctioned by history have dissolved within the mobility and constant newness of American culture. Periodic attempts to create an American aristocracy, such as that of Mrs. William Backhouse Astor in the New York of the 1880's, or the Reverend Endicott Peabody, who founded the Groton School on the English public school model during the same period, ultimately failed before the constant reality of new wealth, and the nation's inherent social mobility.

There were, of course, almost pathological pockets of pseudotradition, especially in the deep South with its culture of mendacity and fake gentility, so brilliantly portrayed in works like John Barendt's non-fictional *Midnight in the Garden of Good and Evil*, and Tennessee Williams' fictional "Streetcar Named Desire." But in the very process of attempting to create the illusion of tradition the South only revealed its underlying social instability and lack of real legitimacy. And this instability and illegitimacy were due entirely to the perennial legacies of slavery and race, and the consequent failure to build a civil society. It is thus no accident that the American South has always been a land marked by violence. Its rates of homicide are much higher than those of any other part of the country, and began to spread to the North and West in the massive emigrations attending World War II. De Tocqueville took special notice of Southern violence as early as the 1830's. Historian Roger Lane, author of *Murder in America*, says, "The whole American scandalously high homicide rates are Southern in origin."[9] That the American South and parts of the West became the primary sources of a call for a "return to traditional values," should not be surprising. No other parts of the country have so consistently deluded themselves about the social character of an America rooted in civil modes of rational mutuality. And no other parts of the country have been so heavily impacted by social and economic change in the last two generations. The leaders of this summons of return to traditional values were also, almost without exception, people who had not grown up with the real experience of these values. Their lives were often, in fact, marked by extremes of social, economic, and geographic transformation.

Ronald Reagan, America's first divorced president, had notably distant and conflicted relations with his own children, and on occasion could not recognize them. He may have grown up in a small town in the "heartland," but the struggles of his mother to maintain a family's dignity and stability amidst her husband's alcoholism left its mark on her son, who spent most of his life two thousand miles away from the place of his youth in a cinematic wonderland of denial called "Hollywood." Reagan began his long career as the vessel into which, and out of which, others poured meaning. His "traditional America" may have been as thin and transparent as the film that embodies his acting career, but it anesthetized a nation reeling from the humiliations of Vietnam, Watergate and Iran. When Reagan's official biographer, Edmund Morris, chose a fictionalized narrative to present his decade of research he only confirmed, according to the *New York Times* journalist who covered the White House in the Reagan era, that "Ronald Reagan lived in a world of his own fictions, far more extensive than the fictions of Edmund Morris. Who better to plumb a phantom subject than a phantom narrator?"[10]

Newt Gingrich, who as college lecturer and House Speaker, championed a "restoration of American civilization," came from an itinerant army family of divorce, is himself thrice-married, and has a Lesbian activist half-sister. When Representative Bob Barr, Gingrich's Georgia colleague, sponsored The Defense of Marriage Act, he did not specify which of his three marriages he was attempting to defend. Neither William Bennet, whose best-selling *Book of Virtues* is something of a manifesto for the return to traditional values; nor Jerry Falwell, who founded The Moral Majority; nor GOP presidential candidate Gary Bauer, ex-president of the conservative Family Research Council; nor Ralph Reed, former head of the Christian Coalition, was raised in a "traditional family."

The right in America is characterized by its sense of nostalgia for an America that never really existed, combined with a paranoia that it is being stolen by ungodly secular humanism, liberal "big government" and media dominated by countercultural values. As one begins to understand the biographies of leading "traditional values" advocates one cannot escape the image of noses pressed up against the glass, of outsiders wanting very much to be inside an unfamiliar world — and fearful of regressing into the unstable world of social marginality from which so many of them had come. The black underclass was a threatening specter that haunted their lives — and their rhetoric — because it summoned images of failure to achieve this imagined world. Christian religious fundamentalism made an alliance with "free market" capitalism to save this fancied world, so that they could continue their pursuit of it.

It may be this that accounts, at least in part, for what might be called the "Timothy McVeigh Syndrome," after the notorious bomber of the Oklahoma City federal building who killed more than one hundred people. In the last generation a new sort of discontent has arisen among a class of men who subsist at the margins of America's white working class; men who feel that America no longer has a place for them.[11] They have formed the backbone of "Promise Keepers," an evangelical Christian movement to put men back in charge of their families, and in charge of America. They populate the various "militias" and extreme, survivalist "Christian identity" movements. They are at the core of the "gun lobby." White males, approaching middle age, usually with high school educations or less, they often come from working-class, small-town, or rural backgrounds. A generation ago they would have entered the military after high school or gotten a factory job. They could have supported a wife and family in the security of the small-town environments familiar to them. The abolition of the military draft and the downsizing of the armed forces coincided with the largest loss of well-paying industrial jobs in American history. The collapse of small family farms as global competition lowered crop prices in the 'eighties contributed other members to this alienated group, whose lives were disrupted by the delocalization of their economic and social subsistence. White rap star, Eminem (Marshall Mathers), symbolizes the resulting rage. The product of a de-industrialized Detroit working-class family, his fulmination against "the system" in general (and women and homosexuals in particular) sells millions of records that chronicle his disinheritance and anger.

Thus the Timothy McVeighs of America found their world disappearing into the global political economy. Often they abandoned their family's traditional allegiance to the Democratic Party and became "Reagan Democrats," willing to blame liberals, "big government," feminists or racial minorities for their situation in a changing America. Their support for "traditional American values," sometimes to the point of bombing women's clinics, gay bars, synagogues and federal buildings, is the final act in a tale of what they regard as cultural betrayal. Blacks may have been the first to feel the full impact of a globalizing economy, but working class whites began to feel the same pressures. Right-wing talk radio and figures like Gingrich and Buchanan made their discontent a focus of their political "culture war" to "restore American civilization" — which meant, in effect, to restore their lost lives.

The illusions of Christian fundamentalist religion and the economic fundamentalism of *laissez-faire* became allies in the culture war against those who were viewed as subverters of traditional values. In this they were aided by what may be described as the Augustinian-Calvinist strain in American thought. This strain, while by no means dominant or universal, has nevertheless been formative in basic parts of American history and of the American character. Augustine had taught that government was a punishment from God for sin. Without "The Fall" mankind would have had no need for punishment and thus no need for government. The Calvinist "Elect" saw government as a means to punish wrong-doers. The Christian Commonwealth is marked by the Elect's empowerment to create a social space where Christian virtue might be lived, an Augustinian "outpost of heaven."

Martin E. Marty, the historian of American religion, called this Protestant version of America the "Righteous Empire."[12] The realm of the righteous in turn required the vigorous suppression of the evil which those predestined for damnation brought with them. Government was inherently both punishment and punishing. Government had no genuine capacity to "do good" by its very nature. Many Americans have been willing to sanction big and intrusive government when, as during Prohibition or the McCarthy period, its function was to punish the depraved and the godless, or during the Cold War, when its function was to protect humankind from atheism and Communism. To them, America's government was God's "Terrible Swift Sword." The tragedy of Prohibition, which is a root of large-scale organized crime in America, or the Vietnam War, which did more to undermine the American social consensus than any other twentieth century event, are ultimately inexplicable outside the American tendency to define the actions of government in these moralistic terms. Biographer and historian Sam Tanenhaus has asserted that, "only in America do religious and political ideals become interchangeable, even indistinguishable."[13] The failure of political realism to take firm root in America is related to this tendency to universalize and idealize what are in fact parochial and essentially *apolitical* values. Political theorist Hans Morganethau wrote, "Political realism refuses to identify the moral aspirations of a particular nation with the moral laws that govern the universe. As it distinguishes between truth and opinion, so it distinguishes between truth and idolatry."[14]

What historian Richard Hofstadter called the "paranoid style" in American politics has much to do with this Calvinist tendency to divide society into the "Elect" and the "Damned," "Us" and "Them." The first Puritan settlers in Massachusetts lost little time in deciding that the native people were the seeds of the devil, and that others — dissenters, Quakers, witches — posed a constant threat to Godly people. Thereafter, blacks, immigrants, Catholics, Jews, homosexuals, and various "subversives" became "the other" in the paranoid consciousness. Alterity and "Americanism" defined one another. The fundamentalist Protestant mind says Hofstadter, "is essentially Manichean" because "it looks upon the world as an arena for conflict between absolute good and absolute evil, and accordingly it scorns compromises (who would compromise with Satan?) and can tolerate no ambiguities."[15] Prohibition, an extraordinary public policy almost unimaginable in any other nation, probably had less to do with social reform than with a distaste for immigrants, especially because so many of them were Catholics — and anti-Catholicism has deep roots in American history.[16] "Rum and Romanism" were inseparable in the Calvinist mind. That blacks and Latinos today suffer disproportionately from the government's disastrous and bankrupt "War on Drugs" may at least partly explain why it has become implacably integral to right-wing dogma.

The United States is the only advanced Western nation to maintain capital punishment. This practice has widespread public support, especially on the right, but increasingly alienates Americans from the justice systems of civilized societies. The socio-dramatic taking of (disproportionately minority) human life on the alter of the state remains integral to the cultural witness Americans continue to make to government as fundamentally and ultimately punitive. That Southern states dominate in the number of these ritual executions confirms the incivility of their cultural roots.

If government, ordained by God in the Augustinian-Calvinist mind to punish the ungodly, is incapable of doing good, the role of government must be limited, certainly in economic affairs. Mercifully, God has provided the "invisible hand" of free-market rationality, which makes government interference both unnecessary and, ultimately, immoral. That the United States never had an effective socialist movement (and remains the only industrial country in which there has been no major socialist political party) derives mainly from a cultural distaste for socialism, not so much as ineffective, but socialism as immoral.[17] Socialism assumes that mankind collectively can be redeemed within secular society, which is to deny The Fall itself. This means that basic governmental programs of obvious merit, such as Social Security, have never achieved legitimacy with the right because they challenge the view that no good can come from government. Such government attempts to "do good" also deny the fundamental separation which Calvinists have always insisted upon between the "Elect" and the "Damned." Socialism promises a society where there are only winners. Capitalism as understood by Calvinists requires losers. The marketplace is a great spiritual battlefield upon which the Godly and the ungodly are separated.

That ultimate American Calvinist, the Reverend Norman Vincent Peale, author of the best-selling *The Power of Positive Thinking* gave a sermon called, "How to Make Christ Your Business Partner." This apostle to the Rotarians never saw a Republican president or a market solution he did not like. He was outspokenly critical of the possibility of a Catholic president in 1960. His church, located on Manhattan's Fifth Avenue, could have as well been on the moon in its relations to New York's large black and Latino community. But for his prosperous congregation he had endless *practical* advice. In introducing his *A Guide to Confident Living* he suggested that, "The best place to get a new and workable idea for your business is the type of church service described in this chapter."[18] The same philistine boosterism is common in the appeal of many prominent conservative preachers and their media ministries, which are themselves highly lucrative businesses.

An orientation toward individual economic self-sufficiency in conservative American Protestantism often masks indifference to the plight of the poor, and to the welfare of others outside the church. One study even documented an inverse relation between conservative, fundamentalist church-going and ethical concern for others.[19] America's two most prominent "home-grown" religions, Mormonism and Christian Science, could not be more different from one another, or conventional Protestantism, in their theologies; but on one thing they do agree: the importance of demonstrating material prosperity. Christian Science, which as a system of radical idealism even rejects the "reality" of the world, is nevertheless pervaded by the Calvinist ethos of material success. Sociologist Bryan Wilson concluded that Christian Science is "the religious expression of the well-to-do and comfortable, or those who would be so; it confirms them in the righteousness of their possessions, or of their striving."[20]

Government *qua* government is not distasteful to a large portion of the American conservative community because of its abuses. Government is distasteful to many conservatives because it is a reminder of the unrighteous among us. For these people, all the revered hallmarks of American government and its "checks and balances" — the separation of powers, federalism, the Bill of Rights — do not reflect the need for the people's rights to be protected from government (these revered hallmarks never in fact protected the most vulnerable of the population), but rather they mostly legitimize anti-government ideology for a people who have had very little government. Americans under British sovereignty never even began to suffer the misrule which many Europeans endured. Since independence in 1776 government at all levels and with few exceptions has been remarkable for its lack of intrusion, and its inability to do so. Many Americans insist on unfettered private gun ownership (with a resultantly appalling homicide rate) because the monopoly on the right to use force characterizes government more than any other quality. The "right to bear arms," as fanatically insisted upon by the American right, has little to do with self-defense (which gun ownership in no way effectively furthers), but with a deeper animus of deligitimizing government as such.[21] Similarly, Americans, who have nearly the lowest tax rates in the industrial world, have made taxes a paramount ideological issue. America seems to be unique in the number of groups with the word "taxpayer" in their organizational names. Only in America do the media report on an annual "Tax Freedom Day" — that statistical day when the average American will have paid all of his taxes and can as a consequence begin "to work for himself" rather than "for the government." For many Americans saying, "I am a taxpayer," is equivalent to saying, "I am a sinner": confessing the condition is integral to resisting the act. The ability to tax is probably second only to the monopoly of force as a signifier of government. Every tax paid is an unwelcome reminder that government exists and that it is legitimate. That the government's power to tax, in effect to punish, is used to support programs for the poor and minorities (and the ungodly) is especially galling to the Calvinist temper.

This body of attitudes may explain the chasm which characterizes the right's insistence on domestic free markets, while vigorously opposing global "free trade." For the right, the face which America uniquely presents to the world is the face of God's righteousness. Presenting America, and Americans, as only other elements within a globalized humanity freely interacting with one another undermines this vision of American singularity. This singularity was enunciated as early as 1630 by Puritan leader John Winthrop, who exhorted his fellows to build a Godly "city on a hill," asserting that "the eyes of all people are upon us." There are few terms of distaste in the vocabulary of the American right that equal "one worlder." The appeals to economic nationalism of Patrick Buchanan and others derives from the prior assumption of the unique localization of God's grace in America.

Each of these elements conspires to promote a culture of incivility.

Civil government, and an inclusive civil society, were hardly known in the American South, and thus civility was not included in the canons of Southern culture because of the vast shadow which slavery and racism has cast over its development. Those vaunted Southern manners, especially because this etiquette was part of a pattern of systematic discrimination and oppression, hardly qualify as civil. The Southern obsession with race required that this basic pattern of social domination and submission be replicated and legitimized, in the name of unquestioned tradition, in all spheres of life, including gender and religion. The South was rural with few urban traditions. The experience of slavery and the culture of racial segregation required that elementary civil rights, such as voting, be sharply restricted. One-party (segregationist) government was universal throughout the South for nearly a century, leading to effective minority rule in states like Mississippi, which had large black populations. Local sources of authority, particularly the sheriff and the courts in the rural areas, were hand-picked by a few powerful, local interests. "Lynch law" and para-military organizations such as the Klu Klux Klan silenced effective democratic discourse on basic social issues. The fundamentalist Christian Churches, particularly the Southern Baptists (formed in defense of slavery and a bastion of resistance to integration) were an integral part of this culture of incivility. Fundamentalist religion did much to suppress any thoughtful discourse on important issues, and replaced it with the know-nothing anti-intellectualism (and such absurdities as "scientific creationism") which characterizes much of Southern church life to this day.

The repressive incivility of Southern culture coalesced with broader elements within the American character during the 1960's to produce the New Right. By the 1980's it was dominant within the Republican Party, and the "solid South," once solidly Democratic, had become just as solidly Republican. But like the counterculture it needed legitimization if its message and values were to become visible in the larger American society. There was no real Southern intellectual tradition, properly defined (*viz.*, the great stream represented by figures like the Alcotts, Hawthorne, Whitman, Melville, Longfellow, Emerson, Thoreau, Adams and James), and Southern political figures and religious leaders largely lacked the ability, the credibility or the visibility to produce such legitimization. The New Right was to find some of this intellectual legitimization in two unlikely places, producing one of the strangest social alliances in American history. Among the authoritarian conservatives of Catholic background, and the neoconservatives of Jewish background, the essentially anti-Catholic and anti-Jewish Southern core constituency of the New Right found its voice. For what is remarkable (but seldom remarked) about the phenomenon of conservative discourse in contemporary America is the disproportionate role that Catholics and Jews have played within it.[22] Ultimately those conservative voices arose from the ambivalences of an immigrant society, and the processes by which pre-civil, immigrant subcultures are assimilated into the cultural values of the dominant elites in a post-industrial, mass-information society.

Notes to Chapter Thirteen

1. A provocative study of some of these issues is found in Thomas Hine, THE RISE AND FALL OF THE AMERICAN TEENAGER (New York: Bard/Avon Books, 1999)
2. Cf. Ann Charters, KEROUAC: A BIOGRAPHY (San Francisco: Straight Arrow Books, 1973)
3. Norman Mailer, "The White Negro," in ADVERSTISEMENTS FOR MYSELF (New York: G. P. Putnam's Sons, 1966)
4. Janson, *op. cit.,* p. 36
5. Two very insightful studies of postwar Southern life are by Pete Daniel: LOST REVOLUTIONS (Chapel Hill, NC: University of North Carolina Press, 2000), and STANDING AT THE CROSSROADS (Baltimore, MD: Johns Hopkins University Press, 1996)
6. A stimulating analysis of post-war consumer culture among those working class Americans seeking the living standards of the middle class is by Andrew Hurley, DINERS, BOWLING ALLEYS AND TRAILER PARKS: CHASING THE AMERICAN DREAM IN THE POSTWAR CONSUMER CULTURE (New York: Basic Books, 2001)
7. Joseph Epstein, "My 1950's," COMMENTARY (September 1993), p. 42; I favor the more realistic view of the era by David Halberstam, THE FIFTIES (New York: Random House, 1993)
8. Charles Handy, "Toqueville Revisited: The Meaning of American Prosperity," HARVARD BUSINESS REVIEW (January 2001), p. 59
9. Fox Butterfield, "Southern Curse: Why America's Murder Rate is So High," *Week in Review,* THE NEW YORK TIMES, July 26, 1998, p. 1; a parallel phenomenon is the frequency of divorce in the South, 50% above the national average. Aside from the special case of Nevada, divorce rates are highest in Tennessee, Arkansas, Alabama and Oklahoma, "the buckle of the Bible Belt." David Crary, "Oklahoma Tackling Huge Divorce Problem," SAN FRANCISCO EXAMINER (November 12, 1999), p. A14
10. Steven R. Weisman, A review of Edmund Morris, DUTCH: A MEMOIR OF RONALD REAGAN, *The New York Times Book Review,* October 10, 1999.
11. An excellent account of the problems of the white working class in contemporary America is by Ray Teixeria and Joel Rogers, AMERICA'S FORGOTTEN MAJORITY (New York: Basic Books, 2000); Feminist writer Susan Faludi has produced a remarkably sensitive study of men in America: STIFFED: THE BETRAYAL OF THE AMERICAN MAN (New York: W. Morrow and Co., 1999)
12. Martin E. Marty, PILGRIMS IN THEIR OWN LAND (Boston: Little, Brown & Co., 1984). He was, of course, proposing the opposite of Reagan's term, "the evil empire," which described the USSR. A good account of the

contemporary religious right is: William Martin, WITH GOD ON OUR SIDE (New York: Broadway Books, 1996)

13. Sam Tanenhaus, WHITTAKER CHAMBERS (New York: Modern Library, 1997), p. 468

14. Hans J. Morgenthau, POLITICS AMONG NATIONS, 2nd ed. (New York: Alfred A. Knopf, Inc. 1958), p. 10. Numerous studies have shown the general belief of Americans that their country and its economy are uniquely God-given. An Ohio University/Scripps Howard poll in 2000 found agreement among sixty-two percent of Americans that, "God has given special blessings to the United States." Forty-six percent said they believed heaven helped America "become a wealthy nation." MILWAUKEE JOURNAL-SENTINAL, Nov. 23, 2000, p. 24A.

15. Richard Hofstadter, ANTI-INTELLECTUALISM IN AMERICAN LIFE (New York: Vintage Books, 1963), p. 135

16. Cf. Mark J. Hurley, THE UNHOLY GHOST (Huntington, Ind.: Our Sunday Visitor Publications Division, 1992); and Michael Schwartz, THE PERSISTENT PREJUDICE (Huntington, Ind.: Our Sunday Visitor Publications Division, 1984)

17. A good survey of the historical, cultural and social circumstances accounting for the failure of socialism to develop effectively in the United States is to be found in Seymour Martin Lipset and Gary Marks, WHY IT DIDN'T HAPPEN HERE (New York: W.W. Norton & Company, 2000).

18. Norman Vincent Peale, A GUIDE TO CONFIDENT LIVING (New York: Fawcett, 1996), p. viii

19. Rodney Stark and Charles Y. Glock, "Will Ethics Be the Death of Christianity?," TRANSACTION (June 1968)

20. Bryan R. Wilson, SECTS AND SOCIETY (Berkeley: University of California Press, 1961), p. 349; a contemporary American sect is the Church of Scientology. The church focuses it attentions on the desires of its members to achieve personal material success, and has itself become prosperous by charging high fees for its services.

21. Michael A. Bellesiles' meticulous study of American "gun culture" demonstrates both the lack of significant numbers of guns in private hands until after the Civil War, and the failure of state militias to play important roles in defense. The militias would have disappeared altogether, he concludes, except for serving their primary purpose as slave patrols in the South. ARMING AMERICA: THE ORIGINS OF A NATIONAL GUN CULTURE (New York: Alfred A. Knopf, 2000)

22. Although I wouldn't defend the proposition against persecution, it may be that the conservatism of both Catholicism and Judaism is ultimately embedded in a *historical* imagination, a backward-looking which is fundamentally pessimistic about human nature. The Anglo-Saxon Protestant vision, upon

which America was founded, is of a millennial "city on a hill," an optimistic view of the human prospect (if not of human nature) which is *ahistorical* and forward-looking regarding the future of humanity in the New World.

CHAPTER FOURTEEN

INVENTING A TRADITIONAL AMERICA

Catholic conservatives, of whom William F. Buckley Jr. and those associated with his *National Review* are among the most prominent, occupy a troubled place in American society. They come out of an Irish Church transplanted to the New World with the massive immigration occasioned by Ireland's "Great Famine" (1845-1850).[1] The American Catholic Church was subsequently shaped as an Irish church. Authoritarian, puritanical and other-worldly, Irish Catholicism saw itself as exiled and under continuous threat by a materialistic, Protestant America, which often made anti-Catholicism a hallmark of patriotism. Largely eschewing business or agriculture as the road to the good life in America — in Ireland land-ownership and commerce had been the domain of Protestants — Irish Catholics settled in the cities, created political machines, and made their livings as blue-collar workers or in the jobs and patronage that control over city governments made available to them. A number of the most prominent voices on the Catholic right come from such working class backgrounds. The result was a church hierarchy overwhelmingly Irish in background, and described by Boston's Archbishop Cushing in 1947 as "working class": not a single Catholic prelate known to him had a parent who had been to college.

Creating their own parochial schools, commuter colleges, social organizations and hospitals within urban neighborhoods, American Catholics could live a relatively insular Catholic life, traditionally defined, having little commerce with the larger, Protestant culture, and its secular and pluralistic expressions. And they were armed with the church's vigorous denunciation of "modernism," (with its roots in secular rationalism, individualism and materialism), first condemned by Pope Pius IX in his *Syllabus of Errors* [1864]. From these urban redoubts of traditional custom and belief occasional attempts were made to purify the larger culture of offending influences, using such devices as

Hollywood's Hays Office and the National Legion of Decency. This relative cultural isolation and conservatism was balanced by often-liberal political ties, especially through the Democratic Party and the labor movement. It was through city machine politics that Catholics began to play significant roles within the Democratic Party. Although Catholics did not begin to hold important national offices in any numbers until after World War II, they were central to the Democratic governing coalition during the New Deal. Similarly, as urban blue collar workers, Catholics played an important part in the rise of labor unions before and after World War II.[2] A number of Irish and/or Catholic figures, like Dorothy Day, of the Catholic Workers movement, and Michael Harrington, the socialist writer, even brought a touch of radical dissent to what were essentially liberal orientations in economic matters. It was from cultural conservatism and economic New Deal liberalism that a number of Catholic intellectuals, such as Daniel Patrick Moynihan, emerged into public life.

Catholics in Ireland had stood in ambiguous relation to political authority. Irish opposition to English, Protestant rule (the Catholic majority had been denied civil rights, including the franchise and public office, until the 1830's) made loyalty to Catholicism an extension of national identity: to be Irish was to be Catholic. If Anglo-Protestants controlled national government and politics in Ireland, Catholics became highly skilled in using legendary interpersonal and rhetorical skills for organizing local communities, often within the secret societies which saturated the countryside. Irish day to day experience was a primal life of subsistence, and of reaction to the powerlessness of social dispossession. The depredations of an Anglican squirearchy produced in the poor, rural Irish a style of life remarkable for its parallels with America's black underclass: a people enclosed by spirituality (and superstition), with remarkable verbal skills capable of producing charismatic personalities. The Irish also had a passion for gambling and sport; a talent for loquacious and charming mendacity ("blarney"); a disposition toward pugnacity ("donnybrooks"); and for entertaining in song and dance. The culture of death, reflected in the traditional "wake," was a dramatic focus for community life. The Irish were also a people plagued with familial disorganization and gender tensions, expressed in a society of bachelors, spinsters, deserted marriages, and matriarchal families — every married man a member of "the secret order of broken spirits," in the words of poet Seamus Heaney. To these circumstances were added forced emigration and dislocation; debilitating alcoholism; and pervasive discrimination ("No Irish need apply"). Such realities supported an overarching cultural fatalism and lassitude, stifling initiative and entrepreneurship. "I'd rather be inspired by idleness than bullied by 'busyness'," said playwright Sean O'Casey.

While the black church in America largely reflected and confirmed the lives of primal fluidity which characterized its underclass members, the Catholic Church in Ireland and America played a very different role. It provided the elements of tradition — the roles and rules within hierarchies — which structured Irish experience, especially in building a system of education: the vast, unparalleled parochial school system. The church was the vessel within which the fluidity of primal lives was given a shape and boundaries. Unlike the black church, which has probably been a net absorber of resources, the Catholic Church in America, with its sacrificing and self-investing priests, sisters and brothers, was the institutional basis for much of the cultural capital the immigrant brought to his assimilation into the American economic system. Especially among Irish immigrants in places like New York City, where primal disorder pervaded everyday life (thousands of abandoned Irish children causing mayhem in the streets) the church made heroic efforts to provide stability and structure. Father Flanagan's *Boy's Town* reminds us of that era.

In Ireland the parish and its priests had been the real connection of the average person to the church and its authority. The semi-legitimate Catholic parish was often the center of community organization before Catholic Emancipation [1830] had permitted a national hierarchy to be formed. But while the church enjoyed the reflected benefits of traditional Irish opposition to British rule, it distanced itself from Irish political resistance, fully understanding that opposition to political authority could easily mutate into opposition to clerical authority. Richard O'Connor has described "centuries of history when the church appeared to be the shield of the people, comforting them in subjugation, even while instructing its followers that they must be loyal to the government of the conquerors."[3] The church also understood that its relations to power and its privileges after Emancipation ultimately rested on the preservation of a status quo which often offered poverty and suffering as central to the Christian life. Consequently, the Irish episcopate vigorously opposed agrarian reform and such tenant organizations as the Land League, founded by (Protestant) Charles Parnell to break the absolute power of landlords. The Pope himself denounced as sinful the tenant "boycott" (which entered English vocabulary from these events), while he permitted Irish Catholics to eat meat on a Friday to celebrate Queen Victoria's jubilee.[4] Before Emancipation, Catholic clergy were educated abroad, and after Emancipation the church hierarchy was notable for both its distance from the lives of ordinary people, and for its closeness to Rome, which dictated unswerving loyalty to British rule "at all times and places."[5]

The Irish in America and their religious leaders carried these ambivalences toward economy and authority into American politics, simultaneously using local, machine politics to advance their economic interests — developing patronage into a high art — but also tending either to resist government as a system of "foreign" rule, or to approach it with unquestioning loyalty. There was never a full embrace of civility, which regards politics as the realm of critical citizenship, of limited, *individual* reflection and discourse concerning public matters. The tendency of Catholic conservatives to join anti-government, *laissez-faire* ideology to patriotism (such business figures as William F. Buckley Sr., Joseph Kennedy Sr., John Simon and Peter Grace being exemplary) was often an extension of this ambivalent embrace of American political democracy. Civility and authority seldom found common ground in a political world which tended to bifurcate between the pragmatic particularism of electoral patronage ("All politics is local," said Speaker Tip O'Neil), and the authoritarian universalism of Catholic dogma.

World War II began to diminish this Catholic, immigrant world. The new Irish-American middle class and other Catholics, like the rest of white urban America, began to see home ownership in the suburbs as the reward for the deprivations of the Depression and World War II. Post-war prosperity and mass communications brought them into fuller contact with Protestant, Anglo-Saxon values, and with civil society. This meant that the young William F. Buckley both embraced the possibilities of an education at the citadel of WASP privilege, Yale University, and was also so appalled by the lack of authoritative religious and social values there that he wrote a book, *God and Man at Yale* [1951], lamenting their absence. How was one to be as American as Yale, but as authoritatively Godly as the Irish Catholic ghetto? The anti-Communist crusades of the 1940's and 1950's provided a powerful answer.

The structure of globalized power relations was bipolar in the post-war world, dominated by two military superpowers, the United States and the Soviet Union, their allies and satellites. The localized manifestation of this global bipolarity was a system of "permanent purge" within the communist bloc, where anything except Stalinist orthodoxy was ruthlessly repressed. In the United States global bipolarity was manifested in an increasing tendency toward political and social conformism — "Americanism" — within which any dissent was viewed as at least latent disloyalty.[6] Constantly shifting interpretations of Stalinist orthodoxy in the eastern camp, and of the real meaning of Americanism in the United States only heightened the pervasive atmosphere of uncertainty and threat, expressed in Hollywood's obsession with nuclear holocaust and "alien" invasions. As social relations were fractured and individuals faced isolation, a desire for stability and certainty threatened the forces of pluralist conversation within civil society. Conservative Catholics found themselves amidst political and social conditions highly convivial to the moral siege mentality which had often pervaded immigrant Catholic communities. At last they could fully demonstrate to suspicious Protestants how American they really were. They would often, in fact, question the patriotic loyalties of the "liberal" WASP establishment (who had dominated the New Deal), and suggest that they themselves were the real repositories of America's past.

As eastern Europe, especially its predominantly Catholic areas (e.g., Poland and Hungary) fell under the Soviet heel, and historically Catholic France and Italy saw the growth of large and influential Communist parties, the American Catholic Church under the leadership of figures like Francis Cardinal Spellman of New York made anti-communism the *sine qua non* of committed Catholicism. Garbed in a military chaplain's uniform, Spellman embodied "the Church Militant," appearing among American troops, side by side with their generals, at Asian and European front lines during the Cold War. From the pulpit he urged Italian-American parishioners to communicate to their families in Italy the importance of voting against the Communists in the 1948 elections. Hungary's Cardinal Minzcenty and Yugoslavia's Cardinal Stepanak were portrayed by him as contemporary martyrs. His close association with Pope Pius XII in the fight against global communism was highlighted in publications.

At the end of World War II the Reverend John Cronin, working on behalf of American Catholic bishops, had issued a report, "The Problem of American Communism in 1945." Cronin was to become an intimate of the FBI, and the source of information to such figures as Richard M. Nixon of the House Un-American Activities Committee in their quest to root out "communist subversion." Similarly, members of the Church hierarchy became staunch supporters of such anti-Communist figures as FBI Director J. Edgar Hoover and Secretary of State John Foster Dulles, whose son, the Jesuit priest Avery Dulles, would ultimately earn a cardinal's hat for his papal loyalties. Joseph McCarthy himself was encouraged by professors at Jesuit Georgetown University to make anti-communism the focus of his political advancement.

In their respect for unquestioned values and the hierarchies within which those values functioned, and within an elevation of political figures like Hoover, Dulles, and McCarthy to positions of unquestioned authority, conservative Catholics melded their traditions with this new Americanism, typified by such works as Buckley's *McCarthy and His Enemies*. Whittaker Chambers, an ex-communist and Christian convert, and his best-seller, *Witness*, were widely promoted within Catholic circles. It was Chambers more than anyone who voiced the view that the anti-communist struggle was nothing less than a historical confrontation between what is Godly and what is ungodly, between what is archtypically good and archtypically evil. For Chambers had declared, in the words of his biographer, "that anything less than total commitment, than moral absolutism, is a failure of nerve, of imagination, of historical grasp."[7]

Dean Clarence Manion, of the University of Notre Dame, and his national radio program, "The Manion Forum," formed a focus for the Catholic right. His book, *The Key to Peace*, proposed "a formula for the perpetuation of real Americanism," a formula of uncompromising religious faith and unquestioning political loyalty.[8] The Jesuit magazine, *America*, promoted the same premise. Bishop Fulton Sheen's popular television program represented a most visible sign of the merger of crosier and flag. The founding of *The National Review* in 1955 by Buckley, William Rusher, and other conservative Catholics extended this trend into broader, non-Catholic conservative discourse. The later establishment of the *New Oxford Review* and *First Things* provided a continuing focus for Catholic conservatism within the broader social dialog.

It was as anti-Communists that a number Catholic figures first emerged fully into American public life. Some of these figures were converts to Catholicism, and this suggests the passion for certainty they brought with them. Writer Clare Booth Luce, wife of the fervently anti-communist publisher of *Time*, became a very visible and influential spokesperson for the Catholic right, after her conversion by Bishop Sheen. Former leftists and even communists, like Louis Budenz (who had been editor of *The Daily Worker*), converted to the Catholic camp, demonstrating that there was much the two movements had in common apart from authoritarian organization, particularly righteous certitude and feeling part of an occult but triumphalist minority. Budenz advanced the view that the chief aim of communism was to destroy the Catholic Church, the only firm bastion of social morality.

Anti-communism also supported the elevation of conservative political philosophy — Russell Kirk being the almost unchallenged voice — with free market economics. Buckley had set the tone early in his attack on liberal higher education at places like Yale for its refusal to defend capitalism as a system of morality as absolute as the sovereignty of God, while simultaneously soliciting the philanthropy of capitalists to propagandize their children. Leo Strauss and the Chicago school of *emigre* theorists had a particularly strong impact in Catholic intellectual circles because they also rejected large portions of the Enlightenment legacy, which Catholics saw as the root problem of modernist values. Friedrich von Hayak's *Road To Serfdom* became canonical in conservative Catholic circles, in part because of its almost Thomistic reduction of economic theory to first principles, the absolute right of private property and *laissez-faire* markets. Ludwig von Mises was to be especially influential in Catholic conservative economic thought later represented by figures like Michael Novak, who asserted that the sin of "envy" lay behind attempts to fetter capitalists. George F. Gilder was to go even further, celebrating American capitalism as a form of altruism, an extension of Christian giving.[9]

Conservative Catholic discourse was also characterized by a Thomistic emphasis on reason and disputation, perhaps the greatest legacy of those commuter, Jesuit universities to American public life. This disputation was usually refreshingly free of the anti-Semitism of the Fr. Coughlin type, which was the curse of the traditional American right. And Buckley, for one, used his growing prestige in conservative circles to vigorously challenge anti-Semitism whenever it appeared. Catholic tradition had prepared these conservative figures, if not with refined intellectual values, with the tools of advocacy which Protestant fundamentalist education, especially in the South, did not. War horses of the political right, writers and media figures like Phyllis Shlafly, John McLaughlin, Richard Viguerie, Paul Weyrich and Patrick Buchanan, emerged from this traditional, authoritarian Catholic strain of the Cold War years. Hofstadter remarked a generation ago: "Indeed, one of the most striking developments of our time has been the emergence of a kind of union, or at least the capacity for cooperation, between Catholic and Protestant fundamentalists, who share a common Puritanism and a common mindless militancy on what they imagine to be political issues, which unite them in opposition to what they repetitively call Godless Communism."[10] The effective disappearance of Godless Communism as an issue has merely switched this mindless militancy to other imagined political issues: the subversion of "family values" in the forms of pornography, feminism, abortion and gay rights.

The Second Vatican Council [1962-1965], with its emphasis on "renewal" and ecumenism, represents something of a benchmark of change for the American Catholic Church. On one hand, it opened up the church to dialog with the larger community in the United States. Catholic higher education was significantly impacted by the new freedom, and Catholic universities like Georgetown and Notre Dame began to build academic reputations equivalent to many of the best non-Catholic institutions. The lack of an inquisitive intellectual tradition in America among Catholics was one of the great weaknesses asserted in John Tracy Ellis's landmark, "American Catholics and the Intellectual Life"[1955]. Under the leadership of President Theodore

Hesburgh of Notre Dame, the "Land O'Lakes Statement" committed American Catholic higher education to standards of academic freedom and excellence indistinguishable from other first-rate universities. Figures like Daniel Patrick Moynihan and Michael Novak emerged as a new sort of Catholic intellectual, more broadly engaging their non-Catholic colleagues, in part because of their exposure to secular universities like Tufts and Harvard. This was especially the case regarding their interactions with Jewish intellectuals: both Moynihan and Novak established relations with *Commentary*, published by the American Jewish Committee, and later a leading voice for neoconservative ideas.

Simultaneously, the loyalty of American Catholics to the institutional church and its unquestioned authority began to decline.[11] Attendance at mass and the sacraments saw a steep attrition, and Catholic young people embraced the youth culture, including the "sexual revolution," with as much energy as their non-Catholic peers. Intermarriage with non-Catholics was one manifestation of the dissolution of the city ghettos in suburban prosperity. Catholic divorce and remarriage rates began to approach national averages. Most ominously, the exit from service to the church of significant numbers of priests, sisters and brothers, and a precipitous decline in religious vocations over the next decades, imperiled the ability of the church to reach its members. The closing of many parochial schools because of the lack of sisters and brothers to staff them threatened the introduction of children to Catholic culture. Since many of the new Catholic immigrants (especially Hispanics) did not bring their native clergy with them, they were often lost to Protestant sects. Also striking was the rise to prominence of a number of Catholic clergyman, like the Berrigan brothers, Robert Groppi and Robert Dornan, who became liberal activists. By the 'seventies, numbers of Catholics began to question the spirit of reform within the church, and trends within American society generally.

A key figure to emerge from the Catholic right in the 1960's was Paul Weyrich, who established the Free Congress Foundation and the Heritage Foundation, and who was an influential voice in other conservative forums. The offspring of an immigrant, working-class family, he laid some of the intellectual foundations for the Christian fundamentalists and other social conservatives who came to dominate the Republican Party. With the indispensable financial support of the scion of another immigrant German family, Joseph Coors, Weyrich pioneered the conservative "think tank" as an alternative to the dominantly liberal intellectual establishment found in the universities, philanthropic foundations and elsewhere. Weyrich identified the cultural crisis which lay at the basis of dissent within the American Catholic Church, and the moral shift which had occurred in the 1960's as Vatican II reformist trends merged with counterculture trends in the wider environment. It was Weyrich who coined the phrase, "the moral majority," to describe the traditional values of "real" Christians and "real" Americans, who dissented from the liberal minority who he believed had come to dominate public discourse. But it was Jerry Falwell, who founded the first major, conservative Christian political action group, The Moral Majority, as well as Pat Robertson (founder of the Christian Coalition) and other Southern Protestant fundamentalists, who used their media ministries and their access to thousands of evangelical churches to provide the organizational framework within which this position was advanced.

The failure of the right to make much political progress on moral issues of central importance like abortion, in spite of winning the White House under Reagan, and both branches of Congress under Newt Gingrich, caused some conservative Catholics, like Richard Neuhaus, to question whether Christians could regard the American government as legitimate, or whether Christians could hold allegiance to it. These feelings of deep discontent on the right reached their apogee in the striking failure of conservatives successfully to use impeachment to remove President Clinton from office. The morality agenda of the right in the 1998 congressional elections cost the Republicans a historically unprecedented loss of seats in the House, and ultimately the Speaker and his designated successor their jobs and their seats. The acquittal of President Clinton in his trial, in the face of overwhelming support for him from the American electorate, was the occasion of deep despair from Weyrich and the conservatives, who now were forced to re-examine their basic premise that the political process could be used to reorient American culture. Weyrich told conservative Christian activists in April 1999: "What I am trying to tell my brethren is that this strategy has failed. If there ever was a moral majority — and I'm not now sure that there ever was — it has ceased to exist. We have had a major cultural shift in this country."[12]

The dilemma of Weywich, Buckley and other conservative Catholics lay in the absolutism of Catholic culture. It did not easily adjust to constantly changing modern circumstances because of its authoritarian and dogmatic premises. This meant that while individual Catholics might pragmatically alter their beliefs and practices to accord with modern realities, Catholic intellectuals had a more difficult situation. Michael Novak, who early in his career as a theologian had embraced the heady atmosphere of "renewal" advanced by Vatican II, found himself retreating into orthodoxy once he realized the challenge to authority and dogma itself which had been implicit in any significant change. Those Catholic intellectuals, like Karen Armstrong, who could not accept this retreat thus often left the church entirely to pursue an independent course. In the case of intellectuals like Mary McCarthy, a marked tone of rejection and bitterness toward anything Catholic characterized their memories of Catholic life. For others, like John Murray Cuddihy, there was an appreciation for the Catholic culture of their youth, but also an understanding that no final compromise of intellectual independence with Catholic authoritarianism was possible. As Thomas Merton — who was forbidden to publish by church authorities in the late 'sixties — was to discover, there were no half-way houses between orthodoxy and apostasy. For American Jewish intellectuals, on the other hand, it was the proliferation of such intellectual half-way houses which characterized their assimilation into modern life.

For conservative Catholic intellectuals, coming from a traditional, immigrant, working-class church, the crisis they face presents itself as a crisis of authority. The church, its hierarchy and the parish had provided the wall of certainty against the dynamics of modernity and rapid change in American society. The dogmatic basis of Catholic belief had a face in these human institutions. Conservative Jewish intellectuals face a somewhat different version of the same problem. Since Jews as a *Diaspora* people have lacked authoritative institutions, authority has had to rest on a bedrock of law and custom; and these were mediated within strong traditional families. To be sure, other religious and ethnic groups stressed the family as the basis for social values and order. But Catholics, in particular, always had to moderate this stance with an over-riding respect for life-long virginity, and for their own celibate leadership and religious orders. A Jewish life outside the framework of family and marriage, on the other hand, was all but unimaginable. Rapid changes in the size and structure of Jewish families, related to education, affluence and social mobility, thus threatened the future of Jewish identity itself. Growing intermarriage with gentiles especially threatened the future existence ("continuity") of Judaism in many eyes. The rapid decline of Jews as a percentage of the American population as affluent, educated couples had only one or two children, had, for many, threatening implications because the Jewish population was not replacing itself.[13] This environment of success confronting survival provided a context for the rise of the Jewish right. What Catholic intellectuals had brought to the right in the 'forties and 'fifties, the neoconservative Jewish intellectuals brought in the 'sixties and 'seventies. They provided at least the patina of sophistication to what were often essentially pre-civil values.

The term "neoconservative" was brought into prominent use by Norman Podhoretz.[14] It was Podhoretz's magazine, *Commentary*, that was an important focus of this emerging brand of thought. Neoconservatives, like the word itself, were an uneasy marriage of the old with the new. Most neoconservatives once considered themselves to be liberals, or even of the left. "Conservative" in America had usually included the anti-Semitism of the Henry Ford stripe. Since many Jews had been associated with the left, and had been prominent within the Communist Party, American Jewry was wary. The anticommunism of American Jews was always moderated by the fear of anti-Semitism, which at least indirectly infused some anticommunist rhetoric. The emergence of the Jewish neoconservatives is remarkable because of this background, and because the Jewish community in America, even the wealthy part of it, has been marked by its liberal, even radical, social stances and politics. This remains stubbornly so even today. There is the suspicion, widespread within the attentive Jewish community, that American conservatism holds no lasting place for them; that, in the end, the conservative agenda is anti-Semitic. As one skeptical Jewish observer put it, if neoconservatism is not anti-Semitic, "it should be." When the Southern Baptist Convention, the nation's largest Protestant denomination, whose ministers have played important roles in conservative Republican politics, recently committed themselves to special efforts to proselytize America's Jews, many of these suspicions seemed to be confirmed. Patrick Buchanan, especially in his attacks on the Israel lobby in Congress, was the object of reproval from William F. Buckley and other conservatives.

But it was not economics or even politics, narrowly defined, which brought a number of Jewish intellectuals into the camp of the right. Even Irving Kristol, who most interested himself in economic issues, could only manage *two* cheers for capitalism. It was a deeper dissatisfaction with the trend of society in America. It was the specter of cultural decay, especially as it manifested itself in its impact on families, which animated the neoconservatives. Podhoretz underlines this when he says, "Indeed, I suspect that revulsion against the counterculture accounted for more converts to neoconservatism than any other single factor."[15] For these were figures who could still remember the traditional society which typified the Jewish ghetto, a life marked by its commonalties and certainties in every direction. Jewish immigrant life was imbued with standards, understood hierarchies within which behavior and achievement could be measured and acknowledged. In a countercultural world, where, as the rock lyric has it, "Everything is beautiful in its own way," neither standards nor achievement were ultimately recognized. This rejection of social norms implied avoiding the responsibility for meeting them, constructing a world with no successes and thus no failures. Jewish intellectuals had functioned at those cultural boundaries where social change was enabled, challenged and directed. It was the lack of such boundaries that characterized the fluid, postmodern counterculture, and this threatened as a consequence the social role of Jewish intellectuals. There was also an ambivalence toward immigrant Jewish life itself in the neoconservative revulsion against the counterculture. Countercultural expressions, as a kind of "acting up" — represented notoriously by Allen Ginsberg's poem, "Howl" — posed the specter of regression into the incivility and vulgarity of immigrant life and manners, from which Jews often self-consciously disassociated themselves in their quest for social advancement.

The neoconservative intellectuals were New York intellectuals, if not always by birth or residence, by aspiration and by focus. Born in the 'twenties and 'thirties, they were of the first generation of upwardly mobile strivers, often the first of their generation of Jews to be admitted to elite universities with "Jewish quotas," or to previously "restricted" clubs and apartment houses. This made them peculiarly insular as well as cosmopolitan. Given the city's huge Jewish population, it was possible to grow up in some Brooklyn and Lower East Side neighborhoods knowing few gentiles. The public schools effectively closed for Jewish holy days. An immigrant Jewish culture, tracing itself to the great eastern European immigration which began in the 1880's, created worlds of *Yiddishkeit*, of kosher markets and delicatessens, of social clubs and resorts, of Yiddish theaters and newspapers, of yeshivas and synagogues. This self-contained universe, at once difficult and magical, sometimes terribly poor but also infinitely rich, was brilliantly chronicled by Irving Howe in *World of Our Fathers*.[16]

The hold of the Jewish ghetto on its members was different from that of other immigrants, even the Irish. Other immigrants to America, as Christians and as western Europeans, were not asked to cross the same social chasm as Jews were expected to do to become "real Americans." Giving up at least part of one's Irish Catholic identity by adopting WASPish ways (as did the Buckleys and the Kennedys) was easier to do than to give up one's Jewish identity. In part, this had to do with history. By the time the Irish began to leave their neighborhoods ("parishes") in large numbers in the post World War II environment, large-scale immigration had long ended, and they had been in America for a century. When the Jews began to face these same pressures and opportunities most were still parts of extended families where some members spoke Yiddish and were observantly Orthodox. Never in America have a group of people experienced such a rapid change of social, economic and cultural circumstances as the first and second generations of New York Jews. They in fact had a powerful and *real* traditional world, which they now faced losing as a consequence of their emergence into civil life. That some of them retreated when their assimilation into modern and secular American culture was finally tested in the 1960's should not be surprising.

Jews brought a number of cultural advantages to this problem of assimilation into America and its civil culture. The Jews were a "People of the Covenant," a culture rooted in the *Torah*. Jewish cultural modes and America's own covenant-based society were especially convivial to one another. Americans — as Pilgrims, as slaves, as Mormons — often self-consciously acted out the Jewish historical venture of freedom, of exodus into a promised land. The intellectual arts and education, so central to the Jewish tradition, were a path to success in a society as flexible and mobile as America's, as they were not in other places. Excellence in teaching and learning were to be the vehicles by which many Jews prospered in America. Traditional Jewish experience in small trades and businesses made transitions to the larger business economy more possible. This was especially so when combined with the cultural talent for "making distinctions," which translated into an ability to read environments and their possibilities. Jewish community organization and capacities for solidarity were already present in the ghettos and *shtetl's* (Jewish towns) of eastern Europe. Jews had something of an urban tradition when they settled in America's burgeoning cities. When necessary there was some collective ability to influence the larger, often-hostile, social environment. In short, Jews as a *Diaspora* people were to some degree culturally adapted to life among strangers, a core component of civil society. Finally, there was a competitive spirit, sometimes perceived as brash by outsiders, which made success a value to be pursued for its own sake. Elena Lappin calls this imperative the *Eleventh Commandment*, "written especially for and by generations of American Jews: Thou Shalt Succeed."[17] This passion for success formed a perfect meld with characteristics dominant in the American environment. Norman Podhoretz wrote a memoir called *Making It*, in which he owned up to "the dirty little secret" of his generation: they wanted success in the larger culture.

But there was a hidden price to be paid for this rapid mobility by New York's Jewish intellectual elite. Because of New York's large Jewish population it was possible to affect some of the style of the gentile environment without really losing one's traditional values; that is, to assimilate only superficially. In Manhattan after World War II the prosperous white population became increasingly Jewish as the Christian middle classes left for the suburbs. By the 1960's the two most animating elements in Manhattan's resident population were the Jews, mainly prosperous and educated, enjoying (and often providing) all the advantages of one of the world's most stimulating and creative environments, together with a growing underclass of blacks, Latinos and other Third World people, struggling to make a bare living. Between blacks and Jews, in particular, there was a growing irritation as the 'sixties progressed. In the arts and entertainment, publishing, education, medicine and law, not to mention realty, retailing, small manufacturing, and investment banking, Jews had become very visible, and often very successful. Black people only became more alienated and more militant as the industrial economy and urban life decayed around them; and they found a succession of preachers, from Malcolm X to Al Sharpton, to voice their anger. The transformation of New York Jewish liberals (who experienced this urban decay from a different perspective) into Jewish conservatives can be followed in such works as Myron Magnet's *The Dream and the Nightmare*.

Also very important in supporting the New York intellectual's perception that he had in fact "made it," that his values were modal and universal rather than parochial and Jewish, was the rise of intellectual modernism, which became ascendant with the advance of Jews in the city's intellectual life during and after World War II. Even those Jewish intellectuals who did not embrace all modernist expressions, like Lionel Trilling who dissented from much of the "New Criticism" in literature, nevertheless were shaped and advanced by the dominant modernist conversation which pervaded New York intellectual life beginning in the 1940's. If modernism was a central threat to traditional Catholic life in its encounter with America, modernism was to many Jews an effective weapon in that encounter.

Modernism was from the beginning a psychological and social temper as much as an intellectual and esthetic movement. As a sensibility it was intimately related to the *fin de siecle* explorations of European literary and artistic figures, but also to the philosophical questing in figures like Nietzsche, who argued for the transcendence of all values in a new kind of human being. The desolation of World War I confirmed this direction in the art of writers like Joyce, Eliot, Kafka and Hemingway, and in the art and architecture of figures like Picasso and Mies. The *Bauhaus* movement, which sprung up amidst the social and economic dislocation of post-World War I Germany, attempted not just to advance new, modernist styles in architecture, art and industrial design, but to champion a whole new way of living. That most members of the Bauhaus were socialists and communists suggests the flavor of the life they envisioned.

The great American modernist critic, Lewis Mumford, combined these powerful tensions in his own life and vision. Raised in a Jewish Brooklyn neighborhood, he was the illegitimate son of a Jewish father and a difficult, distant gentile mother. He found in the extended Jewish immigrant family of his wife, Sophie, the model of community he wanted for America. Deeply influenced by European trends as well, he called for nothing less than a new, organic way of thinking and feeling that recognizes "the inner and the outer, the subjective and the objective, the world of personal intuition and that described by science [as] a single experience."[18] Because it began "anew," from a base line that was less historical than existential, the modernist sensibility was particularly attractive to the emerging Jewish elites in the Western world. Modernism presented itself not as a new style, but rather as a new truth, rather like Marxism and Freudism, its sibling sensibilities among many Jewish intellectuals. It was in fact anti-style, and deeply adversarial in its insistence on sincerity without artifice. It spoke the language of individual questing and integrity, of *seriousness*. Modernism was an ethic as well as an esthetic, and thus like Marxism and Freudism particularly attractive to secularizing Jews in the commitment it demanded.

The god of modernism was a jealous god, who did not permit attendance at other altars. But he was honored under a number of names: "integrity," "honesty," "authenticity," "simplicity," "sincerity," "austerity," "functionality." Because of its focus in abstract technique, means rather than ends, modernism was a radical reflection on the traditional past that in fact delegitimized large portions of it. By replacing traditional Western cultural forms with abstract ones, Jewish modernists were often asserting their freedom from a history they did not feel was theirs, except in its oppressions. Architecture critic Herbert Muschamp proposes: "For 20th-century artists, abstraction was not a purely aesthetic matter. Liberation from explicitly historical motifs held social meaning. It conveyed the idea that assimilation into the Western tradition did not require submission to archaic and undemocratic forms of previlege."[19]

In elevating authentic, abstract form the modernist could neglect content, or at least leave content intact if it could be made consonant with expression. The function (the "how") eclipsed the form (the "what"). *How* something means, not *what* something means became the imaginative focus of modernist esthetics. "A rose is a rose is a rose," wrote modernist poet, Gertrude Stein. A philosophical expression of modernism was the rise of analytic philosophy, deriving from the work of Ludwig Wittgenstein and his followers. "Logical positivism" and its variants began to dominate philosophy in post-war America, and to concern itself narrowly with linguistic issues and mathematical proofs. Traditional Western philosophy, with its concern for the total human universe of meanings, was abandoned (as "non-sense") in favor of a narrow, almost Talmudic didacticism; of a self-referential game concerned only with the formal consistency of its own rules. Its assertions to be "value free" resisted the moral claims of the dominant culture. Karl Deutsch and positivist social science represented the same emerging trend in the 1950's. The followers of Arnold

Schoenberg and the "Serialists" also rejected traditional musical form, and began composing anew atonally, or with a twelve-tone scale. This produced a completely closed and pedantic musical system which could be appreciated only by audiences indoctrinated into its premises.

In modernist criticism, both artistic and literary, apprehension of form was not ultimately directed inwards toward content, but outward toward effect, the individual expression and experience of the artist and of the work. In modern art and architecture form often became the functional medium itself: the frank expression of heating ducts, engineering devices and lighting elements in buildings; the texture of the sculptor's clay, the application of paint on canvas, or the canvas itself in art — and the focus of critical investigation for figures like Clement Greenberg. The subject-object separation was completed in this abstract formalism, where the work of art had no meaning apart from itself. Modern literature expressed the same sentiment in that it became almost an extension of the behavioral in writers like Lawrence, Proust and Hemingway. Modernist literary criticism expressed itself in a very close reading of texts; the uses (and invention) of language; and the nature of character construction, rather than upon narrative or historical context. In this closed world of narrow judgments the modernist motto could have been, "Guilty, until proved innocent of the past." A number of neoconservative critics, including Hilton Kramer, Joseph Epstein and Podhoretz himself, had begun their careers in this modernist milieu.

Modernism was especially convivial to Jews who wished to believe that they were in the *avant garde*, not the ghetto. Newly-educated and prosperous eastern European Jews often embraced modernism as evidence of their cultivation, without the unwelcome Christian connotations. The Jewish modernists tended to believe that their special access to modernist forms and statements, not easily understood by the "man in the street," set them apart not as pariahs, but as an elite intelligentsia. Modernism, sharing roots with the European *refuses* and *secessionists*, was in fact itself a counterculture echoing the pledge of James Joyce: "I shall not submit." And like the communists and socialists, who reserved their strongest invectives for each other rather than capitalism, modernism and postmodernism are alternative countercultures in collision.

But the line between *avant garde* and *parvenu* is a thin one. It was the crisp, defining borders of modernism which separated the *avant garde* intellectual from the *parvenu* Jew in the mind of New York's emerging Jewish intelligentsia. They could have their cake and eat it too: from modernist glass houses they could cast stones at the unenlightened surrounding culture, and thus avoid the ordeal of seeking to be fully part of it. They created their own modernist counterculture which would set the standards for enlightened society as a whole. They would "make it," strive for the "dirty little secret of success," without surrendering to the values of the dominant society, thus confirming their pariah status. They would in fact enact Max Weber's definition of Jews as "aristocratic pariahs." The "little magazines," particularly the *Partisan Review*, helped to establish a new elite attitude where modernist standards were advanced. At the elite universities, increasingly open to them as students and teachers, as Columbia was to Trilling and art critic Meyer Shapiro, Jewish intellectuals began to influence the future direction of American culture. A modernist world was created, as brilliant as it was hermetic and ultimately solipsistic. The intellectuals it produced were a hothouse variety so hybrid that they could thrive only in the modernist glass buildings that began to occupy more and more of their island world of Manhattan.

In painting the leading critics and connoisseurs of modern art, especially Abstract Expressionism, were Meyer Shapiro, Harold Rosenberg, and above all, Clement Greenberg. They promoted this art to the point that by the late 1950's no corporate headquarters lobby or well-appointed apartment would hang other than Pollock or Rothko, de Kooning or Motherwell. As Tom Wolfe suggested in *The Painted Word*, this art was particularly attractive to Jewish critics and clients because it was not representational — which also meant that it lacked most overt references to the surrounding world, especially the past. Thus this art had more in common with a text *to be read* than a canvas to be viewed, every line and passage of paint full of meaning and countermeaning requiring commentary. Ultimately the "painterliness" of these abstract works, especially those of the "action painters" (the term is Rosenberg's), focused the viewer's attention outward on the artist as well as the art. The artist as questing hero, as in the near-cults of Picasso, Eliot and Hemingway, was an element in modernist ethics and esthetics, as well as in its commercial nature.

This new art had a pronounced commercial dimension, and Greenburg, for one, promoted it very much as an entrepreneur. To be sure, in the past figures like Berenson and Duveen had become wealthy as advisors to the likes of Mellon and Widener in building their collections of old masters. But in the post-war environment of New York critics, gallery owners and auctioneers became prosperous indeed in promoting the work of living artists, some of whose output was selling for very large sums, often to a new class of wealthy Jewish collectors. Associated with this was the rise of publishing and criticism as an ever-more commercial process, cultivating "big name" authors and large advances. The post-war culture industry, in art, writing and theater, and its media handmaidens, provided an important milieu of success for New York intellectuals.

Sociologist John Murray Cuddihy, in his incisive analysis, *The Ordeal of Civility: Marx, Freud, Levi-Strauss and the Jewish Struggle with Modernity*, suggests that some of the formative Jewish intellectuals of the modern age, in the very process of confronting that modernity, rejected it. As European ghetto walls came down in the course of the nineteenth century, opening civil life to Jews for the first time, there was a deep loss as well as a gain. The comfortable, enclosing certainties of traditional Jewish life now confronted the more rational, but more fragmented and uncertain world of modern civil society. "I have nothing in common with the Jews," wrote that exemplary modern Jew, Franz Kafka. "Most days I have nothing in common with myself." The alternative worlds proposed by such figures as Marx, Freud and Levi-Strauss consequently hovered somewhere between ghetto and *galut*. Communism, psychoanalysis, and structuralism had as their basic premises the deligitimization of the cultural foundations of the Western world, especially those which rested within achieved Christian civilization: religious belief, custom, law and morality.

Offered in their place were new forms of what amounted to *Yiddishkeit*: of a self-contained, tribal communalism resting in deeper, more abstract and obscure laws authentically interpreted by a new intellectual elite, and where the individual and his society were at one. Civility, that body of cultural norms essential to the establishment of the right tension between the individual and his society in modern civilization through institutions, was thus negated. What replaced civility were polemic, critique and analysis, mediated by a mutated rabbinical elite armed with new texts, the texts of "science." This polemical stance, which has characterized much Jewish intellectuality, also underlines its basic incivility. Marx and Freud, for example, quarreled and ultimately broke relations with most of their colleagues within their respective movements. Contention in the domain of ideas challenged the monist absolutism of modernist ethics, and consequently the contention of ideas almost inevitably became personal contention as well. The civility of a more detached life among strangers eluded them.[20]

By the middle 1960's modernism had run its course. Like many styles in their last days, it seemed completely ascendant. Psychoanalysis, almost arcane today, was then widespread, and everyone in New York seemed to be, like Philip Roth's protagonist Alexander Portnoy, "in analysis." Even Marxist theories were gaining credibility, with radical criticism of the underpinnings of American society having become almost mainstream as the language of "struggle," "oppression" and "liberation" came into wide currency on college campuses — and figures like Herbert Marcuse and Norman O. Brown emerged as cultural heroes — and in new publications like *The New York Review of Books*. In philosophy, "less is more" eventuated in journals like *Analysis*, containing articles of one or two pages narrowly focused in argument and rebuttal on this or that technical issue, in what was an almost pointless *pilpul*. This approach was increasingly rejected in the 'sixties as students, in particular, demanded moral "relevance" in what they studied, especially in the "value free" social sciences. In schools of architecture such as Harvard's Graduate School of Design — which had been under the complete sway of Walter Gropius and the *Bauhaus* — modernist premises were increasingly scrutinized.

Countertrends were challenging modernist assumptions. Robert Venturi, Charles Jencks and other critics saw modernism for what it was: an ideology of dissent masking yet another set of social styles.[21] In architecture, the formal and pithy absolutes so dogmatically asserted by the *Bauhaus* and other sources of modernism were revealed to be specific to a place and time like other styles, and subject to the same transitions. Probably because of its late arrival from Europe prior to World War II, and its inherent minimalism, American modernism, as an articulated sensibility, had less to say — and that was said relatively quickly. Important shifts in artistic patronage were also having their effects. Earlier patrons of art and architecture with names like Singer, Woolworth, Chrysler, and Rockefeller had sought monuments to their success, and were willing to pay for them. Modernist minimalism had legitimized an economical (and often banal) solution to rising building costs in a post-war environment dominated by the faceless multinational corporation.

These new realities encouraged architects, in effect, to mass-manufacture their designs and assemble them, unadorned with expensive materials or workmanship. Architecture had almost become a subcatagory of real estate, and buildings were often purposely commissioned to be bland and "general purpose" in their design. More innovative and use-specific designs (like William Pereira's for the ABC building) were rejected so that structures might be easily sold to very different businesses when, for example, tax depreciation and amortization limits made it advisable to sell them. There were also concerns that if a building came to be regarded as distinguished architecture it might be declared an important public landmark, and thus become difficult to tear down or to alter. Buildings for Lever, Seagram and Pepsi-Cola were rare and splendid exceptions to this monotonous rule of budgets, business strategies and the faceless managements which enforced them. In this process architecture lost much of its humanizing context, as an inherent modernist self-referentiality ("integrity") allied itself to the economic requirements of clients. The barren and windy plazas fronting these metal, concrete and glass edifices destroyed many urban streetscapes (an economical solution to zoning regulations) and called for the mass production of gigantic modernist sculptures that few enjoyed, if in fact they even noticed, and almost no one understood.

Art, too, was now considered a corporate asset, which like corporate headquarters buildings, might have to be transferred or liquidated as business requirements dictated. The very large (but mobile) canvases produced during this period were often intended for corporate lobbies (there were few domestic environments where they would fit), and firms like the Chase Manhattan Bank regarded the art they collected and displayed as both tools of public relations and as investments. The abstractness of these works advanced an very urbane sophistication, without offending conservative customers. The same trends pervaded the other arts. The work of painters like Ad Reinhardt and of composers like John Cage and Philip Glass became at once so dense and so simplified as to be almost completely inaccessible. Milton Babbitt asserted that there were perhaps no more than a dozen persons who really understood his compositions — the ultimate in the self-referential. Patronage also played a role in this trend. Many artists supported themselves with grants and university appointments, and thus had little need to seek broad audiences for their work.

Because of its minimalist, monist, and totalist (not to say "totalitarian") premises, modernism lacked defectibility. If not executed, and maintained, to near perfection ("God is in the details") *less is more* became only less, and understatement became no statement at all, mere banality. The cumulative effects of this banality had become very visible in New York by the 'sixties, and a search was begun for alternative visions. That alternative vision, summed in the term "postmodernist," was a negation of modernism. In order to speak with a new voice, the new artist had to break out of the enclosed spaces which modernism had charted. Or, as gallery owner and talent scout Dick Bellamy asserted about abstract expressionism: "This movement was so total it gave the young artist nowhere to go but away."[22] The values of the postmodernists were often the mirror image of modernist ones. If modernism was characterized by its indefectibility, postmodernism was exuberantly defectible. If elitist modernism was inclined toward an entropic and sterile banality, populist postmodernism was inclined toward a superficial and eruptive vulgarity.

The emerging sensibility of the late 1950's and early 1960's, exemplified by "Pop Art," often looked to the past, and referenced mass culture in particular: flags, comic books, soup cans and movie stars. Robert Rauschenberg, in asserting that he wished his work to fill "the gap between art and life," challenged the self-referentiality of modernism, which had much to do with creating such gaps. Leo Castelli, whose street-friendly and welcoming Soho gallery was the focus of this new trend in art, saw it as a quintessentially American phenomenon, unlike modernism, which was an extension of elite European trends. His focus on new artists (and not the lucrative secondary market for known artists) differentiated his approach from older, more established art dealers. Postmodern architecture began to reference Palladio and the American "shingle style" of the last century, in the emergence of new figures like Michael Graves and Robert A.M. Stern. Philip Johnson, who had been an early champion of modernism, turned in this direction in his building for AT&T, with its neo-baroque pediment. (He would later playfully title himself an architectural "whore," going where clients were to be found.) In literature, the day of the "big," serious novel (like those of Saul Bellow) seemed to be coming to a close, eclipsed by other genres, such as the reality-fantasy of Kurt Vonnegut's *Slaughterhouse Five* and Truman Capote's "non-fiction novel," *In Cold Blood*. Postmodern criticism, introduced to the United States by figures like Paul De Man, began to tie literature to the contingencies of the surrounding world (it was now viewed as socially "constructed"), with the same vigor as modernism had separated itself from them.

The new painting was often a window on the ordinary world of the man in the street. It was the opposite of opaque, and yet very detached in its stance. It needed little *explication de texte*. The work of figures like Andy Warhol, Jasper Johns, Roy Lichtenstein, Larry Rivers, Robert Rauschenberg, Claes Oldenberg and David Hockney reveled in the ordinary, and, with its celebration of mass culture, assaulted both the uncompromising seriousness and the elite assumptions of modernism. It, in fact, treated modernism as the essentially *haut bourgeois* style that it was: the art of the self-conscious *parvenu*. Postmodern art was an unmasking art, and an on-going comment on modernism itself. It treated modernism as a kind of facade, often mocking its pretensions. Andy Worhol, in particular, was devastatingly self-deprecating, when he spoke at all, about what he was doing. "High art" and "low art" seemed to be the same to him as long as clients were buying it, and his *Factory* could turn it out fast enough. He was as wordless as the modernist critics were wordy, in essence delegitimizing the high-toned elitism of the New York art establishment, subtly unmasking its self-promoting entrepreneurship and ultimately its commercial nature, while he shamelessly cashed in on it. "Warhol interprets literally the overshadowing of the artwork by the artist;" wrote Rosenberg, "that is, he sees it strictly in terms of the art market."[23]

The artist was now not only an entrepreneur, it was himself that he was selling, the "designer label." Warhol, and other emerging figures, were masters of self-promotion in their understanding of the global media basis for the growing culture of celebrity. Warhol himself had come from the world of commercial advertising as a graphic artist. But the postmodern artists, as they reveled in mass culture and celebrated the ordinary, were the opposite of elitist, which was the sovereign quality of the New York intellectuals. Warhol famously suggested that soon everyone would have his "fifteen minutes of fame." He sensed, exposed, and finally celebrated the banality which so much of modernity (and modernism) had become. "I want everybody to think alike," he told an interviewer.[24] And soon the same people who had collected Franz Klein and Marc Rothko in the 'fifties were collecting Jasper Johns and Andy Warhol in the 'sixties.

Criticism was deeply disoriented by these events, and some of the most visible figures, like James Baldwin, Susan Sontag, Gore Vidal, and Norman Mailer, were as much or more cultural observers and media figures as they were critics. Their writing and self presentation were characterized by a highly personalized and adversarial tone, idiosyncratic and ironic. Sontag and Vidal, in particular, built their reputations through a keen understanding of popular cultural trends, especially in film. Like Baldwin and Mailer they seemed to sense that mass media visibility was essential to remaining an independent, public intellectual. They were evidence that the independent, detached critic (Edmund Wilson being exemplary) was threatened as changed economic conditions required intellectuals to seek different sources of livelihood beyond publishing. The movement of intellectuals into liberal academic environments for support — as did Philip Rahv and the *Partisan Review*, which abandoned New York for Boston University — or into subsidized relationships with conservative patrons was an emerging phenomenon of the period.

Clement Greenburg had ceased the regular writing of criticism by the mid-sixties. The literary modernists were to fade from the scene as well as the 'sixties ended, giving rise to the gender and race orientation of groups like the influential Modern Language Association. To modernist champions like Hilton Kramer, art editor of the *New York Times*, and a frequent *Commentary* contributor, these trends were the marks of a devastating failure: had all the patient educating of the modernist critics in cultivating the tastes of patrons and audiences come to this? In the end, Kramer, too, seemed to have given up altogether. Abandoning art criticism for conservative publishing, he asserted in 1998: "Today, for a museum to 'privilege the contemporary' is to abandon artistic standards and embrace the repulsive detritus that has illegitimately come to be celebrated in art. That is why anyone who really cares about art should support a moratorium on new museum building. Until there is something new worth putting in galleries of contemporary art, museums should concentrate on their original function: to preserve and exhibit the best of the art of the past."[25]

Modernism as a style ultimately succumbed to the forces which had created it. From its dawn in the era of the first world war to its dusk in the 1960's modernism was characterized by its appeal to universals. Its claims rested in ideas and values which transformed the very idea of "culture" from a set of local forms rooted in particular traditions, to a set of global forms resting in universal principles. Modernism in architecture, in fact, was first introduced to Americans as the "International Style." But globalization is as often a fragmenting and delocalizing force as it is a localizing and unifying one, and it is that fragmentation which those intellectuals, seeking in art and society what they had once had in the unified world of the ghetto, resisted at the very core of their self-identifications.

The opportunity for advancement by Jewish intellectuals in the expanding culture industry of post-war New York, driven by wealth, leisure, and mass communications, ultimately presented a double-edged sword. Historian Michael Kammen has proposed that the growth of mass culture also meant the privatization of culture.[26] Pre-war high culture in America had been dominated by public cultural "experts," a small elite speaking to relatively small groups of attentive culture consumers, principally through the written word. Even popular culture was shaped by a relatively small group of book and music publishers, film makers, and theatrical producers. The growth of mass culture and mass media (especially in television and the recording industry) after World War II marked a quantitative and qualitative shift in the scale of cultural production and consumption. The power to shape cultural taste and to move audiences shifted from intellectual experts to profit-driven mass media corporations, which by the end of the century had been merged into a gigantic global industry conflating publishing, computer networking, recording, film-making, cable and telecasting.

New York found itself competing not only with Washington and Los Angeles, but with places like Atlanta as a media center — or, to use the industry phrase, "media market." Markets, as a "bottom up" phenomenon, more often respond to rather than create taste, and the fragmentation, not to say localization, of taste which eventuated from a globalized media environment only reflected the democratic range of cultural consumption which was now possible. In tying themselves to Manhattan as a publishing center, and to conventional media, especially the written word, the New York intellectuals distanced themselves from important trends originating in the West, New

England and elsewhere. Their cultural ends had been decisively defined by their narrowly focused cultural means. Intellectual life and the intellectual class were simultaneously fragmented by these same impulses. The social base of intellectuals was localized by globalized media economics into think tanks and subsidized journals on the right, and into universities and philanthropic foundations on the left. The independent, public intellectual was increasingly delocalized into oblivion. Even traditional cultural institutions, like museums, were caught up in the commerce in culture. This meant, claimed Rosenberg, that "at the top of the art world the cards are mysteriously stacked by arrangements between museum people, dealers, critics, and tax benefiting collectors."[27]

The written word, the abiding strength of Jewish cultural life and the careers which the neoconservatives had built for themselves, was eclipsed in this new globalized media culture. And while it is true that many Jews prospered in this changed world, figures like Michael Eisener, Barry Diller and David Geffen can hardly be called "intellectuals," and in fact were often the focus of conservative intellectual emnity because of their indifference to universal standards in pursuit of profit. For Russell Jacoby, this shift to a globalized mass communications culture marked the decline of the public intellectuals, the small elite concentrated particularly in New York, who had regarded themselves (and the written word) as the shapers and guardians of American culture.[28] The same forces which had opened cultural life to Jewish intellectuals, who had just begun to replace a large portion of the gentile intellectual establishment in post-war New York, were ultimately to undercut economically and socially the sources of that influence. And thus amidst the extraordinary profusion and confusion of cultural expression which blossomed in the 'sixties Irving Kristol lamented the loss of cultural authority in America, and suggested — in a complaint as old as Plato — that every society requires an elite to uphold a high cultural standard. "*Someone* has to be able to say, with assurance and a measure of authority, what is culture and what is not," he wrote. "There must be some group or class that is admittedly competent to decide — not without error, but more wisely than anyone else — questions of moral and cultural value. Otherwise, a necessary and vital element of order in the life of a society will be lacking."[29] At that point in American cultural history, just when New York intellectuals were "making it," the terms of cultural influence were shifting to their disadvantage.

But something deeper was also occurring. For all their apparent urbane sophistication, the intellectual figures around *Commentary* who were to become the neoconservatives were in their own lives anything but *avant garde* or bohemian. Their social values were those of the aspiring Jewish middle-class, the children of garment workers, grocers and milkmen. Theirs was a commerce of ideas; values were their stock in trade. But their orientations were bourgeois all the same. They no longer dwelt in the Brooklyn or Lower East Side ghettos, to be sure. Rather, their values were those of the fancier ghetto of the Upper West Side. Noting the movement of so many Jewish intellectuals from the left of their youth, to the right in their middle age, Jacoby proposes that, "The economic realities of Jewish and immigrant life go far in explaining a vulnerability to conventional success, money and recognition."[30] Their lack of geographical mobility — they were inveterate New Yorkers with occasional nods, beginning during the Reagan years, to that other insular place, Washington, DC — was evidence of their lack of a real cultural mobility as well. As such the place of tradition with its connotations of families, of status, and of roles and rules within hierarchies of understood values was central to their lives. Ultimately, "making it" meant "getting in on it."

This group of critics never seriously questioned gender roles and marriage, parenthood, or the statuses associated with social class or privilege. Podhoretz described his visit to Greenwich Village in the beat era as if he were venturing to a foreign land ("enemy territory"), and noted his wearing of coat and tie, and his refusal to try marijuana, as if these were badges of middle-class honor for a man of proletarian background.[31] Certainly the Jewish neoconservatives opposed ethnic discrimination, because they themselves had been subject to it. Earlier, they had challenged the WASP establishment (and had often embraced leftist economics and politics) because they had not been admitted into it. But this is rather different from a serious critique of the ways others led their lives within social convention, day to day, or the ways in which the accident of having been born Jewish had so fundamentally shaped their own lives and values. On the whole, they lacked the distanced understanding (and self-understanding) of the dissenting, bohemian intellectual. Their social insularity was also reflected in their ultimate lack of creativity. With a few exceptions, their own work, principally composed of criticism and memoirs, lacked real brilliance or originality. Their total cultural production does not match the influence which they claim, or which in fact they have had. The fact that a number of neoconservative intellectuals edited journals (Podhoretz's *Commentary*; Kristol's *Public Interest*; Kramer's *New Criterion*; Epstein's *American Scholar*) may have deceived them as to the actual range of their influence. They overlooked the critical significance of many trends, especially those originating in beat, rock, and pop culture. Norman Cantor says of the New York intellectuals whose careers began in the pages of the *Partisan Review* and other venues beginning in the 1940's: "Their total achievement as theorists and writers is not anywhere as impressive as they themselves claim."[32] Richard Brookhiser agrees, suggesting that "the currents of political and artistic life flowed around them, not through them."[33]

The Jewish neoconservatives were relentlessly married, sometimes to each other. Norman Podhoretz and his wife, Midge Decter; Irving Kristol and his wife, Gertrude Himmelfarb; their children and their in-laws, resembled nothing so much as an extended intellectual clan. By the most important measure of assimilation into the dominant culture, intermarriage, they were completely unassimilated, at a time when increasing numbers of marriages by Jews, especially highly-educated Jews, were to gentiles. For all of their sophisticated trappings — the good educations and the good Manhattan and Hamptons addresses — the *Commentary* crowd was a tight, extended Jewish family, almost a small business, distributing cultural criticism wholesale. They spent much of their time talking to one another, in the pages of *Commentary*, *The New Criterion*, *The Public Interest* and *The Weekly Standard*, and on panels sponsored by various conservative groups, think tanks, and foundations. And they had found wealthy, conservative patrons to serve: people and organizations with (dominantly gentile) names like Murdoch, Olin, Coors, Scaife, Bradley and the American Enterprise Institute. To these new patrons they offered the certainties of criteria and standards, of judgments and distinctions based on conventional boundaries.

And thus, usually unspoken, there was another basis for their revulsion to the new postmodern sensibility which arose in the 'sixties from the writing of the beats, in the work of the pop artists, and in the work of other figures whose output was appearing more frequently on stage, screen and other arenas of culture. Many of the most prominent of these emerging cultural figures were not heterosexual. Their lives and values were a challenge to the one set of assumptions which these New York intellectuals, for all their sophistication, never allowed themselves to question: those values underlying traditional Jewish family life. Critics like Philip Roth and Stanley Kauffmann, in an echo of the traditional right's claim that there is a hidden Jewish domination of the media, began to question if now there was not a hidden homosexual agenda in the arts.[34] Immutable boundaries were being transgressed. The fact that many of the emerging beat, pop, homosexual and feminist figures were themselves Jewish only increased the discomfort. Midge Decter's tract against feminism is an exercise in making distinctions on a large scale indeed. Regarding maternity as essential to mature femininity, she asserted: "There is no more radical nor desperately nihilistic statement than that there are no necessary differences between the sexes. For such differences both issue in and do in themselves constitute the most fundamental principle of the continuation of life on earth."[35] Her husband, Norman Podhoretz, propounded the same thesis: "There can be no abdication of responsibility more fundamental than the refusal of a man to become, and to be, a father, or the refusal of a woman to become, and be a mother."[36]

During the 'seventies and after Decter became something of a crank on the subject of homosexuality, in the pages of *Commentary* and elsewhere. "Male homosexuals, though they often speak otherwise, are moved more primitively by a hatred for women than a love for men," she opined.[37] As managing editor at *Harper's* she published an article by Joseph Epstein, in which he announced that he would wish homosexuality "off the face of the earth," if he could, also suggesting the pain and despair he would feel if one of his sons were to tell him that he was homosexual, and thus condemned to a life of "niggerdom."[38] Hilton Kramer, who became the founding editor of *The New Criterion*, a leading neoconservative voice, took every opportunity to attack, directly and indirectly, the influence of gay writers and artists, even finding himself on the side of Jesse Helms in opposing National Endowment for the Arts funds for the Robert Mapplethorpe traveling exhibit.[39]

As Susan Sontag has observed in her groundbreaking *Partisan Review* essay, "Notes on Camp,"[1964] this newly visible group of homosexual writers and artists, like Oscar Wilde before them, represented a witty, often subtle, but thorough-going assault on all the unquestioned assumptions of the dominant society. They appeared at a watershed in American culture: the fading of the old industrial society and its replacement by the mass information age, with all of its conflicted and ambiguous messages — and attendant anxieties. As urban life declined in the 'fifties and 'sixties, places like New York's Greenwich Village and West Side became havens for sexual minorities who found in them a tolerance lacking elsewhere, and economic opportunities in the expanding culture industry in fields like entertainment, design, publishing and advertising. With this new urban visibility, homosexuality became something of a social lightning rod for the fears raised by changing gender roles and family structures, rising divorce rates, and a powerful emerging youth counterculture. The homosexual was the ultimate stranger, so unspeakable that even "liberals" felt safe in their revulsion.

"Camp," a term apparently of theatrical origin, celebrates a pervasive ambiguity between appearances and reality, and thus had a special place in homosexual subcultures. It was the radical criticism of *camp* especially in its meditations on gender, marriage and sexuality; its juxtaposition of very different media and human domains; its disinterested moral stance; its epicene fluidities and stubborn refusal to make distinctions, that figures like Decter, Epstein and Kramer abhorred in their attacks on feminism and the influence of homosexuals in the wider culture. To those intellectuals, for whom identification with the *avant garde* had always been a bulwark against the subversions of modernity, the elegant and studied illusions of modernism were assaulted by this emerging (often *camp* and sometimes vulgar) sensibility in culture — a sensibility which urged peeking under the apparent to glimpse the real, as in Edward Albee's play, "Who's Afraid of Virginia Woolf?". *Camp* was a "moral solvent": the whole point of *camp* was "to dethrone the serious," asserted Sontag.[40] That seriousness was the substance of modernism as an ethic and a sensibility; and of the claims of its intellectual champions to elite status.

Politically, the neoconservatives had usually been in the past, to the degree that such things really concerned them, liberals, or even men and women of the left. The 'sixties began to move them to the right politically because, to those who shared Norman Podhoretz's perception, people who "hate America" had co-opted liberalism.[41] Podhoretz wrote of "the spreading power" of the left, which he described as "a coalition of Marxists, Africanists, feminists, gay propagandists, and deconstructionists who were united by their hatred of American society and all its works, and intellectually by their rejection of the belief in scholarly or aesthetic standards and objective truth."[42] The Vietnam War, continuing racial confrontation, and countercultural permissiveness had so compromised liberals, in this view, that they had abdicated the principled basis of liberalism to the radicals. In my view, the previous liberalism (and even radicalism) of the Jewish neoconservatives had often been, like their commitment to modernism, primarily a strategic weapon against a status quo rooted in a Christian, often anti-Semitic past, a status quo which conflicted with the ambitions of a new class of intellectuals emerging from the traditional ghetto. Irving Kristol identifies such liberal groups as the American Civil Liberties Union (ACLU) as the means by which Jews hoped to secure a place for themselves in a secular America, at the expense of Christian expression. "Intoxicated with their economic, political and judicial success over the past half-century," he wrote, "American Jews seem to have no reluctance in expressing their vision of an ideal America: a country where Christians are purely nominal, if that, in their Christianity, while they want Jews to remain a flourishing religious community..."[43]

When secular modernism and liberalism had themselves become the status quo in the 1960's, especially among elites in New York, continuing liberalism became a threat to a generation of achievement through dissent, and to Jewish identity itself. Podhoretz, Kristol, Kramer, Epstein and the others, almost without exception, came from working-class or small trade backgrounds, and their former liberalism seemed to function more as a means to social advancement than as an intellectual faith, or that faith would not have been abandoned so easily. In his career, Podhoretz has run the spectrum from radical and liberal to conservative identities, in what appears to be a situational self-absorption, rather than any continuing social ethic. Thus, the next step in modern advancement was one Podhoretz and his colleagues could not bring themselves to take: the effective abandonment of their Jewish roots, with their source in the roles and rules of the traditional family, and a defining identification with other Jews, and with Israel. They could not embrace civility and secular modernity as had so many Jews because they could not free themselves finally of the powerful pull of an enclosing traditional past. Decter and Kristol, in particular, began to emphasize the importance of religious faith as a basis for both family and social life — and this created an alignment with conservative Catholics like Richard Neuhaus and his magazine, *First Things*.[44] It was in fact becoming apparent that only religion could effectively define Jewish identity in a materialistic, secular America. As a consequence there was within American Jewry a parallel (and polarizing) struggle between the secular and the Orthodox to define the meaning of Judaism.[45] The question becomes: How can those Jewish intellectuals, whose formation rests so solidly in the Western Enlightenment and its social expressions, authentically participate in this religion-based debate?

The island of Manhattan, which New York intellectuals shared with an increasingly discontented and violent Third World under-class, was getting smaller. The City University of New York, which had been the route of upward-mobility for so many Jews, declared "open admissions." Columbia University, Podhoretz's *alma mater* and an important arena of Jewish academic success and social advancement, became a center of unrest and dissent, in part because of its relations with the adjacent black ghetto of Harlem. The public school system, in which Jews were prominent, faced demands from minority groups for "community" control. Such policies as affirmative action discounted the striving of Jews who had succeeded by meeting high standards. The specter of quotas for minority students in admission to the more prestigious private universities only reminded Jewish intellectuals of the quotas of exclusion many of them had faced. But more than this, the broad attacks on America as a "racist" and "oppressive" society devalued the striving by Jews to succeed within it. "Making it" was made to seem collusionist and opportunistic. The crudely anti-Semitic voices of some black spokesmen gave substance to their feelings

It was the radically altered position of Israel in global politics that probably had the most influence on the movement of some New York intellectuals into the camp of the political right. Support for Israel was easy and automatic for most Americans, not just Jewish Americans, in the 1940's and 1950's, when the Holocaust was fresh in memory, and when Israel could present itself as a David sustained against the Goliaths of the Arab world by a combination of democracy, idealism and righteous passion. Jewish support for Israel was submerged within this larger American consensus. As the 'sixties proceeded and the Soviet Union increased its active support of Israel's Arab adversaries militarily and diplomatically, and particularly after the 1967 ("Six Day") war, the situation changed substantially. Israel, which had decisively defeated the alliance against her three times in battle, began to look less like David. Israel's occupation of the West Bank and Gaza brought millions of Palestinians under her often harsh and repressive control, typified by the settlement of Jews on confiscated Palestinian land. Israeli politics, once dominated by liberal, secular Jews of European birth, began to drift toward the right, especially in courting the support of the militantly Orthodox and the non-Western Sephardim, many of whom were openly racist in their attitudes toward Arabs in general and Palestinians in particular. Since Isreal itself sprung from pre-civil premises, its fate seemed to fall back inevitably into pre-civil hands.

Many American Jews were deeply alienated by these trends, as well as by the continuing refusal of the Israeli Orthodox establishment to recognize the religious status of the majority of American rabbis. Zionism was in its maturity revealing itself to be, like Marxism and Freudism, one more exhausted nineteenth-century ideology in the passage out of the European ghetto; an ultimately roofless half-way house. For Israel was born out of the European social devastation of World War II, which itself terminated the Western belief in the folk-based state which Zionism represents. The alternative justifications for Israel's existence — religion and/or ethnic nationalism — all but disappeared among Western intellectual elites. In Israel, as in America, the definition of Judaism became a reflection of the larger quarrel between tradition and modernity, or, in Yoram Hazony's formulation, the struggle between Zionists and Jewish intellectuals who reject Zionism.[46] As Jewish particularism confronts Enlightenment humanism in what is an inherently unresolvable dilemma — leaving Israel without a defining constitution fifty years after its founding — Jewish neoconservatives reflect the distances yet to be traveled between local ghetto and global *galut* .

Among the growing number of Third World states in the United Nations and other forums it was becoming easier for Soviet diplomacy to win friends as the protector of the Middle East from Zionist "imperialism" and "colonialism," and from Israel's ally, America. Soviet repression of internal Jewish dissent by identifying it as the disloyalty of Zionists solidified the connection, as did the U.S. "Jackson Amendment," which sanctioned the Soviet Union for not allowing Jewish emigration to Israel. As America came under international leftist attack, in part because of its unstinting support for Israel, the Jewish neoconservatives became unstinting champions of America. Anti-communism became indistinguishable from Zionism in the 'seventies, as anti-communism had become indistinguishable from Catholicism in the 'forties and 'fifties. The strident anticommunist agenda of the Jewish neoconservatives, evidenced by such groups as The Committee for the Free World (chaired by Midge Decter), represented not so much a belated recognition of the menace of "international communism" by former liberals, but their need to cover sectarian support for Israel with a broader mantel.

The collapse of Soviet communism and the end of the Cold War thus presented something of a problem for the neoconservatives. For now America's unqualified support for Israel could no longer be pursued with Cold War *realpolitik* as its defining justification. As Israel's repressive actions in the occupied territories, and such disasters as its occupation of Lebanon, which directly and indirectly killed dozens of Americans, became harder to defend, the response of the neoconservatives became irrational as well. No American Jew has the right to criticize Israel, suggested Podhoretz, since he does not live there and does not bear the consequences.[47] An alliance with the Christian right, which vigorously defends Israel as the fulfillment of the Biblically-prophesized in-gathering and conversion of the Jews before the Second Coming of Christ, became another absurdity in this neoconservative dynamic.

The alliance of the New Right to restore a "traditional" American world, which has never existed, with those fighting to save immigrant Jewish and Catholic worlds, which are quickly disappearing, is not a very promising one. It is an "anti-" alliance, held together by common complaints: against "liberals," against modern government, against feminism and gay rights, against ambiguity, uncertainty and social disorder, in short, against modernity itself. As intellectuals like Norman Podhoretz, Irving Kristol, and Hilton Kramer more often find themselves in bed with the likes of Pat Robertson, Jesse Helms and Jerry Falwell, who have seldom been accused of being thoughtful, and whose attitudes towards Jews in the long run are at least uncertain, the mutual discomfort can only increase. In recent years, Podhoretz in particular has shown an inclination to declare the ideological and social war with liberalism to have been won (offering as suggestive evidence the desire of homosexuals to marry), and to disengage himself from neoconservatism as a movement which is no longer needed.

For conservative Catholic intellectuals the problems are likely to take a somewhat different form. As the crisis of modernity continues to erode the authority of the Vatican in Europe and North America among many Catholics, who continue to reject the church's teachings, especially concerning sex and the sexes, Catholic intellectuals will find themselves making choices between loyalty to Rome and having a significant American following among educated Catholics. And to the degree that they remain loyal to Rome, they might become disloyal to their American patrons. The Pope has condemned the sovereignty of market economics as frequently as he has communism. George Weigel's biography of John Paul II is consequently hagiographic in its praise for the Pope's uncompromising stance upholding traditional Catholic teachings, and for his role in the defeat of communism. At the same time, Weigel (like Novak before him) is almost dismissive of the Pope's extensive writings on the failures of capitalism as the out-of-touch views of someone who has had no life experience with Western market economies.[48]

The post-World War II era represented the end of the dominant industrial economy which had reached its apogee during the war. Strong labor unions, social legislation, and an American economy without real global competitors produced a standard of living and a kind of social equity which millions had never before experienced. These trends masked the crucial changes in American society, especially regarding race and gender, which had occurred during the previous decades. When the 'sixties arrived the intellectuals of two pre-civil, immigrant cultures, facing fundamental change, were able to give voice to those who felt threatened by those changes, especially because the benefits of the old industrial order had only been recently attained by them. Catholic conservatives and Jewish neoconservatives sought the restoration of an orderly world which was being irretrievably lost.

NOTES TO CHAPTER FOURTEEN

1. Cf. John Tracy Ellis, AMERICAN CATHOLICISM, 2nd ed. (Chicago: University of Chicago Press, 1969); see also, Thomas Gallagher, PADDY'S LAMENT: IRELAND 1846-1847 (New York: Harcourt Brace Jovanovich, Publishers, 1982); and Karl S. Bolligheimer, IRELAND AND THE IRISH (New York: Columbia University Press, 1982)

2. Cf. Walter J. Ong, AMERICAN CATHOLIC CROSSROADS (Westport, Conn.: Greenwood Press, 1981)

3. Richard O'Connor, THE IRISH (New York: G.P. Putnam's Sons, 1971), p.120

4. Conor Cruise O'Brien, STATES OF IRELAND (New York: Pantheon Books, 1972), p. 20

5. The phrase is from the directive of the Vatican's College of Propaganda. Cf. O'Connor, *op.cit.*, p. 120

6. An excellent study of the Cold War mentality, focused on Pennsylvania, is Philip Jenkins and Philip Jenkins, THE COLD WAR AT HOME (Chapel Hill, NC: University of North Carolina Press, 1999)

7. Tanenhaus, *op.cit.*, p. 468

8. Clarence Manion, THE KEY TO PEACE (Chicago: Heritage Foundation, 1950).

9. Cf. Michael Novak, THE CATHOLIC ETHIC AND THE SPIRIT OF CAPITALISM (New York: The Free Press, 1993); George F. Gilder, THE SPIRIT OF ENTERPISE (New York: Simon & Schuster, 1984)

10. Hofstadter, *op.cit.*, pp. 140-141

11. Cf. Andrew Greeley, AMERICAN CATHOLICS: A SOCIAL PORTRAIT (New York: Basic Books, 1977)

12. Joan Lowy, "The Religious Right Wrestles With Doubt," SAN FRANCISCO EXAMINER (April 14, 1999), p. A-18

13. Cf. Alan Dershowitz, THE DISAPPEARING AMERICAN JEW (New York: Little, Brown & Co., Publishers, 1997)

14. On the history of the neoconservative movement, see Norman Podhoretz, "Neoconservatism: A Eulogy," COMMENTARY (March 1996); and Irving Kristol, NEOCONSERVATISM: THE AUTOBIOGRAPHY OF AN IDEA (New York: Basic Books, 1995); it was Kristol who apparently coined the term "neoconservative." Non-Jewish figures like Michael Novak and Daniel Patrick Moynihan have sometimes been included among those termed "neoconservative." While they have had associations with COMMENTARY and Jewish neoconservative writers, it seems to me that Novak's brief flirtation with liberalism early in his career makes him less "neo" than in the mainstream of postwar Catholic conservative thought. Moynihan (together with Daniel Bell and Nathan Glaser) strikes me as less a neoconservative than a social

science positivist, whose prudence and caution are often confused with conservative ideology.

15. *Ibid.*, p. 22
16. Irving Howe, WORLD OF OUR FATHERS (New York: Harcourt, Brace and Company, 1989)
17. Elena Lappin, a review of Gerald Shapiro, BAD JEWS AND OTHER STORIES, in *The New York Times Book Review* (October 17 1999), p. 35
18. Cf. Donald L. Miller, LEWIS MUMFORD: A LIFE (New York: Weidenfeld & Nicholson, 1989), p. 166
19. Herbert Muschamp, "Spirit of Jazz Infuses Plan for Columbus Center," THE NEW YORK TIMES (June 29, 2000), p. B5; Harold Rosenberg wrote that modernism "is inherently polemical; it declares the obsolescence of the heritage of earlier times..." ART ON EDGE (New York: Macmillan Publishing Co., Inc. 1975), p. 282
20. In the American context, a parallel phenomenon was the rise of "objectivism," the thought of Ayn Rand (nee Alice Rosenbaum), its proponents, especially Nathaniel Branden (ne Nathan Blumenthal) and the near-cult surrounding Rand. Composed almost entirely of Jews of eastern European background, including Alan Greenspan, later Federal Reserve chairman, the objectivist movement was an early version of conservatism among assimilating Jews. Ironically calling themselves "the collective," this group met in New York one evening each week with Rand to read and comment upon (but never to criticize) her writings. Condemning religion as irrational, the Randians extolled capitalism as an "unknown ideal," subverted by liberals and other "altruists," and proposed instead a radical individualism based in reason and consent. Rand eventually broke relations with almost every one of these followers, accusing them of "irrationality" and disloyalty. Cf. Barbara Branden, THE PASSION OF AYN RAND (Garden City, NY: Doubleday & Company, Inc., 1986)
21. Robert Venturi, CONTRADICTION AND COMPLEXITY IN MODERN ARCHITECTURE (New York: Museum of Modern Art, 1977); Charles Jencks writes: "Modern architecture suffered from elitism. Post-modernism is trying to get over that elitism not by dropping it, but rather by extending the language of architecture in many different ways - into the vernacular, towards tradition and the commercial slang of the street." THE LANGUAGE OF POST-MODERN ARCHITECTURE (New York: Rizzoli International Publications, Inc., 1977), p. 8
22. Quoted in Charlotte Willard, "Dealers-Eye View," ART IN AMERICA (April 1964), p. 122
23. Rosenberg, *op.cit.*, p. 99
24. Harold Rosenberg, "After Next, What?," ART IN AMERICA (April 1964), p. 72

25. Hilton Kramer, "Notes & Comments," THE NEW CRITERION (January 1998), p. 3

26. Michael G. Kammen, AMERICAN CULTURE, AMERICAN TASTES (New York: Alfred A. Knopf, Inc., 1999)

27. Rosenberg, ART ON EDGE, *op.cit.*, p. 283

28. Russell Jacoby, THE LAST INTELLECTUALS (New York: Basic Books, 1987)

29. Irving Kristol, "High, Low, and Modern," quoted in Kammen, *op.cit.*, p. 147

30. Jacoby, *op.cit.,* p. 89

31. Norman Podhoretz, "My War With Allen Ginsberg," COMMENTARY (August 1997)

32. Norman F. Cantor, TWENTIETH-CENTURY CULTURE (New York: Peter Lang, 1988), p. 216

33. Richard Brookhiser, a review of Norman Podhoretz, EX-FRIENDS (1999) in *The New York Times Book Review* (February 21, 1999), p. 7

34. Philip Roth, "The Play That Dares Not Speak Its Name," NEW YORK REVIEW OF BOOKS (February 25, 1965); Stanley Kauffmann, "Homosexual Drama and Its Disguises," THE NEW YORK TIMES, January 23, 1966

35. Midge Decter, THE NEW CHASTITY AND OTHER ARGUMENTS AGAINST WOMEN'S LIBERATION (New York: Coward, McCann & Geoghegan, Inc., 1972), p. 180

36. Norman Podhoretz, BREAKING RANKS (New York: Harper and Row, 1979), pp. 362-363

37. Decter, *op. cit.*, p. 87

38. Joseph Epstein, "Homo/Hetero: The Struggle for Sexual Identity," HARPER'S (September 1970)

39. Typical of Kramer's writing is his attack on the dean of American architects, Philip Johnson, in which the latter's homosexuality is a subtext: "Philip Johnson's Brilliant Career," COMMENTARY (September 1995)

40. Susan Sontag, "Notes on Camp," in AGAINST INTERPRETATION (New York: Dell Publishing Co., 1969), p. 289; see also: John D'Emilio, SEXUAL POLITICS, SEXUAL COMMUNITIES (Chicago: University of Chicago Press, 1983); Stephen O. Murray, AMERICAN GAY (Chicago: University of Chicago Press, 1996)

41. Podhoretz recounts his break with his liberal past and his intellectual associates in BREAKING RANKS, *op.cit.*

42. Norman Podhoretz, "Liberalism and the Culture: A Turning of the Tide?," COMMENTARY (October 1996), p. 30

43. "Are Jews 'Politically Foolish'?," exerpted in THE WILSON QUARTERLY (Winter 2000), p. 87

44. Cf. Irving Kristol, "Why Religion is Good for the Jews," COMMENTARY (August 1994)

45. Cf., Samuel G. Freedman, JEW VS. JEW (New York: Simon & Schuster, 2000)
46. Yoram Hazony, THE JEWISH STATE: THE STRUGGLE FOR ISREAL'S SOUL (New York: Basic Books, 2000)
47. Norman Podhoretz, "A Statement on the Peace Process," COMMENTARY (April 1993); Podhoretz was to regret this stance later when he himself criticized the Israeli government's moves toward compromise with the Palestinians. His acknowledgment that his views are influenced by the residence of his children and grandchildren in Israel only confirms that his policy views are pre-civil in their premises.
48. George Weigel, WITNESS TO HOPE (New York: Cliff Street Books, 1999)

Chapter Fifteen

Confronting the Naked Self

Underlying the discontents of the right in America lies a deeper dissatisfaction: a dissatisfaction with the naked self. Its most superficial manifestation is an obsession with sex generally and particularly with pornography, which covers as much as it shows of real selves. The naked self which sears the soul of the right is the nakedness of self-examination, the attempt to come to terms with the truth of one's individual existence. The passion for "traditional values" is nothing so much as a flight from an individual self, of the necessary reflection and psychological growth which coming to terms with an authentic self through engagement and introspection implies. The mindless dogma of fundamentalist religion; the unquestioned certainties of the "free market system;" the God-defined roles of "man," and "woman;" are all evasions of this most basic of human problems. Psychologist Gordon Allport insisted: "Maturity, we feel, means that we should become aware of, and in some way partner to, all the discordant conditions of our own existence."[1]

Human maturity thus requires that life itself be experienced as a problem. And that problem is how to become fully human. Humanity is neither a collective nor an achieved fact, but rather an individual and a social process. It is an aspiration lived out day by day as individuals realize in experience and reflection who they are becoming, while engaging their human environment. Having transcended the primal and the traditional, man defines man within the rational freedom of his civil world, and the individual defines himself within his own life, and within the faith that authentically living that life gives him. And that faith must ultimately be an individual achievement, not an unquestioned inheritance. "By its very nature," suggests Reynolds Price, "any sustained thought about a transcendent Creator and judge can only originate in the thoughts and experience of single human beings."[2] This ultimate, individual autonomy within secular society is our heritage from the Age of Reason, especially from Rousseau and Kant, as summarized by Leo Strauss: "Moral and political ideals are established without reference to man's nature: man is radically liberated from the tutelage of nature."[3] The conservative obsession with abortion thus has less to do with the ways in which reproductive rights support the autonomy of women (although the submission of women is central to their hierarchy of values), than to their insistence that humanity is a given — a given which serves as the foundation for a host of other unquestioned givens.

Existentially, full humanness, living authentically by one's own thought, judgment and action, can be realized only in open engagement of the world. This is inherently risky because what is received and known is wagered in the quest for further autonomy. Paul Tillich asserted in *The Courage to Be*: "Man's vitality is as great as his intentionality [his capacity to create meanings]; they are interdependent. Vitality is the power of creating beyond oneself without losing oneself. The more power of creating beyond itself a being has the more vitality it has. [...] Only man has complete vitality because he alone has complete intentionality."[4]

Humanity is, as a consequence, always defined in relation, not absolutely. It is mediated through the evidence of experience and reason, in conversation with one's fellows in civil society. It is civil society that permits humans to transcend the claims of the given, "the natural," as these are encoded in the primal and traditional worlds. The vigor of humanity is evidenced in the vigor of civil life — our capacity for encounter and conversation. Anything less than this higher life rooted in civility is ultimately existence by recipe, an ephemeral life taken off the shelf like a canned computer program. (Most people, observed Oscar Wilde, live someone else's life.) If we do not fully live in civility, among strangers, we lose the possibility of an authentic self and become strangers in our own lives. The realm of unquestioned certitudes, of rigid rules and roles, and strict value hierarchies, is ultimately worldless and thus lifeless. It is the articulation of the many pathologies which afflict individuals and societies experiencing rapid and unmanaged change as the past confronts modernity. In attempting to make brothers of strangers, the Christian right — as much as the countercultural left — challenges the civil world.

The raw material from which we create who we are is experience. Because human life is social life, the nature of our interaction with other human beings ultimately influences our choices about the persons we become. If our experiences with others are essentially primal — that is unmediated and reactive — our self-definitions as individuals are difficult. Primal modes are too diffuse to enable individual people. Traditional modes, even in those non-urban, non-technological societies where they predominate, can at best provide some useful boundaries, e.g. man or woman, within which to discover a genuinely individual self. But ultimately it is only in a civil world, in which boundaries are understood as changeable boundaries of conversation and convention that we begin to discover an irreducible self. A self with no civil world within which to seek these definitions becomes a lost self, a parody of authentic life.

Andre Malraux asserted that, "The Individual stands in opposition to society; but he is nourished by it. And it is far less important to know what differentiates him than what nourishes him."[5] The idea that we are always individual and social in relation is at least as old as Aristotle, and the heart of the idea of a virtuous life — that is, a life worthy of *vir*: man. Concepts of virtue thus focus, according to British literary critic and social theorist Terry Eagleton, "upon the shape, texture and quality of a whole life in its practical social context. Virtue is a matter of the proper, pleasurable fulfillment of one's human powers, both a practice and a matter of practise. Being human is a set of techniques, something you have to get good at like tolerating bores or playing the harmonica, and you cannot do it on your own more than you could carry out major surgery simply by instinct."[6]

The decline of civil norms and institutions in the United States and elsewhere has weakened the historical house of consciousness of the individual. Left to itself, individual life becomes solipsistic and narcissistic. Historian Christopher Lasch has described what he calls a growing "culture of narcissism," in which individuals begin to define the world exclusively within such self-referential terms.[7] Lacking the real dynamics of encounter provided by a vigorous civil world, individuals turn inward toward their isolated selves, seeking to find that "real" and "happy" person. Narcissism is the inability to see or to establish boundaries between oneself and one's environment; an inability to distinguish between one's own feelings, needs and values and those of others. The tragedy of the mythical Narcissus was not that he fell in love with his own image, but that he did not know it was his own image that he loved. Much of this narcissistic self-seeking focuses, with obsession, on the dynamics of romantic love. It is so much the focus of popular culture and media that we usually are not aware of how compellingly romance-obsessed modern society has become. Perhaps because human intimacy is so completely nourished in primal modes, it is this loss of intimacy which we most feel as we ascend the needs hierarchy to lead highly-evolved, modern lives.

Romantic love has become the cipher for the all-embracing intimacy of a diminished primal past. It is in fact our secular religion: we dress ourselves and groom ourselves with a romantic orientation. We attend shows and concerts, view films and read books there vicariously to experience the pleasure/pain of romantic love. Our commercial culture and its media adjuncts are overwhelming centered in the ideals of romance. Young people define themselves, and others, on the basis of their favorite bands. For many people romantic love is a career, the sum of a life-quest focused in therapy and an enormous self-help literature, of which John Gray's popular *Men Are From Mars, Women Are From Venus* is typical. In romantic love we seek simultaneously to confirm our self-absorption and to escape from it. This fusion of two selves "into one" promises the end to our isolation and alienation without attaching us to anything outside of that relationship, as marriage, for example, traditionally did. The phrase, "You can't love others until you love yourself" has become so much a part of this narcissism that it is seldom questioned. In fact, of course, the reverse is true: one cannot love oneself until one loves others. It is in encountering the authentic "other" that the authentic "self" emerges and begins to have operative boundaries. The loved and loving self is the product of these loving experiences. "The other" remains a romantic self-obsession, always tested, never trusted, without this growing, loving self. The "he who is" confronting "the him who is not" existentially and authentically, not romantically and narcissistically, makes genuine encounters with others possible.

The culture of narcissism has a vital economic and commercial dimension. As one ascends the needs hierarchy one's dissatisfactions and one's aspirations may become more peripheral in their concerns but more central in their focus. The passion for romantic love — never of much consequence in primal or traditional cultures where the needs of individual and social survival and continuity are compelling — can dominate the lives of people in modern societies who "have it all," but are not happy because they are not "in love." Others obsess about their looks — body tone, weight, hair (the lack of it or its color), clothing — and spend billions to improve them. Modern commercial culture depends on the relentless dissatisfaction of consumers who must continuously acquire and replace goods to feed these complaints. And this occurs because, in what John Kenneth Galbraith termed "the affluent society," characterized by large discretionary spending, any hesitancy or reallocation of spending by consumers can be disruptive to the economy. Poor societies have no need of "consumer confidence indexes" because elementary needs are predictably continuous. In modern societies creating new "needs" is essential to maintaining the demand which fuels investment and spending. The culture of narcissism and its media expressions are the allies of consumer society in this process. The rise of the "name brand," especially in highly discretionary and replacement consumption like apparel and cosmetics, produced the phenomenon of the "designer label," prominently displayed. As in post-modern art, the designer was often more important than the design, and in fact major figures like Calvin Klein made their fortunes not from their own creations, but from licensing their names to other designers. Marketing has become the essence of style itself.[8]

The culture of narcissism has also found an ally in contemporary management literature. "Taylorism," the older view that workers are almost infinitely malleable within ever more efficient industrial management structures, has been eclipsed by "McGregorism," the view that treating workers as individual and whole persons with life-goals leads to greater productivity. This shift mirrors the move from the old industrial economy to the new service and information-based economy. Industrial consultant and MIT professor Douglas McGregor developed the now-famous "Theory Y," where worker behavior is understood within this context of the existentially autonomous development of individuals.[9] "Therapeutic management," as evidenced in Maslow's pioneering *Eupsychian Management* [1965], generated a booming economy of clinics, workshops and seminars for managers and employees, of which "sensitivity training" around such issues as race and gender are only a small part. Motivational speakers, seminars, books and tapes became a multibillion dollar industry.

As mass society promoted the exchangeability of individuals it diminished genuine individuality, which was often displaced by narcissistic eccentricity. This trend was greatly exacerbated in business environments by computer technology and the "digital revolution," which produced the new class of "digerati" or "cybernerds" in an information society. In this intellectual, high-tech culture human relations are increasingly abstracted, encoded and experienced in "cyberspace." The result is what Paulina Borsook calls a "psychologically brittle" culture which is fundamentally unsociable and uncivil; anti-institutional and antigovernment; and which manifests itself in "a lack of human connection and a discomfort with the core of what many of us consider to be human." In its place the *digerati* promote an almost anarchic libertarianism, which "reduces everything to the contractual, to economic rational decision making."[10] In cyberculture Bill Gates became both the world's wealthiest individual and the symbol of this libertarian class of *digerati*.

As the twentieth century drew to a close, the world of work became a more fluid and less structured place. Employment with the same firm, or even within the same industry, was replaced with a work ethos of independent "consultants" and "contractors." Individuals began to lose the sense of connection to places of work and to colleagues. Work became more opportunistic, "flexible" and isolated, and increasingly youth-oriented, especially in the new "dot-com" economy, where great success was expected before the age of thirty. The process of human exchange within institutions was increasingly replaced by isolated and self-directed activity experienced through modems or on cell phones, often at home, by internet interface. "Private" and "public" became even more conflated in this process, as did the distinction between reality and "virtual reality" in the minds of cyber-obsessed youth. These conditions placed ever greater strains on conventional social forms, especially the family and the community organizations of civil society, which have always rested on long-term identifications within committed relationships. They have also eroded political life. "A society of self-fulfillers, whose affiliations are more and more seen as revocable, cannot sustain the strong identification with the political community which public freedom needs," asserts Charles Taylor.[11]

The culture of narcissism also cultivated its own philosophical foundations in the critical theory of postmodernism. In postmodernist thought, the individual, in his existential and cognitive isolation, becomes the solitary source of truth and knowlege, each of us wrapped in his own "narrations." Claims to a larger, objective reality are dismissed as "metanarratives," constructions which reflect the differing conditions of power — of domination and submission — within society. It should not be surprising that the two individuals most prominently associated with the development of postmodernist theory were Frenchmen of personal and social exile: Michel Foucault, masochistic and homosexual, and Jacques Derrida, an Algerian Jew. Multiculturalism with its attendant "diversity" focus is intimately related to the postmodernist critique in that plurality becomes the only truth, its articulations irreducibly singular, personal and local, each "narration" the result of the individual's experience of the constructions of race, class and gender. Humanity begins to lose any authentic social dimension in the ways this has been understood since Aristotle pronounced it for the Western world. A person's social identity — the constructions imposed upon him — are the vantage point from which he tells his individual story; the only truth with any "objective" validity in his life; the "thereness" from which he narrates his "isness." Ironically, race, class and gender — constructions of no ultimate reality — become the most important circumstances of his condition because they form its narrative ground.

My own take on this stance is that it is ultimately mindless; and since it makes any notion of authentic communication between individuals futile, one wonders why so much is said and written by postmodernists. Like the graffiti it often celebrates, postmodernism in the end inhabits a world of random gossip which no amount of semiotic analysis can decode. More importantly, by undercutting the essential human capacity for objective rationality, it also undercuts its own moral claims as a bastion of the dispossessed. The capacity of people to meliorate the human condition is wedded to the capacity for fellow-feeling, which has an inescapable rational and social basis. Eagleton asserts: "Objectivity means among other things a decentered openess to the reality of others, and as Platonists see is in its more affective reaches closely linked with love. The fact that this is probably in any full sense impossible should not deter us from trying it on. Reason at its best is related to generosity, to being able to acknowledge the truth or justice of another's claims even when its cuts against the grain of one's own interests and desires."[12]

While "the individual" is an abstraction, and an ultimately important one, there is no totally abstract, disembodied self. Like the images on a radar screen, our perceptions of the world bounce off something more than constructed, something ultimately "real," our hazy mental configurations of it not withstanding. There is a *there*, there, which can be increasingly understood empirically.[13] This is the material from which we create our lives. As the existentialists tell us, "Existence precedes essence." What we are becoming essentially emerges *in* existence; in our engagement of the world, especially other people; in the freedom to promise, of which Nietzsche speaks; and in the freedom to act, which Sartre and the existentialists so insist upon. A life partly lived "in public" was the acknowledgment which we made that our fellows had claims to make on us; that our individual lives were lived in tension with theirs as we confronted the common problems of social life. The complex language of civility enabled the habitual identification of a public geography within which each of us engaged, acted and took responsibility. The language of that public life was rooted in reason, and public, rational discourse became the means by which we overcame the isolation of a purely private life.

As America faces the new millennium its concerns seem to be increasingly private. When all is said, the Clinton-Lewinski affair reflected the poverty of public life as it was almost completely privatized within narcissistic self-absorption. The presidential pardons controversy embodied the same dissolution of the boundaries of civility which mark the distinction between public and private matters, money as the universal solvent. That individuals increasingly treat public spaces as if they were private is evidence of the deterioration of public life itself. Until the 1960's it was unusual to see a man in public without a hat; coat and tie were customary even at sporting events. Now people dress (or undress) in public as they do in private. Rude T-shirts announce the opinionated presence of yet one more sovereign voice amidst a herd of individuals. Individuals (self-absorbed by sundry complaints, eccentricities and addictions) feel free to set up housekeeping in public places. Sometimes they live out of improvised tents, cardboard boxes, or shopping carts, in parks or graffiti-tagged streets and squares, using the gutters as privies. Public confessions of private indiscretions ("sharing pain") have become something of a popular, redemptive religion, with television talk-show formats based upon them. Mass voyeurism, a kind of reflected narcissism, produces "blockbuster" *cinema verite* TV hits like "Survivors." Corroded by incivility, public life has increasingly become not mutual exchange, as Aristotle insisted, but rather as William Grieder has phrased it, "mutual contempt." "Instead of a politics that leads the society sooner or later to confront its problems, American politics has developed new ways to hide from them."[14]

Defining the various contexts — referential totalities — within which human existential encounters can take place fruitfully is the function of the worlds of human experience — primal, traditional, civil, and individual — which find their focus in this study. That a robust civil life is what makes modern civilization a culture of creative freedom has been a persistent theme. Civility is in fact the prerequisite of individuality itself. The decline of civil life is the failure to build and sustain the foundations of civil freedom in institutions. Public life has declined in quality and in its capacities to arrest the attentions of individuals as it has become increasingly remote from them, and has concerned itself with merely instrumental values, especially the distribution of material wealth. In part this has to do with the privatization of public life by market relations. Government has to a great extent become merely an extension of private economic interests as public/private boundaries have become blurred. In part this is related to democratization. As the sheer number of people admitted to public life has increased the institutional capacities for dialog within the structures of pluralistic society have also become increasingly burdened.

The coming of technological society has created situations where individuals feel they have no relevance let alone control, like Kafka's protagonist who is on trial for a crime unknown to him. These faceless encounters support an *anomie* in which "hype" and "spin" rooted in scandal replaces common discourse in public life. Political parties, the media, especially television, and interest groups become less the transmission lines of pluralist discourse than the creatures of vast sums of money tied to special interests. As a consequence American electoral politics has come "to resemble a political arms race," charges political scientist Hugh Helco.[15] Daniel Lazare writes in his troubling appraisal of the American polity, *The Frozen Republic*:

> Americans must stop thinking of democracy as a legacy of the Founders and a gift of the gods, something that allows millions of voices to cry "me! me! me!," while politicians and judges divide up the spoils according to some time-honored formula. Rather, they'll have to think of it as an intellectual framework that they create and continuously update, one that allows them to tackle the problems of the modern world not as individuals but as a society. If democracy is to survive, it must grow.[16]

Only if Americans rediscover public life, and the civil world which invigorates and sustains it, will they build and rebuild the institutions of rational persuasion, decision, and responsibility which are indispensible to democratic pluralism.

The widespread anomie which Americans feel as they face public questions underlies one of the most significant phenomena of the last generation: the ascendancy of "identity politics." The paralysis of contemporary American public life both reflects and reinforces the tendency of the citizen to define himself by sets of given boundaries: gender, race, sexual orientation, ethnicity, handicap. Such given selves are then perceived and defined as marginalized and disempowered by "the system." Every turn in human events is viewed through these identity lenses, which ultimately mirror the self as a victim. Civil discourse is impaired to the degree that citizens do not see the common ground they share and the common solutions available to them. Vigorous engagement of one another within the institutions of civil society is the way in which this happens.

The tendency of individuals to identify not with those intermediating institutions, which attach them to civil society, but rather with given identities (and identity movements) which differentiate them from it, weakens civility. Thus what had begun as citizens asserting their civil rights (for participation *in* the system) became campaigns for "liberation" (*from* the system): first of blacks, then of women, then of homosexuals and finally of almost everyone. That middle-class, heterosexual, white men would found an identity movement, a "fire in the belly," of their own was a final articulation of this dynamic. "Diversity" is consequently an ultimately insidious phenomenon eroding the basis of the civil world. In its celebration of what is accidental in human life — e.g., gender or ethnicity — it closes growth into the higher reaches of human freedom, which is made possible precisely to the extent that these self-descriptions are seen for what they are: flights from full responsibility for one's own life. To the degree that one says, "I am a woman, therefore" (or "black, therefore," or "a Jew, therefore") one diminishes one's own real choices and the ability of society to make common, inclusive choices. Identity politics asserts that, "the personal is political." In that statement the very basis of politics as mutual exchange is negated, for the point of politics — real politics — has always been to transcend purely personal concerns, and to enable a higher self, the citizen, through civil discourse. Civil life makes it possible to enlarge concepts of the self and of self-interest, to take a longer-range view of them. Identity politics is a kind of dysfunctional localization of mass society (or delocalization of the citizen, depending on perspective) that has contributed to the decline in those multiple and common spaces of conversation and action in community organizations.

In America, the community organizations of civil society have always been a central, indeed distinguishing feature of public life. Participation in service organizations defined the man of business as much as his participation in the market. Through them much has been achieved, where programs of civil government have been non-extent or have failed. The decline and fragmentation of vital community organizations reflects the fragmentation of the citizenry and the consequent rise of large, increasingly bureaucratic government from which identity groups and others seek to extract advantage. Political scientist Robert B. Putnam has documented the steady erosion of membership in American community organizations — the PTA, Kiwanis, Shriners, Jaycees — in the last quarter-century.[17] Hannah Arendt alluded to the same problem when she asserted a generation ago that, "The trouble lies in the lack of public spaces to which the people at large would have entrance and which an elite could be selected, or rather, where it could select itself."[18] In a word, the spaces within which exchange in its highest expression, transactions in ideas and values, can take place have eroded with the emergence of mass society, identity politics, and narcissistic individualism. Without leadership in the form of elites who are responsible to constituencies of opinion and action, public life in the widest political sense surrenders to a narrower politics of personality, of electioneering and hype. Without such leadership, individuals have become politically *anomic*, that is disconnected from meaningful contact with public life, losing the identity of citizenship. Voting in American national elections is at it lowest levels since the 1920's. This lack of voter participation reflects not only apathy and the need for better "voter education," but the increasing failure of public life to provide any meaningful basis for voting.

As the tangled elections of 2000 seem to indicate, the American political process has taken on the flavor of Third World intrigue and deadlock, corruption and nepotism, with power passed from father to son, from husband to wife in a closed system of institutionalized extortion and bribery (called political "fund-raising") where venality is relieved only in banality. In such a system power and responsibility become ever more estranged. The organs of elected, responsible government become gridlocked as contending (monied) interests neutralize effective policy-making. Power then seeks the safe harbor of those non-elected officials who cannot as easily be held accountable to any constituency. The chairman of the Federal Reserve becomes, in effect, an economic czar whose every word draws close attention, and appointed federal judges with life-time tenure decide the big issues which actually affect individual lives.

Economically, the American system in the last generation has increasingly favored those at the top of the society. A general slowing in the productivity of the American economy from the mid-1960's to the mid-1990's, together with its increasing globalization, has given various portions of the population very different stakes in it by systematically widening the income gap, and economic security generally. Those toward the middle and lower income levels have seen their incomes stagnate or drop. "It is not merely that we are getting richer more slowly than before;" suggests economist Robert J. Samuelson, "the rich are getting rich faster than the poor."[19] This growing economic inequality reinforces the fragmenting tendencies of identity politics, and the result is that America becomes "progressively more and more balkanized and more and more embittered."[20] The forces of globalization have been deeply implicated in this process. As Europe and Japan recovered their places in the world economic system beginning in the 1960's, the relative role of the United States of necessity declined. Much of the growth of the American economy and of the new post-war middle class had been fueled by a global economy of reconstruction (and remilitarization) in which the United States had no real competitors. The subsequent rapid economic growth of Europe and Japan thus occurred at the expense of this American middle class: first, the "blue-collar aristocrats," whose strong labor unions could no longer extract concessions from owners as they competed with a globalized labor force; then the white-collar professionals and middle managers, who were merged and "down-sized" out of jobs by the imperatives of global competition in the 'eighties. The underclass of minorities had, of course, been the first and most vulnerable to these delocalizing trends.

Throughout the world economic elites have come to have more in common with one another than with the citizens of their own national states. They have become citizens of a global economy rather than of a global polity, their fates intertwined in the dynamics of common markets united by information technology, rather than shared institutions resting in national cultures. These elites are joined by the common bias they have come to share: the bias toward the values of production rather than of distribution within the global economic system. This is not simply a matter of the spread of market "supply-side" ideology since the late 1970's when the effects of "stagflation" became apparent globally. It is also a matter of ineffective global institutions, especially the trade, finance and development regimes. Distributive economics requires far more sophisticated and intrusive administrative capabilities — at the national or international levels — than does the economics of production rooted in the more flexible and decentralized marketplace. The economics of production wins by default because, at least in the short term, it is administratively simpler and thus easier.

Global economics has increasingly become subject to the historical weakness of capitalism: the lack of a viable and dynamic equilibrium between the capacity to produce, on one hand, and the capacity to distribute, on the other, because of widely disparate income levels. Greider summarizes:

> The new reality of global competition generates a vicious economic trap for worldwide prosperity: a permanent condition of overcapacity in production that insures destructive economic consequences. Simply put, the world existing structure of manufacturing facilities, constantly being expanded on cheap labor and new technologies, can now turn out far more goods than the world's consumers can afford to buy. That is, more cars, computers, aircraft, appliances, steel and so forth are made than the marketplace can possibly absorb.[21]

Global productive capacity is concentrated in Western Europe, Japan and North America, all but the latter with stagnant or even declining populations. The rest of the world, particularly much of Asia and Africa, continues to experience population growth, but with mostly stagnant or declining incomes. In short, potential consumers are where the income which produces effective demand is not.

This asymmetry is mitigated only by the ability of those with high incomes to increase their standards of living by acquiring and/or replacing more goods. Much of the continuing prosperity of the Western world lies in the replacement of the old industrial infrastructure with new high-information infrastructure in the rapidly growing computer and telecommunications industries. In an environment of slowing or stagnating global consumption, many industrial firms make their profits by taking market share from one another, often through predatory practices made possible by their national political-economic arrangements (*viz.* Japan), or by reducing costs, principally by eliminating well-compensated employment through down-sizing/merger activity and intensive applications of technology (*viz.* United States). The global economy is increasingly driven by the imperatives of cost-reduction at the micro-economic level of the firm, and by the cost-reductions gained at the macro-economic level of the state through dismantling institutional impediments to the free movement of goods, capital and people, such as the WTO, European Union and NAFTA.

The problem is that one man's cost is usually another man's income, and the means of replacing lost income are not so easily at hand in complex economies which are both global in extent and knowledge-based. The forces of global delocalization have triumphed over those of global localization for a substantial portion of America's middle class, the majority of whom have seen no real rise in their standard of living since the 'seventies, and are working longer and harder to maintain that. It is this complaint which brought thousands of protesters to the streets of Seattle in 1999 and Quebec City in 2001 to protest the "free trade consensus," represented by the World Trade Organization, which has neglected the interests of ordinary working people. In contrast, America's academic institutions and the information-based industries they have spawned — *viz.* Boston's Route 128; San Francisco's Silicon Valley; North Carolina's Research Triangle — are examples of the localization of a globalized information culture that is producing unprecedented prosperity for those equipped to capture its benefits. And even here tenured senior professors confront a growing academic under-class of poorly paid and insecure "gypsy" faculty caught up in "cost-containment." In an environment which consistently rewards cost-reduction the mastery of rapid information processing is the key to competitive success. As Peter Drucker points out, especially in traditional businesses, from retailing to banking to hospital supply, the consistent competitive champions have harvested the cost advantages of successful information processing.[22]

An inextricable part of this cost-driven global information economy is also the movement of populations to the centers of production: from Latin America and Asia to North America, and from Africa and Asia to Europe. People become more mobile as goods become less so. Thus the problem of diverse populations sharing a territory but not common cultural premises occurs simultaneously with the weakening of institutions to deal with the inherent conflicts rooted in cultural pluralism. The widening structural distances between production and distribution, and between localization and delocalization in a globalized environment have profound cultural implications, not the least of which is this phenomenon of mass immigration. And even commentators like Samuel P. Huntington, who can hardly be called xenophobic, warn the West of the cultural threat which these trends portend. "Promoting the coherence of the West," he asserts, "means both preserving Western culture within the West and defining the limits of the West. The former requires, among other things, controlling immigration from non-Western societies, as every major European country has done and as the United States is beginning to do, and ensuring the assimilation into Western culture of the immigrants who are admitted."[23]

NOTES TO CHAPTER FIFTEEN

1. Gordon W. Allport, BECOMING (New Haven: Yale University Press, 1955), p. 79
2. Reynolds Price, a review of Robert Coles, THE SECULAR MIND, *The New York Times Book Review* (July 25, 1999) p. 18
3. Hilail Gildin, ed., AN INTRODUCTION TO PHILOSOPHY: TEN ESSAYS BY LEO STRAUSS (Detroit: Wayne State University Press, 1989), p. 92; Strauss, of course, refuses this fundamental legacy of the Enlightenment.
4. Tillich, *op.cit.,* p. 81
5. Callahan, *op.cit.*, p. 355
6. Terry Eagleton, THE ILLUSIONS OF POSTMODERNISM (Oxford: Blackwell Publishers, Ltd., 1996), p. 109
7. Christopher Lasch, THE CULTURE OF NARCISISM (New York: W.W. Norton & Co., 1991)
8. Marketing literature has begun to distinguish between "brands" and "brand leadership," through which a name or label becomes only a cipher for differing strategic-cultural interpretations of the same product. "Global brand leadership means using organizational structures, processes, and cultures to allocate brand-building resources globally, to create global synergies, and to develop a global brand strategy that coordinates and leverages country brand strategies." David A. Aaker and Erich Joachimsthaler, "The Lure of Global Branding," HARVARD BUSINESS REVIEW (November-December 1999)
9. Douglas McGregor, THE HUMAN SIDE OF THE ENTERPRISE (New York: McGraw-Hill, 1960)
10. Paulina Borsook, CYBERSELFISH, (New York: Public Affairs Press, 2000), p. 82
11. Charles Taylor, *op.cit.*, p. 508
12. Eagleton, *op.cit.,* p. 123
13. Philosopher of science Ian Hacking has written an especially insightful criticism of "deconstruction" and its advocates. THE SOCIAL CONSTRUCTION OF WHAT? (Cambridge, MA: Harvard University Press, 1999)
14. William Grieder, WHO WILL TELL THE PEOPLE (New York: Simon & Schuster, 1992), p. 15
15. Hugh Helco, "Hyperdemocracy," THE WILSON QUARTERLY (Winter 1999), p. 67

16. Daniel Lazare, THE FROZEN REPUBLIC (New York: Harcourt, Brace & Company, 1996), p. 299
17. Robert D. Putnam, BOWLING ALONE: THE COLLAPSE AND REVIVIAL OF AMERICAN COMMUNITY (New York: Simon and Schuster, 2000); see also Francis Fukuyama, TRUST: THE SOCIAL VIRTURES AND THE CREATION OF PROSPERITY, (New York: The Free Press, 1995)
18. Hannah Arendt, ON REVOLUTION (New York: The Viking Press, 1963), pp. 281-282
19. Robert J. Samuelson, THE GOOD LIFE AND ITS DISCONTENTS (New York: Times Books, 1995), pp. 70-71; British observer Charles Handy writes: "The standard of living has remained unchanged over the last 25 years for 70% of American families or, to put it another way, it now requires two incomes to live as well, comparatively, as a family with one income did in the last generation." Handy, *op.cit.*, p. 60; an excellent summary of these issues is: Jeffrey Madrick, THE END OF AFFLUENCE (New York: Random House, 1997)
20. *Ibid.*, p. 236
21. Grieder, *op.cit.*, p. 399
22. Peter F. Drucker, "Beyond the Information Revolution," THE ATLANTIC MONTHLY (October 1999)
23. Huntington, "The West: Unique, Not Universal," *op.cit.*, p. 45

CONCLUSION

> Modernization invades our sentiency, demanding wider modes of feeling congruent with the civil modes of behavior needed for living among strangers.
>
> — *John Murray Cuddihy*

The premise that "Westernization" and "modernization" are intimately related is the point at which this study began. The organization of the visible, material world — including its underlying social and economic relations — is governed by powerful cultural structures which are coherent in both time and space. Variations in the characters of individual societies should not obscure these underlying, formal systems. Westernization is a variety of modernization, neither identical nor alternative to it. Huntington suggests that, "The attitudes, values, knowledge and culture of people in a modern society differ greatly from those in a traditional society. As the first civilization to modernize, the West is the first to have fully acquired the culture of modernity."[1] Westernization and modernization are related in a process of wide-ranging historical evolution, and it is illusory to think that major, defining elements of traditional society can endure, as Huntington and others assert, in the face of these transformative cultural forces which modernization brings with it. Yet it is precisely this which many spokesmen, in the less developed world in particular, seem to affirm.

A prominent voice in this debate has been that of Dr. Mahathir Mohamad, Malaysia's long-time and authoritarian prime minister. His book, *The Voice of Asia,* is something of a manifesto for those, especially the so-called "Asian Tigers," which intend to become modern without losing their traditional cultures. A marked critic of contemporary Western culture, Mahathir Mohamad asserts in his book: "Western societies are riddled with single-parent families, which foster incest, with homosexuality, with cohabitation, with unrestrained avarice, with disrespect for others and, of course, with rejection of religious teachings and values."[2] The Malaysian government's economic development program, called "Vision 2020," is aimed at fully industrializing the country two decades into the new millennium. Explicit in this vision is the belief that Malaysia will continue as a very conservative Muslim country with traditional values, especially those identified with traditional families. The fundamental question remains: is it possible to pursue economic and technological development selectively, relatively detached from the larger social and cultural context? Is the phenomenon of exchange ultimately parsed in such segmented ways?

Hannah Arendt has posited that, "Men are conditioned beings because everything they come into contact with turns immediately into a condition of their existence."[3] Every element of human exchange with the environment, including the material environment, defines the totality of the human world. This is the case because in shaping the objects of nature for use, humans imbed in them *and derive from them* sets of values which do not subsist in isolation. Malaysia's economic development has two major sources: the export of raw materials and commodities, especially rubber, palm oil, tin and timber; and electronics manufacturing, especially computer chips — of which Malaysia is the world's largest exporter. As Malaysia's ecology is being profoundly changed by the deforestation of the countryside, and the transformation of subsistence farming into plantation agriculture, people's relations to the objective, natural world are being transformed as well. Similarly, the lives of Malaysian young people, especially young women who make up the bulk of the workforce in the electronics factories, are also being profoundly changed, incrementally and irrevocably. Malaysians are being "conditioned" in exchange in ways not conceived of in Mahathir Mohamad's anti-Western posturing. In tying Malaysia's traditional rural economy to plantation wages and export-driven world commodity prices, its leadership has tied Malaysia to Western societies. This is even more the case for the export-driven electronics industry and its workers, now tied to modern technology. Marion Levy, Jr. proposed that: "The structures of relatively modernized societies cannot be imported entirely piecemeal. Whether introduced by force or voluntary means, more is introduced than is bargained for or understood."[4] This assertion echoes Marcel Mauss, who described modernization as a "total phenomenon," dynamic and systemic. James A. Bill and Robert Springborn also assert that the patterns that constitute "the modernization syndrome" are "mutually reinforcing."[5]

❖ ❖ ❖

The policies of Western nations, biased by their own civil modes as they have dealt with the non-West, have tended to focus on institutional structures and systems without paying sufficient heed to the "total phenomenon" of the cultural contexts which enable them. The International Monetary Fund (IMF), as an example, has throughout its history predicated financial aid to the economies of Africa, Asia and Latin America on premises which were evolved in a post-World War II Western context. It assumes that monetary problems reflect institutional and policy environments that need "reform." It assumes, for example, that banking structures are merely and mostly instruments of policy, and that instrumental adjustments to policy regarding banks will change destabilizing monetary practices. In failing to understand that banks and banking policy outside Europe and North America are usually intimately related to cultural values which are non-Western in character it has provoked as much political and economic crisis as it has resolved. The case of Indonesia is illustrative of these failures in cultural perspectives.

The Suharto regime, which had been in power in Indonesia for over thirty years, maintained itself with rapid economic growth. This growth was initially based on the oil revenues produced during the heyday of inflated OPEC oil prices in the 1970's, and then by Japanese and Western investment in the rapid, oil-fueled growth of the following decades. At the heart of this political economy was a system of institutionalized theft and nepotism within the Suharto family and its allies. The real, but highly localized, business talent and energy within the Indonesian economy was provided by the resident Chinese merchant class, who make up only 4% of the population, but control 70% of the country's liquid wealth. The animosity this Chinese population attracts from other Indonesians resulted in 500,000 deaths in the "year of living dangerously" that brought the Suharto regime to power. On the other hand, half of the stock market by capitalization is in the hands of only ten families. Jean-Pierre Lehmann of the International Institute for Management Development in Switzerland suggests that in many respects Asia's capitalist structure could best be described as "feudal." David Wall of Cambridge University agrees that Asian family-based capitalism "is stronger than ever."[6] Any investment in Indonesia was an investment in a typically Asian system of globalized nepotism and localized ethno-capitalism. This proto-market system by its very nature deformed market rationality, however defined. "Crony capitalism" increasingly rewarded overinvestment in state-controlled elements of the economy, and in those sectors with the largest and most immediate flows of wealth to the Suharto family and its allies, particularly construction and real-estate. The Chinese-controlled segments of the economy, especially small businessmen and their retail prices, were especially vulnerable to capital flight at the first signs of a downturn, and to currency inflation, which came in the summer of 1997.

The structural "imbalances" in Indonesian public and private debt identified by the officials of the IMF as "problematic" were in fact central to the system itself, not some deficiency which could be resolved by such mechanisms as controlling the money supply, tightening credit or balancing government budgets. Because the large inflows of capital in previous years had often been more speculative than real, based as they were on the fortunes of the Indonesian political regime and its relations to the international economic system which the IMF represents, the cessation of these investments (and speculative outflows) brought this inherently unstable system to its knees. The problem of Indonesian public life, as in other pre-civil societies, is that there is no cultural confidence in the institutions which permit individuals to take a longer-range view of their self-interests, that is, to contextualize their lives within the civility which makes public life possible. James C. Scott, in his classic work *Comparative Political Corruption*, asserted the general principle: "*the more uncertain and insecure the environment, the shorter the period over which individuals seek to maximize gains.* Under conditions of great uncertainty, those who pursue long-term strategies are penalized while those who pursue short-run strategies, where risks are smaller and more calculable, are more likely to succeed."[7] Long-term family identification both reflects and reinforces short-term civil ties. A culture of civility is essential to sustaining the formal environment within which long-term gains may be rationally pursued.

The Indonesian political and economic system was thus highly localized in time and space, lacking both the long-term perspective and the ability to tie itself to the structures of truly globalized enterprise which the transnational financial system, its institutions and the IMF represent. The photograph of the Managing Director of the IMF, Michel Camdesus, standing with his arms folded behind the seated Suharto as the latter initialed an IMF bail-out plan said it all. The situation was presented as akin to a school-master correcting an errant pupil. The subsequent collapse of the Suharto regime, with the enormous destruction of property and the death of hundreds that accompanied it, suggest that something far deeper was at stake. What was at stake was the clash of two cultures: that of the IMF, rooted in civil modes of market rationality, institutional stability and pluralistic politics, and that of a non-Western regime, resting in kinship loyalties, authoritarian government and pre-civil institutional modes.

This same pattern of conflict has evidenced itself throughout the non-West. In Russia, in Africa, and in much of Latin America and Asia precivil societies are interpreted in civil modes unsuited to them. Political scientist Crawford Young, in reviewing the devastation visited on Nigeria, Africa's largest state, by thirty years of corruption, repression and misrule, says: "Nigerians are by no means alone in their collective self-doubt. With a debilitating economic decline completing its second decade in many African lands, the remorseless pressures of globalization and world capital markets, and the frustration that endless 'structural adjustments' have engendered, even the indisputable headway in African political liberalization cannot dissipate the apprehensions."[8] No number of "structural adjustments" can address a malaise deeply embedded in cultural values. An election here, and an IMF loan there, will have the same effects as they have had in the forty years of African independence without a deep analysis of these underlying cultural constraints. Yet even Young suggests only that, "Democratization, with its many limits and flaws, remains the only path extending beyond impasse, in Nigeria as elsewhere."[9]

As I have suggested in this study, "democracy" is the end, not the beginning, of a very deep and complex process of social differentiation and abstraction which allows people to place their faith in, and mediate their lives through, the forms and institutions of civil life. Democracy is closely related to the lessening of kinship loyalties in both economics and politics. It assumes the rational individual as the normative unit of civil society. It also assumes his imaginative as well as his social mobility. Fundamentally, democracy assumes that the individual is already participating in those other basic changes which democratization and pluralistic institutions reflect. In the West, economic and social development initiated those forces of modernization which were reflected in democratic, pluralistic values and institutions. This process is reversed in the non-West. It is largely traditional institutions that are initiating and sustaining economic and social modernization, to the degree that it occurs at all. Most individuals in traditional societies are, as Lerner suggested, nonparticipant: political institutions thus have the burden of mobilizing the mass of the population to participate in socio-economic change.

The military has played a dominant role in many traditional societies as they face the forces of global modernization. In part this may be because only the military has the capacity for force to induce minimal levels of social order and discipline. But this also may occur because military structures enable participation of many sectors of the population on a number of levels, as well as establish at least minimal connections to world technological change. In this regard, Japan's experience can be regarded as a successful instance of a more general case. In the Meiji Revolution the *samurai* military class adapted its traditional structures to guide both political and economic modernization in the context of global engagement. In those societies where the military has not become, usually by default, the mechanism for confronting social change, the single-party system dominated by leftist intellectuals attempts a more active and systematic mass mobilization. Beginning with Leninist Russia in the 'twenties, and continuing in such figures as Nehru and Mao in Asia, Torre and Nkrumah in Africa, and Castro in Latin America, these single-party "socialist" systems had as their central purpose the mobilization of the population into the structures of global modernity. But in every case these single-party socialist systems failed. Rather than serving their people by localizing civil society and market development, they at best buffered the delocalization of traditional social and economic modes by providing short-term substitutes for them. Thus the church became the party, and the plantation became the collective farm, but cultural attitudes were hardly touched in this basically conservative process.

Superficial cultural analysis, especially that so often connected with "multiculturalism," suggests that human experience is a sort of banquet of diverse cultural dishes which enrich each of us through their sampling. It has been suggested, for example, that the modern West has much to learn from other cultures about the importance of intimate kinship relations, non-rational modes of apprehension, or traditional medicine. Anthropologist Frederique Marglin and her husband, economist Stephen Marglin, have extolled what they call the "embedded way of life" as experienced in traditional, rural India, where individual and social, home and workplace, poetry and traditional medicine interpenetrate — in contrast to the "polarized," "bureaucratized," and "dehumanized" values of Western society.[10] The poverty, disease, caste-based inequality and very low status of women are either ignored as somehow extrinsic to the culture — or, in effect, extolled, as when Stephen Marglin notes with approval the religious traditions which exclude menstruating women from the workplace.[11] This sort of romanticizing of non-Western culture is as old as the adversary stance of French intellectuals in the late eighteenth century.

If my thesis is correct that modern science and the concept of human rights are the result of a cultural evolution inextricably tied to the weakening of "embedded" ties and the ascendancy of rational empiricism, then the inherent contradictions of multiculturalism begin to emerge. Modernity and civility are by their very nature adversaries to primal and traditional ties and values. Levy calls modernization a "universal social solvent."[12] Modernity and civility do not altogether abolish primal and traditional modes, but they necessarily undermine their cultural integrity and their associated social structures. When Dankwart Rustow describes modernization as a process of "rapidly widening control over nature through closer cooperation among men"[13] he describes the necessarily growing distance between man and the natural world, and the closer association of people in highly mediated, abstract thought and complex institutional arrangements. This distance from nature both undermines kin-based sociality and enables alternatives to it within the forms of civil society. Describing modernization as "inevitable and omnipresent," Bill and Springborg, summarize its far-reaching affects on premodern societies: "Modernization is an unsettling, disruptive, painful process. The comforts of traditional habits are lost as these habits are uprooted. In modernizing societies, new processes and institutions seem always to be trapped in a state of becoming, and as a result, the expected uncertainties of the past have given way to the more frightful and unknown securities of the present."[14]

This is in many ways the tragedy of modernity. As the word itself suggests, modernity is a pervasive cultural temper, a *mood*, which informs everything it touches. When first understood in the West by writers like Kierkegaard, Marx, Nietzsche, Eliot and Joyce, modernity, with its dissolution "into thin air" of all previous formulations of human values, was often accepted as an inevitability rather than as a liberation. The freedom from the claims of the past which modernity brought with it was viewed as an existential problem, or in the case of Franz Kafka, as an existential torment. Modernity is a problem of wholeness, or more specifically, the loss of wholeness. Nietzsche wrote: "The men with whom we live resemble a field of ruins of the most precious sculptural designs where everything shouts at us: come, help, perfect ... we yearn immeasurably to become whole."[15] The loss of wholeness, or "embededness," may be the great human tragedy of modernity, but also its majesty. In acquiring the greater capacity to live by its own reason, judgment and action — to seek wholeness from "the inside out" — humankind severs its ties to much in its pre-modern past which was authoritatively given, that is, its ties to tradition and "nature" with their inhibitions of the highest human capacity, the capacity for freedom. The locus of this capacity is the autonomous individual, who can look at the past with regret and nostalgia or as an object of contemplation, but if he is to be authentic, not as something that can be restored. Tradition cannot be fully appreciated in modern societies, let alone actually recovered, by listening to Indian chants, experimenting with traditional African herbs, wearing ethnic dress, or "celebrating diversity." All of these, it seems to me, are evasions of the problem that the individual in relation to modernity has been since it was first identified.

In the American context, Southern "traditionalists," conservative Catholics and neoconservative Jews have attempted such an evasion to the detriment of individual freedom and, ultimately, the further erosion of civility in the United States. Similarly, liberal advocates of ethnic identity, such as "Afrocentrism," as a basis for economic and social uplift, or for improving the lives of black youth through ethnic awareness, contribute little to the future prospects of these kids in a highly technological, civil society and its globalized environment.[16] For Harvard sociologist Orlando Patterson this "particularist" attitude has been a disaster for black people, "for the simple sociological truth is that the main source of the problems among black Americans is their isolation from the overarching capitalist culture that their leaders misleadingly identify with white society."[17] Simply put, the cultural environment of many black Americans has been delocalized and thus isolated from those globalizing forces which are transforming economic relations in contemporary society. Likewise, Africa has little to teach contemporary Africans as they confront global trends, let alone to teach people who are centuries removed from their African roots. Afrocentrism primarily advances victim ideology and the illusions of academics who carve out such ultimately self-serving career niches. "Only by taking a deep breadth and devoting as much attention to the cultural problem as we currently do to victimhood," asserts Berkeley linguist John H. McWhorter, "can we really start black students on the path to doing as well in school as anyone else — something that has become alarmingly inconceivable to many Americans, black and white."[18] That "cultural problem," with its roots in the anti-intellectualism which pervades the lives of many black Americans — especially those in the underclass — derives from the lack of substantive and analytical boundaries intrinsic to the primal world.

Ethnocentric values have consequences, often negative, in a pluralistic modern society. The spread of multicultural and "diversity" ideology is adversely affecting actual lives, especially those of children, as a recent court case in Chicago illustrates. A drug-abusing, single, black mother had three children taken from her by child welfare authorities. One child, addicted to crack cocaine, was taken from this mother at birth and placed with white foster parents, who tried to adopt the child three years later. The birth mother (photographed in African costume) was granted custody of this child who had never known her as a mother. The judge in the case said she must take into account the racial heritage of the child. "Unless the position of the [child welfare] department is that there is no such thing as Afro-American culture, this issue deserves more attention than to check the box that says 'not applicable'."[19] Had the judge contemplated the possible roots of many of the behaviors of this woman and others like her in the primal cultural modes which characterize the black underclass? "Altered states of consciousness," however induced, are central to primal culture, not accidental to it. An unreflective life of spontaneous expression and "possession;" a reactive life of unmediated interpersonal engagement, which cannot create boundaries or capture the future consequences of impulsive (or addictive) behavior, encourages irresponsible child-bearing, and substance abuse in a modern, urban context. The cultural phenomenon of drug addiction, unplanned pregnancy, and fluid child/parent relations is too pervasive to be only accidental in individual lives. A focus on cultural particularism ultimately only obscures, and even advances, maladaptive behaviors intrinsic to pre-civil cultures as they confront a civil world. Public figures and others have delineated these particularist cultural realms, and their ideological expressions, as another variation of the American preference for special interest politics at the expense of citizenship. As Patterson has suggested, "'Ethnic diversity' and 'cultural pluralism' are the buzz words of deception on this [liberal] side of the spectrum. Certainly on college campuses, diversity no longer means genuine cultural exchange, but the promotion of differences; in politics the protection of ethnic turfs is at stake."[20]

The pervasive emphasis on cultural localization and identity in the American academy has become so corrosive that some intellectuals are reverting to traditional concepts of entitlement by birth as the basis for their core conceptions of justice, of which "affirmative action" is only the most obvious manifestation. The distributive bias of primal economics allies itself to the particularist politics of "diversity" in university ethnic and cultural studies departments to become the focus for what psychologists call "injustice collecting," or what McWhorter calls "victimology." This focus on victimization has defined ethnic scholarship itself, most notably in the specious debate about the putative African origins of classical Greek (and Western) civilization.[21] Elazar Barkman, in his *The Guilt of Nations*, and others (including Harvard's Henry Louis Gates, Jr.) have begun to argue the merits of reparations to the descendants of American slaves.[22] A condition of birth replaces the citizen and civil society in this scheme of social equity. Wendy Kaminer asserts that this notion of "historical justice" is a retrogression to the traditional, reflecting "some of the premises of the aristocracy it attacks. It allows the past to define our entitlements in the present; it relies on a belief in the justice of inheritance. [...] If equality is a birthright, you don't have to purchase it with the sufferings of your ancestors, any more than you should be able to purchase privileges with your ancestors' achievements."[23]

The basic forces which continue to transform the world — especially science, technology and market economics — are rooted firmly in the civil and individual worlds and cannot be abolished without abolishing both the individual and civil society. There can be no ultimate compromises between tradition and modernity, and thus all attempts to preserve traditional cultures or meaningful fragments of them in a modern context are ultimately doomed to failure. Where the primal and the traditional endure in modern societies, it is usually within marginalized subcultures — social "reservations" — which are often caricatures of themselves. When the Iranian ayatollahs tell us they want an "Islamic Republic," or a society "both Muslim and civil," they might as well seek to be half pregnant. The dynamics of civility and the dynamics of orthodox, traditional religion exclude one another because the essence of civility is consent and equal exchange. No orthodox religion truly asks for the consent of adherents to its doctrines, or postulates equality in exchange between adherent and religious authority, let alone between deity and worshiper or between one religion and another. The essence of orthodox religion is that it is revealed and given. Its sources of authority, be it Bible or Koran, bishop or ayatollah are not subject to other authority, and certainly not to the dynamics of conversation and consent which are at the heart of civil society. When the Vatican decreed in 1998 that discussion was closed on the question of a married clergy or the ordination of women; and in 2000 that ecumenism did not mean that other Christian sects were equal to the one, true Church of Rome, it behaved in ways totally consistent with traditional authoritarianism, but utterly inconsistent with civility. At best, one can imagine various forms of truce between traditional religion and civil society as they assert their claims on individual lives and individual judgments. The same point should be made for those who imagine localized forms of "democracy" which are essentially non-Western, be it Indonesian "guided democracy," or Chinese "people's democracy" combined with "market socialism." Such oxymoronic formulations are at best intellectual evasions or cynical forms of propaganda.

These issues are particularly important for universities. The search for truth cannot be mitigated by dogmatically-imposed formal restrictions on learning in the name of orthodoxy, or other forms of intellectual compromise. "Civility dies with the death of dialogue," suggested Jesuit theologian John Courtney Murray. Universities are realms of civility in its highest expression when they are based on dialogue, and when nothing is excluded from the conversation except that which would end the conversation itself. Truth should be understood as unitary and universalized, not as fragmented and localized, and thus it is impossible to take certain topics off the table of discussion without diminishing the search for truth itself. This culture of civility can be misused, and has sometimes been misused in the name of "diversity," or "postmodern" criticism. As equality in exchange is the basis of civility, the inclusion in academic dialog of issues which are inherently not subject to a common language of discourse undermines dialogue. For the secular humanist and the fundamentalist Christian to dialogue with each other or third parties about matters which are based, on one side in empirical rationalism, and the other in revealed and "inerrant" scriptures, is an exercise in futility. Their premises originate in what Stephen Jay Gould has termed different and incompatible "majesteria."[24] The encounter is little more than *reportage* (or, to use a postmodernist term, "narrative") and often indistinguishable from the charismatic: there is no truth apart from the tellers. When conservative clergy like Richard Neuhaus complain that religiously-based views and values are being excluded unfairly from the public space, including the university, they must also address this issue.[25]

It is for this reason that I find the arguments of Stephen Carter, who wishes to make religion the focus of a return to civility, to be basically wrong-headed.[26] Civility is not based on the capacity of individuals to give themselves to some transcendent reality, as Carter argues. Such self-sacrifice is the basis of every form of modern totalitarianism. Civility requires that the individual form values with an intelligent regard for the needs of others. Civility is the capacity to create the dialogue necessary to bring these needs, of the self and of others, into fruitful balance. Dialogue requires common premises, and that the premises themselves be ultimately open to systematic, critical inquiry. Religion, properly so-called, precisely because its premises are given and received, is inherently incapable of creating these common, rational premises which support civil dialogue — unless everyone in society shares the same religion. Perhaps that is why so many issues raised in American public discourse degenerate into attempts by individuals to convert others to their religious assumptions. To celebrate religious attitudes in the public realm is consequently to undermine the possibilities of civility, not to advance them. In our civil encounters with Kierkegaard's "confident knight of faith" we might suspect that he is motivated by his religion, but that individual faith will not reveal itself in public spaces in his discourse. As Kierkegaard understood so well, since the Enlightenment gave birth to modernity persons of traditional faith inhabit (or leap into) a parallel universe to that of secular, civil society. They must live, as Kierkegaard said, in "absurdity," simultaneously in the finite and the infinite. As a citizen the person of faith respects the boundaries between these universes, and does not treat the civil space as if it were a tent meeting, a place of primal, charismatic testimony, aimed in fact at convincing oneself as much as others.

Similarly, postmodernist conceptions of society in general and the university in particular which are based on a presumption that there is no knowable ground for asserting common truths make a mockery of dialogue and of civility itself. It is the sort of self-indulgence a portion of the intellectual class has always allowed itself as it assumes a socially adversary stance in the name of sympathy for the voiceless, the "wretched of the earth." From the privileged and secure halls of academe it is easy to deny the value of the West's cultural achievement, and to posit that Bantus and Belgians are separated only by differing states of oppression and privilege. Terry Eagleton asserts in his incisive analysis of postmodernism: "Those who are privileged enough not to need to know, for whom there is nothing politically at stake in reasonably accurate cognition, have little to lose by proclaiming the virtues of undecideability. There is no reason why literary critics should not turn to autobiography or anecdotalism, or simply slice up their texts and deliver them to their publishers in a cardboard box, if they are not so politically placed as to need emancipatory knowledge."[27] Multiculturalism is the twin of postmodern criticism: if there is no ground for truth, all possess it (and lack it) in equal measure. In "celebrating diversity," we celebrate the democracy of ultimate ignorance which is the human condition in its multitude of "constructions." Thus, as a practical consequence, it is possible love all mankind in general while denigrating individuals in particular — the "imperialists," "elitists," "racists," "classists," and "sexists" whose claims to real knowledge and more evolved cultural values are dismissed, while the very real suffering of human beings outside privileged and "deconstructed" spaces continues unabated.

At the end of the day universities which surrender to multiculturalism have to face this issue, or it will come back to haunt them as it has Yale University. After seeking to be "inclusive" by ignoring its fundamental mission, Yale faced a law-suit from four Orthodox Jewish students who did not wish to live, as is required, in the university's residential colleges, or to be exposed to other influences which might offend the myriad mandates of their Orthodox faith. "These students want the education, but they don't want the encounter," complained Yale's president Richard Levin.[28] In fact these students did not want an education, either, for there is no genuine education without encounter. Rather, what they seemed to seek was vocational training attached to the prestige of a Yale degree. Anyone who already had at hand as much truth as Orthodoxy had given these students had no need of a liberal education rooted in the rigorous search for it. Yale became a prestigious university in the very process of giving up the religious orthodoxies of its founders, who intended to train ministers. Education means an opening up of students to important and influential (not *all*) values and ideas. It is to live as an individual among strangers in pursuit of truth, and the ultimate freedom that truth brings with it. In seeking to enable virtuous human beings the university asks them to reflect on the best and the highest, and this means universities have to make initial judgments about what those might be. That is, it must iterate initial boundaries. As an existential encounter liberal education frees the whole person, and as such is by its very nature inaccessible to those whose lives are closed as a matter of principle, religious or otherwise.

If Yale's soundly-based requirements of all undergraduate students, central to its liberal arts mission, discriminated against these students on account of their religion, as the lawsuit alleged, hen houses discriminate against foxes with their fences. Because its rigorously selective admissions process, which includes an interview with prospective students, did not make manifest the incompatibility of the goals of these Orthodox students with Yale's educational mission, one has to suspect that a thoughtless "celebration of diversity" on the part of the university, or artful dissimulation by these students, or both, had something to do with their admission in the first instance. Could their non-admission have been considered prejudicial at an institution where approximately one-quarter of the student body is Jewish, and where a large proportion of the faculty and administration, including the president himself, is Jewish? If civility is the articulation of boundaries, rationally and consensually chosen, as I have asserted, the civil world, of which the university is paradigmatic, rejects the received boundaries of orthodoxy as well as the borderless world of intellectual postmodernism and multiculturalism.

As the Yale case suggests, multiculturalism poses a problem which is often balanced uneasily between the intellectually trivial and the intellectually subversive. On one level, one can stress the global realities which unite humankind as does Martha C. Nussbaum when she asserts, "The present-day world is inescapably multicultural and multinational. Many of our most pressing problems require for their intelligent, cooperative solution a dialogue that brings together people from many different national and cultural and religious backgrounds. Even those issues that seem closest to home — issues, for example, about the structure of the family, the regulation of sexuality, the future of children — need to be approached with a broad historical and cross-cultural understanding."[29] Few would doubt the animus of these wise words, but many would ask what it is that good universities have been doing these many years. All of the fields in which "multicultural" topics center (from literary criticism and history, to linguistics and sociology) are the products of the last two centuries in Western universities. No non-Western culture, as far as I know, has been as curious about other peoples and societies or studied them as closely as has the West, or been so willing to interact with them and their values. This does not mean the West has fully understood non-Western cultures or has not often seen them through biased eyes. But work in comparative ethnography, religion, language, politics, art and philosophy has been an important part of the Western critical imagination for a long time. It is this which accounts for the fact that everywhere in the world the Western model of academic life is, at least formally, completely ascendant — certainly in the physical and social sciences, medicine and engineering, and increasingly in other fields, such as business management, as well. The Western university has provided the model of cross-cultural interaction: its view of the world has been global for many generations.

Thus, the current movement for multicultural studies seems to have different motivations. And those seem to lie in an attempt to include in the core undergraduate curriculum cultural perspectives which are non-Western, on an equal footing with Western thought. Given the fixed time within which an undergraduate degree is gained, this inclusion necessarily excludes some of what is now in the required curriculum. That the university has not accorded the same intellectual status to non-Western thought in providing a sound, undergraduate liberal arts education is thus not entirely ethnocentric. In its attempts to find what is truly universal (what postmodernism denigrates as "metanarrative") in humanity, liberal education has necessarily accorded priority to those modes of thought which are based on a universal, empirical and rational system of inquiry, and on those ideas and values which have most deeply influenced the history of mankind and continue to rapidly transform the planet. Those influences and modes of thought are overwhelmingly to be found in Western civilization, past and present. That is why a university must ultimately be a *uni*versity and not a *multi*versity. Few would seriously question that there is only one physics, and not American physics or Chinese physics. Theoretical differences in physics are obviated by the universal empirical methods which continue to advance the field. Yet "Western Thought" and "Nonwestern Thought" are often distinguished from one another: sometimes on the basis of their equal validity; sometimes on the basis of the greater value of the latter, as have the Professors Marglin.

Only by making an unfounded epistemological discontinuity between ways of knowing in the natural sciences, on one hand, and in other areas of human knowledge, on the other, is such a stance possible. This stance is often taken, I believe, only because of the self-evident and transformative role Western science has had on the globe, and the refusal of some to believe that the same Western cultural values which have created modern science apply equally to all other areas of inquiry. Realizing that this schizophrenic epistemology is ultimately untenable, extreme deconstructionists now deny that any "objective" truth is possible at all. Some of these critics, like Andrew Pickering, find themselves (not a little uneasily) in such anti-intellectual company as the "creationists" in their attacks on science,[30] and radical feminists in their attacks on freedom of expression. They imagine a "multiversity" where all perspectives are viewed as "constructed," and have equal analytical and substantive legitimacy. They except, of course, those "constructions" which "oppress" — it being left to the self-defined oppressed to decide what is legitimate opinion and what is not. And thus, in the end, it is only the diversity of ideas which must be restricted. In postmodernism mass culture seems to have produced a mass epistemology, one derived from the fragmenting assault on the senses and the cognitive processes of a high information society. "The epistemology of the disco or shopping mall is hardly the epistemology of the jury, the chapel, or the voting booth," Eagleton says. "In these circumstances, we might expect to find forms of subjectivity dramatically at odds with each other, as human subjects too stolidly self-identical to be open to otherness came eye-ball to eye-ball with human subjects too decentered to have much to open up in the first place."[31]

That we live in an increasingly globalized environment and that all of us are in some sense "citizens of the world" is obvious.[32] But we must not become the victims of our metaphors. As I have stressed in this study, phenomena should be understood within their dynamic contexts: a "citizen" is visible in terms of his "world," as a world is in terms of its citizens. These terms are mutually extensive. The citizen first emerged within the context of Western civil culture and its institutional public spaces. The very idea of citizenship is meaningless outside the public world of civil culture. And there is no globally ascendant civil culture, with its attendant public institutions, to form a *world* within which a *citizen* can function. Rational, discursive, consensually-based global institutions are either non-existent or too weak to constitute an operative world. Our individual interactions with other peoples, cultures and socio-economic systems are consequently mediated not through global citizenship, but through other, more institutionally discrete and *localized* systems, such as the nation-states, corporations, and universities, which interact with them. Within the context of our citizenship in states, corporations or universities, what many have resisted is the notion that other cultures *qua other cultures* have something deep and truly important to offer to us which is now unknown, or at least unknowable outside of "multicultural perspectives." That our cultural differences make us stronger has become one of the supposedly self-evident bromides of American public rhetoric which is equally resisted by thoughtful observers. And properly so if it means that the very principles of citizenship and of learning are involved.

In dealing with epistemological questions the Western world has built its public life and its house of consciousness in a long process, often painful, which has systematically and necessarily excluded many alternative ways of knowing and living. In suggesting that we need other cultures for alternative models we overlook the fact that every model being offered by the non-West was once, or still is, a part of Western life as well — be it the extended kinship system, intuitive understanding, mystical religion, alternative sexualities, or communal economic models. It may be said that the West has "been there" and "done that." Differences in cultural presentation, while interesting in themselves, should not deflect us from deeper comprehension of cultural modes. In the university, or in other analytic environments, it is to the universal and not the particular that our attention should be drawn. "Diversities" should interest us as they interest the scientist: not as something to be celebrated, but as a problem to be solved; not *as* diversities, but as avenues to unified understanding. Cultural diversity should also concern us at the appropriate level of analysis. Anyone who has visited Britain, France and Germany senses the differences among these cultures, which require appropriate adaptations for successful interactions within them. But anyone who experiences these national cultures in any depth also knows that they are unified by common attributes which have evolved from centuries of shared experience within Western history. At this deeper level of analysis, each of these nations is a mature civil society, rooted in respect for individual persons; in environments of free and rational exchange; in consensual relations rooted in positive law and covenants.

Suggesting that non-Western alternative models of human inquiry should be acknowledged and included in the canon of liberal education on the same basis as the system of careful, empirical and rational inquiry that characterizes the West at its best is subversive, and — as many suspect — only the extension of an old and on-going attempt, especially within the academy, to discredit the very bases of value formation as it exists in the West. At a more intellectually trivial level this impulse expresses itself in the desire to make students of various cultural backgrounds comfortable by "seeing themselves" in the works they study. This stance undermines the great Socratic tradition of liberal learning, which is intrinsically oriented toward producing discomfort in students. Liberal ("liberating") learning asks students to question the particular identities and values in their lives, especially those which derive from the accidents of birth — such as social class, religion, ethnicity or gender. We also stereotype individual students when we assume that the gene pools from which they come should bear any necessary relationship to their self-identifications, ideas or value systems. When students believe they must promote and defend particular ideas or values because of these contingencies in their lives, they relieve other students, with other contingencies, of the obligation to view these ideas and values with critical detachment.

The word "curriculum" suggests that students should be offered liberal courses of study, not a multicultural smorgasbord. Like individual societies, individual persons must reconcile in themselves contending influences. But like individual societies there are limits to the contradictions that can be accommodated on an on-going basis. For the student from a traditional society, as for the traditional society itself, picking and choosing those aspects of modern civil culture which he finds useful, convenient or inoffensive while rejecting what remains is in the long term an exercise in prolonging the mentality of the ghetto, a highly localized subculture. Levy asserts: "The myth of easy independent selectivity from among the structures of highly modernized societies must be recognized for what it is and has always been — a hybrid of wishful thinking and sentimental piety."[33]

If any single, autonomous element has shaped the condition of humanity on a global scale it is technology. Technology is autonomous because it is the independent variable which incrementally transforms all the social structures and values with which it has contact in mostly uncontrollable ways — in spite of the Luddites who have attempted to slow or destroy technology, and the Mohatir Mohammads who embrace it thinking they can simultaneously preserve their traditional cultures. The forces of globalization, driven by technology, ultimately defeat any localization of culture or institutions which contradict them. Robert Strauz-Hupe was prophetic when he wrote: "Throughout history attempts have been made to curtail technological development, military and civilian. These crude interventions against one or the other device were invariably unsuccessful. Technology needs to be integrated as a whole phenomenon."[34] While understanding the cultures the West impacts is important, much more important is understanding this culture of modernity with its inescapable technological underpinnings.

Thus, global understanding does not mean a towering Babel of voices coexisting in a democracy of multiculturalism. Increasingly it means that attentive elites around the world acknowledge that the core elements of the Western model of human development are most fulfilling for human beings given inherently unalterable trends which have dominated the planet for several centuries. The occasional reactionary revolts of local intellectual elites, such as those in China or Iran, turn out to be only small retreats into isolation — an isolation which is undermined every day by the inexorable forces of modern science, technology, economics and mass communications. As the disastrous case of Africa illustrates, attempts to develop models of modernity which are essentially indigenous (local) rather than Western (global) produced societies which took the worst from Africa — its tribal divisions, animistic irrationality, and charismatic dictatorships — and combined them with the worst of the West — material greed, misuse of technology, and militarism. As a result, in most parts of Africa humanity is worse off in every dimension than when European colonialism retreated in the early 1960's. Tyranny, war, disease, ecological neglect and increasing poverty have killed, and are killing, millions. According to Paul Collier of the World Bank, only 15% of Africans today live in "an environment considered minimally adequate for sustainable growth and development." The Economic Commission for Africa concluded that most African states lack the basic structures needed to develop.[35]

The great disasters of the modern age did not result from the failures of either civility or modernity, but from the failed attempts to escape from their demanding claims. The enslavement and death of millions in the Fascist attempt to return to some traditional, folk-based, organic society, or the Communist attempt to recover the egalitarian and stateless condition of primal society, were precisely tied to such an attempted escape from the complexities and responsibilities of modern life. That they were attempted, at horrendous human costs, in societies which had recently begun to emerge from the traditional world, is an important observation to make. The tortured, fractured faces which look out at us from Picasso's "Guernica," an emblematic icon of modernity, announce the futility of facile escape. Likewise, the triumph of commercial society was not the triumph of the "laws of market economics" over Fascism or Communism. Rather, it was the proof of the ability of civil culture and individual values as the highest expressions of human nature to prevail against the powerful pull of the primal and traditional past.

The lessons here for business are important ones. As the processes of globalization continue to universalize the elements underlying commercial society, it is a mistake to believe that jobs and technology can be transferred into a traditional environment without undermining its social integrity. When computer chip manufacturing was transferred to places like Malaysia a process was set in motion which began to undermine traditional values. Most of the workers brought by the multinational corporations into electronics factories were young, rural girls and women with traditional Muslim values. They were chosen precisely because their youth, gender and traditional values produce a nimble, submissive work force. The companies that employ them exhibited no "cultural sensitivity" by providing Muslim prayer rooms where breaks from the assembly lines might be taken. In the process of living together in company dormitories, concentrated in entirely unfamiliar ways by age, class and gender, of spending eight to twelve hours a day, six or seven days a week, encased in antiseptic suits while standing before machines producing computer chips, these girls experience literal "culture shock." Many workers collapse into hysterical screaming on the factory floors. Executives at National Semiconductor, Motorola, and Hewlett-Packard may convince themselves that they are offering these girls a chance to improve their lives (while "respecting their traditional culture") — but is that in fact what is transpiring? Will these young women ever have a chance to marry and have children, living in a gender-segregated urban environment so removed from traditional sociality? Their rural families have come to depend on the wages they earn and send home. The work these girls do as machine operators is largely unskilled. What is their future if the multinationals decide to move elsewhere for even cheaper labor as relentless globalization "rationalizes" labor markets? Will it be on the streets as beggars or prostitutes as in so many other societies where the traditional family base and economy have been severely eroded?

Malaysia's traditional Muslim past is being irrevocably challenged without a clear vision of where modernity — if it truly arrives — will take it. The traditionalist pieties of the Malaysian leadership and the "cultural sensitivity" nostrums of corporate leadership are no substitute for this realistic vision. Only rapid economic growth, around eight per cent each year, has kept the Malaysian system from imploding, and recent economic troubles have challenged it. The economic crisis in Asia is revealing the ways in which superficial modernity covers a system still nepotistic and kin-based, institutionally weak and governed by concepts of authority which are pre-civil. No amount of "cultural sensitivity training" of Western managers or multicultural advocacy will conceal the basic forces of social disruption which are being released because of decisions made in corporate headquarters in Silicon Valley, Wall Street or Tokyo. In fact, an analytical focus on cultural diversity in the name of more effective, tactical management of multinational operations only mitigates a real, strategic view of global markets.[36]

A more responsible approach would from the beginning assume that a total social transformation, including the passing of traditional society itself, is the consequence of globalized business operations. If this passage is not wisely managed through the building of transformation-based institutions the global market system itself will be adversely impacted. George Soros, the investor, irresponsibly blamed by Malaysia's prime minister for much of South East

Asia's financial crisis by "encouraging speculation and capital flight," seems to be one of the few businessmen to understand the cultural and institutional roots of the crisis: "We can have a market economy but we cannot have a market society. In addition to markets, society needs institutions to serve such social goals as political freedom and social justice. There are such institutions in individual countries, but not in the global society. The development of a global society has lagged behind the growth of a global economy. Unless the gap is closed, the global capitalist system will not survive."[37]

Globalization is driven by underlying forces rooted in technology and economics, but its possible expressions and forms are various. "Globalization is not destined," asserts Martin Wolf, "it is chosen."[38] Global citizenship rests on the cumulative choices of the world's policy interests and elites, which are reflected in the institutional development of international organization. Global citizenship requires, ultimately, the institutionalization of a globalized civil culture. This requires the opposite of multicultural perspectives. It requires the unifying perspectives which inhabit the civil world of human experience. Without such effective global institutions to mediate between the energetic dynamism of globalized businesses, and their continuous evolution of new technologies, the existent social and cultural structures of global commerce will largely direct themselves. And an ultimately dysfunctional pattern of investment and trade flows related to differing cultural modes becomes apparent.

Among those societies where primal cultural modes tend to dominate, as in much of Africa, participation in the globalized economy is lowest, and thus economic conditions are the most dysfunctional and delocalized. By the most important criteria of participation, foreign direct investment (FDI), Africa south of the Sahara absorbs slightly more than 1% of the total. Almost all of the world's poorest countries, as measured by per capita gross domestic product (GDP) are located in this region of Africa. On all sides the visitor is confronted by disorder and decomposition; by societies seemingly unable to build and maintain any permanent substance. Such primal fluidity creates high levels of risk for investors. Investment in Africa, both domestic and foreign, is heavily centered in commodities, especially extractive industries, for two reasons. First, political, social, and institutional instability in this region promote high risks, and thus require high returns for investment. Since climate and natural resource endowments are not transferable, multinational companies invest in these regions only to access these resources — but to add value elsewhere in more capital-intensive, down-stream operations. True wealth-creation from its resources thus takes place outside of Africa rather than within it. Second, extractive industries (e.g. oil in Nigeria, or iron in Liberia) can be most effectively localized within their own relatively stand-alone infrastructures, operated by trained foreign managers, and requiring little in the way of the advanced financial, communications and workforce supports which these environments make difficult to provide. Thus Nigeria, a major oil producer, must import gasoline because the few local refineries are often inoperative, in part because of the theft of vital component equipment. From ancient Sumeria to modern Japan we have noted that it is resource scarcity combined with social capital (in the form of skilled, well-organized human beings) which stimulates sustainable wealth creation. Africa is rich in everything except this indispensable social capital and the cultural values to build and sustain it. "Companies have nothing against Africa," suggested UN Development Program economist Salim Jehar, "It's that stability, infrastructure, and skills are not there."[39]

Africa is a primal economy of distribution writ large. The continent's horrendous international debt loads are not, finally, the result of poor weather, poor resource endowments, dysfunctional institutions, or even the secular decline in global commodity prices. Rather, a constitutive cultural inclination toward feast and famine rests, like the *potlatch* and similar phenomena among primitive peoples, in the consumption and destruction of goods in a life of extravagant self-presentation — perhaps best symbolized in Congolese dictator Mobuto's gold bathtub; the tiny Central African Empire's $50 million coronation extravaganza for "Emperor Bokasa I;" or the extravagant "copy" of Rome's St. Peter's basilica erected in the Ivory Coast. The new "reform" government of Nigeria confronted massive debts, a crumbling infrastructure and pervasive corruption by approving a $350 million soccer stadium, and a fleet of private jets for itself. The "expressive life-style" is evidenced again as the adversary of wealth-creation. Even the few rich Africans are domestically poor to the extent that their wealth is distributed to accounts in Europe and North America, where it benefits only the already wealthy. The relation of such a primal system to the globalized economy is inherently one of deficit. Any international forgiveness of these debt loads, without a cultural transformation which relates Africa to the world economy on the basis of real investment, and value-added wealth production, will only eventuate in another debt load requiring more forgiveness. Until that happens, Africa will remain the textbook example of economic delocalization, a continent incapable of maintaining even a subsistence economy in the face of the inexorable forces of globalization. Carole Rakodi concludes, "Whatever the terms and outcomes of its integration into the world economy, world politics, and the cultural-ideological world system, Africa is, like it or not, part of that system. On balance, [...] Africa has in the past and continues in the present to lose more than it gains; for much of the continent, dependency, marginalization, and lack of policy autonomy are the main outcomes of its incorporation."[40]

Global investment in more advanced, but traditional societies combines commodity production with low-skill manufacturing. The countries of Asia which have developed most quickly are essentially manufacturing platforms primarily directed toward consumption in Western markets. Manufacturing, as a relatively mechanical and rote activity, can employ large numbers of people in a traditional, authoritarian environment which provides the stability multinational firms require before investing. In Malaysia, for example, the government provides a relatively stable institutional presence, and favorable public policies, such as forbidding electronics workers to organize labor unions. With a few notable exceptions (e.g., software development in India) these countries play only marginal roles in those service, finance and information-based sectors which really drive the world economy.[41] While these traditional societies have greater participation in the global economy than primal societies, and thus rising incomes, their development brings with it rising cultural conflict between indigenous and modern (Western) values. Regime legitimacy is always a central and pressing social issue, as in all traditional societies, sometimes leading to regime collapse, *viz.* the Shah's Iran, Marcos' Philippines and Suharto's Indonesia.

Overwhelmingly, global investment, economic productivity, and wealth remain centered in a relatively small number of countries centered in North America and Western Europe.[42] This basic reality has not changed substantially since the first great globalization took place in the seventeenth and eighteenth centuries. The same societies which were the focus of the historic intellectual, technological and commercial transformations which created the modern world centuries ago still play this role. To the degree that Russians, Indians, Japanese or Chinese play significant parts in the on-going process of globalization can be attributed to their adoption or adaptation of the Western model of economic, technological and social development. But even in the West, the forces of globalization are forcing painful adjustments. What has made those adjustments possible is the culture of civility, evolved over the centuries, which underlies the creation of new socio-economic policies and the institutions to support them.

The states which compose the European Union (EU) have experienced extraordinary social, economic and political pressures after the Treaty of Rome [1957] laid the basis for a united Europe — a transforming response to powerful forces of economic globalization in the post-war world.[43] Since the Single Europe Act [1987] especially, and the introduction of a single currency (the *euro*) in 1999, the societies of Europe have had to cope with a historical transformation equivalent in its way to globalizing trends elsewhere. Social democratic states like Germany, Norway, Denmark and Sweden — which achieved the world's highest living standards in the post-war period — have been torn between maintaining the structures of state sovereignty and the policies which made this high degree of social equity possible, and dismantling them to meet the demands of an integrated Europe. Norwegians have declined membership in the European Union, fearing a loss of the autonomy which produced a successful social democracy; but they now face increasing isolation in Europe. Denmark and Sweden have joined the EU, but have resisted monetary integration to avoid altering the national budget structures which enabled the advanced welfare state. Britain has declined the *euro*, to preserve its special cultural character, and the social policies evolved since the Thatcher era. But it has also adopted the Bill of Rights, rooted in the European Declaration of Human Rights, causing a transformation of its legal system as profound as any since the adoption of *Magna Carta* in 1215.

Previously poor states, like Ireland, have seen vigorous economic growth since joining the EU and adopting the *euro*. But Ireland must now cope with labor shortages; growing income disparities; immigration (rather than emigration); the marked erosion of its Catholic culture; and the loss of policy autonomy to deal with issues like inflation. The introduction of new states from central Europe into the EU promises more such disorientations. But what remains remarkable in this forty-year movement toward the unification of Europe and its globalization — especially given its bloody, destructive history between 1914 and 1945 — is the ability of Europe (and the West as a community) to call upon its centuries of evolution into civility to manage this extraordinary change.

A phenomenon integral to these globalizing European trends toward a continental civility, resting on transnational values and institutions, is a parallel trend toward regional cultural localization. As Brussels, Frankfort and Strasbourg have become the centers of supranationalism in Europe, eclipsing the traditional nation-state, a number of cultural *superregions* have emerged. The term "superregion" is Darrell Delamaide's. It was he who documented the increasing interdependence of transnational economic-cultural regions.[44] Thus, Barcelona (in Spain), Marseilles (in France), and Genoa (in Italy) have more in common with each other than they do with, respectively, Madrid, Paris and Rome. These similarities in cultural styles and interests based on common economic histories (as Mediterranean ports with ties to Africa and the Near East) unites them into what Delamaide calls, "The Latin Crescent." Similar superregions elsewhere on the continent have begun to build the institutions and communications networks which bind their localized experiences and interests. In each case it is the non-governmental organizations (NGO), trade associations, chambers of commerce and transnational corporations which are driving this regional integration. And it is an ancient culture of civility — characterized since Greek times by the capacity to generate such intermediating groups, and institutional forms with changing contents — which provided the experience and the values to sustain it. A once-dominating form, the nation-state, is exchanged for two others: Pan-Europeanism and regionalism.

It is from this vantage point that the world "culture clash" asserted by Huntington and others must be appraised. We have to treat with caution Huntington's notion that the West is so unique that its values are basically incompatible with those of other peoples. An inference of this stance is that the West needs to isolate itself from these non-Western values if it is to preserve its cultural integrity, thus negating the irresistible forces of globalization themselves. My analysis suggests that the West and the non-West confront each other in globalization at differing stages of cultural development, and that these differences are apparent and temporal rather than culturally absolute. It may be that the non-West will not develop from essentially primal and traditional into civil and individual modes (as Japan has not), but there is no compelling reason to suggest that they cannot or will not. The West may have taken the form which it did with a good deal of contingency, but the underlying impulses toward human actualization, which civility and individuality represent, are integral to the species, not to any particular ethnic or cultural group. We need to avoid the excesses of multiculturalism, which assumes that a more humane world can be fabricated only from the fragmented "diversity" of localized cultures, rather than from the human universals — actual and potential — embedded in each of them.

If it is true, as Levi-Stauss asserts (confirming Rousseau), that culture "is based on the aptitude of man to perfect himself," the role of commerce in this self-perfection becomes central.[45] This study has indicated that markets plays few, or only marginal formative roles in the primal and traditional worlds. Commerce and markets begin to occur as a central and legitimate activity only with the rise of civil culture. And the dominant characteristic of civility is its public character. The civil world supersedes human ties of blood and tradition, which being entirely accidental and non-consensual are private in character, with ties of contract. Contracts have a public character because they are typified by the establishment of relations "outside" — with non-kin, in an unnatural world of strangers. Public life is also rational in character because reason is the basis upon which strangers can begin to communicate: it presumes no shared culture except that of rationality itself. Contracts are witnessed in public places to enforce their rational and covenantial, rather than prescriptive character. In short, the public world is the place where rational human purpose becomes fully visible — and can therefore be acknowledged and authenticated. The public world is also the summit of exchange as a distinctly human enterprise which connects the individual, the civil, the traditional and the primal. In exchange human subjectivity and objectivity mutually define themselves, making a genuine self possible.

In the primal world exchange is charismatic and highly localized, and is characterized by symbolic transactions in both goods and words reflecting the immediacy and allocentricity which localization mandates. Language is the primary instrument of existential visibility, and therefore represents primarily charismatic and expressive rather than instrumental values. These produce symbolic worlds which are intrinsically adversarial to markets and material accumulation. In the traditional world exchange is authoritarian, and is characterized by ritual exchange, including exchanges of goods, within understood hierarchies. Decorum (as rectitude) is the principle means of existential visibility focused in, and legitimized by, group identity. Commercial values exist in pronounced tension with other cultural values in the traditional world. In the civil world exchange is mercantile, and is characterized by the mobility of goods and people in markets. Contracting (promising) in rational exchange in public spaces is the principle means of existential visibility, focused in the citizen, whose sense of self worth is both supported and evidenced in public life. In the world of individuals exchange is intellectual and normative, characterized by the autocentric, subjective transactions in values and judgments of individuals as ultimately autonomous moral beings: "he who is not" in the presence of "him who is." Creativity and insight are the principal modes of existential visibility.

The relation of the public space to the visible world is essential to its function in enabling self-esteem, that human motive which occupies pride of place within it. Only those humans thought to require such esteem for their self-definition — in effect, until contemporary times, adult free men — were admitted to a public life. What made free persons visible was their attachment to property (in the broadest sense, including education and skill), the *trope* which gave evidence of their autonomous existence, and which forms the basis of action in public — the action of exchange. A life focused in rational exchange made it possible for civility in its highest form — the commerce of ideas and values in public life — to take place. The person, and subsequently the individual, arose as responses to the complex demands of a life lived in public, focused in dialogue and reason, rewarded with self-defining esteem. In their work and its enduring products individual human beings become visible in the world and are able to engage in the exchange which begins to bring both full social visibility and the esteem of others. Self-esteem, the final expression of a life lived in the esteem of others, is the ultimate prize of a public life, and as Riker has suggested, the essential normative purpose of democracy. Societies which deny their members the possibility of a public life thwart this important manifestation of human fulfillment. There is consequently no alternative, fully human life without institutionalized public spaces where humankind's highest values are realized. These human values have reached their highest expression in the civil, commercial societies of the West. But they are only apparently "Western" values. They are human values first evidenced in the cultures of the Western world which developed along lines that enabled them.

If it is through culture that man perfects himself, achieves the *species being* that distinguishes him from other animals, it is in advancing humanity to higher need fulfillment that Western commerce has played a central role. In sundering its ties to tradition, and by committing itself to civility, Western humanity embraced a sense of purposive time. The future became a quest as well as a fact, because the future became a matter of choice. The troubling and disorientating distractions of the present age — the great wars, the rise and fall of empires and ideologies — are subordinated to these deeper, epochal forces animated by trends in Western culture during past centuries. I. R. Sinai, an important British theorist of modernization, wrote a generation ago: "It is only in the West that man has made a conscious and persistent effort to separate himself from nature and has opposed, to the idea of nature as imprisoning, the concept of his own individual freedom (precarious though it may be) within it, shaped by his own adventurous intelligence and vital energy."[46]

The West has impacted the rest of the globe as it transforms itself within this altered understanding of man as a spiritual entity removed from the world, while living within it. Those ideologies of retreat, of a return to a life of human "embededness" — which is in the last analysis what calls for "traditional values," "multiculturalism" and exhortations to "diversity" become — inevitably make of humankind an object rather than a subject. But if the past is prologue, this reflects an underestimation of the great forces transforming the planet. Would anyone have believed even a decade ago that the mighty Soviet Union would become the collection of shattered states and poor, disoriented societies which it has in fact become? Or that Mao Tse Tung's body would lie entombed only steps away from the golden arches of MacDonald's? The phenomenon of exchange has been irresistibly globalized. "All over the world, in fact," asserts Sinai, "decaying elements of the past are being destroyed or will have to be destroyed, and all over the world millions of human beings have to prepare themselves for new beginnings, and new thrusts in sociological functioning, for a radical remodeling of their ways of social life."[47] In the culture of free commerce we see the vitality of human life at its best: curious, inventive, risk-taking, rational, exchange-based, covenantial — and committed to a human future understood as different (and better, however defined) from the past. Mature commercial life was conceived within the widest range of these higher human capacities. The reduction of commerce to a set of economic laws (and their attendant *laissez-faire* ideologies) may thus diminish human life as much as attempts to abolish commercial society itself. Commerce has historically unfolded as a cultural value, a set of human self-definitions, intimately tied to the human capacity for freedom.

No contemporary thinker has understood the human issues underlying the debate about tradition and modernity (or the debate between modernists and postmodernists) better than Jurgen Habermas. His theory of "communicative action" has had a major impact on modern thought in a number of fields. Habermas asserts that in human exchange, in the form of speech, are located the premises of a moral universe which advances freedom and the individual person. Human speech itself constructs moral relationships between and among human beings. For in speech humanity rationally persuades, and can thus authentically make the pledges and promises which constitute civil life. In this stance, it seems to me, Habermas is the heir of Nietzsche. If the essence of human morality in exchange is the capacity to make promises, as Nietzsche suggested, it is the active and persistent capacity *to remember* these pledges that maintains the moral universe. Nietzsche wrote in *The Genealogy of Morals*: "This involves no mere passive inability to rid oneself of an impression, no mere indigestion through a once-pledged word with which one cannot 'have done,' but an active desire not to rid oneself, a desire for the continuance of something desired once, a real memory of the will: so that between the original 'I will,' 'I shall do this' and the actual discharge of the will, its act, a world of strange new things, circumstances, even acts of will may be interposed without breaking this long chain of will."[48]

The on-going social conversation, the heart of the civility from which promising comes, is undermined by the tendency to forget — in effect to flee from our own freedom by undermining the complex of covenants which ultimately sustains it. The horrors of Fascism and Communism can be traced to the substitution of imagined pasts and futures for a remembering present. This failure of memory is abetted by the dissolution or lack of communication structures within which the civil conversation is made effectively continuous. It is the silence of forgetfulness which lies at the center of so many modern social tragedies. When humanity becomes socially mute — unable to refresh the chain of memory within the civil conversation, and thus constrained from speech in its fullest expression — sociality is diminished. It is of this silence that philosopher Albert Camus warned: "And for all who can live only in an atmosphere of human dialogue, and sociability, this silence is the end of the world."[49] The constraints of ideology on the left and tradition on the right, to the extent that these so often produce fundamentally inarticulate people, promote the noncommunicative inhumanity which inhibits or destroys the institutional foundations of speech itself. Man is, as Aristotle suggested, a speaking animal, and his public life is the place of his self-realization in speech. For Habermas, as for Hannah Arendt before him, modern civility can be defended and advanced through "the formation of autonomous public spheres, which...enter into communication with one another as soon as the potential for self-organization and the self-organized employment of communication media is made use of."[50] All the bases of this human capacity for self-organization lie within the Western tradition, especially the ascendance of empirical rationalism since the Enlightenment, in Habermas's view. The irreducible basis of this human capacity is the ability of human beings to think in rational terms, and to communicate rationally through institutions.

The model of rational exchange in communication lies in the commerce of goods. For markets, as they developed fully within civil society, were the means by which rational individuals, and the various spheres of judgment and action in which they participated, entered into conversation with one another through the dynamics of public exchange — of pledging and remembering. The history of market exchange is one of the institutionalization of these rational premises through more advanced forms of abstract and mediated thought, reaching its summit in science. Alphabetical language, money, positive law and secular courts are only some of the institutional abstractions which rational exchange in commerce produced, and without which advanced commerce in ideas and values would not have been possible. Because markets resist, by their nature, any final institutionalization, any canonization, they also model the endless quest which distinguishes civil life and Western civilization from contemporary traditional and primitive societies. Markets from their historical inception in the Near East millennia ago were also impelled by the forces of globalization, overcoming the localizing forces of geography, politics and culture in the quest for advantagous exchange.

What has also characterized advanced human economic activity in the West is the substitution of increasingly mediated and abstract forms of thought for material mass and effort. "In one way or another," asserts economist Thomas Petzinger Jr., "wealth-creating innovations ultimately substitute knowledge for energy or materials."[51] In practical terms, this has meant that in the last half of the twentieth century America has tripled the real value of its material economic output with no increase in the total weight of the goods produced. And, in a perverse symmetry, much of the Third World (especially Africa) has produced more material mass (in the form of commodities) with a net loss of real wealth. The cybernetics which increasingly define the modern global economy, with its winners and its losers, are propelled by this extraordinary ability of human beings in Western societies to increasingly imbed in everything they touch ever more complex, dense and interactive symbolic systems. Globalization and complex, mediated abstraction have been, from the inception of commercial culture, allied forces challenging cultural localization in all of its expressions.

Institutions marry the fundamental human capacity for abstraction to the fundamental human capacity for advanced forms of sociality. Within these mediating institutions rational speech as an ultimately moral enterprise of human engagement is secured at its highest levels. This vital capacity for speech continues to lack the institutional architecture — globally, regionally and nationally — it needs to confront the dynamically complex symbolic world which man has created for himself. Martin Wolf asserts that, "as the world economy continues to integrate and cross-border flows become more important, global governance must be improved."[52]

It is the failure of human institutional development to keep pace with the human capacity for symbolization which characterizes the major social and moral failures of the past century. It is within business environments more than any other that human beings have been impelled by challenging circumstances to innovate socially and institutionally. Commerce and modern corporate life have provided the plurality of models necessary for humanity to make critical institutional choices as it faces change. The future of human self-realization consequently continues to be, and has historically always been, linked to the development of commerce — not only as the means by which higher levels of human subsistence are advanced in the exchange of goods — but in the ways human culture as rational and moral communication is advanced in the building of human institutions.

NOTES TO CONCLUSION

1. Huntington, *op.cit.*, pp. 27-28
2. Walter Russell Mead, "Asia Devalued," THE NEW YORK TIMES MAGA-
   ZINE (May 31, 1998), p. 38
3. Arendt, *op.cit.*, p. 11
4. Levy, *op.cit.*, p. 128
5. James A. Bill and Robert Springborg, POLITICS IN THE MIDDLE EAST,
   4th ed. (New York: HarperCollins College Publishers, 1994), p. 4
6. Alan Wheatley, "Calls for Reform Slow to Change Asia's Family-Based
   Capitalism," SAN FRANCISCO EXAMINER (October 17, 2000), p. A15
7. James C. Scott, COMPARATIVE POLITICAL CORRUPTION (Englewood
   Cliffs, NJ: Prentice-Hall, Inc., 1972), p. 84
8. Crawford Young, "The Impossible Necessity of Nigeria," FOREIGN
   AFFAIRS (Nov/Dec 1996), p. 143
9. *Ibid.*
10. S.A. Marglin and F. Appfel Marglin, eds. DOMINATING KNOWLEDGE
    (Oxford: Clarendon Press, 1993); a similar romanticizing of American Indians
    is Calvin Luther Martin's claim that the Western mind is "deeply detached
    from participation with the earth," in contrast to the "remarkable courtesy
    rendered plants and animals" by native Americans; THE WAY OF THE
    HUMAN BEING (New Haven, Conn.: Yale University Press, 1999); an
    excellent rejoinder to this sort of paen to "the primal" is Sephard Krech's THE
    ECOLOGICAL INDIAN: MYTH AND HISTORY (New York: W.W. Norton
    & Company, 1999)
11. S.A. Marglin, "Losing Touch: The Cultural Conditions of Worker Accommo-
    dation and Resistance," *ibid.*, pp. 217ff
12. Marion J. Levy, Jr., MODERNIZATION: LATECOMERS AND SURVI-
    VORS (New York: Basic Books, 1972)
13. Dankwart A. Rustow, A WORLD OF NATIONS: PROBLEMS OF POLITI-
    CAL MODERNIZATION (Washington, D.C.: The Brookings Institution,
    1967), p. 3
14. Bill and Springborg, *op.cit.*, p. 5
15. Walter Kaufman, NIETZSCHE (New York: Meridian Books, Inc., 1956),
    p.149
16. Asa G. Hilliard is representative of a group of "Afrocentric" educators who
    believe, on the basis of very thin and questionable scholarship, that Africa in
    general and ancient Egypt in particular, have something to teach black
    children, who learn in ways unique to their heritage. Suggesting that "cultural
    diversity and democracy go hand in hand," he asserts: "Coercive cultural unity
    is undemocratic as well as unhealthy. Democracy is not merely freedom of

movement but freedom to be a people." THE MAROON WITHIN US (Baltimore: Black Classic Press, 1995) p.82; Wade W. Nobles also suggests that "the ultimate question becomes how do we educate (reproduce and define) African children to become authentic human beings." Introduction to Asa G. Hilliard, SBA: THE REAWAKENING OF THE AFRICAN MIND (Gainesville, Fla: Makare Publishing Company, 1998), p.xvii.

17. Orlando Paterson, "The G.O.P. Isn't the Only Party to Dissemble on Race," *The Week in Review*, THE NEW YORK TIMES (August 6, 2000), p. 15

18. John H. McWhorter, *op.cit.*; Kieth B. Richburg, a black reporter who covered African affairs for the *Washington Post*, challenged many of the myths underlying "Afrocentrism," in his OUT OF AMERICA: A BLACK MAN CONFRONTS AFRICA (New York: Basic Books, 1997)

19. Dirk Johnson, "Former Cocaine User Regains Child in Racial Custody Case," THE NEW YORK TIMES, March 9, 1999, p. A18

20. Patterson, *op.cit.*; see also, David A. Hollinger, POST-ETHNIC AMERICA (New York: Basic Books, 1996)

21. An excellent, and highly scholarly, summary of this issue is contained in Mary R. Lefkowitz and Guy MacClean Rogers, eds., BLACK ATHENA REVISITED (Chapel Hill, NC: University of North Carolina Press, 1996)

22. Cf. Elazar Barkan, THE GUILT OF NATIONS (New York: W.W. Norton, 2000); see also, Randall Robinson, THE DEBT (New York: E.P. Dutton, 2000)

23. quoted in Diane Cardwell, "Seeking Out A Just Way To Make Amends for Slavery," THE NEW YORK TIMES (August 12, 2000), p. A19

24. Stephen Jay Gould, ROCKS OF AGES: SCIENCE & RELIGION IN THE FULLNESS OF LIFE (New York: Ballantine Books, 1999)

25. Richard J. Neuhaus, THE NAKED PUBLIC SQUARE (Grand Rapids, MI: William B. Eerdmans, Publishing, Co., 1984); see also his AMERICA AGAINST ITSELF (Notre Dame, IN: University of Notre Dame Press, 1992)

26. Stephen L. Carter, CIVILITY (New York: Basic Books, 1998)

27. Eagleton, *op. cit.*, p. 5.

28. Cf. Samuel G. Freedman, "Yeshivish at Yale," THE NEW YORK TIMES MAGAZINE (May 23, 1998)

29. Martha C. Nussbaum, CULTIVATING HUMANITY (Cambridge: Harvard University Press, 1997), p. 8

30. Cf. Andrew Pickering, CONSTRUCTING QUARKS (Chicago: University of Chicago Press, 1984)

31. Eagleton, *op. cit.*, p. 15

32. This phrase, originally from Diogenes, was adopted by Nussbaum. *ibid.*, p. 50ff

33. Levy, MODERNIZATION AND THE STRUCTURE OF SOCIETIES, *op.cit.*, p. 252-253

34. Robert Strausz-Hupe, "Society and Ecology," AMERICAN BEHAVIORAL SCIENTIST (No. 6, 1968), p. 2

35. "Africa: The Heart of the Matter," THE ECONOMIST (May 13th-19th, 2000), p. 22; Thomas Sowell cites "cultural capital" as essential to economic development in Africa and elsewhere. RACE AND CULTURE: A WORLD VIEW (New York: Basic Books, 1995)

36. A good example of managerial "diversity" analyis is that of Jack N. Behrman, who claims that, "Cross-cultural sensitivity is a decided comparative disadvantage for American managers; even the Japanese have sought to understand foreigners, and the Europeans are hard-pressed to do so by their proximity to each other. With increasing competition in the global economy, ability to match products and services to consumer wants will be decisive; these can be understood only by deep cultural understanding. To achieve this requires observation, appreciation, tolerance, enjoyment, and unity. Through these, not only will there be greater acceptance of diversity, but also a recognition that at the most fundamental level - the spiritual - the world is one and should be treated as such." "Why and How Managers Must Develop Greater Cross-Cultural Sensitivity," GLOBAL OUTLOOK (Vol. 11; No. 1, 1999), p. 9

37. George Soros, "Toward a Global Open Society," THE ATLANTIC MONTHLY (January 1998), p. 24

38. Martin Wolf, "Will the Nation-State Survive Globalization?," FOREIGN AFFAIRS (January/February 2001), p. 182

39. Pete Engardio and Catherine Belton, "Global Capitalism: Can It Be Made to Work Better," BUSINESS WEEK (November 6, 2000), p. 76. It is ironic that African spokesmen often point to the high average returns on investment (ROI) in Africa — in the rage of 25% — to attract foreign investors. Those high ROI's reflect the great risks involved, and thus also the scarcity of realistic opportunities to realize those high returns. The World Bank continues to be surprised that "iron-clad" transparency provisions in loans to African states are violated. In financing an oil pipeline in Chad, the bank had secured the agreement of the government that revenues would go to social programs. The very first receipts from the pipeline were in fact diverted to the military, upon whose support the government depends. Douglas Farah and David B. Ottaway, "World Bank Jolted by Chad Leader's Diversion of Funds for Pipeline Deal," SAN FRANCISCO CHRONICLE (December 6, 2000), p. C20

40. Carole Rakodi, "Conclusion," in Carole Rakodi, ed., THE URBAN CHALLENGE IN AFRICA (Tokyo: United Nations University Press, 1997), p. 555

41. India is an exception that may prove the cultural rule. As in other traditional societies, the Brahmin elite in India abhorred physical work, and institutionalized this disdain in its rigid caste system. This thwarted industrial development

in India, and since political independence in 1947 the ruling Congress Party embraced socialism as a modern canonization of the anti-business values of the traditional elites. The coming of the global information economy advantaged India in that it played to a strong suit: economic productivity tied to intellectual imagination, relatively detached from physical work. It was an easy transition from Brahmin spiritual space, in which mathematics especially thrived, to cyber space. Globalization abetted this. Many of the entrepreneurs of Silicon Valley are Indian emigres, who brought the Indian genius for spiritual abstraction to the new information economy, and have stimulated the boom in software development in India itself. See Gurcharan Das, INDIA UNBOUND (New York: Alfred A. Knopf, 2001)

42. Cf. Paul Knox & John Agnew, "Patterns in the Economic Landscape," in Knox & Agnew, THE GEOGRAPHY OF THE WORLD ECONOMY, 2nd ed. (London: Edward Arnold, 1994), p. 16ff; also, The World Bank, WORLD DEVELOPMENT REPORT (New York: Oxford University Press, 1999)

43. Cf: John McCormick, THE EUROPEAN UNION, 2nd ed. (Boulder, Colo: Westview Press, 1999); Andrew Morawesik, THE CHOICE FOR EUROPE (Ithaca, NY: Cornell University Press, 1998)

44. Darrell Delamaide, THE NEW SUPERREGIONS OF EUROPE (New York: E.P. Dutton, 1981); Delamaide's work recalls a similar study by Joel Garreau, THE NINE NATIONS OF NORTH AMERICA (Boston: Houghton Mifflin, 1981)

45. Levi-Strauss, TOTEMISM, *op.cit.*, p. 100

46. I.R. Sinai, THE CHALLENGE OF MODERNISATION (New York: W.W. Norton & Company, Inc., 1964), p. 12

47. *Ibid.*, p. 10

48. Nietzsche, *op.cit.*, p. 58

49. Albert Camus, "Neither Victims nor Executioners," (Dwight McDonald, trans.), in Paul Goodman, ed., SEEDS OF LIBERATION (New York: George Braziller, Publisher, 1964), p. 301

50. Cf. Tracy B. Strong and Frank Andreas Sposito, "Habermas's Significant Other," in Stephen K. White, ed. HABERMAS (Cambridge: Cambridge University Press, 1995), p. 263

51. Thomas Petzinger, Jr., "So Long, Supply and Demand," THE WALL STREET JOURNAL (January 1, 2000), p. R31

52. Wolf, *op.cit.*, p. 190

SELECTED BIBLIOGRAPHY

ARTICLES

Abbott, Susan, "Gender, Status, and Values Among Kikuyu and Appalachian Adolescents," in Thomas S. Weisner, Candice Bradley, and Philip L. Kilbride, AFRICAN FAMILIES AND THE CRISIS OF SOCIAL CHANGE (Westport, CT: Bergin & Garvey, 1997)

Barnett, H.G., "The Nature of the Patlatch," AMERICAN ANTHROPOLOGIST (July/August 1938)

Bellah, Robert N., "Religious Evolution," AMERICAN SOCIOLOGICAL REVIEW (June 1964)

Bower, Bruce, "Yours, Mine and Ours," SCIENCE NEWS (March 28, 1998)

Brookhiser, Richard, review of Norman Podhoretz, EX-FRIENDS, NEW YORK TIMES BOOK REVIEW (February 21, 1999)

Butterfield, Fox, "Southern Curse: Why America's Murder Rate is So High," *Week in Review,* THE NEW YORK TIMES (July 26, 1998)

Camus, Albert, "Neither Victim nor Executioner," (Dwight MacDonald, trans.) in Paul Goodman, ed., SEEDS OF LIBERATION (New York: George Braziller, Publisher, 1964)

Carlson, Donal E., "An Evironmental Explanation for Race Differences in Basketball Performance," JOURNAL OF SPORT AND SOCIAL ISSUES, 7 Summer/Autumn 1983)

Chie, Nakane, "Hierarchy in Japanese Society," Daniel I. Okimoto and Thomas P Rohlen, INSIDE THE JAPANESE SYSTEM (Stanford, CA: Stanford University Press, 1988)

de Laszlo, Violet, "Introduction," THE BASIC WRITINGS OF C.J. JUNG (New York: The Modern Library, 1959)

Diamant, Alfred, "The Nature of Political Development," Jason L. Finkle and Richard W. Gable, eds., POLITICAL DEVELOPMENT AND SOCIAL CHANGE, (New York: John Wiley and Sons, 1966)

Dicken, Paul, "Global-Local Tensions: Firms and States in the Global Space-Economy," ECONOMIC GEOGRAPHY (No. 70, 1994)

Drucker, Peter F., "Beyond the Information Revolution," THE ATLANTIC MONTHLY (October 1999)

Epstein, Joseph, "Hetero/Homo: the Struggle for Sexual Identity," HARPER'S (September 1970)

_____, "My 1950's," COMMENTARY (September 1993)

Ferrell, Jeff and Sanders, Clinton, R., "Culture, Crime and Criminology," in Jeff Ferrell and Clinton R. Sanders, CULTURAL CRIMINOLOGY (Boston: Northeastern University Press, 995), pp. 3 and 4

Freedman, Samuel G., "Yeshivish at Yale," THE NEW YORK TIMES MAGAZINE (May 23, 1998)

Goody, Jack R., "Polygyny, Economy, and the Role of Women," in Jack R. Goody, ed., THE CHARACTER OF KINSHIP (Cambridge: Cambridge University Press, 1973)

Guignon, Charles B., "Introduction," HEIDEGGER, Charles B. Guignon, ed. (Cambridge: Cambridge University Press, 1993)

Guilford, J.P., "A Revised Structure of Intellect," REPORTS FROM THE PSYCHOLOGICAL LABORATORY, No. 19

Guyer, Jane, "Lineal Identifies and Lateral Networks: the Logic of Polyandrous Motherhood," in Caroline Bledsoe and Gilles Pison, ed., NUPTUALITY IN SUB-SAHARAN AFRICA (Oxford: Clarendon Press, 1994)

Handelman, Stephen, "The Russian 'Mafiya'," FOREIGN AFFAIRS (March/April 1994)

Handy, Charles, "Tocqueville Revisited: The Meaning of American Prosperity," HARVARD BUSINESS REVIEW (January 2001)

Hayes, William C., "Daily Life in Ancient Egypt," in EVERYDAY LIFE IN ANCIENT TIMES (Washington, D.C.: National Geographic Society, 1951)

Hideo, Tanaka, "The Role of Law and Lawyers in Japanese Society," Daniel I. Okimoto and Thomas P. Rohlen, INSIDE THE JAPANESE SYSTEM (Stanford, CA: Stanford University Press, 1988)

Holtom, D.C., "The Centrality of *Kami* in Shinto," in H. Byron Earhart, ed. RELIGION IN THE JAPANESE EXPERIENCE (Belmont, CA: Wadsworth Publishing   Company, 1974)

Horton, John, "Time and Cool People," in Lee Rainwater, ed., SOUL, (Chicago: Aldine Publishing Co., 1970)

Huntington, Samuel P., "The West: Unique, Not Universal," FOREIGN AFFAIRS (Nov./Dec. 1996)

Ignatieff, Michael, "On Civil Society," FOREIGN AFFAIRS (March/April 1995)

Jacobsen, Thorkild, "Mesopotamia," in Henri Frankfort, et.al., BEFORE PHILOSOPHY (Baltimore: Pelican Books, 1949)

Jaffe, Greg, "Appalachian Trails," THE WALL STREET JOURNAL (April 8, 1999)

Johnson, Dirk, "Former Cocaine User Regains Child in Racial Custody Case," THE NEW YORK TIMES (March 9, 1999)

Johnson, George, "Science and Religion: Bridging the Great Divide," THE NEW YORK TIMES (June 30, 1998)

Kaplan, Robert D., "Travels into America's Future," THE ATLANTIC MONTHLY (July 1998)

_____, "The Coming Anarchy," THE ATLANTIC MONTHLY (February 1994)

Kauffmann, Stanley, "Homosexual Drama and Its Disguises," THE NEW YORK TIMES (January 23, 1966)

Kierkegaard, Soren, "The Knight of Faith and the Knight of Infinite Resignation," A KIERKEGAARD ANTHOLOGY, Robert Bretall, ed., (New York: The Modern Library, 1946)

_____, "The Present Age: A Literary Review," *Ibid.*

Knox, Paul and Agnew, John, "Patterns in the Economic Landscape," in Paul Knox and John Agnew, GEOGRPAHY AND THE WORLD ECONOMY, 2nd ed. (London: Edward Arnold, 1994)

Kochman, Thomas, "Rapping in the Ghetto," in Lee Rainwater, ed., SOUL (Chicago: Aldine Publishing Co., 1970)

Kramer, Hilton, "Philip Johnson's Brilliant Career," COMMENTARY (September 1995)

_____, "Notes & Comments," THE NEW CRITERION (January 1998)

Kristol, Irving, "Why Religion is Good for the Jews," COMMENTARY (August 1994)

Kristov, Nicholas D., "A Man with a Plan? Japanese Prefer Premiers Who Speak Softly and Hold a Lot of Meetings," THE NEW YORK TIMES (July 20, 1998)

Lagerfeld, Steven, "Who Knows Where Time Goes?," THE WILSON QUARTERLY (Summer 1998)

Lappin, Elena, a review of Gerald Shapiro, *BAD JEWS AND OTHER STORIES*, NEW YORK TIMES BOOK REVIEW (October 17, 1999)

Lowry, John, "The Religious Right Wrestles With Doubt," SAN FRANCISCO EXAMINER (April 14, 1999)

Makino, Catherine, "Japan Bullies Unwanted Employees," SAN FRANCISCO CHRONICLE (March 19, 1999)

Marglin, S.A., "Losing Touch: The Cultural Conditions of Worker Accommodation and Resistance," S.A. Marglin and F. Appfel Marglin, eds., DOMINATING KNOWLEDGE (Oxford: Clarendon Press, 1993)

Mead, Walter Russell, "Asia Devalued," THE NEW YORK TIMES MAGAZINE (May 31, 1998)

Morse, Dan, "Shirts for the Dead Are the New Rage in Some Inner Cities," THE WALL STREET JOURNAL (February 4, 1999)

Nettl, J.P., "Ideas, Intellectuals and Structures of Dissent," Philip Rieff ed., ON INTELLECTUALS (New York: Doubleday & Company, 1970)

Rosenberg, Harold, ART ON THE EDGE (New York: Macmillan Publishing Co., Inc. 1975)

Shils, Edward, "The Intellectuals and the Powers: Some Perspectives for Comparative Analysis," COMPARATIVE STUDIES IN SOCIETY AND HISTORY (The Hague: Mouton & Co., 1958)

Simmel, Georg, "The Lie," in Kurt H. Wolff, ed., THE SOCIOLOGY OF GEORG SIMMEL (Glencoe, Ill: The Free Press, 1950)

Skinner, G.W., "Marketing and Social Structures in Rural China," JOURNAL OF ASIAN STUDIES (November 1964)

Soros, George, "Toward a Global Open Society," THE ATLANTIC MONTHLY (January 1998)

Stanner, W.E.H., "The Dreaming," in William Lessa and Evon Z. Vogt, eds. READER IN CONTEMPORARY RELIGION (Evanston, Ill: Row, Peterson Publishers, 1958)

Stark, Rodney and Charles Y. Glock, "Will Ethics Be the Death of Christianisty?," TRANSACTION (June 1968)

Strong, Tracy B. and Sposito, Frank Andreas, "Habermas's Significant Other," in Stephen K. White, ed., HABERMAS (Cambridge: Cambridge University Press, 1995)

Suzuki, Daisetz, "The Role of Nature in Zen Buddhism," H. Byron Earhart, RELIGION IN THE JAPANESE EXPERIENCE (Belmont, Cal: Wadsworth Publishing Company, 1974)

Takeo, Doi, "Dependency in Human Relationships," in Daniel I. Okimoto and Thomas P. Rohlen, INSIDE THE JAPANESE SYSTEM (Stanford, CA: Stanford University Press, 1988)

Van Wolferen, Karel, "Japan's Non-Revolution," FOREIGN AFFAIRS (September/October 1993)

Weisman, Steven R., a review of Edmund Morris, Dutch: A Memoir of Ronald Reagan, NEW YORK TIMES BOOK REVIEW (October 10, 1999)

Whorf, Benjamin L., "Language Mind and Reality," in John B. Carroll, ed., LANGUAGE, THOUGHT AND REALITY (Cambridge, MA: The M.I.T. Press, 1956)

_____, "The Relation of Habitual Thought and Behavior to Language,"in Carroll, *ibid.*

_____, "Science and Linguistics," in Carroll, *ibid.*

Whyte, Martin King, "The Chinese Family and Economic Development: Obstacle or Engine," ECONOMIC DEVELOPMENT AND CULTURAL CHANGE (October 1996)

Wilson, Edward O., "Is Everything Relative?," THE WILSON QUARTERLY (Winter 1998)

Wilson, John A., "Egypt," in Henri Frankfort, et. al. BEFORE PHILOSOPHY (Baltimore: Pelican Books, 1949)

Wolf, Martin, "Will the Nation-State Survive Globalization?," FOREIGN AFFAIRS (January/February 2001)

Young, Crawford, "The Impossible Necessity of Nigeria," FOREIGN AFFAIRS (November/December 1996)

BOOKS

Abegglen, James C. and Stalk, George Jr., KAISHA: THE JAPANESE CORPORATION (New York: Basic Books, Inc., Publishers, 1985)

Adler, Mortimer, ed., THE SYNTOPICON: AN INDEX TO THE GREAT IDEAS (Chicago: Encyclopedia Brittannica, 1990)

Aeschylus, THE ORESTEIA, Robert Fagles, trans. (New York: Penguin Books, 1979)

Alport, Gordon, BECOMING (New Haven: Yale University Press, 1955)

Aptheker, Herbert, AMERICAN NEGRO SLAVE REVOLTS (New York: International Publishing Co., 1993)

Arendt, Hannah, BETWEEN PAST AND FUTURE, rev. ed. (New York: The Viking Press, 1968)

_____, ON REVOLUTION (New York: The Viking Press, 1963)

_____, THE HUMAN CONDITION (New York: Doubleday Anchor Books, 1959)

Aristotle, THE POLITICS, T.A. Sinclair, trans. (Baltimore: Penguin Books, 1962)

_____, NICHMACHEAN ETHICS, Martin Ostwald, trans. (New York: Macmillan Publishing Company, 1962)

Aubet, Maria Eugenia, THE PHOENICIANS AND THE WEST (Cambridge: Cambridge University Press, 1996)

Augustine, CONFESSIONS, R.S. Pine-Coffin, trans. (New York: Penguin Books, 1961)

Aveni, Anthony, EMPIRES OF TIME (New York: Kodansha America Publishing Co., 1989)

Bacon, Edmund N., DESIGN OF CITIES, rev.ed. (New York: Penguin Books, 1974)

Bagehot, Walter, THE ENGLISH CONSTITUTION (Ithaca, N.Y.: Cornell University Press, 1966)

Baines, John and Malek, Jaromir, ATLAS OF ANCIENT EGYPT (New York: Facts on File Publications, 1980)

Baldwin, James, GO TELL IT ON THE MOUNTAIN (New York: Dial Press, 1963)

Barkan, Elazar, THE GUILT OF NATIONS (New York: W.W. Norton, 2000)

Barnet, Richard J. and Cavanagh, John, GLOBAL DREAMS (New York: Simon & Schuster, 1994)

Barshay, Andrew E., STATE AND INTELLECTUAL IN IMPERIAL JAPAN (Berkeley, Cal: University of California Press, 1988)

Barsook, Paulina, CYBERSELFISH (New York: Public Affairs Press, 2000)

Basham, A.L., THE WONDER THAT WAS INDIA, (New York: Grove Press, Inc. 1959)

Bellah, Robert N., RELIGION AND PROGRESS IN MODERN ASIA (Ann Arbor, Mich.: University of Michigan Press, 1965)

_____, TOKUGAWA RELIGION (New York: The Free Press, 1985)

_____, and Hammond, Phillip E., VARIETIES OF CIVIL RELIGION (San Francisco: Harper & Row, Publishers, 1980)

Bellesiles, Michael A., ARMING AMERICA: THE ORIGINS OF A NATIONAL GUN CULTURE (New York: Alfred A. Knopf, 2000)

Benedict, Ruth, PATTERNS OF CULTURE (Boston: Houghton Mifflin Company, 1934)

Berberoglu, Berch, THE POLITICAL ECONOMY OF DEVELOPMENT (Albany, N.Y.: State University of New York Press, 1992)

Bill, James A. and Springborg, Robert, POLITICS IN THE MIDDLE EAST, 4th ed. (New York: Harper Collins College Publishers, 1994)

Blake, Peter, FORM FOLLOWS FIASCO (Boston: Little, Brown and Company, 1977)

Bledsoe, Caroline and Pison, Gilles, eds., NUPTUALITY IN SUB-SAHARAN AFRICA (Oxford: Clarendon Press, 1994)

Bloomer, Kent C. and Moore, Charles W., BODY, MEMORY, AND ARCHITEC-TURE (New Haven: CT: Yale University Press, 1977)

Bok, Sessela, LYING (New York: Vintage Books, 1999)

Bollighemer, Karl S., IRELAND AND THE IRISH (New York: Columbia University Press, 1982)

Boorstin, Daniel J., THE DISCOVERERS (New York: Vintage Books, 1985)

Branden, Barbara, THE PASSION OF AYN RAND (Garden City, NY: Doubleday & Company, Inc., 1986)

Braudel, Fernand, THE WHEELS OF COMMERCE, 3 vols., Sian Reynolds, trans. (New York: Harper & Row, Publishers, 1986)

Brinton, Crane, THE SHAPING OF THE MODERN MIND (New York: New American Library, 1950)

Buber, Martin, I AND THOU, R.G. Smith, trans. (New York: Charles Scribner's Sons, 1958)

Burton, J.W., SYSTEMS, STATES, DIPLOMACY AND RULES (Cambridge: The University Press, 1968)

Butler, Johnella E. Butler and Walter, John C., TRANSFORMING THE CURRICULUM (Albany, N.Y.: State University of New York, 1991)

Callahan, John F., ed., THE COLLECTED ESSAYS OF RALPH ELLISON (New York: The Modern Library, 1995)

CAMBRIDGE ECONOMIC HISTORY OF EUROPE, Vols. 1-III (Cambridge: Cambridge University Press, 1941-1963)

Cantor, Norman, TWENTIETH-CENTURY CULTURE (New York: Peter Lang Publishing, 1988)

Carter, Stephen L., CIVILITY (New York: Basic Books, 1998)

Casson, Lionel, THE ANCIENT MARINERS, 2nd. ed. (Princeton, NJ: Princeton University Press, 1991)

Castledon, Rodney, MINOANS (New York and London: Routledge, 1993)

Chadwick, John, THE MYCENAEAN WORLD (Cambridge: Cambridge University Press, 1978)

Charters, Ann, KEROUAC: A BIOGRAPHY (San Francisco: Straight Arrow Press, 1973)

Choat, Pat, AGENTS OF INFLUENCE (New York: Alfred A. Knopf, Publishers, 1990)

Chomsky, Noam, SYNTACTIC STRUCTURES (The Hague: Mouton & Co., 1957)

Cohen, Edward E., ATHENIAN ECONOMY AND SOCIETY (Princeton: Princeton University Press, 1992)

Coser, Lewis A., MEN OF IDEAS (New York: The Free Press, 1965)

Crawford, Harriet, SUMER AND THE SUMERIANS (Cambridge: Cambridge University Press, 1991)

Cuddihy, John Murray, THE ORDEAL OF CIVILITY (New York: Dell Publishing Co., Inc., 1974)

Dale, Peter N., THE MYTH OF JAPANESE UNIQUENESS (New York: St. Martin's Press, 1986)

Daniel, Pete, LOST REVOLUTIONS (Chapel Hill, NC: University of North Carolina Press, 2000)

_____ , STANDING AT THE CROSSROADS (Balitimore, MD: Johns Hopkins University Press, 1996

_____ , THE SHADOW OF SLAVERY (Champagn, Ill: University of Illinois Press, 1990)

Das, Gurcharan, INDIA UNBOUND (New York: Alfred A. Knopf, 2001)

Dash, Leon, ROSA LEE: A MOTHER AND HER CHILDREN IN URBAN
    AMERICA (New York: Plume, 1996)
De Rougemont, Denis, LOVE IN THE WESTERN WORLD, Montgomery
    Belgion, trans. (Princeton: Princeton University Press, 1983)
_____ , MAN'S WESTERN QUEST, Montgomery Belgion, trans. (New
    York: Harper & Brothers, Publishers, 1957)
De Soto, Hernando, THE MYSTERY OF CAPITAL (New York: Basic Books,
    2000)
Decter, Midge, THE NEW CHASTITY AND OTHER ARGUMENTS AGAINST
    WOMEN'S LIBERATION (New York: Coward, McCann & Geoghegan, Inc.,
    1972)
Dehaene, Stanislas HOW THE MIND CREATES MATHEMATICS (Oxford:
    Oxford University Press, 1997)
Delamaide, Darrell, THE NEW SUPERREGIONS OF EUROPE (New York: E.P.
    Dutton, 1994)
Delaney, Samuel R., THE MOTION OF LIGHT ON WATER (New York: New
    American Library, 1988)
Dershowitz, Alan, THE VANISHING AMERICAN JEW (New York: Little,
    Brown & Co., Publishers, 1997)
Diamond, Jared, GUNS, GERMS, AND STEEL (New York: W.W. Norton & Co.,
    1999)
Dillard, J.L., BLACK ENGLISH (New York: Random House, 1972)
Donahue, Ray T., JAPANESE CULTURE AND COMMUNICATION (Lanham,
    MD: University Press of America, 1998)
Drucker, Peter, POST-CAPITALIST SOCIETY (New York: HarperCollins,
    Publishers, 1993)
DuBois, W.E.B., DUSK OF DAWN ESSAYS (New York: The Library of
    America, 1986)
Eagleton, Terry, THE ILLUSIONS OF POSTMODERNISM (Oxford: Blackwell
    Publishers, Ltd., 1996)
Eisenstadt, S.N., MAX WEBER ON CHARISMA AND INSTITUTION BUILD-
    ING (Chicago: University of Chicago Press, 1968)
Eitzen, Stanley D. and Sage, George H., SOCIOLOGY OF NORTH AMERICAN
    SPORT, 5th ed. (Madison, Wis.: Brown & Benchmark, 1993)
Elegant, Robert S., THE CENTER OF THE WORLD, 2nd ed., rev., (New York:
    Funk & Wagnalls, 1968)
Eliade, Mercea, MYTH AND REALITY (New York: Harper and Row Publishers,
    1963)
Ellis, John Tracy, AMERICAN CATHOLICISM, 2nd ed. (Chicago: University of
    Chicago Press, 1969)

Fagan, Brian M., THE AZTECS (New York: W.H. Freeeman and Company, 1984)

Faludi, Susan, STIFFED: THE BETRAYAL OF THE AMERICAN MAN (New York: W. Morrow and Co., 1999)

Festinger, Leon, Henry W. Riecken and Stanley Schacter, WHEN PROPHECY FAILS (Minneapolis: University of Minnesota Press, 1956)

Frankfort, Henri, *et. al.*, BEFORE PHILOSOPHY (Baltimore: Pelican Books, 1949)

Fraser, Caroline, GOD'S PERFECT CHILD: LIVING AND DYING IN THE CHRISTIAN SCIENCE CHURCH (New York: Metropolitan Books, 1999)

Freud, Sigmund, CIVILIZATION AND ITS DISCONTENTS, James Strachey, trans. (New York: W.W. Norton & Co., Inc., 1961)

Fried, Morton H., THE EVOLUTION OF POLITICAL SOCIETY (New York: Random House, 1967)

Fromm, Erich, MAN FOR HIMSELF (New York: Holt, Rinehart & Winston, 1947)

Fukuyama, Francis, TRUST: The Social Virtues and the Creation of Prosperity (New York: The Free Press, 1995)

Gardiner, Sir Alan, EGYPT OF THE PHAROAHS (New York: Oxford University Press, 1964)

Garlan, Yvon, SLAVERY IN ANCIENT GREECE, Janet Lloyd, trans. (Ithaca, NY: Cornell University Press, 1988)

Garreau, Joel, THE NINE NATIONS OF NORTH AMERICA (Boston: Houghton Mifflin, 1981)

Geertz, Clifford, THE INTERPRETATION OF CULTURES (New York: Basic Books, 1973)

Genovese, Eugene D., ROLL, JORDAN, ROLL: THE WORLD THE SLAVES MADE (New York: Vintage Books, 1976)

Gilden, Hilail, ed., AN INTRODUCTION TO PHILOSOPHY: TEN ESSAYS BY LEO STRAUSS (Detroit: Wayne State University Press, 1989)

Gilder, George F., THE SPIRIT OF ENTERPRISE (New York: Simon & Schuster, 1984)

Goody, Jack R., ed., THE CHARACTER OF KINSHIP (Cambridge: Cambridge University Press, 1973)

Gould, Stephen Jay, ROCKS OF AGES (New York: Ballantine Books, 1999)

_____, TIME'S ARROW (Cambridge: Harvard University Press, 1987)

Greeley, Andrew, THE AMERICAN CATHOLIC: A SOCIAL PROFILE (New York: Basic Books, 1977)

Grieder, William, WHO WILL TELL THE PEOPLE (New York: Simon & Schuster, 1992)

Grier, William H. & Cobbs, Price M., BLACK RAGE (New York: Bantam Books, 1968)

Hacking, Ian, THE SOCIAL CONSTRUCTION OF WHAT? (Cambridge, MA: Harvard University Press, 1999)

Halberstam, David, THE FIFTIES (New York: Random House, 1993)

Hall, Edward T., BEYOND CULTURE (Garden City, N.J.: Anchor Books, 1977)

_____, Hall, Edward T., THE SILENT LANGUAGE (New York: Doubleday & Co., 1959)

Hamilton, Edith, THE GREAT AGE OF GREEK LITERATURE (New York: W.W. Norton and Company, 1930)

_____, THE GREEK WAY (New York: W.W. Norton, Publishers, 1993)

Hauser, Arnold, THE SOCIAL HISTORY OF ART (New York: Vintage Books, 1957)

Heidegger, Martin, TIME AND BEING, Joan Stambaugh, trans. (Albany: State University of New York Press, 1996)

Heilbroner, Robert and Milberg, William THE MAKING OF ECONOMIC SOCIETY, 10th ed. (Upper Saddle River, NJ: Prentice-Hall, 1998)

Hendry, Joy, WRAPPING CULTURE (Oxford: Clarendon Press, 1995)

Herlihy, David, THE BLACK DEATH AND THE TRANSFORMATION OF THE WEST (Cambridge, Mass: Harvard University Press, 1997)

Herm, Gerhard, THE PHOENICIANS, Caroline Hillier, trans. (New York: William Morrow & Company, Inc., 1975)

Hertz, John H., INTERNATIONAL POLITICS IN THE ATOMIC AGE (New York: Columbia University Press, 1962)

Hilliard, Asa P., THE MAROON WITHIN US (Baltimore: Black Classic Press, 1995)

Himmelfarb, Gertrude, ONE NATION, TWO CULTURES (New York: Alfred A. Knopf, 1999)

Hoberman, John, DARWIN'S ATHLETES (New York: Houghton Mifflin, 1996)

Hoffman, Michael A., EGYPT BEFORE THE PHARAOHS (New York: Dorset Press, 1979)

Hofstadter, Richard, ANTI-INTELLECTUALSIM IN AMERICAN LIFE (New York: Vintage Books, 1966)

Hollinger, David A., POST-ETHNIC AMERICA (New York: Basic Books, 1996)

Hooper, Finley, GREEK REALITIES (Detroit: Wayne State University Press, 1978)

Hotchkiss, Carolyn, INTERNATIONAL LAW FOR BUSINESS (New York: McGraw-Hill, Inc., 1994)

Howe, Irving, WORLD OF OUR FATHERS (New York: Harcourt, Brace and Company, 1989)

Hughes, Robert, CULTURE OF COMPLAINT (New York: Oxford University Press, 1993)

Huisinga, J., THE WANING OF THE MIDDLE AGES (New York: Anchor Books, 1954)

————, Johan, HOMO LUDENS (Boston: Beacon Press, 1955)

Huntington, Samuel P., THE CLASH OF CIVILIZATIONS AND THE SHAPING OF WORLD ORDER (New York: Simon & Schuster, 1996)

————, and Lawrence E. Harrison, eds., CULTURE MATTERS: HOW VALUES SHAPE HUMAN PROGRESS (New York: Basic Books, 2000)

Hurley, Andrew, DINERS, BOWLING ALLEYS AND TRAILER PARKS (New York: Basic Books, 2001)

Hyde, Lewis, THE GIFT (New York: Vintage Books, 1983)

Ishihara, Shintaro, THE JAPAN THAT CAN SAY NO, Frank Baldwin, trans. (New York: Simon & Schuster, 1989)

Ishinomori, Shotaro, JAPAN, INC., introd. by Peter Duus (Berkeley: University of California Press, 1988)

Jacobs, Jane, CITIES AND THE WEALTH OF NATIONS (New York: Random House, 1984)

Jacoby, Russell, THE LAST INTELLECTUALS (New York: Basic Books, 1987)

Janson, H.W., HISTORY OF ART (New York: Harry N. Abrams, Inc. 1962)

Jencks, Charles, THE LANGUAGE OF POST-MODERN ARCHITECTURE (New York: Rizzoli International Publications, Inc, 1977)

Jenkins, Philip, Jenkins, Philip, THE COLD WAR AT HOME (Chapel Hill, NC: University of North Carolina Press, 2000)

Kammen, Michael G., AMERICAN CULTURE, AMERICAN TASTE (New York: Alfred A. Knopf, Inc., 1999)

Kaufman, Walter, NIETZSCHE (New York: Meridian Books, Inc., 1956)

Keegan, John, A HISTORY OF WARFARE (New York: Alfred A. Knopf, 1993)

Kemp, Barry J., ANCIENT EGYPT: ANATOMY OF A CIVILIZATION (New York: Routledge, 1998)

Keuls, Eva C., THE REIGN OF THE PHALLUS (New York: Harper & Row, Publishers, 1985)

Kitto, H.D.F., THE GREEKS (New York: Penguin Books, 1957)

Knox, Paul L., and Taylor, Peter J., eds. WORLD CITIES IN A WORLD SYSTEM (Cambridge: Cambridge University Press, 1995)

Kohlberg, Lawrence, THE PHILOSOPHY OF MORAL DEVELOPMENT (San Francisco: Harper & Row, 1981)

Kramer, Samuel Noah, THE SUMERIANS (Chicago: University of Chicago Press, 1971)

Krech III, Shepard, THE ECOLOGICAL INDIAN: MYTH AND HISTORY (New York: W.W. Norton & Company, 1999)

Kristol, Irving, TWO CHEERS FOR CAPITALISM (New York: New American Library, 1978)

_____, NEOCONSERVATISM: THE AUTOBIOGRAPHY OF AN IDEA (New York: Basic Books, 1995)

Kuhn, Thomas, THE STRUCTURE OF SCIENTIFIC REVOLUTIONS, 3rd ed. (Chicago: University of Chicago Press, 1996)

Lancel, Serge, CARTHAGE: A HISTORY, Antonia Nevill, trans. (Oxford: Blackwell Publishers, 1995)

Landes, David S., THE WEALTH AND POVERTY OF NATIONS (New York: W.W. Norton & Co., 1998)

Lasch, Christopher, THE CULTURE OF NARCISSISM (New York: W.W. Norton & Co., 1991)

Lazare, Daniel, THE FROZEN REPUBLIC (New York: Harcourt, Brace & Company, 1996)

Lemann, Nicholas, THE PROMISED LAND (New York: Vintage Books, 1992)

Lerner, Daniel, THE PASSING OF TRADITIONAL SOCIETY, (New York: The Free Press, 1964)

Levenson, Joseph R., MODERN CHINA AND ITS CONFUCIAN PAST (New York: Doubleday & Company, Inc, 1964)

Levi-Strauss, Claude, TOTEMISM, Rodney Needham, trans. (Boston: Beacon Press, 1963)

_____, THE SAVAGE MIND, (Chicago: University of Chicago Press, 1966)

Levy, Marion J., Jr., MODERNIZATION AND THE STRUCTURE OF SOCIETIES (Princeton: Princeton University Press, 1969)

_____, MODERNIZATION: LATECOMERS AND SURVIVORS (New York: Basic Books, 1972)

Lipset, Seymour Martin and Marks, Gary, WHY IT DID'T HAPPEN HERE (New York: W.W. Norton & Company, 2000)

Lopez, Robert S., THE COMMERCIAL REVOLUTION OF THE MIDDLE AGES, 950-1350 (Englewood Cliffs, NJ: Prentice-Hall, INC., 1971)

Luther, Martin, CHRISTIAN LIBERTY, W.A. Lambert, trans. (Philadelphia: Fortress Press, 1957)

Lynd, Helen Merrill, ON SHAME AND THE SEARCH FOR IDENTITY (New York: Harcourt, Brace & Co., 1958)

Madrick, Jeffrey, THE END OF AFFLUENCE (New York: Random House, 1995)

Magnet, Myron, THE DREAM AND THE NIGHTMARE (San Francisco: Encounter Books, 2000)

Mailer, Norman, ADVERTISEMENTS FOR MYSELF (New York: G.P. Putnam's Sons, 1966)

Manion, Clarence, THE KEY TO PEACE (Chicago: Heritage Foundation, 1950)

Mannheim, Karl, IDEOLOGY AND UTOPIA, Louis Wirth and Edward Shils, trans. (New York: Harcourt, Brace & World, Inc., 1936)

Marable, Manning, BLACK LEADERSHIP (New York: Columbia University Press, 1998)

Marglin, S.A., and Marglin, F. Appfel, eds. DOMINATING KNOWLEDGE (Oxford: Clarendon Press, 1993)

Martin, Calvin Luther, THE WAY OF THE HUMAN BEING (New Haven, Conn.: Yale University Press, 1999)

Martin, William, WITH GOD ON OUR SIDE (New York: Broadway Books, 1996)

Marty, Martin E., PILGRIMS IN THEIR OWN LAND (Boston: Little, Brown & Co., 1984)

Maslow, Abraham H., EUPSYCHIAN MANAGEMENT (Homewood, Ill.: R.D. Irwin, 1965)

_____, TOWARD A PSYCHOLOGY OF BEING, 2nd ed. (New York: Van Norstrand, 1966)

Mauss, Marcel, THE GIFT, Ian Cunnison, trans. (London: Cohen and West, 1954)

May, Rollo, THE DISCOVERY OF BEING (New York: W.W. Norton & Co., 1983)

McClelland, David, THE ACHIEVING SOCIETY (New York: Ivington Publications, 1961)

McCormick, John, THE EUROPEAN UNION, 2nd ed. (Boulder, Colo: Westview Press, 1999)

McGregor, Douglas, THE HUMAN SIDE OF MANAGEMENT (New York: McGraw-Hill, 1960)

McWhorter, John H., LOSING THE RACE (New York: Basic Books, 2000)

Merton, Thomas, CONTEMPLATION IN A WORLD OF ACTION (Garden City, NY: Doubleday & Co., 1971)

Miller, Donald L., LEWIS MUMFORD: A LIFE (New York: Weidenfeld & Nicholson, 1989)

Morawisik, Andrew, THE CHOICE FOR EUROPE (Ithaca, NY: Cornell University Press, 1998)

Morganthau, Hans J., POLITICS AMONG NATIONS, 2nd ed. (New York: Alfred A. Knopf, Inc. 1958)

Morley, David and Kuan-Hsing Chen (eds.), STUART HALL: CRITICAL DIALOGUES ON CULTURE (London: Routledge, 1996)

Morris, Edmund, DUTCH: A MEMOIR OF RONALD REAGAN (New York: Random House, 1999)

Moscati, Sabatino, THE FACE OF THE ANCIENT ORIENT (Garden City, NY: Anchor Books, 1962)

_____, THE WORLD OF THE PHOENICIANS (New York: Frederick A. Praeger, 1968)

Muir, Edward, CIVIC RITUAL IN RENAISSANCE VENICE (Princeton: Princeton University Press, 1981)

Mumford, Lewis, TECHNICS AND CIVILIZATION (New York: Harcourt, Brace & Company, 1934)

Myerdahl, Gunnar, AN AMERICA DILEMMA (New York: Harper & Brothers, 1944)

_____, A CHALLENGE TO AFFLUENCE (New York: Pantheon Books, 1962)

Neuhaus, Richard J., THE NAKED PUBLIC SQUARE (Grand Rapids, MI: William B. Eerdmans Publishing Co., 1984)

_____, AMERICA AGAINST ITSELF (Notre Dame, IN: University of Notre Dame Press, 1992)

Niebuhr, Reinhold, MORAL MAN AND IMMORAL SOCIETY (New York: Charles Scribner's Sons, 1960)

Nietzsche, Friedrich, ON THE GENEALOGY OF MORALS, Walter Kaufmann, trans. (New York: Vintage Books, 1989)

Novak, Michael, THE CATHOLIC ETHIC AND THE SPIRIT OF CAPITALISM (New York: The Free Press, 1993)

Nussbaum, Martha C., CULTIVATING HUMANITY (Cambridge, Mass.: Harvard University Press, 1997)

Oates, Joan, BABYLON (London: Thames and Hudson, 1979)

O'Brien, Conor Cruise, STATES OF IRELAND (New York: Pantheon Books, 1972)

O'Connor, Richard, THE IRISH (New York: G.P. Putnam's Sons, 1971)

Org, Walter J., AMERICAN CATHOLIC CROSSROADS (Westport, Conn.: Greenwood Press, 1981)

Paglia, Camille, SEXUAL PERSONAE, (New York: Vintage Books, 1991)

Palley, Thomas I., PLENTY OF NOTHING (Princeton: Princeton University Press, 1998)

Parsons, Talcott, THE SOCIAL SYSTEM (Chicago: The Free Press, 1951)

_____, SOCIETIES: EVOLUTIONARY AND COMPARATIVE PERSPEC- TIVES (Englewood Cliffs, NJ: Prentice-Hall Inc., 1966)

Parsons, Talcott, and Bales, Robert, FAMILY SOCIALIZATION PROCESS AND INTERACTION PROCESS (New York: The Free Press, 1955)

Payne, Robert, THE MAKING OF THE CHRISTIAN WORLD (New York: Dorset Press, 1966)

Peale, Norman Vincent, A GUIDE TO CONFIDENT LIVING (New York: Fawcett Books, 1996)

Pickering, Andrew, CONSTRUCTING QUARKS (Chicago: University of Chicago Press, 1984)

Podhoretz, Norman, BREAKING RANKS (New York: Harper & Row, 1979)

_____, EX-FRIENDS (New York: The Free Press, 1999)

_____, MAKING IT (New York: Random House, 1967)

Poggiloi, Renato, THE THEORY OF THE AVANT-GARDE, Gerald Fitzgerald, trans. (Cambridge, Mass.: Harvard University Press, 1968)

Polyani, Karl, THE GREAT TRANSFORMATION (Boston: Beacon Press, 1980)

Putnam, Robert D., BOWLING ALONE: THE COLLAPSE AND REVIVAL OF AMERICAN COMMUNITY (New York: Simon & Schuster, 2000)

Pye, Lucian W., CHINA (Boston: Little, Brown and Company, 1972)

Pyle, Kenneth B., THE NEW GENERATION IN MEIJI JAPAN (Stanford: Stanford University Press, 1969)

Radin, Paul, THE WORLD OF PRIMITIVE MAN, (New York: E.P. Dutton & Co., Inc., 1971)

Rakodi, Carole, ed., THE URBAN CHALLENGE IN AFRICA (Tokyo: United Nations Press, 1997)

Reader, Ian, RELIGION IN CONTEMPORARY JAPAN (Honolulu: University of Hawaii Press, 1991)

Redford, Donald B., EGYPT, CANAAN, AND ISREAL IN ANCIENT TIMES (Princeton: Princeton University Press, 1992)

Reid, T.R., CONFUCIUS LIVES NEXT DOOR (New York: Random House, 1999)

Richburg, Kieth B., OUT OF AMERICA (New York: Basic Books, 1997)

Riker, William H., DEMOCRACY IN THE UNITED STATES (New York: The Macmillan Company, 1953)

Robinson, Randall, THE DEBT (New York: E.P. Dutton, 2000)

Rohde, Peter, ed., THE DIARY OF SOREN KIERKEGAARD (New York: Carol Publishing Group, 1993)

Rostow, W.W., THE STAGES OF ECONOMIC GROWTH (Cambridge: The University Press, 1960)

Roszak, Theodore, THE MAKING OF A COUNTER CULTURE (Garden City: NJ: Anchor Books, 1969)

Rustow, Dankwart A., A WORLD OF NATIONS: PROBLEMS OF POLITICAL MODERNIZATION (Washington, D.C.: The Brookings Institution, 1967)

Rybcezynski, Witold, HOME: A SHORT HISTORY OF AN IDEA (New York: Penguin Books, 1986)

Sagan, Carl, THE DRAGONS OF EDEN (New York: Ballantine Books, 1977)

Sahlins, Marshall and Service, Elman R., eds., EVOLUTION AND CULTURE (Ann Arbor, Mich.: University of Michigan Press, 1960)

Sahlins, Marshall, STONE AGE ECONOMICS (New York: Aldine De Gruyter, 1972)

Samuelson, Robert J., THE GOOD LIFE AND ITS DISCONTENTS (New York: Times Books, 1995)

Sansom, G.B., JAPAN: A SHORT CULTURAL HISTORY, rev. ed. (New York: Appleton-Century-Crofts, 1962)

_____, THE WESTERN WORLD AND JAPAN (New York: Alfred A. Knopf, 1968)

Schama, Simon, THE EMBARRASSMENT OF RICHES (New York: Alfred A. Knopf, 1987)

Schlesinger, Authur, Jr., THE DISUNITING OF AMERICA, rev.ed. (New York: W.W. Norton, 1998)

Schulz, David A., COMING UP BLACK (Englewood Cliffs, N.J.: Prentice-Hall, Inc. 1969)

Scott, James C., COMPARATIVE POLITICAL CORRUPTION (Englewood Cliffs, NJ: Prentice-Hall, Inc. 1972)

Scott-Maxwell, Florida, WOMEN AND SOMETIMES MEN (New York: Harper & Row, Publishers, 1971)

Sennett, Richard, AUTHORITY, (New York: Alfred A. Knopf, 1980)

Shactel, E.G., METAMORPHOSIS (New York: Basic Books, 1959)

Shils, Edward, THE INTELLECTUAL BETWEEN TRADITION AND MODERNITY (The Hague: Mouton & Co., Publishers, 1961)

Sinai, I.R., THE CHALLENGE OF MODERNISATION (New York: W.W. Norton & Company, Inc. 1964)

Sombart, Werner, THE JEWS AND MODERN CAPITALISM, Mordecai Epstein, trans. (New Brunswick, NJ: Rutgers University Press, 1982)

Sontag, Susan, AGAINST INTERPRETATION (New York: Dell Publishing Co., 1969)

Sowell, Thomas, RACE AND CULTURE: A WORLD VIEW (New York: Basic Books, 1995)

Stampp, Kenneth M., THE PECULIAR INSTITUTION (New York: Random House, 1990)

Stack, Carol B., ALL OUR KIN (New York: Harper & Row, 1974)

Susman, Warren I., CULTURE AS HISTORY (New York: Pantheon Books, 1984)

Tasker, Peter, THE JAPANESE (New York: E.P. Dutton, 1988)

Tawney, R.H., RELIGION AND THE RISE OF CAPITALISM (Magnolia, Mass.: Peter Smith Publisher, Inc., 1990)

Taylor, Charles, SOURCES OF THE SELF (Cambridge, Mass.: Harvard University Press, 1989)

Teilhard de Chardin, Pierre, THE PHENOMENON OF MAN, Bernard Wall, trans. (New York: Harper Brothers, Publishers 1959)

Teixeria, Ray and Rogers, Joel, AMERICA'S FORGOTTEN MAJORITY (New York: Basic Books, 2000)

Terpstra, Vernon, THE CULTURAL ENVIRONMENT OF INTERNATIONAL BUSINESS (Cincinnati, O.: South-Western Publishing Co., 1978)

Thomlinson, John, CULTURAL IMPERIALISM (Baltimore: The Johns Hopkins University Press, 1991)

Thucydides, HISTORY, A.E. Zimmern, trans. (Oxford: Clarendon Press, 1911)

Thurow, Lester, THE FUTURE OF CAPITALISM (New York: Penguin Books, 1996)

Tillich, Paul, THE COURAGE TO BE (New Haven: Yale University Press, 1952)

Trilling, Lionel, THE LIBERAL IMAGINATION (New York: Harcourt, Brace, Jovanovich, 1979)

Van Seters, John, IN SEARCH OF HISTORY (New Haven, Conn.: Yale University Press, 1983)

Venturi, Robert, CONTRADICTION AND COMPLEXITY IN MODERN ARCHITECTURE (New York: Museum of Modern Art, 1977)

Veyne, Paul, BREAD AND CIRCUSES, Brian Pearce, trans. (New York: Penguin Books, 1990)

Wallace, Anthony F. C., CULTURE AND PERSONALITY (New York: Random House, 1961)

Watts, Alan W., THE TWO HANDS OF GOD (New York: Collier Books, 1969)

Weber, Max, THE PROTESTANT ETHIC AND THE SPIRIT OF CAPITALISM (Los Angeles: Roxbury Publishing Company, 1996)

_____, THE SOCIOLOGY OF RELIGION, Ephraim Fischoff, trans. (Boston: Beacon Press, 1963)

Weigel, George, WITNESS TO HOPE (New York: Cliff Street Books, 1999)

Wheatley, Paul, PIVOT OF THE FOUR CORNERS, (Chicago: Aldine Publishing Co., 1971)

White, Jon Ewbank Manship, and White, J. Manship, ANCIENT EGYPT: ITS CULTURE AND HISTORY (Mineola, NY: Dover Publications, 1970)

White, Leslie, THE EVOLUTION OF CULTURE (New York: McGraw Hill Publishers, 1959)

White, Ruth, THE FIRST CITIES (New York: E.P. Dutton, 1977)

Whitman, Walt, COMPLETE POETRY AND COLLECTED PROSE (New York: Literary Classics of the United States, 1982)

Williams, Jonathan, ed., MONEY: A HISTORY (New York: St. Martin's Press, 1997)

Wilson, A.N., PAUL (New York: W.W. Norton & Co., 1997)

Wilson, Bryan R., SECTS AND SOCIETY (Berkeley: University of California Press, 1961)

Wilson, James Q. and Herrnstein, Richard J., CRIME AND HUMAN NATURE (New York: Simon and Schuster, 1985)

Wilson, John A., THE CULTURE OF ANCIENT EGYPT (Chicago: University of Chicago Press, 1951)

Wilson, William J., WHEN JOBS DISAPPEAR (New York: Random House, 1996)

Wimsatt, William Upski, BOMB THE SUBURBS (Chicago: Subway and Elevated Free Press of Chicago, 1994)

Wittfogel, Karl A., ORIENTAL DESPOTISM (New Haven: Yale University Press, 1957)

Wolfe, Tom, THE PAINTED WORD (New York: Bantam Books, 1982)

Wood, Michael, IN SEARCH OF THE TROJAN WAR (New York: New American Library, 1985)

Woodward, C. Vann, THE BURDEN OF SOUTHERN HISTORY (Baton Rouge, LA: Louisiana State University Press, 1960)

_____, THE STRANGE CAREER OF JIM CROW (New York: Oxford University Press, 1955)

X, Malcolm (with Alex Haley) THE AUTOBIOGRAPHY OF MALCOLM X (New York: Ballantine Books, 1964)

Yamamura, Kozo, A STUDY OF SAMURAI INCOME AND ENTREPRENEUR-SHIP (Cambridge, Mass.: Harvard University Press, 1974)

Ziemba, William T. and Schwartz, Sandra L., POWER JAPAN (Chicago: Probus Publishing, 1992)

Zimmer, Heinrich, PHILOSOPHIES OF INDIA, Joseph Campbell, ed. (Cleveland, O.: The World Publishing Co., 1956)

Zumthor, Paul, DAILY LIFE IN REMBRADT'S HOLLAND, S.W. Taylor, trans. (New York: Macmillan and Company, Publishers,

INDEX

Some entries that appear throughout the book, such as *culture*, *globalization*, and *localization*, are not listed in the Index. Unless otherwise specified, all references to *U.S.* and *United States* refer to the United States during nation-building.

ABOUT THE AUTHOR

G. Eric Hansen (Ph.D., The Fletcher School of Law and Diplomacy, Tufts University) is Professor of International Political Economy at Saint Mary's College of California. After serving on the faculties of Haverford, MIT and Wellesley, he became a dean and member of the graduate faculty of Saint Mary's College of California. His articles and reviews have appeared in The Journal of Politics, Pacific Affairs, Orbis, American Political Science Review, and in edited collections. He lives in San Francisco and on Cape Cod.